T0331955

COVID-19 and the Informal Economy

UNU World Institute for Development Economics Research (UNU-WIDER) was established by the United Nations University as its first research and training centre and started work in Helsinki, Finland, in 1985. The mandate of the institute is to undertake applied research and policy analysis on structural changes affecting developing and transitional economies, to provide a forum for the advocacy of policies leading to robust, equitable, and environmentally sustainable growth, and to promote capacity strengthening and training in the field of economic and social policy-making. Its work is carried out by staff researchers and visiting scholars in Helsinki and via networks of collaborating scholars and institutions around the world.

United Nations University World Institute for Development Economics Research—
UNU–WIDER
Katajanokanlaituri 6B, 00160 Helsinki,
Finland
www.wider.unu.edu

COVID-19 and the Informal Economy

Impact, Recovery, and the Future

Edited by

MARTHA ALTER CHEN
MICHAEL ROGAN
KUNAL SEN

A study prepared by the United Nations University World Institute for Development Economics Research—UNU–WIDER

OXFORD
UNIVERSITY PRESS

OXFORD
UNIVERSITY PRESS

Great Clarendon Street, Oxford, OX2 6DP,
United Kingdom

Oxford University Press is a department of the University of Oxford.
It furthers the University's objective of excellence in research, scholarship,
and education by publishing worldwide. Oxford is a registered trade mark of
Oxford University Press in the UK and in certain other countries

© United Nations University World Institute for Development Economics Research (UNU-WIDER) 2024

The moral rights of the authors have been asserted

Some rights reserved. No part of this publication may be reproduced, stored in
a retrieval system, or transmitted, in any form or by any means, for commercial purposes
without the prior permission in writing of Oxford University Press, or as expressly
permitted by law, by licence or under terms agreed with the appropriate
reprographics rights organization.

This is an open access publication. Except where otherwise noted, this work is distributed under the terms of
a Creative Commons Attribution-Non Commercial-ShareAlike 3.0 IGO licence (CC BY-NC-SA 3.0 IGO),
a copy of which is available at https://creativecommons.org/licenses/by-nc-sa/3.0/igo/.

Enquiries concerning reproduction outside the scope of this licence
should be sent to the Rights Department, Oxford University Press, at the address above

Published in the United States of America by Oxford University Press
198 Madison Avenue, New York, NY 10016, United States of America

British Library Cataloguing in Publication Data

Data available

Library of Congress Control Number: 2023951091

ISBN 9780198887041

DOI: 10.1093/oso/9780198887041.001.0001

Printed and bound by
CPI Group (UK) Ltd, Croydon, CR0 4YY

Links to third party websites are provided by Oxford in good faith and
for information only. Oxford disclaims any responsibility for the materials
contained in any third party website referenced in this work.

Foreword

Informal workers in low- and middle-income societies face a variety of shocks to their livelihoods, from economy-wide shocks—such as sudden increases in food prices or prolonged recessions—to uncertain and volatile demand for their labour, and myriad government restrictions on their ability to earn a living, especially if they are self-employed. However, rarely have informal workers faced generalized shutdowns of economic activity such as occurred during the COVID-19 pandemic. The pandemic affected the economic life of informal workers through the increased the risk of falling ill with the virus if households went about their normal working lives. The pandemic also affected informal workers' livelihoods through the introduction of lockdown policies by national governments in developing economies, which shut down economic activity for prolonged periods of time.

In 2021, the second year of the COVID-19 pandemic, United Nations University World Institute for Development Economics Research (UNU-WIDER) partnered with Women in Informal Employment: Globalizing and Organizing (WIEGO) to launch a multidisciplinary research project to answer some key questions on increasing informality during times of crisis. What have we learned about the impact of the COVID-19 pandemic on the livelihoods of informal workers in developing countries? What is the future of labour markets in developing countries in the post-pandemic period? What have been the policy measures for relief and recovery that developing countries have followed, and how could they have been improved? What lessons can we learn from the impact of the COVID-19 pandemic on the livelihoods of informal workers in the Global South, and what can be done to make sure that informal workers do not take the brunt of the next pandemic?

This book brings together well-researched contributions which examine the future of labour markets in the light of the COVID-19 pandemic and how policy measures can protect informal workers and reflect on the lessons learned from the largest shock to the global labour market in generations, as well as the ongoing disruption to global supply chains.

I wish to sincerely thank my fellow co-editors, for not only their cornerstone contributions to the work but also helping to bring this vitally important research to realization. The chapter authors contributed their vast knowledge on informality to the body of work now before the reader. The professional collaboration is very much appreciated. I would also like to thank Lorraine Telfer-Taivainen,

UNU-WIDER Editorial and Publishing Associate, for her steadfast support and remarkable commitment in preparing the manuscript.

Kunal Sen
Director, UNU-WIDER
Helsinki, January 2024

Acknowledgements

WIEGO would like to acknowledge core funding from the William and Flora Hewlett Foundation, the Ford Foundation, and Sweden, represented by Swedish Sida. Without the generous support of these donors, WIEGO's work in supporting organizations of workers in informal employment would not be possible. WIEGO and its local research partners would also like to acknowledge the support of the Canadian International Development Research Centre (IDRC), which funded the study on COVID-19 and its impacts on workers in informal employment in 11 cities. Finally, WIEGO would like to recognize the incredible sacrifices that workers across the world have made to protect their livelihoods during the COVID-19 pandemic.

UNU-WIDER gratefully acknowledges the support and financial contribution to its work programme by the Institute's core donors of the governments of Finland and Sweden. Without this vital funding, our research and policy advisory work would be impossible.

Martha Chen, Michael Rogen, and Kunal Sen
January 2024

Contents

List of Figures

List of Tables

List of Abbreviations

ACTED	Agency for Technical Cooperation and Development
AFP	Agence France Presse
ASD	Asian Development Bank
BBS	Bangladesh Bureau of Statistics
BIGD	BRAC Institute of Governance and Development
CAP	Coronavirus Alleviation Programme
CBR	central bank rate
CGD	Center for Global Development
CGS	credit guarantee scheme
CHT	Chattogram Hill Tracts
CBK	Central Bank of Kenya
CLEAR	Civic Leadership Education and Research
CMSME	cottage, micro-, small-and-medium enterprises
CPHS	Consumer Pyramids Household Survey
CRAM	Coronavirus Rapid Mobile Survey
CREAW	Centre for Rights Education and Awareness
CRR	cash reserve rate
CSAE	Centre for the Study of African Economics
CSG	Child Support Grant
DB	defined benefit
DC	defined contribution
DFID-UK	Department for International Development-United Kingdom
DIGESTYC	*Dirección General de Estadística y Censos* (General Directorate of Statistics and Census)
DPRU	Development Policy Research Unit
EHPM	*Encuesta de Hogares de Propósitos Múktuokes* (Multi-purpose Household Survey)
ENAHO	*Encuesta Nacional de Hogares* (National Household Survey)
ENE	*Encuesta Nacional de Empleo* (Labour Force Survey)
ENOE	*Encuesta Nacional de Ocupación y Empleo* (National Occupation and Employment Survey)
EPR	extended producer responsibility
ESC	Emergency Social Committee
ESID	Effective States and Inclusive Development
ESS	Extension of Social Security
FCDO	Foreign, Commonwealth & Development Office
FSAP	Financial Sector Assessment Programme
GDP	gross domestic product

GIGA	German Institute for Global and Area Studies
GIZ	German Agency for International Cooperation
GlaD	Globalization and Development
GSPS	Ghana Socio-economic Panel Survey
GST	goods and services tax
HH	household
HIES	Household Income and Expenditure Survey
HSRC	Human Sciences Research Council
IBRD	International Bank for Reconstruction and Development
ICCCAD	International Centre for Climate Change and Development
ICLS	International Conference of Labour Statisticians
ICT	information and communication technology
IDA	International Development Association
IDRC	International Development Research Centre
IDS	Institute of Development Studies
IEJ	Institute for Economic Justice
IGA	income-generating activity
IHME	Institute of Health Metrics and Evaluation
IIED	International Institute for Environment and Development
ILC	International Labour Conference
ILO	International Labour Organization
IMF	International Monetary Fund
INE	*Instituto Nacional de Estadisticas* (National Institute of Statistics)
INEGI	*Instituto Nacional de Estadisca y Geografia* (National Institute of Statistics and Geography)
INEI	*Instituto Nacional de Estadistica e Informatica* (National Institute of Statistics and Informatics)
ISSER	Institute of Statistical, Social and Economic Research
ITUC	International Trade Union Confederation
IUSSP	International Union for the Scientific Study of Population
IWHC	International Women's Health Coalition
IZA	Institute of Labor Economics
KNBS	Kenya National Bureau of Statistics
LEAP	Livelihood Empowerment against Poverty
MBO	membership-based organization
MENAFN	Middle East North Africa Financial Network
MMDCE	metropolitan, municipal district chief executive
MSME	micro, small, and medium enterprises
MSW	municipal sanitation workers
NADMO	National Disaster Management Organization
NALSU	Neil Aggett Labour Studies Unit
NBER	National Bureau of Economic Research
NBSSI	National Board for Small Scale Industries
NGO	non-governmental organization
NICD	National Institute for Communicable Diseases

NIDS	National Income Dynamics Study
ODI	Overseas Development Institute
OECD	Organisation for Economic Co-operation and Development
OHCHR	Office of the High Commissioner on Human Rights
PARI	People's Archive of Rural India
PDS	public distribution system
PLAAS	Institute for Poverty, Land and Agrarian Studies
PMT	payment
PNAD	*Pesquisa Nacional por Amostra de Domicílios Contínua* (National Sample Survey of Households)
PPE	personal protective equipment
PPI	Progress out of Poverty Index
PPRC	Power and Participation Research Centre
QLFS	Quarterly Labour Force Survey
RCT	randomized controlled trial
REPO	repurchase agreement
RMG	ready-made garment
RWA	resident welfare association
SALDRU	Southern Africa Labour and Development Research Unit
SDGs	sustainable development goals
SEIU	Service Employees International Union
SHG	self-help group
SME	small and medium-scale enterprise
SOAS	School of Oriental and African Studies
SPACE	Social Protection Approaches to COVID-19 Expert Advice Service
SPAP	Social Protection Assessment Programme
SRDG	Social Relief of Distress Grant
SSA	sub-Saharan Africa
SSRN	Social Science Research Network
TCB	Trading Corporation of Bangladesh
TERS	Temporary Employer/Employee Relief Scheme
TIN	tax identification number
UBPL	upper-bound poverty line
UCT	University of Cape Town
UIF	Unemployment Insurance Fund
UNDP	United Nations Development Programme
UNGPs	UN Guiding Principles on Business and Human Rights
UNIFEM	United Nations Development Fund for Women
UNRISD	United Nations Research Institute for Social Development
UNU-MERIT	United Nations University-Maastricht Economic and Social Research Institute on Innovation and Technology
UNU-WIDER	United Nations University-World Institute for Development Economics Research
URT	upper respiratory tract
USP	universal social protection

VAT	value-added tax
WFP	World Food Programme
WIEGO	Women in Informal Employment: Globalizing and Organizing
WPR	working poverty rate

Notes on Contributors

Laura Alfers is Director of the Social Protection Programme at Women in Informal Employment: Globalizing and Organizing (WIEGO) and a research associate at the Neil Aggett Labour Studies Unit at Rhodes University in Makhanda, South Africa. Her research focuses on the intersections of social policy and informal employment, on which she has published widely. She holds a PhD from the University of KwaZulu-Natal and an MPhil in Development Studies from Cambridge University.

Jan Breman is Professor Emeritus of Comparative Sociology at the University of Amsterdam since 2001 and continues his academic work as Honorary Fellow at the International Institute of Social History in Amsterdam. He specialized in South and Southeast Asian Studies, and the themes of his research concern labour in the presence or absence of the social question in the setting of globalized capitalism from the colonial to the postcolonial era.

Deepita Chakravarty is a professor of development studies at the School of Development Studies, Dr B.R. Ambedkar University Delhi. Her areas of research are gender, work and family, labour market behaviour of women and men in South Asia, and industrial organization and institutions. She has published widely in all these fields.

Martha Alter Chen is a lecturer in public policy at the Harvard Kennedy School, an affiliated professor at the Harvard Graduate School of Design, and senior advisor of the global research-policy-action network WIEGO. An experienced development practitioner and scholar, her areas of specialization are employment, gender, and poverty with a focus on the working poor in the informal economy. Before joining Harvard in 1987, she had two decades of resident experience in Bangladesh working with BRAC (now the world's largest non-governmental organization) and in India, where she served as field representative of Oxfam America for India and Bangladesh. Dr Chen received a PhD in South Asia Regional Studies from the University of Pennsylvania. She is the author and editor of numerous books, including *The Informal Economy Revisited: Examining the Past, Envisioning the Future* (co-edited with Francoise Carre), *Bridging Perspectives: Labour, Informal Employment, and Poverty* (co-edited with Namrata Bali and Ravi Kanbur), *The Progress of the World's Women 2005: Women, Work and Poverty* (co-authored with Joann Vanek, Francie Lund, James Heintz, Renana Jhabvala, and Chris Bonner), *Mainstreaming Informal Employment and Gender in Poverty Reduction* (co-authored with Marilyn Carr and Joann Vanek), *Women and Men in the Informal Economy: A Statistical Picture* (co-authored with Joann Vanek and others), and *Perpetual Mourning: Widowhood in Rural India*. Dr Chen was awarded a high civilian award, the Padma Shri, by the government of India in April 2011 and a Friends of Bangladesh Liberation War award by the government of Bangladesh in December 2012.

Michael Danquah is a development economist and a research fellow at United Nations University-World Institute for Development Economics Research (UNU-WIDER). He is a co-chair of the International Union for the Scientific Study of Population (IUSSP) Scientific Panel on Population, Poverty and Climate Change and a visiting research fellow at the Transfer Project. His research interest is in economic development in sub-Saharan Africa, primarily focusing on issues such as informality, inclusive growth, climate change, and productivity growth, among others. His research has been published in journals such as *Journal of Development Studies, Journal of Economic Behavior & Organization, Small Business Economics, and Energy Economics*, among others.

Amina Ebrahim is a research fellow at UNU-WIDER. Her research interests include labour and public economics, focusing on employment, tax, and social policies. Her recent research has focused on evaluating South Africa's youth wage subsidy policy using tax data from South Africa. Her works focus on making large administrative tax data available for research and collaboration with African revenue authorities.

Avinno Faruk is a senior research associate at BRAC Institute of Governance and Development (BIGD), BRAC University, and a graduate student at Duke University. Her past publications focus on labour economics, poverty, and the economics of gender.

Jayati Ghosh is a professor of economics at the University of Massachusetts Amherst. Prior to that, she taught at Jawaharlal Nehru University, New Delhi for more than three decades. Her research interests include international macroeconomics and the political economy of gender and development.

Erofili Grapsa is a statistician and data analyst with many years' experience in analysing complex data sets and applying advanced statistical methodologies and modelling in health, labour market, gender research, time use, and social sciences in general. Over the course of her career, she has worked as a researcher for a variety of organizations and universities and collaborated with multicultural and diverse teams. She is interested in developing and expanding research methodology by implementing cross- and inter-disciplinary methods and providing support for evidence-based policymaking.

Barbara Harriss-White is Emeritus Professor and Fellow, Wolfson College, Oxford University. Since 1969, she has studied and taught Indian political economy, making long-term field-studies of agrarian change, non-metropolitan capitalism, market-mediated deprivation, and related areas of policy, publishing widely in these fields. She now works on the economy as a waste-producing system.

Md Saiful Islam is a lecturer at the Department of Economics, University of Dhaka. He started his career at BRAC (BIGD), BRAC University, in July 2019 as a research associate. He is experienced in conducting quantitative data collection and analysis, randomized controlled trials (RCTs) and field-based experiments. His main areas of interest include development economics, public health, and labour economics.

Ghida Ismail is a researcher with WIEGO. She has also worked with international organizations, such as the United Nations Development Programme (UNDP), UN Women, and the World Bank, on generating data and evidence to better inform the design of policies and development programmes. Her research has covered diverse social and economic issues in the Middle East, East Africa, and South Asia, including social protections for informal workers, women's access to affordable transportation and the labour market, social cohesion, and farmers' empowerment.

Florian Juergens-Grant is Global Social Protection Advisor at WIEGO, based in London. Prior to this, Florian worked as Global Social Protection Advisor at HelpAge International and with the International Labour Organization in Malawi. He holds an MSc in Public Policy and Human Development with specialization in Social Protection Policy, Design and Finance, from the United Nations University-Maastricht Economic and Social Research Institute on Innovation and Technology (UNU-MERIT) and the Maastricht Graduate School of Governance.

Ravi Kanbur is T.H. Lee Professor of World Affairs and Economics at Cornell University. He has served on the senior staff of the World Bank, including as Chief Economist for Africa. He is Co-Chair of the Food System Economics Commission. The positions he has held include chair of UNU-WIDER, president of the Human Development and Capability Association, and president of the Society for the Study of Economic Inequality.

Imran Matin is Executive Director of BIGD, a social research and teaching Institute of BRAC University. Trained as a development economist, with professional positions in development research and management, his research interests are in the area of livelihoods, financial inclusion, and economic empowerment, with a focus on global southern development knowledge.

Siviwe Mhlana is a researcher at the University of the Witwatersrand and a PhD candidate in the Department of Economics at the School of Oriental and African Studies (SOAS) University of London. She has worked as a consultant for organizations such as WIEGO and the International Women's Health Coalition (IWHC). Siviwe also serves on the board of the Institute for Economic Justice (IEJ), and holds positions a research associate in the Rhodes University Department of Economics and Economic History and a member of the Neil Aggett Labour Studies Unit (NALSU). Siviwe holds an MA in Social Policy and Labour Studies from Rhodes University. Her research interests include international development, labour economics, social policy, and gender.

Rachel Moussié is WIEGO's Director of Programmes. Since 2016, she has worked with WIEGO's Social Protection Programme, where she led on the Child Care Initiative, a project looking at women informal workers' need and lack of access to quality childcare. Rachel brings a gender and feminist analysis to her research and engagement with informal workers' organizations. This builds on her years as a women's rights policy manager at ActionAid International, where she explored participatory research methodologies to understand women's time use and the impact this has on their economic security and rights. Rachel is from Mauritius and holds an MSc in Development Management from the London School of Economics and a BA from McGill University.

Nandini Nayak is an assistant professor of development studies at the School of Development Studies, Dr B.R. Ambedkar University Delhi. Her research interests include the following thematic areas: political economy of development; political sociology of development; social exclusion, inequality, and poverty; and gender and development. She has published widely in these fields.

Robert Darko Osei is an associate professor at the Institute of Statistical, Social and Economic Research (ISSER), University of Ghana, Legon and also Dean for the School of Graduate Studies at the University of Ghana. Robert has published widely in edited volumes and top international journals. His main areas of research include evaluative poverty and rural research, macro- and micro-implications of fiscal policies, aid effectiveness, and other economic development policy concerns. He is currently involved in a number of research projects in Ghana, Niger, Burkina Faso, and Mali.

Sophie Plagerson is a visiting associate professor at the Centre for Social Development in Africa, University of Johannesburg, South Africa. She is currently based in the Netherlands, working as an independent consultant. She holds a PhD in Epidemiology from the London School of Hygiene and Tropical Medicine. Research interests include social protection, state–citizen relations, and social development theory.

Atiya Rahman is an associate research fellow at BIGD, BRAC University and a PhD student at the University of East Anglia. Her research interests include poverty, financial inclusion, youth development, and intra-household conflict.

Hossain Zillur Rahman has degrees in economics and political sociology and is Founder-Chair of the Power and Participation Research Centre (PPRC) and Chairperson of BRAC. He has held multiple policy positions and written extensively on poverty, social protection, governance, urbanization, and the sociology of development.

Sarah Orleans Reed is Director of Strategy Research for the Worker Rights Consortium. During the period 2020–22, she coordinated the WIEGO COVID-19 and the Informal Economy Study, supporting quantitative and qualitative research with informal workers across 11 cities globally. In her previous roles, she supported research and worker organizing with HomeNet Thailand in Bangkok and the Street Vendor Project and Service Employees International Union (SEIU) 32BJ in New York. Prior to working in the field of labour rights, her work focused on climate resilience and urban development, primarily in Southeast Asia.

Sally Roever has a PhD from the University of California at Berkeley and has served as International Coordinator of WIEGO since 2018. As a scholar-activist, she has produced groundbreaking research on informal employment and supported organizations of workers in informal employment for over two decades. Her current research focuses on the risks and vulnerabilities associated with own-account work in the urban informal economy, the role of urban infrastructure and public space in supporting informal livelihoods, and innovations in urban legal frameworks regarding informal employment.

Michael Rogan is an associate professor in the Department of Economics and Economic History and in NALSU, both at Rhodes University in South Africa. Since 2011, he has been a research associate in the Urban Policies Programme of the global research policy action network WIEGO. During the period 2014–16, he was an honorary research fellow at the South African Human Science Research Council, where he led a national research programme on labour markets. His work over the past five years has been concerned largely with informal employment, gender, poverty, food security, education and skills development, and survey design. In recent years, he has contributed chapters on informal employment to a number of edited volumes. These include *The Oxford Handbook of the South African Economy*, *The South African Informal Sector: Creating Jobs, Reducing Poverty*, *The Informal Economy Revisited: Examining the Past, Envisioning the Future*, *Migrant Labour after Apartheid: The Inside Story*, and the *Handbook of Social Policy and Development*. He has also published numerous journal articles and his research appears in, *inter alia*, *Development Southern Africa*, *Social Indicators Research*, the *Journal of Human Development and Capabilities*, the *Journal of Development Studies*, and *World Development*. In addition to his research activities, Dr Rogan has served in advisory roles with national government departments (the Department of Labour and the Department of Higher Education and Training) in South Africa as well as with a number of research and funding agencies (the Overseas Development Institute, the Ford Foundation, and the National Research Foundation).

Simone Schotte is an applied microeconomist with research interests in development and labour economics, working specifically at the interface of poverty, inequality, and employment dynamics research. She joined UNU-WIDER as research associate in February 2019. Before coming to Helsinki, she worked at the German Institute for Global and Area Studies (GIGA) and was a consultant to the World Bank. She holds a PhD in economics from the University of Göttingen, Germany, where she was a member of the Globalization and Development (GlaD) research training group. At UNU-WIDER, Simone's main research focus is on questions related to understanding the drivers and livelihood implications of transitions between different types of formal and informal work as well as the interlinkage between occupational change and earnings inequality dynamics in developing countries. Simone's research has been published in journals such as *World Development*, the *Journal of Economic Inequality*, the *Journal of Development Studies*, *Kyklos*, and *International Migration Review*, among others.

Kunal Sen is Director of UNU-WIDER, and a professor of development economics at the Global Development Institute, University of Manchester. Formerly, he was joint research director of the Department for International Development-UK (DFID-UK) funded Effective States and Inclusive Development (ESID) Research Centre. His current research is on the political economy of development. He has performed extensive research on international finance, the political economy determinants of inclusive growth, the dynamics of poverty, social exclusion, female labour force participation, and the informal sector in developing economies. His research has focused on India, East Asia, and sub-Saharan Africa. Kunal is also a research fellow at the Institute for Labour Economics in Bonn. He has also served in advisory roles with national governments and bilateral and multilateral development agencies, including the UK's DFID, the Asian Development Bank (ADB), and the International Development Research Centre (IDRC). Kunal's recent authored books are *The Political Economy of India's Growth Episodes* and *Out of the Shadows? The Informal Sector in Post-Reform India*. He has published over 100 journal articles, including chapters in the *Journal of Development Economics*, the *Journal of Development Studies*, and *World Development*. He won the Dudley Seers Prize in 2003 and the Sanjaya Lall Prize in 2006 for his publications.

Caroline Skinner is a senior researcher at the African Centre for Cities at the University of Cape Town and Director of the Urban Policies Programme within the global research policy action network WIEGO. For over 15 years, her work has interrogated the nature of the informal economy, with a focus on informing advocacy processes and livelihood-centred policy and planning responses. She has published widely on the topic.

Marcela Valdivia is a policy analyst at the Organisation for Economic Co-operation and Development's (OECD's) Employment, Labour and Social Affairs Directorate, where she conducts research on the labour market and social inclusion of migrants, with a particular focus on women. Between 2020 and 2022, she collaborated with WIEGO as the COVID-19 study officer. She has also worked as a consultant with the German Agency for International Cooperation (GIZ), the UNDP, and the Inter-American Dialogue, working towards the financial inclusion of migrants and their families and understanding structural development challenges underpinning migration. She holds two master's degrees—one in development economics and the other in international relations—from Sorbonne University (Paris) and Georgetown University (Washington DC), respectively.

Joann Vanek is Emeritus Director and Senior Advisor of the Statistics Programme of the global network WIEGO. Her work has focused on developing statistics to inform social and economic concerns and making them easily accessible. She worked in the United Nations Statistics Division for 20 years, where she led the development of the gender statistics programme and coordinated production of three issues of the global report, *The World's Women: Trends and Statistics*.

Mohammad Abdul Wazed has a long experience in the Bangladesh Civil Service and is Director General of the Bangladesh Bureau of Statistics. He has a special interest in the areas of governance, social protection, recovery of livelihoods of disaster-affected people, and climate change adaptation. As a consultant and senior fellow at the PPRC, he has been involved in action research programmes. Mr Wazed is also a part-time teacher in the Department of Disaster Science and Climate Resilience of the University of Dhaka.

Maureen Were is a researcher at the Central Bank of Kenya. Prior to this, she was a research fellow at UNU-WIDER. She was the focal point for UNU-WIDER's collaborative research project with the Institute of African Leadership for Sustainable Development, also known as UONGOZI Institute in Tanzania. She is an expert in macroeconomic modelling, analysis, and forecasting—design and application of analytical models for policy analysis and forecasting.

Umama Zillur has a master's degree in public policy candidate from the University of Chicago, Harris School of Public Policy and is a fellow at the Pearson Institute of the Study and Resolution Global Conflict. As a research associate at the PPRC, she has been studying urban poverty in Bangladesh with a specific focus on the gendered impact of multidimensional poverty. She is the founder of Kotha, a feminist youth organization working on the root causes of gender-based violence.

Rocco Zizzamia is a development economist focusing broadly on social protection and labour, development, and behavioural economics. He has led research projects in South Africa and Bangladesh, which have used a wide variety of methods—including household surveys, field experiments, qualitative studies, and behavioural lab experiments. He has consulted for the International Labour Organization and the World Bank and held appointments at the Southern African Labour and Development Research Unit. He has also worked with the South African government on the targeting approach used for dispensing cash grants as a relief measure during the initial COVID-19 lockdowns. He received an MPhil in Development Studies from the University of Oxford, where he is currently a DPhil student and incoming post-doctoral researcher.

Introduction

Martha Alter Chen, Michael Rogan, and Kunal Sen

1. The COVID-19 Crisis in Context

It has now been more than three years since the start of the COVID-19 pandemic and hopes for a global labour market recovery have not yet materialized. While some of the livelihoods and jobs that were lost at the outset of the pandemic in 2020 have been restored, the second half of 2021 was characterized by a stalled and uneven recovery (ILO 2022). A further setback in the form of low or negative economic growth in 2022 was accompanied by the beginning of a cost-of-living crisis. Estimates from the International Monetary Fund (IMF) suggest that global inflation reached 8.8 per cent in 2022, while emerging and developing economies saw inflation reach levels of 11 per cent (IMF 2022). In emerging and developing countries, working hours actually decreased further in 2021 compared with 2020 (e.g. by between 5.7 and 7.4 per cent in the third quarter of 2021, respectively), while working hours showed signs of recovery in early 2021 in developed countries before stalling again (ILO 2021). Thus, even before the Russian invasion of Ukraine and the onset of rampant inflation, the employment recovery in developing countries in 2021 was already far more muted, and significantly, these are the countries in which 70 per cent of all employment is informal (ILO 2018).

By the end of 2022, the picture did not look much better, with medium-term expectations for employment suggesting that emerging and developing economies would experience average losses of 4.3 per cent for output and 2.6 per cent for employment in 2024 (IMF 2022). Compounding matters is the existence of an ongoing 'fiscal stimulus gap' between emerging and developing countries, on the one hand, and developed countries on the other (ILO 2022). As a result, poverty levels (and working poverty rates) have increased for the first time in decades, and development progress (including progress towards the sustainable development goals (SDGs)) is now under threat (ILO 2022). Global inequality is also likely to rise as one of the consistent themes over the pandemic and post-pandemic periods has been the widening of pre-existing fault lines and vulnerabilities, especially between the capitalist class and the working poor (Alon et al. 2020; ILO 2021).

As a result, and due to the unpredictability of the pandemic's trajectory combined with unprecedented increases in global food and energy prices, the global

Martha Alter Chen, Michael Rogan, and Kunal Sen, *Introduction*. In: *COVID-19 and the Informal Economy*. Edited by: Martha Alter Chen, Michael Rogan, and Kunal Sen, Oxford University Press. © Martha Alter Chen, Michael Rogan, and Kunal Sen (2024). DOI: 10.1093/oso/9780198887041.003.0001 outlook remained unstable and uncertain in 2022 (ILO 2022). This high level of uncertainty notwithstanding, there are two conclusions that can be drawn concerning the impact of the pandemic on the global labour market. First, both the short- and medium-term effects of the pandemic and accompanying government restrictions to contain its spread have been highly differentiated. In many developed countries, the effects of the pandemic have given rise to even greater levels of flexible work arrangements, decreases in labour supply, and the continued expansion of the 'gig economy'. In contrast, much of the early evidence suggests that, in emerging and developing countries, informal workers have borne the brunt of job losses and have been left, in large part, to fend for themselves (ILO 2020). Second, it has become clear that the events of 2020 and 2021 are likely to reshape labour markets in the long term. Shifts in the structure of employment, the advent of remote working, the 'great resignation' (or the great 're-shuffle') of 2021, more flexible work arrangements, changes in market demand, and the catastrophic loss of employment and earnings, particularly among the informally employed, will likely have enduring implications for labour markets.

This volume aims to shed new light on both of these themes, and its publication is timely. Detailed evidence on the impacts of the pandemic on regional and national labour markets is only now becoming available. At the same time, there is emerging research which illustrates precisely how differentiated the magnitude of job and earnings losses have been in different contexts and for different sectors and types of workers. While a complete picture of the shorter-term impacts of the pandemic on employment will only emerge in the years to come, it is crucial to understand the longer-term implications for labour markets. This volume brings together a number of contributions which aim to examine the future of labour markets, how policy measures can protect informal workers, and to reflect on the lessons learned from the largest shock to the global labour market in generations as well as the ongoing disruption to global supply chains.

The remainder of this introductory chapter is structured as follows. Section 2 sets out the context by providing an overview of the health dimensions of the crisis as experienced by informal workers. Next, Section 3 offers an overarching framework for defining informal employment and provides an overview of the size and structure of informal employment in different regions. Section 4 offers a brief assessment of the evidence base on the impact of the pandemic on informal employment from a range of contexts and based on a number of different data sources. Section five provides an overview of the contributions to the volume and offers some context for the regions and countries which are included in respective chapter analyses.

2. A health and employment crisis

The focus of this volume is on the employment and economic impacts of the COVID-19 pandemic and associated restrictions and economic downturns on informal workers and their livelihood activities. However, to provide some context, it is important to understand the health impacts of the crisis on informal workers and their families. The challenge, in this regard, is that the evidence remains limited and available statistics are often puzzling, if not misleading. Studies which focus on the differential health impact of the crisis on different population groups tend to use demographic or socio-economic indicators, not employment indicators, to differentiate between groups. Moreover, the estimates of mortality due to the virus vary significantly depending on whether the estimates are of reported deaths, total deaths, or excess deaths, that is, the difference between total deaths and expected deaths due to common causes in non-crisis years, such as influenza. The estimates also differ by source. In mid-2022, the Institute of Health Metrics and Evaluation (IHME), one of the most credible sources of global data, estimated 6.9 million recorded deaths from the virus and 17.2 million excess deaths worldwide since the beginning of the pandemic (IHME 2022).

2.1 The statistical puzzle: Inverse relationship between informality and mortality rates

During the pandemic, the rates of recorded deaths in Europe and North America (where rates of informal employment are relatively low) were higher than in developing regions (where rates of informal employment are very high). In part, this is because estimates of reported deaths tend to be disproportionately high in rich countries and regions due to higher levels of both testing for infections and reporting deaths. But in some developing countries, there was an inverse relationship between informality and mortality rates during the pandemic, even using estimates of total or excess deaths.

Consider Africa for instance. In mid-2022, the reported death rate in Africa was relatively low at 165 deaths per million in mid-2022. But the IHME estimated that the total death rate for Africa was ten times higher at 1,774 deaths per million (IHME 2022). However, even comparing total deaths, Africa had the second-lowest regional death rate in the world (Sachs et al. 2022). Yet, sub-Saharan Africa and South Asia have the highest rates of informal employment at 77 and 78 per cent, respectively (ILO 2018). Meagher (2022) has interrogated this puzzle in her review of COVID-19, informality, and social policy in Africa. Among the factors that could explain the relatively low mortality rates, Meagher identified a young population profile which reduced the likelihood of dying from the virus, an underlying disease profile that limited vulnerability to the virus, quick action at the start of the pandemic by public health systems with experience in tracking and tackling infectious disease outbreaks, and climatic factors conducive to a prevalence of open-air activities (Meagher 2022 citing Birner et al. 2021; Ghosh et al. 2020). Meagher also focuses on subregional differences in the size and structure of the informal economy and the nature of the state, including the ability to deliver health care, in different countries. Meagher (2022: 1212) concludes that the evidence 'suggests an inverse relationship between the size and complexity of informal economies, and the capacity of states to administer complex social provisioning arrangements'.

Before turning to the ability of informal workers to access health care during the pandemic, it should be noted that the largest wave of the virus around the world in terms of deaths (recorded, total, and excess) was the Delta wave in 2021 (Sachs et al. 2022). This wave resulted in extremely high mortality, with an estimated two million deaths worldwide between April and June 2021 of which an estimated 1.6 million were in India alone (IHME 2022). During the first wave in India in 2020, which led to a nationwide lockdown, informal workers across India (and around the world) lamented, 'We will die from hunger before we die from the virus' (Chen et al. 2021). During the Delta wave a year later, most informal workers across India (and around the world) were more concerned about the spread of the virus than outright hunger as many were back at work, albeit for fewer days per week and with lower earnings (Alfers et al. 2022). After the Delta surge, cases in India decreased markedly and vaccination efforts accelerated; by September 2022, more than 70 per cent of the eligible population of India was fully vaccinated (Sachs et al. 2022). But within India, affluent states like Delhi and Goa had higher rates of both testing and reported deaths than poor states like Bihar and Uttar Pradesh (Roy 2021). However, during the Omicron wave in January 2022, deaths in India overall (recorded, total, and excess) remained relatively low (Sachs et al. 2022).

2.2 Reality on the ground: High exposure to health risks, low access to health care for informal workers

Most studies which identified population groups who were particularly vulnerable during the pandemic did not consider whether these groups were informally employed. For instance, a Lancet Commission on the crisis identified a long list of 'heavily burdened' groups based on its review of available studies: from essential workers, to minority and low-income communities, to women who face employ-ment and income losses, to migrants and displaced populations, to people without access to quality and affordable health care (Sachs et al. 2022). Before the pan-demic, it is very likely that the majority of working persons in each of these groups were informally employed (ILO 2018).

One exception was a study in Colombia of confirmed cases of the virus, which found that the risk of dying was higher among males and people over 60 years of age as well as among indigenous peoples, those with subsidized health insur-ance, and those from the two lowest socio-economic strata (Cifuentes et al. 2021). The authors pointed out that those with subsidized health insurance are likely to be informally employed and highlighted the association between poor working conditions and high exposure to infections as follows, citing their own as well as others' studies:

> People in the more disadvantaged working groups have lower-paid work and are more likely to work in key basic services (food, cleaning, delivery or public ser-vices) that require them to work in person and commute across the cities (Ribeiro and Leist 2020). In contrast, people with higher-paid work are more likely to work from home with lower exposure to COVID-19 infection.
> (Bambra et al. 2020; Cifuentes et al. 2021: Discussion)

Some studies have highlighted the difficulties that specific population groups faced in accessing health care, both before and during the pandemic: such as Blacks and other people of colour in the United States (Millet et al. 2020). But few of these studies focused on the specific difficulties informal workers faced in accessing health care.

One exception is the 11-city study led by Women in Informal Employment: Globalizing and Organizing (WIEGO), which is featured in Chapters 1 in this volume. In regard to preventative health care, this study found that many informal workers, especially street vendors and waste pickers, had no access to water where they worked and that most respondents had to buy their own personal protec-tive equipment (PPE). Also, COVID-19 vaccine coverage among informal workers and their families was generally low, even by the second half of 2021, despite the fact that the workers were often obliged to get vaccinated by employers and local authorities (Braham 2022). This low vaccine coverage was due to common fac-tors (such as lack of vaccines, inequities in the distribution of vaccines, the cost of getting vaccinated and vaccine hesitancy) but also to specific barriers faced by informal workers in getting vaccinated: notably, the lack of time to register for vac-cinations and concern about the side effects of vaccines as few informal workers are entitled to paid sick leave and, therefore, cannot afford to miss work (Braham 2022).

In regard to curative health care, the 11-city study found that the majority of respondents faced difficulties accessing health care, even when they were confirmed to be infected with COVID. After trying to deal with overburdened public health systems, many respondents had no option but to take infected family members to private hospitals, despite the high costs involved. Those that did so struggled to pay for private treatment because they had no health insurance and few financial resources as they were earning less and had drawn down savings during the pandemic recession. Some informal workers had to forgo medical treatment for themselves or a family member, including around a quarter of respondents in Lima and Mexico. Further, some respondents (notably domestic workers) were not allowed to seek health care. In Lima and Mexico City, some domestic workers were forced to work, despite being ill, and others were laid off if they missed work due to illness; and many live-in domestic workers were not allowed to leave their employer's house for medical appointments or to get vaccinated (Braham 2022).

Furthermore, in cities with particularly severe waves of COVID-19, respondents also spoke about how the deaths of immediate family and community members impacted them. A domestic worker in Lima who lost several family members and friends reported, 'it has been disastrous, shocking. To see people die so often shocks one's nerves; seeing so much pain is shocking' (Alfers et al. 2022: 22).

The impacts of COVID-19 on the health and livelihoods of informal workers were interlinked. On the one hand, the barriers to, and costs of accessing, health care; the inability to care for—or even see—family members; and the loss of family members compounded the economic and financial stress. On the other hand, becoming ill, or the fear of becoming ill, were significant obstacles to being able to work. Nearly 30 per cent of respondents in the 11-city study reported being unable to work at some point over the past year due to being ill or out of fear of becoming ill (Alfers et al. 2022: 22). One woman home-based worker in Bangkok reported the lingering impacts of COVID-19 infection on her ability to work, suggesting that some had suffered from 'long COVID': 'For those who got COVID, although they recovered . . . their health is different from before. They are easily tired, and when they get tired, they have to stop working immediately' (Alfers et al. 2022).

3. Informal employment: Definitions and the structure of global employment

3.1 An international definition of informal employment

At the beginning of a volume which is concerned with the impact of the pandemic on informal employment, it is important to provide a definitional framework and overview of the structure and scope of informal employment in developing and emerging economies. As a point of departure, the International Labour Organization's (ILO's) International Conference of Labour Statisticians (ICLS) provides recommendations for a comprehensive and internationally comparable definition of informal employment. In broad terms, the ICLS recommended definition is inclusive of all types of employment that lack any type of legal recognition or protection and where workers do not have secure employment contracts, workers' benefits, social protection, or workers' representation (Hussmanns 2004; ILO 2013). Informal-sector employment, a subset of informal employment, is defined as all employment within unregistered or unincorporated enterprises. This includes self-employment and wage employment as well as contributing family work. These two definitions—informal employment and informal-sector employment—are operationalized at the country level and then reported to the ILO based on the analysis of official household surveys such as a labour force survey.

In this volume, informal employment is conceptualized within the parameters of the ILO definition, but each chapter approaches the definition based on the available data. Two chapters, Danquah et al. (Chapter 3) and Rogan and Skinner (Chapter 4), present an analysis based on an official national household survey (or a subsample of one) and, as such, define (explicitly) informal employment in line with the ICLS recommendations. Other chapters examine informal employment through the lens of specific groups of workers, such as the self-employed (the majority of informal workers in many contexts) and domestic workers (who are largely employed informally) as well as informal workers engaged in activities such as waste collection, home-based work, and street and market trade. In short, each of the empirical chapters in the volume concentrate their analysis on a segment of the workforce that is broadly identifiable as informal under the international ICLS guidelines.

3.2 Informal employment in a global context

In the mid-1900s, it was widely assumed that economic growth would be accompanied by a structural transformation of the economy from agriculture to manufacturing and services (Kuznets 1955) and of labour markets from self-employment in traditional labour-intensive activities to wage employment in modern, capital-intensive activities (Lewis 1952). However, in some countries, economic growth outpaced structural transformation, and in others, structural transformation took different directions.

Today, labour markets differ significantly not only between developed and developing countries but also between developed and emerging countries as economic growth has outpaced the growth of formal wage employment in many countries, which recently graduated from developing to middle-income countries.

Globally, the majority of all workers (61 per cent) are informally employed: a total of 2 billion workers—90 per cent of all workers in developing countries, 67 per cent in emerging countries, and 18 per cent in developed countries (ILO 2018).

This volume focuses on COVID-19 and informal employment in primarily developing and emerging economies. To provide some context, what follows is a summary overview of labour markets in developing and emerging economies grouped by geographic region but excluding developed countries in the regions. Data on three key indicators of the composition of labour markets are presented and briefly discussed: share of total employment that is informal as well as percentage distribution of total and informal employment across different branches of industry and status in employment, including differences between women and men.

All the data in this summary are from calculations by the ILO of household survey micro-data sets from around 2016 in ILOSTAT, the ILO database, for a statistical brief by the ILO and WIEGO in 2019 (Bonnet et al. 2019). Several outliers are excluded in the regional averages presented here: China from East and Southeast Asia and three Southern African countries from sub-Saharan Africa (SSA) for which data are available (Botswana, Namibia, and South Africa).

The share of informal employment in total employment varies across regions: from around 90 per cent of total employment in South Asia and SSA to three-quarters of total employment in East and Southeast Asia to over two-thirds in the Middle East and North Africa, over half in Latin America and the Caribbean, and over one-third in Eastern Europe and Central Asia (Table 1). The share of informal employment in non-agricultural employment is lower than in total employment (by 5–10 percentage points) in all regions and follows the same general rank order.

3.3 Branch of industry

Total employment
Services is the predominant branch of total employment in most regions, except in South Asia and SSA, where it represents around 30 per cent. *Industry* represents 28 per cent or less of total employment in all regions: as low as 9 per cent in SSA (Table 1).[1] *Agriculture* is the predominant branch of employment only in SSA, at 60 per cent of total employment. Agriculture comprises 36 per cent of total employment in East Asia and Southeast Asia, only 16 per cent of total employment in Eastern Europe and Central Asia, and 18 per cent in Latin America and the Caribbean.

---

[1] The branch or category *Industry* includes not only manufacturing but also mining and quarrying; electricity, gas, steam, and air conditioning supply; water supply; sewerage and waste management and remediation activities; and construction.

Table 1 Total and informal employment by geographic regions and branch of economy: percentage distribution with regions ranked by percentage of informal employment

Geographic regions (%) (excluding developed countries)*	Agriculture		Industry		Services	
	T	I	T	I	T	I
Sub-Saharan Africa** (92)	60	65	9	8	31	27
South Asia (88)	43	48	28	24	32	27
East and South-East Asia*** (77)	36	45	23	20	41	35
Middle East and North Africa (68)	24	34	23	25	52	41
Latin America and the Caribbean (54)	18	23	22	20	62	57
Southern Africa (40)	10	17	22	19	68	64
Eastern Europe and Central Asia (37)	16	33	26	24	58	43
Developed countries (18)	3	10	22	19	75	71

Note: T = total employment; I = informal employment; * = regions rank-ordered according to rate of informal employment (% in parentheses); ** = excluding Southern African countries; *** = excluding China.
Source: 2018 ILO calculations based on household survey micro-data sets in ILOSTAT; presented in Bonnet et. al (2019).

Informal employment

The percentage distribution of informal employment across the three broad branches of the economy is different than for total employment in several ways. *Services* represent a lower share of informal employment than of total employment in all regions with a low of just over 30 per cent in South Asia and SSA. *Industry* represents roughly the same share of informal employment as of total employment in all regions (within three percentage points). *Agriculture* represents a greater share of informal employment than of total employment in all regions with a high of 65 per cent of informal employment in SSA followed by 48 per cent of informal employment in South Asia.

In sum, as the regional rate of informality decreases, the proportion of both total and informal workers in agriculture decreases while the proportion in services increases and the proportion in industry varies. But across all regions, compared to total employment, the proportion of informal workers in agriculture is higher and the proportion of informal workers in services and industry is lower, except in the Middle East and North Africa, where the proportion of informal workers in industry is slightly higher. Notably, among the three branches of the economy, industry represents the lowest share of both total and informal workers: between 20 and 30 per cent in all regions, except in SSA, where it comprises less than 10 per cent of total and informal workers.

3.4 Status in employment

Total employment

Employers (those who hire others) represent a very low percentage of total employment, ranging from 1 per cent in South Asia to 5–6 per cent in Southern Africa, Latin America and the Caribbean, the Middle East and North Africa, and Eastern Europe and Central Asia (Table 2). *Employees* or wage workers represent the predominant share of total employment in most regions, except South Asia and SSA, where they represent just over one-quarter and one-third, respectively. *Own-account workers* (self-employed who do not hire others) represent another major share of total employment: well over half of all workers in South Asia; more than half in SSA; over one-third in East and Southeast Asia; around one-quarter in Latin America and the Caribbean and the Middle East and North Africa; but only 10 and 15 per cent, respectively, in Southern Africa and Eastern Europe and Central Asia. *Contributing family workers* (unpaid workers in family units or on family farms) represent a varying share of total employment across the regions: from 1 per cent in Southern Africa to 15–16 per cent in South Asia, East and South-East Asia, and SSA.

Informal employment

Employers represent a similarly low percentage of informal employment as of total employment, except in the Middle East and North Africa, where they represent a slightly higher share of informal employment than of total employment. The percentage distribution of informal workers across the other three statuses in employment is different than for total employment in important ways. *Employees* or wage workers represent a far smaller share of informal employment than of total employment in all regions: as low as 20 per cent of informal employment in South Asia and 27 per cent in SSA. Conversely, *own-account workers* represent a far higher share of informal employment than of total employment in all regions: as high as 62 per cent in South Asia and 53 per cent in SSA. Also, *contributing family members* represent a far higher percentage of informal employment than of total employment in all regions: as high as 23 per cent of all informal workers in East and Southeast Asia and 17–18 per cent in South Asia and SSA.

In sum, across the regions, as the rate of informality decreases, the proportion of total and informal workers who are employers or employees increases and the proportion who are own-account workers or contributing family workers decreases. Across all regions, compared to total workers, the proportion of informal workers who are employees is lower, and the proportion who are own-account workers and contributing workers is higher. Notably, across all regions, employers represent the lowest share of both total and informal workers: between 1 and 9 per cent, with no clear distribution pattern within this range.

Table 2 Total and informal employment by geographic regions and status in employment: percentage distribution with regions ranked by percentage of informal employment

Geographic regions (%)	Employers		Employees		Own-account workers		Contributing family workers	
(excluding developed countries)*	T	I	T	I	T	I	T	I
Sub-Saharan Africa (92)**	2	2	35	27	53	47	16	18
South Asia (88)	1	1	26	20	58	62	15	17
East and South-East Asia (77)***	4	3	46	39	35	36	5	23
Middle East and North Africa (68)	6	9	60	44	25	36	9	11
Latin America and the Caribbean (54)	5	4	63	45	28	43	4	8
Southern Africa (40)	5	5	84	70	0	22	1	3
Eastern Europe and Central Asia (37)	2	2	79	65	14	23	4	11
Developed countries (18)	6	6	86	51	9	36	1	6

Note: T = total employment; I = informal employment; * = regions rank-ordered according to rate of informal employment (% in parentheses); ** = excluding Southern African countries; *** = excluding China.
Source: 2018 ILO calculations based on household survey micro-data sets in ILOSTAT; presented in Bonnet et. al (2019).

3.5 Women and men

Finally, it is important to consider differences between women and men in total and informal employment and by branches of industry and status in employment. In developing and emerging economies, female labour force participation rates tend to be lower than for men. And, globally, a lower percentage of women workers (58 per cent) than of men workers (63 per cent) are informally employed. However, in developing countries, a higher percentage of women workers (92 per cent) than of men workers (87 per cent) are informally employed. This is because women have higher rates of informal employment than men in three populous geographic regions: SSA (excluding Southern Africa), South Asia, and Latin America and the Caribbean. Considered another way, a higher percentage of women workers than of men workers are informally employed in well over half (56 per cent) of the countries.

Among both formal and informal workers, women are more likely than men to be employed in the service sector in three regions: SSA (including Southern Africa), Latin American and the Caribbean, and Eastern Europe and Central Asia.

Also, in all regions, the rate of formal employment in services is higher for women than for men. By contrast, industry is a greater source of employment—total, formal, and informal—for men than for women across all geographic regions.

Women are far less likely than men to be *employers* in all regions but especially in Southern Africa and the Middle East and North Africa. In marked contrast, across all regions and among both total and informal workers, women are far more likely than men to be *contributing family workers*: more than three times as likely in South Asia, East and Southeast Asia (including China), and the Middle East and North Africa. One exception is Southern African, where the percentages of contributing family workers are extremely low among both women and men in both total and informal employment. Among both total and informal workers, the percentages of women and men in *wage employment* are roughly the same, except in SSA (excluding Southern Africa) and the Middle East and North Africa, where men are more likely to be wage workers/employees. Also, among both total and informal workers, the percentages of women and men who are *own-account workers* are roughly the same, except in South Asia, East and South-East Asia (including and excluding China), and (among formal workers) in the Middle East and North Africa, where men are more likely to be own-account workers.

In sum, labour markets in developing as well as emerging countries defy the earlier predictions of structural transformation from agriculture to industry and services and from low-end self-employment to modern wage employment. Notably, informal employment, particularly own-account work, predominates in the labour markets of emerging and (especially) developing economies. But there are important regional and subregional differences in the percentage distribution of informal employment by branch of industry and status in employment. South Asia and SSA (excluding Southern Africa) have the highest rates of informality and, among informal workers, relatively high rates of own-account work and work in agriculture. But both total and informal workers in South Asia are three times more likely than their counterparts in SSA (excluding Southern Africa) to be employed in industry.

Finally, it is important to highlight that the differences between labour markets in developing and emerging economies pale in comparison to the differences between labour markets in developed countries and those in developing and emerging countries. This is because employment in developed countries is predominantly formal wage employment in (especially) services but also industry, while employment in developing and emerging countries is predominantly informal self-employment in agriculture and services.

4. Early evidence on the impact of COVID-19 on informal employment

Turning now to the theme of this volume, it was evident, even during the earliest stages of the pandemic, that there would be a devastating and disproportionate impact on informal workers. In late April 2020, the ILO estimated that 1.6 billion people employed in the informal economy—preliminary ILO projections suggested that 80 per cent of informal workers were likely to be severely affected—would see their livelihoods destroyed due to the decline in work, working hours, and earnings brought on by lockdowns or other restrictions to curb the spread of COVID-19 (ILO 2020). Since then, a growing body of studies on the impact of the COVID-19 crisis on informal workers has confirmed the ILO prediction: including the studies featured in Part I of this volume.

Among the early studies carried out in 2020, an analysis of data from Burkina Faso, Mali, and Senegal suggest that, by the end of April 2020, across these three West African countries, one-quarter of all workers had lost jobs or were not able to work, and half of all workers had experienced a decline in earnings (Balde et al. 2020). These surveys found that informal workers were at significantly higher risk than formal workers. As of the end of April, in Burkina Faso, 4 per cent of formal workers and 48 per cent of informal workers were unemployed; in Mali, 8 per cent of formal workers and 32 per cent of informal workers were unemployed; and in Senegal, 8 per cent of formal workers and 42 per cent of informal workers were unemployed (Balde et al. 2020). These large differences can be attributed (the authors argue) to the fact that informal workers tend to be over-represented in activities that were disproportionately impacted by lockdown measures—such as the retail trade, restaurants, tourism, hairdressing, and taxi driving (Balde et al. 2020).

While the disproportionate impact on informal workers was anticipated widely, the delay in access to nationally representative surveys, together with the difficulties associated with collecting data during a pandemic, has meant that a complete picture is only now beginning to emerge. In the absence of official labour force data, evidence initially came from two sources (Cueva et al. 2021): simulation models (Cereda et al. 2020; Genoni et al. 2020; O'Donoghue et al. 2020) and specialized 'COVID' telephonic surveys[2] (Benhura and Magejo 2020; Chetty et al. 2020; Montenovo et al. 2021; Ranchhod and Daniels 2020; Rogan and Skinner 2020; Schotte et al. 2021). More innovative ways to capture the pandemic's impact have included the use of financial diaries kept by

---

[2] See, e.g. the World Bank High-Frequency Phone Surveys, https://microdata.worldbank.org/index.php/catalog/hfps (accessed 31 October 2023).

poor households in the pre-pandemic and pandemic periods. The advantage of this method is that it allows us to examine individual diarists' behavioural responses to the pandemic with a granularity that is not possible with large-scale phone surveys (Rönkkö et al. 2022). More recently, national household surveys from several countries have become available in contexts where national statistical offices continued to collect data during the pandemic. In countries such as Peru and South Africa (Cueva et al. 2021; Skinner et al. 2021), these surveys have been collected quarterly and allow for disaggregation between formal and informal employment. Each of these broad methodological approaches to understanding the impact of the pandemic on employment have different strengths and weaknesses. Taken together, however, they suggest that jobs and earnings losses in a number of different developing and emerging country contexts were concentrated among women, low-paid workers, urban dwellers, and informal workers (Cueva et al. 2021). In sum, these studies and the ones featured in this volume confirm the April 2020 ILO projection that the pandemic-cum-lockdowns/restrictions would have disproportionately negative impacts on informal workers, their livelihood activities, and their households. In low-income households, which depend on daily earnings, the imposition of lockdowns and other stay-at-home restrictions to curb the spread of the virus led, almost immediately, to three interrelated crises for informal workers: no work, no income, no food.

However, a more nuanced understanding of the impact of the pandemic on informal employment in developing and emerging countries is still required. Recent evidence suggests that it is important to identify the different pathways or degrees of impact on informal labour markets in different contexts. The most recent ILO report, for example, suggests that there has been a global pandemic-driven increase in self-employment and contributing family work which may be explained by a rise in 'gig work' (ILO 2022) and by a decrease in work orders to subcontracted workers (Chen et al., Chapter 1 this volume). The same report noted that, in a selection of ten middle-income countries, informal wage and self-employment both saw the largest job losses at the beginning of the pandemic but that informal self-employment has recovered[3] at a greater rate over the following four quarters. Thus, there is still much to be learned about the effects on different groups of informal workers across labour markets in developing and emerging countries. For example, a recent World Bank report has argued that informal self-employment may actually increase in developed countries in response to the loss of jobs in the formal sector (Ohnsorge and Yu 2021). While this claim is not based on an empirical analysis, it demonstrates the need for grounded evidence on how the pandemic has

---

[3] At least at the extensive margins. There is still much to be learned about the loss of working hours as well as the impact on earnings and household debt, among the informally self-employed.

impacted different groups of workers as well as how the structures of segmented labour markets in much of the Global South have disadvantaged the majority of the global workforce while leading to unprecedented increases in working poverty.

5. Objectives and outline of the volume

The aims of this volume are twofold. First, it brings together, for the first time, evidence on the differentiated impacts of the pandemic on diverse groups of informal workers from a number of developing and emerging country contexts. In so doing, the volume aims to highlight the nuanced ways in which informal workers have been impacted by the pandemic during its peak (2020–22). Second, the volume aims to reflect on the implications of this unprecedented disruption to informal work for the longer-term structure of employment, with a particular focus on labour markets in the Global South. Lessons from the responses to the pandemic are synthesized in several chapters in order to envision a sustainable economic recovery which includes the majority of the world's workforce.

The volume is structured in three parts. Part one provides timely analyses from a number of recent studies that began collecting data on informal employment as the first wave of the pandemic unfolded in 2020. Chapter authors present analyses based on large data sets (e.g. labour force surveys and national COVID-19 impact surveys) as well as more detailed surveys of distinct groups of informal workers (e.g. WIEGO's 11-city longitudinal study). The aim of these contributions is to investigate the impacts of the crisis on informal workers in general and on different subgroups of workers, differentiated by occupation, status in employment, place of work, and gender.

The geographic scope of this section of the volume includes Latin America (Brazil, Chile, El Salvador, Mexico, and Peru), sub-Saharan Africa (Ghana, Senegal, and South Africa), and Asia (Bangladesh, India, and Thailand). In most of these countries, the majority of employment is informal and the impacts of the pandemic have been severe. There are two chapters on South Africa (Rogan and Skinner (Chapter 4) and Schotte and Zizzamia (Chapter 5)), where the rate of informal employment is relatively low, but which experienced the largest caseload of virus infections, the greatest number of pandemic-related deaths, and what was described at the time (early 2020) as the most severe government lockdown and set of restrictions globally. There are two chapters on South Asian countries (Bangladesh—Rahman et al., Chapter 6) and India—Chakravarty and Nayak, Chapter 7), which analyse the impacts on the working poor in countries where roughly 90 per cent of employment is informal and which endured one of the most severe outbreaks of the pandemic when the Delta variant swept through the region in 2021.

A wider geographic focus is provided by the Chen et al. in Chapter 1, which analyses data from a longitudinal survey, conducted in mid-2020 and mid-2021, of different groups of informal workers from 11 cities from nine countries in five regions (including two cities in the Global North—New York, and Pleven, Bulgaria). Chapter 2 (Chen and Vanek) provides an analysis of recent national labour force data from five Latin America countries.

In Part II, several chapters examine response, recovery, and stimulus measures with a view to understanding their implications for, and impacts on, informal employment. The chapters in this section include country case studies as well as analyses of the economic recovery frameworks in selected contexts. The first chapter in this section (Danquah et al., Chapter 8) analyses, in detail, the country-level responses of Ghana, Kenya, and South Africa and shows there has been an uneven recovery in the labour market in these countries, with informal workers, in particular, lacking support from government. This may be due to the 'moderate' economic stimulus packages introduced in these countries to support individuals and businesses to resume their economic activities.

In view of the growing 'fiscal stimulus gap' between developed countries and the rest of the world, the second chapter in this part of the volume (Mhlana et al., Chapter 9) seeks to provide a broader analysis of economic recovery policies based on a case study of two low-income countries (Bangladesh and Kenya) and two middle-income countries (South Africa and Thailand). The case study of country experiences aims to highlight the diversity of impacts and economic responses against the backdrop of the multilateral economic recovery frameworks which have been promoted throughout the pandemic period. The chapter then positions these national recovery packages within a 'gap analysis' to highlight the mismatches between livelihood erosion among workers in the informal economy and stimulus packages in the selected contexts.

In Part III of the volume, the contributions are forward-looking and reflect on the future of informal employment—and labour markets more generally—post-COVID-19. The pandemic has prompted an almost unprecedented policy focus on social protection, in part due to the lack of social safety nets when earnings came to a standstill in early 2020. The first chapter in this final part (Alfers and Juergens-Grant, Chapter 10) of the volume reflects on the role of social protection during a period in which traditional mechanisms for smoothing or protecting income have failed. The chapter also offer some insights into the way in which social protection systems have been reshaped during the pandemic and how this challenges the traditional links between social protection and employment, particularly in contexts with high levels of informal employment and where the standard employment relationship is not the norm. The second chapter (Chen et al., Chapter 11) makes the case that informal workers need to be included as key partners in a new social contract between state, capital, and labour. In particular, it seeks to highlight the mismatch between the lived realities of informal work and mainstream approaches to social contracts to make the case for a new social contract that includes informal workers as key stakeholders in contracts with the state as well as with capital. A final chapter (Kanbur et al., Chapter 12) presents a set of reflections from four well-known scholars who have dedicated their careers to understanding employment in developing country contexts.

The conclusion examines the future of informal employment through the lens of what has been learned during the COVID crisis, including the disproportionate impact of the COVID crisis on informal workers, the neglect of informal workers in economic recovery and stimulus measures, and the recognition of informal workers as essential frontline workers. It considers the likely structure of labour markets in different contexts going forward and the relationship between largely informal labour markets, economic growth, and poverty. It also envisions the type of economic and social policies which would safeguard the livelihoods of the working poor in the informal economy, extend social protection and economic support to them, and ensure that the gains from growth are distributed more evenly.

References

Alfers, L., C. Braham, M. Chen, E. Grapsa, J. Harvey, G. Ismail et al. (2022). 'COVID-19 and Informal Work: Recovery Pathways amidst Continued Crisis', Women in Informal Employment: Globalizing and Organizing (WIEGO) Working Paper No. 43, Manchester: WIEGO.

Alon, T., M. Doepke, J. Olmstead-Rumsey, and M. Tertilt (2020). 'The Impact of COVID-19 on Gender Equality', National Bureau of Economic Research (NBER) Working Paper No. 26947, Cambridge, MA: National Bureau of Economic Research.

Balde, R., M. Boly, and E. Avenyo (2020). 'Labour Market Effects of COVID-19 in Sub-Saharan Africa: An Informality Lens from Burkina Faso, Mali and Senegal', United Nations University-Maastricht Economic and Social Research Institute on Innovation and Technology (UNU-MERIT) Working Paper No. 2020/22, Maastricht: UNU-MERIT.

Bambra, C., R. Riordan, J. Ford, and F. Matthews (2020). 'The COVID-19 Pandemic and Health Inequalities', Journal of Epidemiology and Community Health, 74: 964–68.

Benhura, M., and P. Magejo (2020). 'Differences between Formal and Informal Workers' Outcomes during the COVID-19 Crisis Lockdown in South Africa', National Income Dynamics Study (NIDS)—Coronavirus Rapid Mobile Survey (CRAM) Report No. 2, Wave 2, Cape Town: NIDS.

Birner, R. et al. (2021). '"We Would Rather Die from Covid-19 than from Hunger" — Exploring Lockdown Stringencies in Five African Countries', Global Food Security 31: 100571.

Bonnet, F., J. Vanek, and M. Chen (2019). 'Women and Men in the Informal Economy: A Statistical Brief', Manchester: WIEGO.

Braham, C. (2022). 'COVID-19 Vaccination and Informal Workers: Immunize, Don't Marginalize', Policy Insights No. 9, Manchester: WIEGO.

Cereda, F., R. Rubião, and L. Liliana (2020). 'COVID-19, Labor Market Shocks, and Poverty in Brazil: A Microsimulation Analysis', World Bank Background Note, Washington, DC: Poverty and Equity Global Practice, World Bank.

Chen, M., E. Grapsa, G. Ismail, M. Rogan, M. Valdivia, L. Alfers et al. (2020). 'How Did COVID-19 and Stabilization Policies Affect Spending and Employment? A New Real-Time Economic Tracker Based on Private Sector Data', NBER Working Paper No. 27431, Cambridge, MA: NBER.

Chen, M., E. Grapsa, G. Ismail, M. Rogan, M. Valdivia, with L. Alfers et al. (2021). 'Distinct Pathways of Impact and Recovery in 11 Cities around the World', Working Paper No. 42, Manchester: WIEGO.

Cifuentes, M.P., L.A. Rodriguez-Villamizar, M.L. Rojas-Botero, C.A. Alvarez-Moreno, and J.A. Fernández-Niño (2021). 'Socioeconomic Inequalities Associated with Mortality for COVID-19 in Colombia: A Cohort Nationwide Study', *Journal of Epidemiology and Community Health*, 75(7): 610–615.

Cueva, R., X. Del Carpio, and H. Winkler (2021). 'The Impacts of COVID-19 on Informal Labor Markets: Evidence from Peru', Policy Research Working Paper No. 9675, Washington, DC: World Bank.

Genoni, M.E., A.I. Khan, N. Krishnan, N. Palaniswamy, W. Raza (2020). *Losing Livelihoods: The Labor Market Impacts of COVID-19 in Bangladesh*. Washington, DC: Poverty and Equity Global Practice, World Bank.

Ghosh, D., J.A. Bernstein and T.B. Mersha (2020). 'COVID-19 Pandemic: The African Paradox', *Journal of Global Health*, 10(2): 1–6.

Hussmanns, R. (2004). 'Measuring the Informal Economy: From Employment in the Informal Sector to Informal Employment', International Labour Organization (ILO) Working Paper No. 53, Geneva: ILO.

IHME (Institute of Health Metrics and Evaluation) (2022). 'COVID-19 Estimates and Related Resources', available at www.healthdata.org/covid (accessed 31 October 2023).

ILO (International Labour Organization) (2013). *Measuring Informality: A Statistical Manual on the Informal Sector and Informal Employment*. Geneva: ILO.

ILO (2018). *Women and Men in the Informal Economy: A Statistical Picture* (3rd edn). Geneva: ILO.

ILO (2020). *COVID-19 and the World of Work: Updated Analysis and Estimates* (3rd edn), ILO Monitor. Geneva: ILO.

ILO (2021). *COVID-19 and the World of Work: Updated Analysis and Estimates* (8th edn), ILO Monitor. Geneva: ILO.

ILO (2022). *World Employment and Social Outlook: Trends 2022*. Geneva: ILO.

IMF (International Monetary Fund) (2022). *World Economic Outlook: Countering the Cost-of-Living Crisis*, Washington, DC: IMF.

Kuznets, S. (1955). Economic Growth and Income Inequality. *The American Economic Review*, 45(1), 1–28.

Lewis, W. A. (1954). Economic Development with Unlimited Supplies of Labour. *The Manchester School*, 22(2), 139–191.

Meagher, K. (2022). 'Crisis Narratives and the African Paradox: African Informal Economies, COVID-19 and the Decolonization of Social Policy', *Development and Change* 53(6): 1200–29.

Millett, G.A., A.T. Jones, D. Benkeser, S. Baral, L. Mercer, C. Beyrer et al. (2020). 'Assessing Differential Impacts of COVID-19 on Black Communities', *Annal of Epidemiology*, 47: 37–44.

Montenovo. L., X. Jiang, F.L. Rojas, I.M. Schmutte, K.I. Simon, B.A. Weinberg et al. (2021). 'Determinants of Disparities in COVID-19 Job Losses', NBER Working Paper No. 27132, Cambridge MA: National Bureau of Economic Research.

O'Donoghue, C., D.M. Sologon, I. Kyzyma, and J. McHale (2020). 'Modelling the Distributional Impact of the COVID-19 Crisis', Institute of Labor Economics (IZA) Discussion Paper No. 13235, Bonn: IZA.

Ohnsorge, F., and S. Yu (2021). *The Long Shadow of Informality: Challenges and Policies*. Washington, DC: World Bank.

Ranchhod, V., and R. Daniels (2020). 'Labour Market Dynamics in South Africa in the Time of COVID-19', NIDS—CRAM, Report No. 9, Wave 1, Cape Town.

Ribeiro, F., and A. Leist (2020). 'Who Is Going to Pay the Price of Covid-19? Reflections about an Unequal Brazil', *International Journal of Equity Health*, 19: 19–21.

Rogan, M., and C. Skinner (2020). 'The Covid-19 Crisis and the South African Informal Economy: "Locked Out" of Livelihoods and Employment', NIDS—CRAM Working Paper No.10, Cape Town.

Rönkkö, R., S. Rutherford, and K. Sen (2022). 'The Impact of the COVID-19 Pandemic on the Poor: Insight from the Hrishipara Diaries', *World Development*, 149: 1–14.

Roy, M.P. (2021). 'Factors Associated with Mortality from COVID 19: Indian Perspective', *Lung India Journal*, 38(5): 501–02.

Sachs, J.D., S.S.A. Karim, L. Aknin, J. Allen, K. Brosbøl, F. Colombo et al. (2022). 'The *Lancet* Commission on Lessons for the Future from the COVID-19 Pandemic', *The Lancet*, 400(10359): 1224–80.

Schotte, S., M. Danquah, R. Osei, and K. Sen (2021). 'The Labour Market Impact of COVID-19 Lockdowns: Evidence from Ghana', IZA Discussion Paper No. 14692, Bonn: IZA.

Skinner, C., C. Skinner, J. Barrett, L. Alfers, and M. Rogan (2021). 'Informal Work in South Africa and COVID-19: Gendered Impacts and Priority Interventions', A Joint UN Women–WIEGO Policy Brief, Pretoria: UN Women–WIEGO.

PART I
IMPACT

1

COVID-19 and Informal Work

Degrees and Pathways of Impact in 11 Cities around the World

Martha Alter Chen, Erofili Grapsa, Ghida Ismail, Sarah Orleans Reed,
Michael Rogan, and Marcela Valdivia*

1. Introduction

In May 2018, the International Labour Organization (ILO) published the first ever global estimates of informal employment. These global estimates show that 61 per cent of all workers worldwide are informally employed—a total of two billion workers (Bonnet et al. 2019: 4; ILO 2018: 13). They also show that the rate of informal employment is highest in developing countries (at 90 per cent), lowest in developed countries (at 18 per cent), and quite significant in emerging countries (at 67 per cent) (Bonnet et al. 2019: 4; ILO 2018: 14).

Two years later, in late April 2020, the ILO estimated that 1.6 billion people employed in the informal economy—80 per cent of the global informal workforce and nearly half of the total global workforce—could see their livelihoods destroyed due to the decline in work, working hours, and earnings brought on by lockdowns or other restrictions to curb the spread of COVID-19 (ILO 2020: 1). Since then, a growing body of studies on the impact of the COVID-19 crisis on informal workers, especially during 2020, has confirmed this ILO prediction.

Despite the attention paid in 2020 to the impact of the COVID-19 crisis on informal workers, there was limited evidence on whether, and how, different groups of informal workers were impacted by the crisis. Further, there have been few longitudinal studies on the impact of the COVID-19 crisis on informal workers during subsequent waves of the pandemic and policy restrictions. Two notable exceptions are the current study in 11 cities and a longitudinal study in Bangladesh by the BRAC Institute of Governance and Development (BIGD) and the Power and Participation Research Centre (PPRC) (Rahman et al. 2020).

* The Women in Informal Employment: Globalizing and Organizing (WIEGO) COVID-19 crisis study team would like to acknowledge our local partners in each study city, the local organizations of informal workers, and the local research teams as well as the informal workers who participated in the study. All of them participated willingly and fully, despite the significant public health concerns and economic hardships they were experiencing at the time.

Martha Alter Chen et al., *COVID-19 and Informal Work*. In: *COVID-19 and the Informal Economy*. Edited by: Martha Alter Chen, Michael Rogan, and Kunal Sen, Oxford University Press. © Martha Alter Chen et al. (2024).
DOI: 10.1093/oso/9780198887041.003.0002

The chapter is structured as follows. Section 2 describes the WIEGO-led study: its design, sample, methods, and value-added. Section 3 summarizes the aggregate impacts of the pandemic recession on the work, earnings, and food security of informal workers across the 11 cities, noting significant differences between cities. Section 4 examines the different degrees and pathways of impact by sector and, within sectors, by key variables. Section 5 presents the coping strategies of the sample households in response to the major impacts of the crisis and inadequate government relief. The chapter concludes with reflections on (a) the nature of the economic crisis triggered by the COVID-19 pandemic, including the disproportionate impact of the crisis on informal workers and the enhanced recognition of the essential goods and services provided by informal workers, and (b) on the implications for economic recovery, social protection, and the social contract going forwards.

2. WIEGO-led study

This chapter presents findings from the two rounds of a mixed-method longitudinal study of informal workers from 11 cities[1] across 5 regions. The quantitative component consisted of a mobile phone survey of 2,231 workers, among whom 1,849 were from four main sectors of urban informal work—domestic work, home-based work, street vending/market trading, and waste picking (Table 1.1). Six additional sectors were surveyed across some of the cities.[2] The survey questionnaire was designed to collect information on the ability to work, working hours, earnings, and sector-specific constraints to livelihoods at different points in time. The questionnaire also collected information on health and safety, food security and hunger, household responsibilities and tensions, household coping strategies, and the role of government and local organizations of informal workers in providing relief and support of other kinds.

Round 1 of the study was carried out between May and early August 2020 with two recall periods—April 2020 (period of peak lockdowns or restrictions in all study cities) and February 2020 (as a pre-COVID-19 reference period). Round 2 of the study was carried out between June and early August 2021, except in Delhi and Ahmedabad, where surveys were delayed to September and October 2021 due to

---

[1] The cities include, in Asia, Bangkok (Thailand) and Ahmedabad, Delhi, and Tiruppur (India); in Africa, Accra (Ghana), Dakar (Senegal), Dar es Salaam (Tanzania), and Durban (South Africa); in Latin America, Lima (Peru) and Mexico City (Mexico); in North America, New York City (United States); and in Eastern Europe, Pleven (Bulgaria). The data from the twelfth city, Dar es Salaam, have been excluded from the analysis in this chapter.

[2] The sample for this analysis consists of 1,938 workers, 1,391 of whom were interviewed in both rounds, 334 in Round 1 only, and 213 in Round 2 only. While the survey included several additional occupational sectors, the sample for the data presented in this chapter includes only the four core sectors—domestic workers, home-based workers, street vendors/market traders, and waste pickers.

the severe Delta variant outbreak mid-year,[3] and included two reference periods—the previous month and the previous 12 months (Table 1.2).

To supplement and help interpret the survey data, the study included two sources of qualitative data: open-ended questions at the end of the survey about the major impacts of the crisis, to allow respondents to answer in their own words, and in-depth interviews with informal worker leaders and other key informants from worker organizations, government, civil society, and academia about the context and impacts. These qualitative data highlight the perspectives of informal workers, providing insights in their own words.

To carry out the study, WIEGO partnered with a local membership-based organization (MBO) of informal workers in each city who helped design the study, identify the local research team, identify the study sample, and interpret the study findings. A team of WIEGO researchers and data analysts oversaw the study, with one researcher assigned as a focal point for each study city.

The sample from each city was drawn from the membership of the informal worker organizations participating in the study and is not intended to be representative of informal workers in the city or even of the sampled groups of informal workers (Table 1.3). As members of local organizations, the sample respondents are more likely than other informal workers in each city to have

Table 1.1 Sample sectors by whether from Round 1 and/or Round 2

	Domestic worker	Home-based worker	Street/market vendor	Waste picker	Total
Both rounds	279	258	509	345	1,391
Round 2	40	10	71	92	213
Round 1	37	26	118	153	334
Total	356	294	698	590	1,938

Source: WIEGO COVID-19 crisis study, 2020 and 2021.

Table 1.2 Two rounds of study

	2020	2021
Dates of survey	May–early August	June–early August
Reference periods	April 2020	Previous year
Pre-COVID baseline	February 2020	February 2020

Source: see text.

---

[3] In the interest of simplifying the presentation of the data, we refer to the Round 2 study period as mid-2021.

Table 1.3 Sample sectors by city

	Domestic worker	Home-based worker	Street/market vendor	Waste picker	Total
Accra	0	0	98	49	147
Pleven	55	73	46	0	174
Dakar	0	0	0	94	94
Ahmedabad	61	55	77	53	246
Delhi	58	64	75	59	256
Mexico City	73	0	58	43	174
New York	0	0	62	65	127
Lima	54	0	67	61	182
Durban	0	0	151	105	256
Tiruppur	0	61	0	0	61
Bangkok	55	41	64	61	221
Total	356	294	698	590	1,938

Source: WIEGO COVID-19 crisis study, 2020 and 2021.

benefited from collective action pre-COVID-19 and to have received relief support during COVID-19.

The findings of the study differ by city and by sector. Some of the differences between cities are attributable to the sample in each city: only three cities studied all four main groups (Ahmedabad, Bangkok, and Delhi), and two cities studied only one group (Dakar and Tiruppur). Other factors which contributed to differences between cities include the severity and duration of different waves of the COVID-19 virus and associated restrictions and the type, coverage, and duration of relief measures.[4] It should be noted that by Round 2, no recovery measures had reached informal workers in any of the study cities.

3. Impact on work, earnings, and food security: Across 11 cities

The findings from the WIEGO-led 11-city study confirm, first and foremost, that the impact of the COVID-19 crisis on the ability of informal workers to work was substantial and that by mid-2021, in most cities and sectors, the livelihoods of informal workers had not recovered to their pre-pandemic levels. Across the cities, nearly two-thirds (65 per cent) of the respondents reported not working at all during the peak lockdowns/restrictions in April 2020. By mid-2020, when severe restrictions had been eased or lifted, most respondents had returned to work, but

---

[4] For a more detailed report on Round 1 findings, including a table with key variables of the study cities (country income group, informal employment rate, government restrictions relief in 2020), see Chen et al. (2022).

over one-third were still unable to work; and in mid-2021, over 20 per cent were unable to work (Figure 1.1).

Prior to the crisis, in February 2020, the sample reported full-time employment at 5.5 days of work per week on average. The most severe disruption to working days occurred in April 2020 and had recovered to 3.4 days per week by the middle of 2020. However, between mid-2020 and mid-2021, the average number of days worked across the city samples increased by only half a day, to 4 days per week in mid-2021 (Figure 1.2).

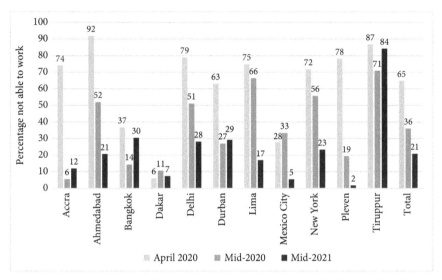

Figure 1.1 Percentage not able to work, by city, April 2020, mid-2020, and mid-2021
Source: WIEGO COVID-19 crisis study, 2020 and 2021.

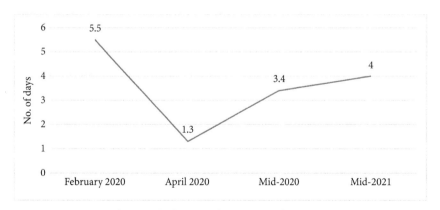

Figure 1.2 Average days worked per week in 2020 and 2021
Source: WIEGO COVID-19 crisis study, 2020 and 2021.

By mid-2021, in New York City and Pleven, the number of working days per week was more than, or close to, pre-COVID levels, whereas in Ahmedabad, Bangkok, Delhi, and Durban, the average working days per week were more than two days below their pre-COVID levels and, in Tiruppur, the respondents averaged less than one day of work per week (Figure 1.3).

Not surprisingly, the slow and uneven return to full-time work coincided with a stalled recovery in earnings. By the middle of 2021, recovery of earnings across the city samples was only 64 per cent of pre-COVID levels (Figure 1.4).[5] While the earnings recovery of respondents in two cities (Pleven and Mexico City) had nearly or fully reached pre-pandemic levels, it was low in the remaining cities.

In Tiruppur in June 2021, near the end of a severe second wave of the virus across India aggravated by the Delta variant, earnings recovery was zero among a sample that consisted almost entirely of subcontracted, home-based garment

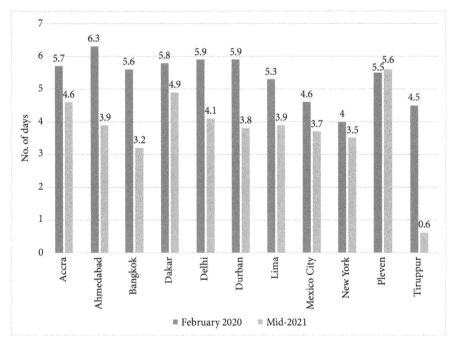

Figure 1.3 Average days worked per week, by city

Source: WIEGO COVID-19 crisis study, 2020 and 2021.

[5] In order to provide a comparable earnings measure across cities and different currencies, we created the ratio of each respondent's median monthly earnings at every time point post-February 2020 to their earnings in February 2020. This represents the share of their earnings at every time point as a proportion or percentage of their February 2020 earnings. All earnings are reported as median (or 'typical' earnings), meaning that half of the sample's earnings as a percentage of pre-COVID earnings was less than or equal to the median. In the analysis of recovery of earnings, we present the median of the individual respondent ratios.

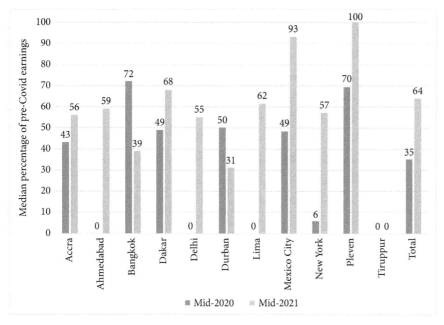

Figure 1.4 Median percentage of pre-COVID earnings, by city
Source: WIEGO COVID-19 crisis study, 2020 and 2021.

workers. Recovery of earnings in the remaining cities was between 31 and 68 per cent of pre-COVID earnings levels.

In all cities except Bangkok, Durban, and Tiruppur (where the Round 2 survey was conducted amidst a COVID-19 wave and/or political crisis), earnings were far closer in mid-2021 to their pre-COVID levels than they were in mid-2020 (Figure 1.4). For the sample as a whole, median earnings were just over one-third (35 per cent) of pre-COVID levels in mid-2020 but had increased to nearly two-thirds (64 per cent) by mid-2021.

Often, the first resort to cope with the loss of work and earnings was to cut back on household expenditures, beginning with food. In the first wave of the crisis, between April and June 2020, in 7 of the 11 cities, more than one-third of workers reported some level of hunger in their household (Figure 1.5). In mid-2021, across the sample as a whole, 29 per cent of respondents reported that an adult in their household had gone hungry over the past month, 27 per cent of households with children reported that a child had gone hungry, and the majority (57 per cent) reported a decrease in dietary diversity or less frequent meals. Food insecurity was greatest in Dakar, Durban, and Lima, where the majority of the respondents reported both hunger and changes in diet.

The significant variation across the cities reflects, first and foremost, the sector composition of the sample in each study city. It also reflects the length and severity

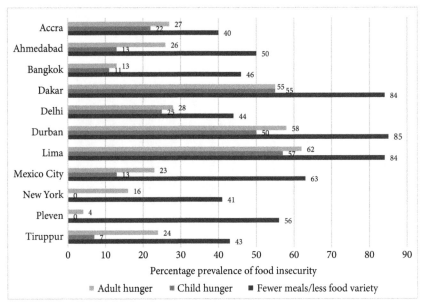

Figure 1.5 Percentage prevalence of food insecurity, by city
Source: WIEGO COVID-19 crisis study, 2020 and 2021.

of successive waves of the virus and of government restrictions on movement, transport, and commerce in the different cities. Consider the situation across the cities when the Round 2 study was conducted: in Accra, Dakar, Lima, Mexico City, and New York, there were few, if any, government restrictions; Ahmedabad, Delhi, and Pleven were coming out of severe waves of the virus and restrictions had only recently been removed; and Bangkok, Durban, and Tiruppur were still experiencing a severe COVID wave with restrictions in place. In the case of Durban, widespread protests and unrest also impacted informal livelihoods.[6] The variation between cities also reflects the ability of local organizations of informal workers to support their members and of different sectors of informal workers—as well as individual workers—to recover.

4. Pathways of impact: By sector and within sectors

While there is growing evidence—and recognition—that the pandemic and lock-downs or restrictions have had a disproportionate impact on informal workers compared to formal workers, there is limited understanding of the degree to which—and the ways in which—the crisis impacted different groups of informal

---

[6] See Chen et al. (2021) for the comparative situation in the study cities in 2021.

workers. In this section, we trace the degrees to which—and the distinct pathways through which—the COVID-19 crisis impacted domestic workers, home-based workers, street vendors/market traders, and waste pickers and, within these sectors, by key sector variables including place of work, status in employment, product or service, and sex.

4.1 Overall impact by sector

The impact of the COVID-19 crisis on informal workers was not uniform: it differed across cities as well as between and within sectors. In terms of ability to work, less than 20 per cent of home-based workers were able to work in April 2020, just over half in mid-2021, and around 60 per cent by mid-2021, due to lack of demand and work orders. Second to home-based workers, street vendors were the least able to work in all periods and faced decreased demand and sales even once they could return to work. Nearly 40 per cent of domestic workers were able to work in April 2020, nearly 60 per cent in mid-2020, and over 80 per cent by mid-2021. Waste pickers were the most able to work in all periods but faced a decline in access to waste and in market outlets and prices for reclaimed waste. Overall, across the study sample, home-based workers and street vendors were the least able to work in mid-2021 and had the lowest recovery in median earnings by mid-2021, although street vendors fared significantly better than home-based workers on both counts (Table 1.4).

In April 2020, all four sectors cited government restrictions on movement and commerce as the most common reason for not working and disruptions in markets and supply chains as the second most common reason. Since mid-2020, government restrictions remained the most significant constraint on the ability of home-based workers and street vendors to work, employer hiring practices remained most important for domestic workers, and health concerns had become of greatest importance to waste pickers (Figure 1.6).

Table 1.4 Percentage not able to work

Sector	April 2020	Mid-2020	Mid-2021
Domestic worker	63	42	18
Home-based worker	82	48	43
Street/market vendor	72	34	20
Waste picker	49	24	11
Total	65	36	21

Source: WIEGO COVID-19 crisis study, 2020 and 2021.

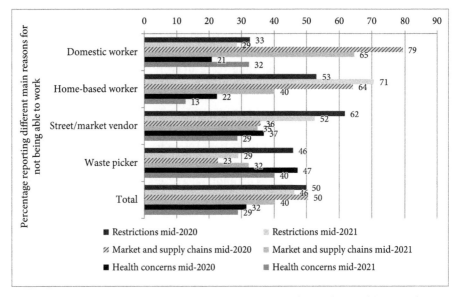

Figure 1.6 Percentage reporting different main reasons for not being able to work, by sector

Note: the reference period in mid-2020 was the previous month, and the reference period in mid-2021 was the previous 12 months. Respondents could report more than one reason.
Source: WIEGO COVID-19 crisis study, 2020 and 2021.

In April 2020, at the peak of the lockdowns and other restrictions across all cities, the median earnings in all four sectors, relative to pre-COVID earnings, was zero. However, there was substantial variation in earnings recovery by mid-2020 and mid-2021 relative to pre-COVID-19 earnings (February 2020) (Figure 1.4). Home-based workers were the hardest hit, with no recovery in earnings by mid-2020 and very limited recovery by mid-2021. The street vendors had the second lowest recovery at both points in time but significantly higher than the home-based workers. The waste pickers had the highest recovery of earnings by mid-2020 and the second highest in mid-2021, while the domestic workers had the second highest recovery of earnings by mid-2020 and the highest by mid-2021.

By mid-2021, the earnings of domestic workers, waste pickers, and street vendors had improved substantially compared with the middle of 2020, when all were earning less than half of pre-COVID earnings (Figure 1.7).

While the earnings of domestic workers had nearly recovered to pre-COVID levels by mid-2021, there was substantial variation between cities. Only in Pleven did domestic workers fully recover their pre-COVID earnings, while in Ahmedabad and Mexico City, the earnings of domestic workers remained less than half of their pre-COVID earnings and, in Delhi, only 10 per cent. Overall, more than one-quarter of the domestic workers (28 per cent) were still earning less than 75

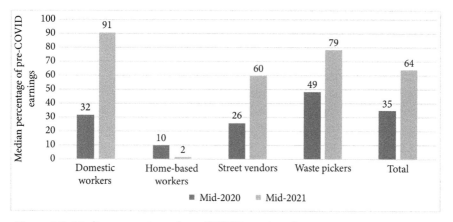

Figure 1.7 Median percentage of pre-COVID earnings, by sector
Source: WIEGO COVID-19 crisis study, 2020 and 2021.

per cent of their pre-COVID earnings. The earnings of waste pickers and street vendors had recovered, at the median, to 78 and 60 per cent, respectively, of their pre-COVID earnings, although 42 per cent of waste pickers and 62 per cent of street vendors were still earning less than 75 per cent of their pre-COVID earnings.

The situation of home-based workers was particularly alarming. This group was the most severely affected in 2020 as supply chains collapsed and work orders dried up, leaving home-based workers, particularly those who were subcontracted, with very little work. By mid-2021, their earnings had further deteriorated to only 2 per cent (at the median) of pre-COVID earnings levels. Indeed, at the city-level in mid-2021, the earnings recovery of home-based workers was zero in all cities where they were studied (Ahmedabad, Delhi, Tiruppur, and Bangkok), with the exception of Pleven.[7] In sum, supply chains remained broken and demand for the goods and services produced by home-based workers was still severely diminished, especially for those who were subcontracted by factories or supply chains and particularly in Asia, the region with the world's highest prevalence of home-based workers (Bonnet et al. 2021).

4.2 Degree of impact: By sector and within sectors

The rest of this section explores the degree and distinct pathways of impact by sector, including changes in demand, supply, prices, wages, and piece rates. It also explores differences within sectors by key sector variables, such as live-in versus live-out domestic workers, self-employed versus subcontracted home-based

---

[7] The dire situation of home-based workers in Asian cities aligns with findings from a HomeNet South Asia study in 12 South Asian cities (HomeNet South Asia 2021).

workers, food versus non-food street vendors/market traders, collection sites for waste pickers, and by gender.

Domestic workers

In my organization, the workers don't know what to do. Some are working as live-ins because they are afraid of losing their jobs. Those who are working as live-out domestic workers are being overloaded with work. They say that before [the pandemic], they simply watched the children, [but] now they have to take care of cooking, washing, ironing, etc.

(Domestic worker leader, Lima, Peru)

Impact on work and income

As noted above, domestic workers had the second highest ability to work, after the waste pickers, during the peak lockdowns/restrictions in 2020, mid-2020, and mid-2021 and enjoyed the highest recovery of earnings in mid-2020 and the second highest, after the waste pickers, by mid-2021.

Key variables

After government lockdowns or restrictions were eased, the attitude and hiring practice of their employers were the key determinant of whether domestic workers were able to work and differed significantly by whether or not the domestic worker lived in her or his employer's home. In general, live-in workers were allowed to continue to work so long as they did not go out (except to shop for their employers), not even to visit their families or to get medical treatment. As a domestic worker leader in Lima explained, 'Sometimes colleagues who are ill and are working can't even go out to a doctor's appointment. So this is also a lack of humanity on the part of their employer, who says to a worker: "You can't go out today, you are working". So they miss that appointment too.' A few live-out workers were able to work, as was the case for some domestic workers in Ahmedabad and Delhi whose employers lived in residential colonies that had a daily screening system in place. The gap in ability to work between live-in and live-out domestic workers was most pronounced during the peak lockdowns/restrictions in April 2020 and narrowed significantly by mid-2020 but increased again by mid-2021 (Table 1.5).

As a consequence, the earnings and earnings recovery of live-in domestic workers were far higher than that of live-out domestic workers in 2020, especially in April 2020, when the earnings of live-out domestic workers were zero. This gap had narrowed considerably by mid-2021, when the earnings recovery of live-in domestic workers reached pre-COVID levels, and the earnings recovery of live-out domestic workers was 88 per cent of the pre-COVID-19 level (Table 1.6)

Table 1.5 Live-in and live-out domestic workers: Percentage not able to work

	April 2020	Mid-2020	Mid-2021
Live-in	32	31	9
Live-out	73	44	18
Total	65	42	16

Source: WIEGO COVID-19 crisis study, 2020 and 2021.

Table 1.6 Live-in and live-out domestic workers: Median percentage of pre-COVID-19 earnings

	April 2020	Mid-2020	Mid-2021
Live-in	78	96	100
Live-out	0	17	88
Total	0	32	95

Source: WIEGO COVID-19 crisis study, 2020 and 2021.

The predicament of live-out domestic workers across the different waves of the virus is captured in the following statement by a domestic worker leader in Mexico City:

> What happened in the first wave is that [domestic workers] were sent home without pay. When they saw that the pandemic continued, the employers did not want to pay them, some of them had their salaries reduced, others were fired. In the second wave of the pandemic, they reduced the days of work or paid them less.

It is important to add that most of the domestic workers who were not allowed to work by their employer were not compensated by their employer.

For those live-out domestic workers who had work, the availability and cost of public transport, as well as the fear of contracting the virus on public transport, were major concerns. A domestic worker leader in Mexico City explained the concerns of live-out domestic workers as follows: 'They can be exposed in public transportation, they can be exposed when going from one house to another, and some employers spread the infection but say nothing.' To avoid possible contagion, some domestic workers in Lima in mid-2020 began walking to work or taking only one bus rather than several, adding to the unpaid hours they spent in their daily commute and to the physical toll of their work.

While live-in domestic workers did not suffer a significant decline in work or earnings, many faced additional demands on their time and energy: cleaning, cooking, and tending to the many family members in their employer's home. Most were not allowed to leave their employer's home or visit their own families and faced reductions in time off. A domestic worker leader in Lima explained the situation of live-in workers as follows: 'They are up early, they are stressed. There was a young domestic worker who said that she had a headache all day long. They are facing a lot of problems associated with stress.'

Home-based workers
'The factories are closed, income has stopped, but the hunger, rent, bills cannot be stopped'—home-based worker, Tiruppur, India.

Impact on work and income
Among the four main sectors in the sample, the home-based workers were hardest hit: the least able to work during the peak lockdowns or restrictions and the slowest to recover by mid-2021. But there was significant variation in the ability to work across the five cities in which home-based workers were surveyed. Home-based workers in Pleven were the least able to work in April 2020 but the most able to work by mid-2021, while the home-based workers in Tiruppur were also badly hit in April 2020 and were the least able to work by mid-2021. By mid-2021 in Tiruppur, the textile and garment factories were still not operating at full capacity due to stagnant demand (domestic and export) and were not, therefore, putting out much work to the homeworkers. A significant share of the home-based workers in Ahmedabad (37 per cent), Delhi (52 per cent), and Bangkok (58 per cent) were not able to work by mid-2021 due to lack of demand and work orders: a sign of the stagnant economic recovery overall and continuing supply-chain disruptions (Figure 1.8).

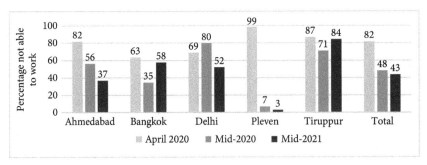

Figure 1.8 Home-based workers: Percentage not able to work by city, April 2020, mid-2020, and mid-2021

Note: respondents could report more than one reason.
Source: WIEGO COVID-19 crisis study, 2020 and 2021.

Key variables

There are two main groups of home-based workers: *subcontracted* workers, who depend on work orders from firms or factories through their intermediaries, and the *self-employed*, who sell to individual customers or buyers. Among the home-based worker sample, more than half were subcontracted in Round 1, while more than half were self-employed in Round 2.

Between the two groups, a slightly higher percentage of subcontracted home-based workers were able to work in April 2020, but a higher percentage of self-employed home-based workers were able to work by mid-2020 and in mid-2021 (Table 1.7). More significantly, the median earnings of the subcontracted workers were zero in April 2020 and had not recovered by mid-2021, while the median earnings of the self-employed recovered to 44 per cent of pre-COVID-19 earnings by mid-2020 but then dropped to 24 per cent by mid-2021 (Table 1.8).

Among subcontracted home-based workers, it is also important to distinguish (where possible) between those who produce for domestic supply chains and those who produce for global supply chains. In Tiruppur, the T-shirt capital of the world pre-COVID-19, most of the garment production is for export markets. Pre-COVID-19, most of the home-based workers were subcontracted by textile and garment factories to do ancillary tasks, especially when export orders were high. But, as of mid-2021, the factories were not operating fully and were putting out less work to the home-based workers: only 16 per cent of the home-based workers had worked, even part-time, the previous month.

Table 1.7 Self-employed and subcontracted home-based workers: Percentage not able to work, April 2020, mid-2020, and mid-2021

	April 2020	**Mid-2020**	**Mid-2021**
Self-employed	84	40	38
Subcontracted	80	58	50
Total	82	48	43

Source: WIEGO COVID-19 crisis study, 2020 and 2021.

Table 1.8 Self-employed and subcontracted home-based workers: Median percentage of pre-COVID-19 earnings, April 2020, mid-2020, and mid-2021

	April 2020	**Mid-2020**	**Mid-2021**
Self-employed	0	44	24
Subcontracted	0	0	0
Total	0	0	3

Source: WIEGO COVID-19 crisis study, 2020 and 2021.

Street vendors and market traders

All the municipal administrations only want to evict us and do not think about what we are going to live on. Without work I cannot pay for my children's studies so that in the future they won't be working on the streets like me. We feel impotent without work, they don't allow us, and we will never get out of poverty if we don't work.

(Male street vendor, Lima, Peru)

Impact on work and earnings

Among the four main sectors in the sample, the street vendors were the second hardest hit after the home-based workers, except in mid-2020, when they had recovered significantly in terms of ability to work. But there was significant variation in their ability to work across the study cities, depending on the intensity and duration of the lockdown and other restrictions, when wholesale markets and vendor markets were allowed to reopen, and whether street-food vendors were deemed essential workers.

Key variables

Pre-COVID-19, across the nine cities which studied street vendors, more than half of the street vendors/market traders sold food items, either fresh or cooked. And pre-COVID-19, vendors/traders who sold food earned significantly more, on average, than street vendors/traders who sold non-food items. During the COVID-19 crisis, in several cities, local governments recognized street-food vendors as essential workers, either implicitly or explicitly, reflecting a high demand for food. By mid-2021, around 80 per cent of all street vendors/market traders were able to work (Table 1.9), but the earnings of food vendors/traders had recovered more than those of non-food vendors (Table 1.10). In part, this was because the tourism sector had not recovered in some cities, and the vendors/traders in those cities who sold non-food items to tourists were still badly affected.

Table 1.9 Food and non-food street vendors/market traders: Percentage not able to work, April 2020, mid-2020, and mid-2021

	April 2020	Mid-2020	Mid-2021
Food	67	30	11
Non-food	81	38	11
Total	73	33	11

Source: WIEGO COVID-19 crisis study, 2020 and 2021.

Table 1.10 Food and non-food street vendors/market traders: Median percentage of pre-COVID-19 earnings, April 2020, mid-2020, and mid-2021

	April 2020	Mid-2020	Mid-2021
Food	0	30	71
Non-food	0	20	64
Total	0	26	70

Source: WIEGO COVID-19 crisis study, 2020 and 2021.

Table 1.11 Women and men street vendors/market traders: Percentage not able to work, April 2020, mid-2020, and mid-2021

	April 2020	Mid-2020	Mid-2021
Women	73	35	20
Men	70	33	18
Total	72	35	20

Source: WIEGO COVID-19 crisis study, 2020 and 2021.

Table 1.12 Women and men street vendors/market traders: Median percentage of pre-COVID-19 earnings, April 2020, mid-2020, and mid-2021

	April 2020	Mid-2020	Mid-2021
Women	0	25	55
Men	0	28	70
Total	0	26	60

Source: WIEGO COVID-19 crisis study, 2020 and 2021.

During both 2020 and 2021, a slightly lower percentage of women street vendors/market traders were able to work (Table 1.11), compared to men. And, while the median earnings of both women and men street vendors/market traders were zero in April 2020, the earnings of men street vendors/market traders had recovered more by mid-2020 and even more so by mid-2021 (Table 1.12)

> Waste pickers
> 'Access to materials is more difficult, especially for the women who go to the dump site. Sometimes, you meet women with their children who work all day but when they come down, they don't have anything to buy to eat. The situation is degrading and really difficult for some'—
> waste picker leader, Dakar, Senegal.

Impact on work and earnings

Among the four main sectors in the sample, the waste pickers were most able to work at all periods of time and enjoyed the second highest recovery of earnings by mid-2021 (after domestic workers), albeit from a relatively low base of earnings and working conditions. Across the nine cities which studied waste pickers, half of the waste pickers were able to work during the peak lockdowns or restrictions in April 2020 (Table 1.13). The three main reasons cited for not being able to work were restrictions on movement and work (75 per cent of respondents), health concerns (40 per cent), and disruptions to the waste supply chain (including the closure of collection and sorting sites as well as waste dealerships) (37 per cent).

By mid-2020, three-quarters of the waste pickers had returned to work. Again, there was significant variation across cities: 92 per cent had returned to work in Accra—where the lockdown was partial and short—compared to only 24 per cent in Lima—where the lockdown was full and long. By mid-2020, the main reasons for not being able to work had shifted since April: health concerns were the major concern for half of the waste pickers, followed by continuing restrictions on movement and closures of collection and sorting sites (Table 1.3). And, by mid-2021, almost 90 per cent of the waste pickers were able to work.

Because of health concerns, some waste pickers stopped collecting waste and shifted to other occupations. One waste picker in Ahmedabad who shifted to doing domestic work described the causes and consequences of the shift as follows:

> Because of this disease, I had to leave the work of waste picking. My family members are reluctant to let me do this work. They say that I should not do such work that invites disease in the house. Thus, I resorted to doing domestic work (sweeping and mopping) in the nearby house. I am very sad.

While contracting the virus through contact with toxic waste materials was a major concern for the waste pickers, the general public tended to see both the waste pickers themselves and the waste they collect as vectors of the disease. A waste picker in Ahmedabad described the dehumanizing indignity of not being able to work due to being stigmatized as a vector of the virus:

> How difficult it can be for a person who works all day, to sit in a corner without any work. Those were the days of compulsion. No one talks to us and those who touch us are clad in plastic clothes. We feel as if we are in some other world. I felt that it would be better if god gave me death instead of this suffering because even the neighbours would look at me with suspicion. People would ask after my well-being while standing far away from their windows. I felt very sad at that time.

Across the four sectors, waste pickers experienced the greatest recovery of median earnings by mid-2020 and the second highest by mid-2021—to 48 and 78 per cent, respectively, of pre-COVID-19 earnings. In part, this is because most waste pickers are self-employed and can operate below the radar of the municipal government. However, it should be noted that, pre-COVID-19, waste pickers earned the least of all sectors in most of the nine cities. But six of the nine cities which studied waste pickers did not study home-based workers and four did not study domestic workers. In two cities which studied all four groups, Ahmedabad and Delhi, home-based workers earned less, on average, than waste pickers pre-COVID-19 in both cities and, compared to waste pickers, their earnings had recovered less in Ahmedabad but more in Delhi by mid-2021. However, domestic workers earned more than waste pickers in Ahmedabad and in Bangkok both pre-COVID and mid-2021.

Key variables
There are key differences between waste pickers according to what tasks they perform and where they collect, sort, or store waste. Women waste pickers tend to be concentrated in primary collection and sorting and are less likely than men waste pickers to be involved in processing or trading in recyclables. Pre-COVID-19, a higher percentage of the women waste pickers collected and sorted waste at dump sites, compared to men, and a higher percentage of men waste pickers collected waste from homes and from businesses, compared to women.

In April 2020, a lower percentage of women than men waste pickers were able to work. This gender gap in ability to work became wider by mid-2020 but had narrowed by mid-2021 (Table 1.14). In mid-2020, the main reasons for not being able to work cited by both women and men waste pickers were that the local government did not permit them to work and/or had closed their collection sites (Table 1.14). But some women waste pickers reported constraints that no men waste pickers reported: public transport was not available or had become too expensive (6 per cent of women waste pickers), the need to care for children and tend to other household chores (13 per cent), and the need to take time off for childbirth and for deaths in the family (3 per cent). Also, a higher percentage of women waste pickers reported the threat of arrests and fines by the police and local authorities, compared to men.

While the median earnings of both women and men waste pickers were zero in April 2020, male earnings had recovered more by mid-2020 and even more by mid-2021. In part, the difference in earnings recovery reflects the gender gap in work rates (Table 1.13). But other factors also contributed to the gender gap in average earnings among waste pickers. Consider the case of waste pickers in Dakar where, pre-COVID, the earnings of women waste pickers were 20 per cent of those

Table 1.13 Women and men waste pickers: Percentage not able to work, April 2020, mid-2020, and mid-2021

	April 20	Mid-2020	Mid-2021
Women	55	32	15
Men	46	16	7
Total	50	25	11

Source: WIEGO COVID-19 crisis study, 2020 and 2021.

Table 1.14 Women and men waste pickers: Percentage reporting different reasons for not being able to work, mid-2021

	Women	Men	Total
Restrictions	37	29	34
Markets and supply chain	26	30	28
Migration	8	6	7
Transport	9	0	5
Health concerns	45	40	43
Care and household responsibilities	18	3	11

Source: WIEGO COVID-19 crisis study, 2020 and 2021.

of men waste pickers. This was attributed by local informants to the disadvantaged status of women waste pickers, relative to men waste pickers, including the physical disadvantage that women face in competing with men for the waste dumped by trucks and in transporting waste, the fact that women are less likely to be self-employed and more likely to work for another waste picker, and the shorter work weeks and work days of women due to their unequal burden of care and other household responsibilities and the lack of day care facilities near the dump sites.

In sum, the waste pickers were most able to work during the peak lockdowns or restrictions in 2020 and in mid-2021 and experienced the second highest recovery in earnings, in part because they are self-employed and were able to operate below the government radar. Domestic workers were the next group most able to work during the peak lockdowns or restrictions in 2020 and in mid-2021 and enjoyed the highest earnings recovery by mid-2021. The status of street vendors was mixed: nearly three-quarters were not able to work during the strict lockdowns and restrictions in April 2020, while 80 per cent were able to work by mid-2021. But their earnings had recovered to only 60 per cent of pre-COVID earnings by mid-2021. Home-based workers were least able to work during the peak lockdowns or restrictions and had recovered least by mid-2021, in terms of both ability to work and earnings.

4.3 Distinct pathways of impact: By sector

As detailed above, restrictions on physical mobility, commercial activities, and public transport had major impacts on the livelihoods of all respondents, especially during the peak period of lockdowns or other restrictions in April–May 2020 but also during subsequent waves of the virus and associated restrictions and recession across the different cities/countries. However, the cumulative impact of the pandemic, restrictions, and recession on the different groups of informal workers worked through distinct pathways. These distinct pathways, captured through the qualitative components of the WIEGO-led study, are summarized in Box 1.1.[8]

5. Household coping strategies

To help cushion the immediate impact of the crisis in 2020, there was a rapid, if uneven, deployment of relief measures by national, state, and city governments: the local organizations of informal workers helped to facilitate the outreach of the government aid and supplement it with their own direct aid. But Round 1 findings showed that three to four months into the pandemic, cash and food relief had reached less than half of survey respondents (Alfers et al. 2020, Chen et al. 2021). By mid-2021, government relief had been reduced or discontinued in most cities/countries. Between mid-2020 and mid-2021, access to cash relief had improved in only four cities (Bangkok, Durban, Lima, Mexico City, and Pleven).[9]

Given the scale of losses in work, working hours, and earnings across the sample and the inadequate and sporadic relief provided, it is not surprising that respondents and their families resorted to different coping strategies to buy food and pay for other essentials (rent, utilities, health care, and education). To cope with the cumulative impact of the pandemic recession, the respondents—and their households—reported a variety of coping strategies between mid-2020 and mid-2021: borrowing money (46 per cent), drawing down on savings (35 per cent), and reducing non-food (26 per cent) and food (23 per cent) consumption. Nearly three-quarters (72 per cent) of all respondents took one or more of these measures (Figure 1.9). The cumulative impact of these strategies is a lower standard of living and nutrition and a reduced ability to recover livelihoods and living standards in the immediate term.

Rates of borrowing were highest in Delhi (72 per cent), Ahmedabad (68 per cent), Mexico City (61 per cent), and Lima (59 per cent), while rates of savings

---

[8] For more details, see WIEGO Working Paper No. 42 (Chen et al. 2021).
[9] For more details on the impact on informal workers of, and policy responses to, the COVID-19 crisis in South Africa, see Skinner et al. (2021).

Box 1.1 Distinct pathways of impact

	Decreased demand	Decreased supply	Unfavourable prices/wages	Restrictive regulations	Lack of public services
Home-based workers: Self-employed	Fewer orders from customers and buyers	Decreased supply of raw materials	Increased prices of raw materials and decreased prices of finished goods	Single-use zoning regulations and insecure housing tenure	Lack of basic infrastructure services at home = workplace + public transport services
Home-based workers: Subcontracted	Fewer work orders from factories and firms	Decreased supply of raw materials—from factories/firms	Decreased piece rates or wages for finished goods	Single-use zoning regulations, insecure housing tenure, and lack of labour regulations	Lack of basic infrastructure services at home = workplace + public transport services
Street vendors	Fewer customers	Closure of wholesale markets and supply-chain disruptions	Increased buying prices for stock and decreased selling prices of goods	Reduced access to public space, closures of natural markets, and restrictive licence/permit systems	Lack of basic infrastructure services at vending site/natural market and public transport services
Market traders	Fewer customers	Closure of wholesale markets and supply-chain disruptions	Buying price of stock and selling price of goods	Plans for and regulation of built markets	Lack of fire safety, basic infrastructure services at built markets, and public transport services
Waste pickers	Fewer waste dealers	Reduced generation of waste and closure of waste-collection sites	Lower prices for recycled waste	Solid waste management systems and rules	Lack of sorting sites or buildings, equipment, and public transport services

Source: adapted from Box 6 in Chen et al. (2021: 33).

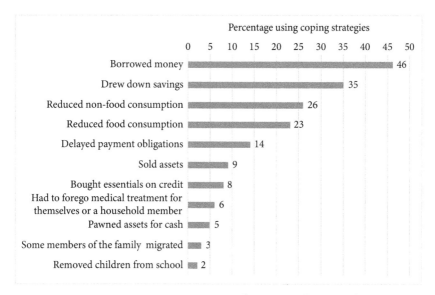

Figure 1.9 Percentage using coping strategies between mid-2020 and mid-2021
Source: WIEGO COVID-19 crisis study, 2020 and 2021.

depletion were highest in Mexico City (69 per cent), New York (57 per cent), and Accra (56 per cent) (Figure 1.10).

In addition, across the 11 cities, many respondent households postponed paying rent, utility bills, and school fees, incurring mounting debt with compounding interest. Overall, the data from the study suggest that, in the absence of comprehensive government support, informal workers were forced to cushion the blow by depleting their already meagre savings or by going into debt and, in some cases, mortgaging or selling physical assets. It is likely that many of the informal workers in these and other cities have taken on unsustainable levels of debt. As a result, economic recovery remains elusive. The vast majority (82 per cent) of respondents who had to draw down on savings since the pandemic recession began were not able to replenish any of their savings by mid-2021: 12 per cent were able to replace less than half of their savings, and 6 per cent had replaced half or more.

6. Concluding reflections

The economic crisis triggered by the COVID-19 pandemic was different in several regards from other global economic crises. First, the impact was felt, first and foremost, in the real economy, not the financial economy. Second, the impact was disproportionately felt by the informal workforce who could not work remotely. And third, the global community came to appreciate a range of basic essential

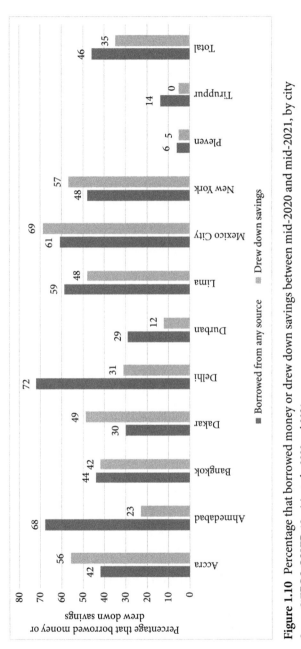

Figure 1.10 Percentage that borrowed money or drew down savings between mid-2020 and mid-2021, by city

Source: WIEGO COVID-19 crisis study, 2020 and 2021.

goods and services—notably, food production and delivery, health care, child and eldercare, house cleaning, street cleaning, waste recycling—and the fact that those who produce these goods or provide these services are often informally employed.

The findings from the 11 cities in this WIEGO-led study confirm that informal workers were severely impacted by the pandemic and lockdowns and deepen our understanding of the different degrees and pathways of impact on distinct groups of informal workers.

The findings also underscore that the ability of informal workers and their households to recover has been triply constrained by the COVID-19 crisis: their meagre resources were depleted by drawing down or depleting savings and pawning or selling assets to meet basic necessities; they went further into debt by borrowing money for basic necessities (including buying food on credit) and postponing payments (often with compounding interest) of rent, utility bills, and school fees; and they faced continued—if not intensified—restrictions and other punitive measures on their livelihoods, including destruction of their workplaces and infrastructure.

For these and other reasons, it will take a long time for informal workers and their livelihoods to recover. But going forwards, the recovery of informal livelihoods is essential to bringing poverty levels and the rate of poverty reduction back to pre-COVID-19 levels. Moreover, economic recovery will be slower and less robust unless it includes informal workers and their livelihoods.

This is a moment to be bold. The increased recognition of informal workers as essential workers should be translated into more inclusive recovery plans and an agenda for transformative change to protect and support these workers and their livelihoods. Most fundamentally, the global community, national and local governments, and other policymakers need to recognize that informal workers and their livelihood activities represent the broad base of the economy producing essential goods and services not only for low-income customers but also for the general public and for the formal economy.

References

Alfers, L., G. Ismail, and M. Valdivia (2020). 'Informal Workers and the Social Protection Response to COVID-19: Who Got Relief? How? And Did It Make a Difference?', Policy Insights No. 2, Manchester: Women in Informal Employment: Globalizing and Organizing (WIEGO).

Bonnet, F., J. Vanek, and M. Chen (2019). *Women and Men in the Informal Economy: A Statistical Brief*. Geneva: ILO and Manchester: WIEGO.

Bonnet, F., F. Carre, M.A. Chen, and J. Vanek (2021). 'Home-Based Workers in the World: A Statistical Profile', WIEGO Statistical Brief No. 27, Manchester: WIEGO.

Chen, M.A., E. Grapsa, G. Ismail, M. Rogan, M. Valdivia, L. Alfers et al. (2021). 'COVID-19 and Informal Work: Distinct Pathways of Impact and Recovery in 11

Cities around the World', WIEGO Working Paper No. 42, Manchester: WIEGO (May), available at www.wiego.org/sites/default/files/publications/file/WIEGO_Working%20Paper%20No%2042%20May%202021.pdf (accessed March 2022).

Chen, M.A., E. Grapsa, G. Ismail, M. Rogan, M. Valdivia, L. Alfers et al. (2022). 'COVID-19 and Informal Work: Evidence from 11 Cities', *International Labour Review*, 161(1): 29–58. https://doi.org/10.1111/ilr.12221.

HomeNet South Asia. (2021). *Impact of COVID-19 on Women Home-based Workers in South Asia*. HomeNet South Asia.

ILO (International Labour Organization) (2018). *Women and Men in the Informal Economy: A Statistical Picture* (3rd edn). Geneva: ILO.

ILO (2020). *COVID-19 and the World of Work: Updated Analysis and Estimates* (3rd edn), ILO Monitor. Geneva: ILO.

Rahman, H.Z., A. Rahman, U. Zillur, I. Matin, S.M. Gain, F. Mohammad et al. (2020). 'Livelihoods, Coping and Recovery during COVID-19 Crisis', Power and Participation Research Centre (PPRC)–BRAC Institute of Governance and Development (BIGD) 2nd Rapid Response Research Report, Dhaka: PPRC and BIGD.

Skinner, C., J. Barrett, L. Alfers, and M. Rogan (2021). 'Informal Work in South Africa and COVID 19: Gendered Impacts and Priority Interventions', WIEGO Policy Brief No. 22, Manchester: WIEGO.

2

Impact of the COVID-19 Pandemic on? Employment

National labour surveys in five Latin American countries and field research in 11 cities around the world

Martha Alter Chen and Joann Vanek

This chapter provides a comparative summary of recent national statistics from five Latin American countries on employment losses and gains during the peak COVID-19 years compared with pre-pandemic levels. As part of its work on the impact of the pandemic on informal workers, the Women in Informal Employment: Globalizing and Organizing (WIEGO) network commissioned analyses of recent national labour force data in Brazil, Chile, El Salvador, Mexico, and Peru and undertook a separate analysis of South African data on employment losses and gains during COVID-19 (see Rogan and Skinner, Chapter 4 in this volume). This chapter also presents, in section 2, micro-evidence from a WIEGO-led study of the impact of COVID-19 on informal workers. This information supplements the national statistics in section 1, with information on the dynamics of employment losses and gains for workers in specific groups of urban informal workers. It is based on a panel study carried out by the WIEGO network in mid-2020 and mid-2021 on the impact of the pandemic on informal workers in 11 cities around the world, using both a survey questionnaire and in-depth interviews (see Chen et al., Chapter 1 in this volume). The chapter concludes with reflections on the use of mixed data sources and research methods and on policy responses to the informal economy going forwards.

1. Impact of COVID-19 on employment: National estimates

This section is based on data from national labour force surveys in five Latin American countries—Brazil, Chile, El Salvador, Mexico, and Peru—as reported in the

Martha Alter Chen and Joann Vanek, *Impact of the COVID-19 Pandemic on Employment*. In: *COVID-19 and the Informal Economy*. Edited by: Martha Alter Chen, Michael Rogan, and Kunal Sen, Oxford University Press. © Martha Alter Chen and Joann Vanek (2024). DOI: 10.1093/oso/9780198887041.003.0003

WIEGO statistical briefs.[1] It provides estimates of employment losses and gains during the COVID-19 pandemic for total employment, informal employment, specific groups of mainly informal workers, and women and men. The peak period of lockdowns and restrictions in all five countries occurred in late March or April 2020, so the estimates of initial employment losses are from 2020.[2] Estimates of employment losses or gains after the initial impact of the pandemic were available for only three of the five countries because the country reports were undertaken at different times, specifically 2021 for El Salvador and Peru and the first quarters of 2021 and 2022 for Mexico.

Informal employment represents a significant share of total employment in the countries considered here. The pre-COVID-19 statistics for three of the countries show that informal employment predominated, comprising 56 per cent of total employment in Mexico, 69 per cent in El Salvador, and 73 per cent in Peru. In the other two countries, informal employment represented a lower but still significant share of total employment: 41 per cent in Brazil and 27 per cent in Chile.

Each subsection begins with summary text (*in italics*) of comparative employment losses and gains across the countries followed by details for each country.

1.1 Impact on total employment

The COVID-19 pandemic, and associated restrictions and recession, had a major impact on total employment, as seen in the percentage and numbers of all workers pre-COVID-19 who lost work during the onset of the pandemic: 7 per cent in El Salvador (around 191,000 workers), 9 per cent in Brazil (8.3 million workers), 12 per cent in Chile (1.1 million workers), 13 per cent in Peru (2.2 million workers), and 19 per cent in Mexico (10.3 million workers).[3] In four of the countries, the percentage losses were significantly higher for women than for men, whereas in El Salvador, they were about the same. By 2021, employment in Peru had reached the pre-COVID-19 level; by 2022 in Mexico, employment had surpassed the pre-COVID-19 level.

Brazil: between 2019 and 2020, 8.3 million workers (nearly 9 per cent of the pre-COVID-19 workforce) lost employment. Out of the 8.3 million workers, 7.6 million (92 per cent) had worked in urban areas. A higher percentage of women workers (11 per cent) than men workers (7 per cent) lost work.

---

[1] See Bouvier and Vanek (2023), Bouvier et al. (2022), Ramírez et al. (2023), Ramírez and Vanek (2023), and Salazar and Vanek (2022). The specific national surveys are listed in the 'Data sources for WIEGO statistical briefs' at the end of this chapter.

[2] The data for the pre-COVID period in Mexico are from the first quarter of 2020 and for the period of peak employment loss from the second quarter of 2020. Employment recovery began in Mexico in the third quarter of 2020 and continued into 2021 and 2022. Data for employment recovery in Mexico are from the first quarters of 2021 and 2022.

[3] Throughout section 1, employment loss refers to 'net loss' as some workers who lost employment may have taken another job before the survey.

Chile: between 2019 and 2020, around 1.1 million workers (12 per cent of the pre-COVID-19 workforce) lost employment. In small towns, the employment loss was greater (41 per cent) than in large cities such as Santiago (9 per cent) and a far higher percentage of women (16 per cent) than men (9 per cent) lost work.

El Salvador: between 2019 and 2020, over 7 per cent of the pre-COVID-19 workforce lost employment. The percentage loss was slightly higher in urban areas (8 per cent). By 2021, the number of workers who were able to work had recovered to around 94 per cent of pre-pandemic levels, except in the capital, San Salvador, where employment continued to decline. There was only a slight difference between women and men (1 per cent or less) in both employment losses and recovery.

Mexico: during lockdown in the second quarter of 2020, 10.3 million workers (19 per cent of the 55.1 million workers pre-pandemic) lost employment. The numbers employed recovered steadily in the second half of 2020 to 50.8 million in the third quarter and 53.1 million in the fourth quarter of 2020. The loss in employment by the first quarter of 2021 compared with pre-COVID-19 levels was just over 2 million workers (4 per cent of the pre-COVID-19 workforce), of which 1.5 million were women and 600,000 men. Nearly two-thirds of the loss (65 per cent) by early 2021 was in urban areas, the majority in Mexico City.

By the first quarter of 2022 in Mexico, employment levels were slightly higher than pre-COVID-19 levels at 102 per cent for all workers (101 per cent for women and 102 per cent for men). However, the employment rate remained slightly lower than that pre-COVID, down from 58 per cent to 57 per cent (from 44 per cent to 42 per cent for women and 74 per cent to 73 per cent for men).

Peru: between 2019 and 2020, 2.2 million workers (13 per cent of the pre-COVID-19 workforce) lost work, virtually all in urban areas and especially in Metropolitan Lima, where 1.2 million (22 per cent of all workers) lost employment. Agriculture helped to cushion the loss, absorbing 629,000 additional workers. By 2021, the numbers employed reached the pre-COVID-19 level, although recovery for women was slightly lower than for men (98 per cent compared with 101 per cent). However, the total employment rate was lower than pre-COVID-19 levels: 68 per cent compared with 70 per cent.

1.2 Impact on informal employment

In four of the countries, the COVID-19 pandemic, and associated restrictions and recession, had a disproportionate impact on informal workers. During the height of the lockdowns and other restrictions, employment loss among informal workers ranged from 8 per cent in El Salvador to around 15 per cent in Brazil and 16 per cent in Chile to 26 per cent in Mexico. In Mexico, between the first and second quarters of 2020, 26 per cent of informal workers and 10 per cent of formal workers lost employment. However, in Peru, although a large percentage of informal workers (10 per cent) lost employment, the percentage of formal workers who lost employment was more than twice as high (21 per cent). Among informal workers, a higher percentage of women than men suffered employment loss, except in El Salvador, where slightly more men (by less than 1 per cent) than women suffered employment loss.

The recovery was uneven across countries and between women and men. In El Salvador, between 2019 and 2021, formal employment recovered to 96 per cent and informal employment to 94 per cent of pre-COVID-19 levels. In Peru, employment gains were significantly higher in the informal than in the formal economy: to higher than pre-COVID-19 levels at 106 per cent for all informal workers (108 per cent for men and 102 per cent for women). In Mexico, by 2022, total employment had recovered to 102 per cent of the pre-COVID-19 level and was slightly higher for formal workers (103 per cent) than for informal workers (101 per cent). Between the first quarters of 2021 and 2022 in Mexico, the number of women in formal employment increased by 6 per cent compared with 5 per cent for men, whereas the number of women in informal employment increased by 11 per cent compared with 3 per cent for men.

Brazil: between 2019 and 2020, 15 per cent of informal workers experienced employment loss compared with 5 per cent of formal workers. Considered another way, 70 per cent of lost employment was among informal workers. Among both formal and (more so) informal workers, a higher percentage of women than men lost employment: 6 per cent of women compared with 4 per cent of men, among formal workers and 18 per cent of women compared with 12 per cent of men, among informal workers.

Chile: between 2019 and 2020, 16 per cent of informal workers and 10 per cent of formal workers experienced employment loss. In urban Chile, the declines were significantly less but also higher among informal workers (3 per cent) than among formal workers (less than 1 per cent). Losses were higher for women than for men in both formal employment (12 per cent compared with 8 per cent) and informal employment (23 per cent compared with 11 per cent).

El Salvador: between 2019 and 2020, around 8 per cent of informal workers and 5 per cent of formal workers lost employment, followed by a slow recovery between 2020 and 2021. The increase in numbers employed was only slightly higher for informal workers than for formal workers. By 2021, informal employment recovered to 94 per cent and formal employment to 96 per cent of pre-COVID-19 levels. Nationally, women led the increase in formal employment and men led the increase in informal employment. In urban El Salvador, informal employment increased by 3 per cent, whereas formal employment increased by 1 per cent. By contrast, in the capital city of San Salvador, there was a decrease in both informal employment (by 4 per cent) and formal employment (by 2 per cent).

Mexico: between the first and second quarters of 2020, 26 per cent of informal workers and 10 per cent of formal workers lost employment. By 2022, informal employment had increased to 101 per cent and formal employment to 103 per cent of pre-COVID-19 levels. In Mexico City, the increase in numbers was higher for formal workers (16 per cent) than for informal workers (12 per cent). Nationally, the recovery between 2021 and 2022 was highest among women informal workers (an 11 per cent increase) followed by women formal workers (6 per cent), men formal workers (5 per cent), and men informal workers (4 per cent).

Peru: between 2019 and 2020, nationally, nearly 10 per cent of informal workers and 21 per cent of formal workers lost employment. In urban Peru, 14 per cent of informal workers and 21 per cent of formal workers lost employment, but in Metropolitan Lima, a similar percentage of informal workers (22 per cent) and formal workers (21 per cent) lost employment. Among both formal and (especially) informal workers, women suffered greater losses compared with men: only slightly higher among formal workers but nearly three times higher among informal workers. Between 2020 and 2021, the number of informal workers increased to a higher level (106 per cent) than pre-COVID-19 levels, with a higher recovery in the number of men informal workers (108 per cent) than of women informal workers (102 per cent).

1.3 Impact on specific groups of informal workers

While the overall impact of COVID-19 on informal workers was quite severe, the impact varied across groups of workers.[4] Among four main groups of (largely) informal workers (domestic workers, home-based workers, street vendors, and market traders), home-based workers were the only group to see a dramatic increase in numbers due to new entrants. Among the other groups, the percentage losses in numbers during 2020, after the onset of the pandemic and associated restrictions, varied across countries. Domestic workers suffered the greatest loss (42 per cent) in Peru compared with 37 per cent in Chile, 20 per cent in Brazil, and 9 per cent in El Salvador. Street vendors suffered the greatest loss (37 per cent) in Peru compared with 24 per cent in Chile and 19 per cent in both Brazil and Mexico.[5] Market traders suffered the greatest loss (40 per cent) in Chile compared with around 21 per cent in Brazil, 19 per cent in Peru, and 16 per cent in Mexico. In the three countries with

---

[4] The specific worker groups included in each country analysis were based on requests by informal worker organizations and on the availability of data. This section focuses on the four worker groups covered in all five of the country analyses: domestic workers, home-based workers, market traders, and street vendors. Not all countries had data on waste pickers or on workers in informal construction and informal transport. However, in countries where data were available, these groups are also included.

[5] The data on specific groups in Mexico are from the first quarters of 2020, 2021, and 2022; thus, any sharp losses in the second quarter of 2020 are not reflected.

data, waste pickers suffered a greater loss (22 per cent) in Peru than in Brazil (17 per cent) and El Salvador (3 per cent).

By 2021 in Peru, the numbers of home-based workers and waste pickers had increased to around 104 per cent of pre-COVID-19 levels compared with around 87 per cent for street vendors and market traders and 81 per cent for domestic workers. By the first quarter of 2022 in Mexico, the number of home-based workers had reached 113 per cent of the pre-COVID-19 number compared with 94 per cent for domestic workers, 91 per cent for market traders, and 90 per cent for street vendors. In El Salvador, the number of workers in these groups, taken together, recovered to a level higher than the pre-COVID-19 level, with an overall gain among home-based workers and waste pickers but a loss for other worker groups, especially for market traders.

Brazil: five groups of (largely) informal workers—domestic workers, home-based workers, market traders, street vendors, and waste pickers—represented 15 per cent of total employment in 2019: 25 per cent of women's employment and 7 per cent of men's employment. In 2020, after COVID-19 hit, the total number of workers in these five groups dropped by around 14 per cent. Excluding home-based workers, whose numbers increased, the other four groups suffered an average loss in numbers of 20 per cent, ranging from 17 per cent of waste pickers, to around 20 per cent of both domestic workers and street vendors, to just over 21 per cent of market traders. Percentage losses were higher for women than for men among domestic workers but higher for men than for women among street vendors and (more so) waste pickers. The losses among market traders were roughly the same for women and men.

Chile: six groups of (largely informal) workers—domestic workers, home-based workers, market traders, street vendors, informal construction workers, and informal transport workers—represented 21 per cent of total employment in 2019: 24 per cent of women's employment and 18 per cent of men's employment. Between 2019 and 2020, the total number of workers in these six groups increased. This is because the number of home-based workers more than doubled as workers in education, finance, real estate, and other services began working at home. Excluding home-based workers, the total number of workers across the other five groups decreased by 27 per cent, ranging from 24 per cent of street vendors, to 37 per cent of domestic workers, to 40 per cent of market traders. Among street vendors and construction workers, a higher percentage of women than men lost employment; among street vendors, 28 per cent of women compared with 20 per cent of men lost employment, whereas among market traders, the same percentage of women and men (40 per cent) lost employment. The notable increase in the number of home-based workers in Chile between 2019 and 2020 (by 390,474 women and 282,000 men) shifted the distribution of home-based work across industries. Education became the predominant industry for women home-based workers (accounting for 31 per cent). At the same time, there was a sharp decline in the percentage of women home-based workers engaged in trade (from 36 per cent to 22 per cent) and in manufacturing (from 30 per cent to 16 per cent). Among men home-based workers, there was a dramatic increase in the percentage engaged in education (from less than 1 per cent to 21 per cent) as well as a significant increase in the percentage in other services (from around 9 per cent to 23 per cent) and a marked decline in the percentage engaged in manufacturing (from around 30 per cent to 13 per cent).

El Salvador: the five groups of (largely) informal workers—domestic workers, home-based workers, market traders, street vendors, and waste pickers—represented 24 per cent of total employment in 2019: 43 per cent of women's employment and 10 per cent of men's employment. Employment numbers in these five groups, taken together, grew by 10 per cent between 2019 and 2020 and declined by less than 1 per cent between 2020 and 2021. The largest changes occurred among home-based workers, whose numbers increased by 21 per cent in 2020 and then dropped by 3 per cent in 2021, and among market traders, whose numbers increased by 19 per cent in 2020 and then dropped by 22 per cent in 2021. The number of street vendors also increased by 9 per cent between 2019 and 2020 and then increased by another 4 per cent by 2021. By 2021, employment in the five groups, taken together, recovered to a level higher than the pre-COVID-19 level (109 per cent) and a slightly higher share of total employment at 28 per cent. Unlike the other countries, employment among market traders and street vendors, not just among home-based workers, increased between 2019 and 2020. However, between 2020 and 2021 in El Salvador, employment decreased among home-based workers (by 3 per cent), market vendors (by 21 per cent), and domestic workers (by 1 per cent) but increased among street vendors (by 4 per cent). The increase in home-based work between 2019 and 2020 in El Salvador was greater for men (31 per cent) than for women (17 per cent) and was followed by a four times higher decrease by 2021 for women (4 per cent) than for men (1 per cent). Of the five groups, waste pickers (the smallest in numbers pre-COVID) lost 6 per cent of employment between 2019 and 2020, mainly among men; the numbers had grown by 59 per cent by 2021, with an increase of 70 per cent for men and 23 per cent for women.

Mexico: six groups of (largely) informal workers—domestic workers, home-based workers, market traders, street vendors, informal construction workers, and informal transport workers—represented 24 per cent of total employment in 2020: 27 per cent of women's employment and 22 per cent of men's employment. The total number of workers in the six groups dropped in 2021 but rose, in 2022, to higher than pre-COVID-19 levels. This pattern is reflected across four of the groups but not among home-based workers and informal construction workers. The number of home-based workers increased between the first quarters of 2020 and 2022, reaching a level of employment in early 2022 that was higher than pre-COVID-19 levels. The number of construction workers rose by just over 3 per cent between the first quarters of 2020 and 2021 and by another 4 per cent between the first quarters of 2021 and 2022. In Mexico, numbers in each of the other four groups declined but to varying degrees: the highest losses by the first quarter of 2021 were among those who provided services both on the streets (by 28 per cent) and in markets (20 per cent), followed by those who sold non-food/beverages on the streets (17 per cent) and in markets (15 per cent), followed by transport workers (13 per cent), domestic workers (13 per cent), and street vendors and market traders who sold food and beverages (10 per cent each). By the first quarter of 2022, home-based workers had the greatest recovery, surpassing the number of workers pre-COVID-19 for both women and men. The number of men in informal construction work and domestic work also increased to higher than pre-COVID-19 levels, whereas the number of women in construction work and domestic work recovered to 75 per cent and 94 per cent, respectively. Among market traders, the number of men recovered to 98 per cent and women to 84 per cent. Among street vendors, the numbers for both women and men recovered to around 90 per cent of pre-COVID-19 levels.

Peru: five groups of (largely) informal workers—domestic workers, home-based workers, market traders, street vendors, and waste pickers—represented 22 per cent of total employment in 2019: 36 per cent of women's employment and 10 per cent of men's employment. Unlike in the other countries, the number of home-based workers decreased during 2020 (by 44 per cent). Among the other groups, domestic workers suffered the greatest loss in numbers employed (by 42 per cent), followed by street vendors (37 per cent), waste pickers (22 per cent), and market traders (19 per cent). By 2021, the numbers for both home-based workers and waste pickers increased to around 104 per cent of pre-COVID-19 levels compared with around 87 per cent for street vendors and market traders and around 81 per cent for domestic workers. Between 2019 and 2020 in Peru, the total employment loss among the five groups of workers was much higher for women than for men. Despite recovery in 2021, women's employment in the five groups did not reach pre-COVID-19 levels, with the exception of home-based workers. There were higher numbers of women home-based workers in 2021 than in 2019, both nationally and in urban Peru. Meanwhile, although the number of men increased in each group, the numbers did not recover to pre-COVID-19 levels in any group.

One of the countries—Brazil—has estimates on the intersection of race and informal employment.[6] In Brazil, a far higher percentage of informal workers than formal workers is Black or mixed race. In 2019, among the five groups of (largely) informal workers, waste pickers had the highest concentration of Black and mixed-race workers (72 per cent), followed by market traders (68 per cent), domestic workers (67 per cent), and street vendors (61 per cent). In each group, a

---

[6] The South Africa data, presented in Rogan and Skinner (Chapter 4 in this volume), also illustrate the intersection of race and informality in determining employment impacts of the COVID-19 pandemic.

higher percentage of women than men were Black or mixed race. All four of these predominantly Black and mixed-race groups suffered significant employment losses. By contrast, even before the new entrants due to COVID, home-based workers had the highest concentration of White workers (45 per cent) and a higher percentage of men (50 per cent) than women (45 per cent) home-based workers were White.

Considering the employment impact of COVID-19 on these different groups of (largely) informal workers, home-based workers stand out as an anomalous group and deserve special attention: see Box 2.1 for further analysis of employment losses and gains among home-based workers in Brazil, Chile, and Mexico.

Box 2.1 Home-based workers in Brazil, Chile, and Mexico: Employment losses, gains, and distribution across sectors

The number of home-based workers increased dramatically during the COVID-19 crisis years as many workers, including white-collar and professional workers, who could work remotely, began working from their homes. Meanwhile, many of those who produced goods and services from in or around their homes pre-COVID-19 were not able to work during the COVID-19 crisis (see section 2 for more details).

In *Brazil*, among home-based workers, the loss of employment was concentrated in the manufacturing sector (for women and men) and also in the trade sector (for men). While the increase in home-based work was in professional, technical, and education sectors (for women and men), the largest increases in home-based work among men were in financial, health, and other services, especially in São Paulo, where the percentage of men home-based workers in these sectors increased from 37% to 46%. Overall, the net impact was that home-based work increased among men (by 10%) and decreased among women (by 3%). The entrance of higher-earning workers into home-based work is reflected in their earnings. In São Paolo, between 2019 and 2020, the percentage of home-based workers earning *three or more* times the minimum wage jumped from 26% to 31%; in the rest of Brazil, where there were presumably fewer new higher-earning entrants into home-based work, the proportion earning the *minimum wage or less* increased from 55% to 60%.

In *Chile*, the number of home-based workers more than doubled between 2019 and 2020, and this dramatic increase in numbers was accompanied by a marked shift in the percentage distribution of home-based workers across branches or sectors of the economy. Among women home-based workers, there was a sharp decline in trade: from 36% to 22% nationally and from 34% to 23% in urban Chile. A similar decline occurred for women in manufacturing.

continued

Box 2.1   Continued

Meanwhile, education became the predominant sector for women home-based workers, from less than 2% in 2019 to 31% nationally. Among men home-based workers, there was a marked decline in manufacturing from around 30% of all men home-based workers in 2019 to 13% in 2020. However, the percentage of men home-based workers in education and other services increased dramatically: in education from less than 1% pre-COVID-19 to 21% and in other services from 10% to around 25%. Another impact of newcomers into home-based work was that the share of home-based workers who were informally employed decreased from 56% to 35% during 2020.

In *Mexico*, where the reference periods were later than in other countries, the increase in numbers and the distribution shift among home-based workers were not as marked as in Brazil and Chile. Between the first quarters of 2020 and 2021, the number of home-based workers increased by around 350,000 workers. By the first quarter of 2022, the percentage of home-based workers who were in manufacturing had decreased to 35% from 41% pre-COVID. Meanwhile, the share of home-based workers in professional services increased to 78% from 46% pre-COVID-19 and the share in other services remained at around 34%.

1.4 Impact on women and men workers

In four of the countries, loss of employment was higher among women than men during the initial year of the COVID-19 crisis: by seven percentage points in Chile and Peru, four percentage points in Brazil, and less than one percentage point in El Salvador. In Mexico, there was a 19-percentage-point loss of employment for both women and men between the first and second quarters of 2020; by the first quarter of 2021, employment had recovered, but losses among women workers were 5 percentage points higher than that among men. As the data also show, the differential impact of the COVID-19 crisis on women and men workers was, in large part, mediated by where women and men workers were situated within the workforce pre-COVID: whether they were formally or informally employed, in which branch of the economy and which goods or services they produced or provided, and where they worked.

Between 2019 and 2020, in three of the countries, the percentage losses were greater for women than for men in both formal and (more so) informal employment. In Brazil, there was a 2 percentage point difference between women and men in formal employment compared with 6 percentage points in informal employment. In Chile, there was a difference of 4 percentage points in formal employment and 13 percentage points in informal employment. In Peru, there was a difference of two percentage points in formal employment and ten percentage points in informal employment. In Mexico, between the first and second quarters of 2020, there was a greater loss among women than among men in informal employment (five-percentage-point difference), but among formal workers the loss was greater for men than for women (six-percentage-point difference in favour of women). There was little difference between loss of employment for women and men informal workers and for women and men formal workers in El Salvador between 2019 and 2020.

In two of the three countries with more recent data, the recovery in women's employment was striking, given the much greater losses they had sustained in the initial period of the pandemic. In Mexico, women's employment increased to 101 per cent of the pre-COVID-19 level, only slightly less than the increase to 102 per cent for men. In Peru, women's employment increased to 98 per cent of the pre-COVID-19 level, whereas men's increased to 101 per cent. Among the informal workforce, employment recovery in Mexico was 99 per cent of the pre-COVID-19 level for women and 102 per cent for men and, in Peru, 102 per cent for women and 108 per cent for men. This reflects a greater percentage increase in total women's employment (by 9 per cent) than in men's (by 4 per cent) between 2021 and 2022 in Mexico, and in Peru by 19 per cent for women and 12 per cent for men between 2020 and 2021. In El Salvador, neither total employment nor informal employment reached pre-COVID-19 levels for women or men.

The four groups of (largely) informal workers were a larger source of employment for women than for men pre-COVID; women's employment in the groups tended to be hit harder than men's during the pandemic. However, among home-based workers, a higher percentage of men than women lost employment, except in Brazil. Also, in Peru during 2020 and 2021, the increases in home-based work were greater for women than for men.

Brazil: between 2019 and 2020, a higher percentage of women (11 per cent) than men (7 per cent) experienced employment loss. However, the gender differences were overshadowed by the difference in impact between formal and informal workers: 5 per cent of formal workers lost employment compared with 15 per cent of informal workers. Nationally, among formal workers, 6 per cent of women and 4 per cent of men suffered loss of employment, whereas among informal workers, 18 per cent of women compared with 12 per cent of men lost employment. In other words, three times as many informal workers, both women and men, faced losses compared with their formal counterparts; among both formal and informal workers, women faced 1.5 times as many losses as men. Women working in the five groups of informal workers were especially hard hit: four times as many women as men in the groups lost employment.

Chile: between 2019 and 2020, a higher percentage of women workers (16 per cent) than men workers (9 per cent) and a higher percentage of informal (16 per cent) than formal (10 per cent) workers lost employment. The gender differences were affected by whether the worker was in formal or informal employment. Among women, 23 per cent of informal workers, compared with 12 per cent of formal workers, lost employment; among men, 11 per cent of informal workers, compared with 8 per cent of formal workers, lost employment. In 2019 in Chile, employment in the four groups (domestic workers, home-based workers, market traders, and street vendors) represented 23 per cent of total employment for women and 16 per cent for men. Between 2019 and 2020, the number of women and men in these groups increased by 121 per cent and 138 per cent, respectively, largely because of the doubling of the number of home-based workers.

El Salvador: between 2019 and 2020, a slightly higher percentage of women than men workers (7 per cent compared with 6 per cent) lost employment. However, between 2020 and 2021, there was a slightly higher recovery among women than men workers (by 2 per cent compared with by 1 per cent). The net result was that, by 2021, the number of women workers was higher than pre-COVID-19 levels, whereas the number of men workers was lower. However, the employment rate of men (75 per cent) remained considerably higher than that of women (44 per cent). In El Salvador, there is little difference in the losses or gains in employment between formal and informal workers and between women and men. Nationally, among formal workers, 6 per cent of women and 4 per cent of men suffered loss of employment, whereas among informal workers, 7 per cent of women compared with 8 per cent of men lost employment. By 2021, among formal workers, there was a 7 per cent employment gain among women and an additional 3 per cent loss among men; among informal workers, there was less than a 1 per cent employment gain among women and 2 per cent among men.

Mexico: although employment had begun to recover in the latter half of 2020, a higher percentage of women (7 per cent) than men (2 per cent) continued to suffer employment loss between the first quarters of 2020 and 2021: the relative loss of employment for women and men in formal employment was similar, but much greater loss was noted for women than for men in informal employment (10 per cent compared with 2 per cent). Moreover, the percentage loss of employment experienced by women informal workers was much higher than those of women formal workers, except in Mexico City where the rates were similar. By the first quarter of 2022, compared with the first quarter of 2021, the percentage increases in employment were greater for women than for men nationally (9 per cent compared with 4 per cent), in urban Mexico (10 per cent compared with 7 per cent), and in Mexico City (18 per cent compared with 11 per cent). The increases were substantial in both formal and informal employment for both women and men and especially among women in formal employment in Mexico City. For women, total employment increased in Mexico City and urban Mexico to levels higher than pre-COVID-19 and nationally to levels only slightly less. For men, who lost less employment than women during the pandemic, employment increased beyond pre-COVID-19 levels in all three geographic areas.

In each of the four groups of (largely) informal workers, the decline in numbers between the first quarters of 2020 and 2021 was greater for women than for men. However, while employment increased for both women and men between 2021 and 2022 in each of the groups, men's employment recovered to a greater degree, except among street vendors, with roughly 90 per cent recovery for both women and men. Among home-based workers, the number of women recovered to 106 per cent of the pre-COVID-19 level, whereas the number of men recovered to 121 per cent.

Peru: between 2019 and 2020, a higher percentage of women workers than men workers lost employment: 17 per cent compared with 10 per cent among all workers and 15 per cent compared with 5 per cent among informal workers. An increase of men in agricultural employment likely contributed to the smaller drop in employment for men. By 2021, there was a significant recovery in informal employment. Women's employment increased more than men's; however, the increase in women's employment in the worker groups did not compensate for earlier losses. As a result, in 2021, women's employment in the worker groups remained below pre-COVID-19 levels while men's employment in the groups recovered to higher than pre-COVID-19 levels. By another indicator, employment rates did not fully recover for women or men and women's employment rate remained substantially lower than men's. Between 2019 and 2021, the employment rate for women decreased from 62 per cent to 59 per cent and for men from 78 per cent to 77 per cent. In Peru in 2019, the four groups of workers represented 36 per cent of women's employment and 10 per cent of men's. Between 2019 and 2021, women's employment in the groups, taken together, increased to 94 per cent of pre-COVID-19 levels and men's to 89 per cent.

Two of the countries—Brazil and Mexico—have data on earnings during the pandemic. In pre-COVID-19 Brazil, average earnings were quite low among informal workers, especially among women. With the onset of the pandemic, among informal workers, the average earnings dropped further still, but the gender gap in earnings remained relatively unchanged. Street vendors as a group were hardest hit: pre-COVID, 59 per cent earned less than the minimum wage; by mid-2020, this had increased to 65 per cent.

The data for Mexico on average hours per week and average earnings for the first quarters of 2020 (pre-COVID), 2021, and 2022 are detailed in Box 2.2.

Box 2.2 Hours of work per week and earnings in Mexico: First quarters of 2020 (pre-COVID), 2021, and 2022

Hours of work per week
In the first quarters of both 2020 (pre-COVID) and 2021, the majority of women in four groups of mainly informal workers (domestic workers, home-based workers, market traders, and street vendors), taken together, worked a short work week of 35 hours or less. But there was a shift in the

continued

Box 2.2   Continued

---

percentage of women working fewer than 35 hours per work week across the specific groups with the exception of home-based workers: an increase for domestic workers (from 54% to 57%) but a decrease for market traders (57% to 52%) and street vendors (68% to 65%). In the four groups, the share of men working fewer than 35 hours per work week was much lower than the share of women pre-COVID-19 but increased by 2021 (from 26% to 29%). Moreover, between the first quarters of 2020 and 2021, there was a decrease in the share of men working more than 48 hours per week and the percentage decrease varied by group: from 35% to 30% for domestic workers, from 23% to 22% for home-based workers, from 37% to 34% for market traders, and from 33% to 29% for street venders. There was also a decrease in the share of women working a long work week: 13% in both 2020 and 2021. However, the percentage of women street vendors working more than 48 hours per week increased from 12% in in the first quarter of 2020 to 15% by 2021.

Average hourly earnings

Pre-COVID, in the first quarter of 2020, among two groups of workers (domestic workers and market traders), men earned a few more pesos per hour on average than women. Among home-based workers, men earned around 15 pesos more per hour than women. However, among street vendors, women earned around 4 pesos more per hour than men. These earnings gaps between women and men across the worker groups remained mixed through 2021. The most notable change was among home-based workers, with an increase of 7 pesos for women and 11 pesos for men. Average earnings for women and men in domestic work went up slightly. Women's earnings in both market trade and street vending declined, while men's earnings in market trade increased (by 5 pesos) but decreased in street vending (by a few pesos). By the first quarter of 2022, average earnings of both women and men increased across all worker groups, except for men in domestic work. Among home-based workers, average earnings increased by an additional 11 pesos for men compared with less than 1 peso for women. Among street vendors, women continued to earn more than men by 6 pesos per hour.

To summarize, the national estimates reveal certain common patterns of employment loss and gain during the COVID-19 pandemic, with only a few exceptions.

- The first year of the COVID-19 pandemic, with its associated restrictions and lockdowns, had a dramatic impact on employment. Around 22 million workers lost employment across the five countries during the pandemic.

The employment losses during 2020 ranged from nearly 7 per cent in El Salvador to 19 per cent in Mexico. Recovery in numbers employed by 2021 was significant: to 94 per cent of the pre-COVID-19 levels in El Salvador, 96 per cent in Mexico, and 100 per cent in Peru. By the first quarter of 2022, employment recovery in Mexico was to 102 per cent of the pre-COVID-19 level.

- The informal workforce suffered a higher percentage loss in numbers employed than the formal workforce in four of the countries but not in Peru, where the losses were greater in formal employment. However, in Metropolitan Lima, the percentage losses were similar in formal and informal employment. Of the three countries with post-2020 data (El Salvador, Mexico, and Peru), informal employment led the recovery in numbers employed nationally. However, in Mexico City and urban Mexico, formal employment led the recovery, and in San Salvador, both formal employment and especially informal employment continued to decline.
- Women workers suffered higher employment losses than men, both in percentage terms and in absolute numbers in Brazil, Chile, and Peru. However, in El Salvador and Mexico, the initial losses in numbers were higher for men than for women, with little difference in the percentage losses. In all three countries with post-2020 data (El Salvador, Mexico, and Peru), the percentage increases for women were higher than for men nationally.
- The difference in employment losses and gains was greater between informal and formal workers than between women and men workers in Brazil, Mexico, and Peru and roughly the same in Chile and El Salvador.
- In four of the countries, with the exception of El Salvador, the differences in employment losses and gains were generally greater between women and men in the informal workforce than in the formal workforce. In Mexico, the difference during the initial loss of employment in 2020 was roughly equal between women and men in formal and informal employment, but by the first quarter of 2021, as the numbers employed began to recover, women workers recovered far less (by 10 per cent) than men workers in informal employment but to the same percentage as men in formal employment.
- Within the informal workforce, traditional forms of home-based work (in manufacturing and trade) and domestic work were particularly hard hit, and women tended to be over-represented in these segments.

2. Impact of the COVID-19 pandemic on informal employment: Insights from 11 cities

This section presents relevant city-level findings from an 11-city study led by WIEGO to supplement and help interpret the national estimates presented in section 1, particularly on specific groups of informal workers (see Chen et al., Chapter 1 in this volume).[7] The micro-evidence will illustrate some of the dynamics behind the employment losses and recovery within four groups of (largely) informal workers (domestic workers, home-based workers, street vendors/market traders, and waste pickers) and between women and men within these groups.[8]

2.1 Impact on informal employment

The 11-city study findings confirm the dramatic initial decline in informal employment plus the slow recovery in numbers of informal workers able to work during the COVID-19 crisis. In addition, estimates of the average days of work per week and the average earnings from work are provided, confirming the national data on these variables from Brazil and Mexico.

Numbers able to work
Across the 11 cities, nearly two-thirds (65 per cent) of the respondents were not able to work at all during the peak lockdowns/restrictions in April 2020. By mid-2020, when severe restrictions had been eased or lifted, over two-thirds were still unable to work, and by mid-2021, over 20 per cent were unable to work.

Days of work per week
Prior to the COVID-19 crisis, the respondents in the 11-city study sample worked 5.5 days per week on average. Their average days worked per week dropped to 1.3 in April 2020 but recovered to 3.4 days per week by mid-2020. However, between mid-2020 and mid-2021, their average days worked per week increased by only half a day to four days per week in mid-2021.

Average earnings
Not surprisingly, the slow return to full-time work was associated with a slow recovery in earnings. For the 11-city sample as a whole, median earnings were just over one-third (35 per cent) of pre-COVID-19 levels in mid-2020 and just under two-thirds (65 per cent) by mid-2021. However, one group—the home-based workers—were earning only 2 per cent of their pre-COVID-19 earnings by mid-2021. It should be noted that the average pre-COVID-19 earnings of the study sample were close to, or below, the national poverty line in most cities.

In sum, among the 11-city study sample of informal workers, recovery measured in terms of numbers able to work was slow and partial but greater than recovery

---

[7] The 11 cities in this study are Accra (Ghana), Ahmedabad (India), Bangkok (Thailand), Dakar (Senegal), Delhi (India), Durban (South Africa), Lima (Peru), Mexico City (Mexico), New York City (United States of America), Pleven (Bulgaria), and Tiruppur (India). The data from these 11 cities are based on a WIEGO-led panel survey conducted in mid-2020 and mid-2021.

[8] Since the sample for the 11-city study includes only informal workers, this section does not consider the impact of the COVID-19 crisis on total employment or formal employment.

measured in terms of average days of work per week and average earnings. These findings are confirmed by the national estimates from Mexico and illustrate the need to understand and study employment recovery, and other employment trends, not simply in terms of numbers able to work or employment rates but also in terms of hours/days of work and earnings.

2.2 Impact on specific groups of informal workers

The 11-city findings confirm that the impact of the COVID-19 crisis on informal workers was not uniform and varied between, and within, different groups of informal workers.

Ability to work

Unlike the national labour force survey samples that contained new entrants into home-based work, the 11-city sample contained only those home-based workers who had been engaged in home-based work pre-pandemic. Unlike the national estimates that showed an increase in the number of home-based workers, the 11-city study found that home-based workers suffered the greatest loss in employment and were the slowest to recover. Less than 20 per cent of home-based workers were able to work in April 2020, just over half in mid-2020, and around 60 per cent by mid-2021 because of the lack of demand and work orders and disruptions in supply chains for raw materials and finished goods. Second to home-based workers, street vendors were the least able to work in all periods and faced decreased demand and sales even once they could return to work. In contrast, over one-third of domestic workers were able to work in April 2020, nearly 60 per cent in mid-2020, and just over 80 per cent by mid-2021. Waste pickers were the most able to work in all periods but faced a decline in access to waste, in market outlets, and in prices for reclaimed waste. Overall, across the study sample, home-based workers and street vendors were the least able to work and had the lowest recovery in median earnings by mid-2021, although street vendors fared significantly better than home-based workers on both counts.

Reasons for loss of work

In April 2020, among the 11-city study sample, all four groups cited government restrictions on movement and commerce as the most significant reason for not being able to work and disruptions in markets and supply chains as the second most significant reason. Between mid-2020 and mid-2021, government restrictions, followed by market and supply-chain disruptions, remained the most significant constraints on the ability of home-based workers and street vendors to work; but as government restrictions were eased, employer hiring practices became the most significant constraint for domestic workers, and health concerns became the most significant constraint for waste pickers.

Average earnings

In April 2020, at the peak of restrictions and lockdowns across all cities, the median earnings in all four sectors were zero relative to pre-COVID-19 earnings. However, there was substantial variation in earnings recovery by mid-2020 and mid-2021. Home-based workers were the hardest hit: with no recovery in earnings by mid-2020 and slow recovery by mid-2021. Street vendors had the second lowest recovery at both points in time but significantly higher than home-based workers. Waste pickers, who had the lowest average earnings pre-COVID, had the highest recovery of earnings by mid-2020 and the second highest in mid-2021, whereas domestic workers had the second highest recovery of earnings by mid-2020 and the highest by mid-2021.

Key differences within groups

Within each group of informal workers, the employment impacts were different for key subgroups.

Domestic workers: there are two main groups of domestic workers in the 11-city sample: *live-in* and *live-out*. Most live-ins were allowed to continue to work but were not allowed to go out on days off or to visit family; most live-outs were not able to work during the peak restrictions, and many were not hired back by their employers once restrictions were eased. As a consequence, during 2020, the average earnings of live-in domestic workers were far higher than those of live-out domestic workers, especially in April 2020, when live-out domestic workers could not work or earn. By mid-2021, the average earnings of live-in domestic workers reached the pre-COVID-19 level, whereas the average earnings of live-out domestic workers were 88 per cent of the pre-COVID-19 level.

Home-based workers: there are two main groups of home-based workers: *subcontracted* workers, who depend on work orders from firms or factories through their intermediaries, and *self-employed* workers, who sell to individual customers or buyers. After the initial restrictions or lockdown, the self-employed fared better than the subcontracted in the ability to work and in average earnings. By mid-2021, mainly due to ongoing disruptions in the supply chains that limited work orders, the median earnings of subcontracted home-based workers were around 0 per cent of pre-COVID-19 earnings compared with 24 per cent for self-employed workers.

Street vendors/market traders: pre-COVID-19, more than half of the street vendors/market traders in the 11-city study sample sold food items, either fresh or cooked; those who sold food earned significantly more, on average, than those who sold non-food items. During the COVID-19 crisis, in several cities, local governments recognized street-food vendors as essential workers, reflecting a high demand for food. By mid-2021, around 90 per cent of all vendors/traders were able to work, but the average earnings of food vendors/traders had recovered more than those of non-food vendors/traders.

Waste pickers: among the four main sectors in the 11-city sample, waste pickers fared the best, although from the lowest base of earnings and working conditions pre-COVID-19 and with the notable exception of those who collected waste from dump sites that were closed during the COVID-19 crisis. By mid-2020, three-quarters of waste pickers had returned to work; by mid-2021, almost 90 per cent of waste pickers had returned to work. Across the four sectors, waste pickers experienced the greatest recovery of median earnings by mid-2020 and second highest by mid-2021: to 48 per cent and 78 per cent, respectively, of pre-COVID-19 earnings. In part, this is because most waste pickers are self-employed and can operate below the radar of the municipal government. However, it should be noted that, pre-COVID-19, waste pickers earned the least of the four sectors in most cities.

2.3 Impact on women and men in informal employment

In terms of the employment impact of the COVID-19 crisis on women and men informal workers, the 11-city study findings confirm what the national estimates found: namely, that women informal workers were hit harder and recovered less well than men informal workers. In part, this is due to the burden of childcare and domestic chores borne by women, although the 11-city study found an increase in care work and domestic work among both men and (somewhat more so) women during the COVID-19 crisis. Additionally, and importantly, the 11-city study findings show that key differences between, and within, groups of informal workers help explain why women informal workers tended to fare worse than men informal workers.

Distribution of women and men across groups

Among the 11-city study sample, the largest group was street vendors/market traders (698), followed by waste pickers (590), domestic workers (350), and home-based workers (294). Of the total sample of just under 2,000 informal workers, 70 per cent were women. Among the samples for the specific groups, women comprised nearly 90 per cent of home-based workers, who fared least well, and nearly two-thirds of street vendors/market traders, who also did not fare well. However, women represented half of the waste pickers, who fared the best relatively, and nearly 100 per cent of domestic workers, who also fared relatively well.

Differences between women and men within groups

Domestic workers and home-based workers: given the predominance of women in the samples for these two groups, the differences between men and women within these groups are not statistically significant. In the study sample, out of 356 domestic workers, only 7 were men, of which one was a live-in (the subgroup more likely to be able to continue working); and out of 294 home-based workers, 33 were men, of which 12 were subcontracted (the subgroup less likely to be able to continue working).

Street vendors/market traders: pre-COVID, women vendors/traders were more likely than men to sell food items and earned less, on average, than men vendors. During both 2020 and 2021, a slightly lower percentage of women than men street vendors/market traders were able to work. While the median earnings of both women and men were very low in April 2020, earnings recovered by mid-2021 to 70 per cent for men and 55 per cent for women compared with pre-COVID-19 earnings. In Delhi and Pleven, the earnings gap between women and men vendors/traders increased between mid-2020 and mid-2021. In Delhi, the 2021 survey was carried out during a festival season when the demand for non-food specialty items increased. In Pleven, as the COVID-19 crisis dragged on, and given their lower earnings pre-COVID, some women vendors could no longer afford to rent a space in street markets or bazaars.

Waste pickers: in April 2020, a lower percentage of women waste pickers than men waste pickers were able to work. This gender gap in ability to work widened by mid-2020 but narrowed by mid-2021. The gender gap was due, in part, to key differences between waste pickers according to what tasks they perform and where they collect, sort, and store waste. Pre-COVID, among the study sample, a higher percentage of women than men collected and sorted waste at dump sites (some of which were closed during the COVID-19 crisis), and a higher percentage of men than women collected waste from homes and from businesses. Also, a higher percentage of women than men waste pickers reported the threat of arrests and fines by the police and local authorities.

In sum, the percentage of women and men in the 11-city samples for specific groups of informal workers partially explains the gendered difference in the employment impact of the COVID-19 crisis as women were over-represented in the two hardest hit sectors, especially among home-based workers (the hardest hit) but also among street vendors/market traders (the largest group in the overall sample). But other factors also contributed to the differential impact on women and men. Among the one group in the sample that was not predominantly female and fared the best (waste pickers), women were worse hit and recovered less than men. Within the sectors, a range of factors helped explain the differential impact on women and men, including place of work, tasks performed, product sold, and treatment by local authorities.

As summarized in this section, the micro-findings from the 11-city study provide important insights into the dynamics of employment loss and recovery within the informal economy, illustrating that branch of industry, status in employment, and place of work of individual workers, plus the goods or services they provide, are key determining factors as well as the policies or practices of government, employers, and dominant actors in supply chains (for more details, see Chen et al., Chapter 1 in this volume). The micro-findings also confirm a common finding in several of the national estimates: namely, that it is the new entrants into home-based work who account for the increased numbers in that sector as the numbers of those engaged in home-based work pre-COVID-19 dropped dramatically early into the COVID-19 crisis and recovered only slowly. The micro-findings also show that the earnings of pre-existing home-based workers dropped even more dramatically and recovered even more slowly than the numbers employed.

3. Closing reflections

The joint findings, national and local, presented in this chapter illustrate that the pandemic, and associated restrictions and recession, exposed and exacerbated pre-existing inequalities within the total workforce, notably between formal and informal workers but also by branch of the economy, by status in employment, and, intersecting with these variables, by gender and (as the Brazil data show) by race.

3.1 Mixed data sources and research methods

The joint findings also illustrate the value of using mixed data sources to inform and illuminate each other. For 25 years, the WIEGO network has been recognized as an informed user of official national data; it works closely with the International Labour Organization (ILO), the United Nations Statistical System, national statisticians, and data analysts to promote improved measurement of informal employment, contributing to the 2018 publication by the ILO of the first ever global estimates of informal employment, which, in turn, contributed to the availability and analysis of recent national data from seven countries reported in this study. And, for 25 years, the WIEGO network has generated multiple multi-site studies on different topics related to the informal economy, such as the 11-city COVID-19 study, using a mix of quantitative (survey questionnaire) and qualitative (focus groups and in-depth interviews) methods. These micro-studies have been used to inform the production and analysis of national data as they illustrate the importance of key variables—branch of the economy, status in employment, place of work—in measuring informal employment. The micro-studies have also served to illustrate the intersection of these key individual variables with wider structural variables—economic trends and crises, economic and urban policies and the practices of government, employers and dominant actors in supply chains—in driving employment outcomes, not just during crises, thereby serving to inform policy towards, as well as measurement of, the informal economy.

3.2 Future policy responses to the informal economy

The joint findings presented in this chapter confirm that informal workers represent a significant share of total employment and were badly affected during the COVID-19 pandemic. They should, therefore, be given priority in economic recovery efforts and in future policies. But this requires a shift in the dominant narratives about the informal economy: from stigmatizing and penalizing informal workers to seeing them as the broad base of the economy providing essential goods and services. Hopefully, the evidence in this and other chapters in this volume will make the case for this necessary shift.

The evidence presented in this and other chapters in this volume also illustrates that policy support to the informal economy requires a differentiated approach to address the dynamics of different segments of the informal workforce. Two chapters in Part III of this volume, one on universal social protection for informal workers (Alfers and Juergens-Grant, Chapter 10) and the other on a new social contract for informal workers (Chen et al., Chapter 11), offer guidelines for a new policy approach that supports, rather than penalizes, informal workers and that recognizes and addresses the heterogeneity of the informal workforce.

References

Bouvier, M., and J. Vanek (2023). 'Informal Workers in El Salvador: A Statistical Profile, 2019–2021', Women in Informal Employment: Globalizing and Organizing (WIEGO) Statistical Brief, Manchester: WIEGO.

Bouvier, M., J. Vanek, and F. Roubaud (2022). 'Informal Workers in Brazil: A Statistical Profile', WIEGO Statistical Brief 33, Manchester: WIEGO.

Ramírez, T., and J. Vanek (2023). 'The Impact of COVID-19 on Employment in Mexico, 2020–2023', WIEGO Statistical Brief No. 37, Manchester: WIEGO.

Ramírez, T., R. Carcelén, C. Roca, and J. Vanek (2023). 'Informal Workers in Peru: A Statistical Profile, 2015–2021', WIEGO Statistical Brief 34, Manchester: WIEGO.

Salazar, J.J.L., and J. Vanek (2022). 'Informal Workers in Chile: A Statistical Profile', WIEGO Statistical Brief 30, Manchester: WIEGO.

Data sources for WIEGO statistical briefs

Brazil: the data are based on the *Pesquisa Nacional por Amostra de Domicílios Contínua* (PNAD, National Sample Survey of Households) which, since 2012, has been the Brazilian Labour Force Survey.

Chile: the data are based on the fourth quarter of the 2017, 2019, and 2020 *Encuesta Nacional de Empleo* (ENE, Labour Force Survey), a quarterly survey of the *Instituto Nacional de Estadisticas* (INE, National Institute of Statistics).

El Salvador: the data are based on the *Encuesta de Hogares de Propósitos Múltiples* (EHPM, Multi-purpose Household Survey), conducted by the *Dirección General de Estadística y Censos* (DIGESTYC, General Directorate of Statistics and Census).

Mexico: the data are based on the first quarters of the 2020, 2021, 2022 *Encuesta Nacional de Ocupación y Empleo* (ENOE, National Occupation and Employment Survey), a quarterly survey of the *Instituto Nacional de Estadisca y Geografia* (INEGI, National Institute of Statistics and Geography). Additional data are also included for the second quarter of 2020.

Peru: the data are based on the annual results of the *Encuesta Nacional de Hogares* (ENAHO, National Household Survey) for 2019, 2020, and 2021 carried out by the *Instituto Nacional de Estadistica e Informatica* (INEI, National Institute of Statistics and Informatics).

3

Impact of COVID-19 on Employment and Earnings in Ghana

Michael Danquah, Robert Darko Osei, Simone Schotte, and Kunal Sen

1. Introduction

1.1 Background

To limit the spread of COVID-19, the infectious disease caused by the novel coronavirus, policymakers around the world enacted stringent containment and closure policies (see Danquah et al., Chapter 8 in this volume for an overview of some of these policies). In April 2020, rules on hygiene and social distancing reshaped daily life. Consequently, schools and businesses were closed, gatherings banned, and almost 2.7 billion workers, representing around 81 per cent of the world's workforce, were affected by partial or full lockdown regulations (ILO 2020a).

In Ghana, the first two cases of COVID-19 were reported on 12 March 2020. As a first response, on 15 March, all public gatherings exceeding 25 people were banned, and all schools and universities were closed until further notice. Following that, the country's borders were closed on 23 March. In the interest of public safety and protection of the population, a partial lockdown was introduced on 30 March in areas identified as 'hotspots' in the country—which included the Greater Accra and Greater Kumasi Metropolitan Areas and contiguous districts. The partial lockdown restricted the movement of persons only in these contagious areas. People in these areas were only permitted to leave their homes for essential items such as food, medicine, water, or to undertake banking transactions. Persons involved in the food value chain (such as those operating in the markets; members of the executive, legislature, and judiciary; staff of utility companies and digital service providers, fisherfolks, and mining workers as well as staff of fuel stations) were exempted from the restrictions. The lockdown was largely meant to facilitate the scaling-up of effective contact tracing of persons who had come into contact with infected persons, test them for the virus, and—if necessary—quarantine and isolate them for treatment. The partial lockdown was lifted after a 21-day period on 20 April, while the other measures remained in effect throughout May 2020 and were only gradually lifted from 5 June onwards.

Michael Danquah et al., *Impact of COVID-19 on Employment and Earnings in Ghana*. In: *COVID-19 and the Informal Economy*. Edited by: Martha Alter Chen, Michael Rogan, and Kunal Sen, Oxford University Press. © Michael Danquah et al (2024). DOI: 10.1093/oso/9780198887041.003.0004

The decision to lift the partial lockdown was largely influenced by mounting concerns regarding the severe economic burden that the restrictions posed—especially on the livelihoods of the urban poor, many of whom had, by that time, run out of money to buy food, due both to the hike in food prices and to the restricted possibilities to earn a living (Asante and Mills 2020).

Across the world, the economic impact of distancing polices and the overall drop in demand were acutely felt in the labour market—triggering job losses, business closures, and underemployment. Informal employment, an activity of last resort that often serves to buffer the impact of adverse economic shocks in developing countries, was suddenly rendered unavailable due to the imposed restrictions. Workers in the informal sector were particularly vulnerable to the crisis as they generally rely on daily sales for their earnings, have limited or no access to health care or social safety nets, lack mechanisms for collective bargaining, and tend to be in activities that are contact-intensive and, thus, particularly affected by the pandemic response measures (Balde et al. 2020; Danquah et al. 2020; ILO 2020b).

In this chapter, we provide an assessment of the early impact of the COVID-19 pandemic on labour market outcomes in urban Ghana using data collected on a subsample of the 2018/19 Ghana Socio-economic Panel Survey (GSPS). The ensuing sections discuss the main objectives and the questionnaire. This is followed by a description of how respondents were impacted by the pandemic response measures in section 2. In sections 3 and 4, we discuss in detail the economic impact of COVID-19 and the labour market impact, respectively. The summary and lessons for policy are presented in section 5.

1.2 Objectives and questionnaire

The GSPS-COVID Panel Survey was implemented with the goal of gaining a better understanding of how workers in urban Ghana were coping with the COVID-19 pandemic, the main challenges they were facing, and how they viewed the response measures adopted by national and local governments.[1] For this purpose, a structured questionnaire was administered by trained local enumerators using

---

[1] To construct the sampling frame for this study, we focused on the GSPS Wave 3 (W3) adult population in urban areas who were heads of household and had been working (outside of smallholder agriculture) in the last survey round. From these, we drew a random sample of 918 respondents, stratified by geographic location, occupational position (wage employee vs self-employed) and formality status (formal vs informal employment). Among those who were contacted, 184 could not be reached, 52 refused to be interviewed, 16 were no longer members of the same household, and 10 could not be unequivocally identified, and in 8 cases, the interview was not completed, leaving us with a sample of 648 respondents, of whom 599 reported having been working in February 2020.

phone interviews. Respondents were asked retrospectively about their household's economic well-being and their own employment situation in February, April, and the seven days prior to the interview, which took place between 19 August and 17 September 2020.

Detailed data were collected on the following four key elements:

- respondents' perception of and compliance with *policy measures* adopted in response to the COVID-19 pandemic;
- the *economic impact* of the pandemic on household income and ability to satisfy basic needs, considering adopted coping strategies and take-up of government relief measures;
- the *labour market impact* of the pandemic, retrospectively capturing respondents' work status in February 2020 (i.e. before the coronavirus had reached Ghana), April 2020 (the month when parts of Ghana were under lockdown), and the seven days prior to the interview;
- households' *health status*, checking for symptoms of COVID-19 as well as risk factors, such as any chronic conditions or other major illnesses.

The data set aims not only to provide a foundation for investigating the immediate and near-term impact of the COVID-19 pandemic on workers' livelihoods but also to allow assessing the extent to which these effects are heterogeneous across various groups of workers, who differ in their exposure to the shock and/or their ability to cope with and adapt to the situation.

Importantly, the data allow the differentiation of workers by

- *location* (e.g. districts subject to different lockdown policies);
- *type of employment* (e.g. wage vs self-employment, formal vs informal employment);[2]
- *demographic characteristics* (e.g. males vs females—other characteristics such as marital status, education level, or household assets are available from earlier waves of GSPS).

The detailed description of the sample design and implementation of the survey can be found in section 1.3 of the online report published by UNU WIDER (Schotte et al. 2021).

---

[2] In this chapter, wage workers with written contracts and any social security withholdings from their salaries (for medical care or retirement provisions) are classified as formal. Self-employed workers are classified as formal if operating an enterprise that is officially registered with relevant national institutions.

2. Pandemic response measures

The survey first asked respondents how much their life had changed due to the coronavirus pandemic on a scale from one (not at all) to ten (completely). The detailed distribution of answers is presented in Figure 3.1. Five out of ten respondents (51.4 per cent) reported substantial changes (scale 8–10), while only one out of ten (12 per cent) reported no or moderate changes (scale 1–3).

Figure 3.2 reports the average rating scores of changes in life due to the coronavirus pandemic reported by different subgroups. Respondents in lockdown districts reported slightly higher changes than those in no-lockdown districts, women tended to report somewhat higher changes than men, and those who had been in informal employment prior to the pandemic appeared to be somewhat more affected than those who had been in formal employment. These differences yet are relatively small and, considering the distribution of responses, are not statistically significant. However, those who had been self-employed prior to the pandemic reported significantly larger life changes attributable to the pandemic than those who had been wage employed.

Figure 3.3 provides a ranking of aspects of the COVID-19 pandemic that, according to respondents, had the largest impact on them personally. Roughly two out of three respondents (62.6 per cent) selected unemployment or loss of income as the aspect of the pandemic that impacted them the most. In addition, 13.6 per cent of respondents reported restrictions on movement as their primary concern, while 12.7 per cent mentioned being sick or fear of getting sick, followed by childcare and/or home schooling (4.1 per cent), shortages in food supply (3.5 per cent), and other concerns (1.2 per cent).

Differentiating between subgroups, Table 3.1 reports the average share of respondents who reported unemployment or loss of income as their main concern. Interestingly, respondents located in lockdown versus no-lockdown districts were equally concerned about unemployment or loss of income. However, the

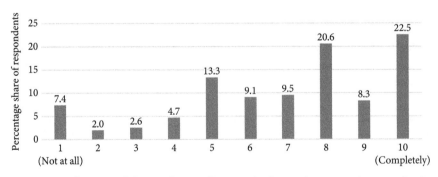

Figure 3.1 Changes in life over the past five months due to the coronavirus pandemic

Source: authors' estimates based on GSPS-COVID-19 survey.

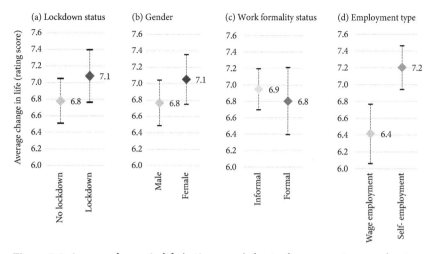

Figure 3.2 Average change in life (rating score) due to the coronavirus pandemic, by subgroup

Note: dotted lines indicate 95 per cent confidence intervals.
Source: authors' illustration based GSPS-COVID-19 survey.

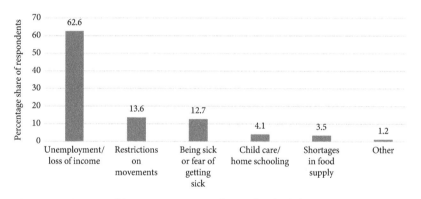

Figure 3.3 Aspect of the coronavirus pandemic that had the greatest impact
Source: authors' estimates based on GSPS-COVID-19 survey.

share of respondents mainly worrying about restrictions on movement or potential health effects was slightly higher in lockdown districts. While differences by gender are small, the data further show that women tended to be less concerned about the economic effects of the pandemic and expressed larger worries regarding their health and childcare and/or home-schooling responsibilities. Yet more substantial and statistically significant differences are observed in the responses of workers depending on their pre-pandemic status in employment—67.6 per cent of respondents in informal work were primarily worried about unemployment or loss of income during the pandemic compared to 54.9 per cent of respondents in formal work. Moreover, 68.7 per cent of the self-employed saw unemployment or loss of income as their main concern compared to 56.8 per cent of those in wage employment.

Next, the survey asked respondents to rate—on a scale from one (very poorly) to ten (very well)—how well the national government had responded to the coronavirus crisis (see Figure 3.4). Two out of three respondents (65.9 per cent) expressed strong satisfaction with the government response (rating 8–10), while only 4.6 per cent were highly critical (rating 1–3).

The way in which different subgroups rated the government response to the coronavirus pandemic is reported in Table 3.2. The average rating score was slightly higher in lockdown districts (8.0) than in no-lockdown districts (7.6), which may suggest that respondents in lockdown districts saw the need for this drastic measure despite adverse welfare effects. The data show no significant differences in rating scores between males and females or by pre-pandemic status in employment.

The survey also asked respondents to rate (on the same scale) how well non-state actors—such as churches, mosques, or non-governmental organizations (NGOs)—had responded to the pandemic. The detailed distribution of answers presented shows that, overall, the rating was slightly less positive than for the national government, with 45.9 per cent of respondents expressing strong satisfaction (rating 8–10) and 7.6 per cent being clearly critical (rating 1–3).

The average ratings, by subgroup, of the response by non-state actors to the coronavirus pandemic are reported in Table 3.3. While the average rating score is very similar in lockdown and no-lockdown districts and between workers in different types of employment, the data show that women (7.1) rated the response by non-state actors more positively than men (6.7), on average.

In a next step, interviewers reminded respondents of specific government response measures that had been introduced in Ghana since mid-March 2020 to control and prevent further spread of the coronavirus. Most of these measures had been lifted by the time of the interview. The list of measures included the ban of all public gatherings; the implementation of social distancing measures (including instructions to wear face masks in public spaces); the closure of bars, restaurants, and schools, including universities; the suspension of religious services; the closure of borders; and the partial lockdown of areas identified as 'hotspots'.

First, respondents were asked to indicate to which degree they supported the implementation of these measures. In line with the overall positive assessment of the government response to the crisis, 95.6 per cent expressed support for the implementation of the listed measures, with 68.7 per cent being strongly supportive and 26.8 per cent expressing moderate support.

Second, respondents were asked to indicate to which degree they supported the gradual relaxation of these measures. Relative to the support for the initial implementation, a slightly smaller—but still very large—share of 84.8 per cent expressed support for the relaxation of the listed measures, with a clearly smaller share of

Table 3.1 Percentage average share who selected unemployment/loss of income as main concern, by subgroup

| Total | Lockdown status | | Gender | | Work formality status | | Employment type | |
	No lockdown	Lockdown	Male	Female	Informal	Formal	Wage employment	Self-employment
62.6	62.6	62.7	64.0	61.1	67.6	54.9	56.8	68.7

Source: authors' estimates based on GSPS-COVID-19 survey.

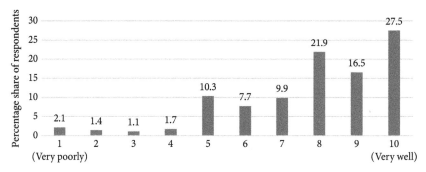

Figure 3.4 Rating of response by the national government to the coronavirus pandemic

Source: authors' estimates based on GSPS-COVID-19 survey.

43.7 per cent being strongly supportive and 40.7 per cent expressing moderate support. Workers located in districts that were under lockdown, male workers, informal workers, and self-employed workers were slightly more supportive of the relaxation of government measures, though these differences are not statistically significant (see Figure 3.5).

Third, respondents were asked how difficult it had been for them personally to comply with the listed measures while they were in place. The responses to this question were more mixed. About 61.4 per cent of respondents found it either easy or very easy to comply with the measures, while 34.3 per cent said it had been difficult or very difficult. Informal workers had more difficulty in complying with government measures (Figure 3.6c).

Finally, the survey asked respondents how many days they had stayed at home in the seven days prior to the interview (conducted in August/September) without going out at all. The responses showed some polarization of answers at the two extremes, with 25.4 per cent reporting leaving the house on all seven days and 15.7 per cent reporting staying at home on all seven days. On average, respondents stayed at home on three out of seven days in the past week. The average was slightly higher in lockdown districts (3.1 days) than in no-lockdown districts (2.9 days).

3. Economic impact of COVID-19

The next section of the survey explored the general economic impact of the pandemic. First, all sources of income to which the respondents' household had access in February 2020 (i.e. before the coronavirus had reached Ghana) were recorded. Subsequently, respondents were asked whether their household had experienced a decline or an increase in any of these sources since the start of the coronavirus pandemic.

Table 3.2 Average rating of government response to coronavirus pandemic, by subgroup

Total	Lockdown status		Gender		Work formality status		Employment type	
	No lockdown	Lockdown	Male	Female	Informal	Formal	Wage employment	Self-employment
7.8	7.6	8.0	7.7	7.9	7.8	7.8	7.6	7.9

Source: authors' estimates based on GSPS-COVID-19 survey.

Table 3.3 Average rating of response by non-state actors to coronavirus pandemic, by subgroup

| Total | Lockdown status | | Gender | | Work formality status | | Employment type | |
	No lockdown	Lockdown	Male	Female	Informal	Formal	Wage employment	Self-employment
6.9	6.8	7.0	6.7	7.1	6.9	6.8	6.7	6.9

Source: authors' estimates based on GSPS-COVID-19 survey.

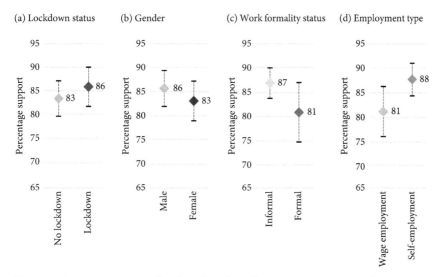

Figure 3.5 Average support for the relaxation of government measures, by subgroup

Note: dotted lines indicate 95 per cent confidence intervals.
Source: authors' illustration based on GSPS-COVID-19 survey.

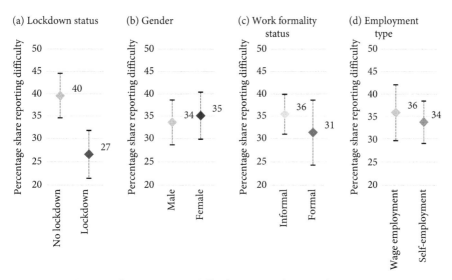

Figure 3.6 Average share reporting difficulty in complying with government measures, by subgroup

Note: dotted lines indicate 95 per cent confidence intervals.
Source: authors' illustration based on GSPS-COVID-19 survey.

The results are reported in Table 3.4. Labour earnings were by far the most important source of household income prior to the pandemic. In total, 92.1 per cent of respondents reported that their household had access to income from the labour market. Specifically, 65.2 per cent reported access to returns from self-employment and 38.0 per cent reported access to earnings from wage employment. Among these, 11.1 per cent had access to labour income from both sources of labour income in their household. Other relevant sources included remittances from friends or family (6.5 per cent), rental income (2.3 per cent), private pensions (2.0 per cent), and government grants (1.7 per cent). Only 1.5 per cent of respondents reported not having access to any type of income in their household.

Overall, 84.3 per cent of respondents reported a decline in household income since the start of the coronavirus pandemic. Remarkably, 93.5 per cent of respondents whose household had access to earnings from self-employment prior to the pandemic reported a decline in this source of income. A strong decline was also observed in rental income (reported by 80 per cent) as well as in private transfers

Table 3.4 Sources of household income

	Share of respondents whose household had access to income from this source in February 2020 (%)	Share of respondents with access in February whose household saw a decline in income from this source (%)	Share of respondents with access in February whose household saw an increase in income from this source (%)
Wage employment	38.0	60.8	4.4
Business/self-employment/selling things	65.2	93.5	3.7
Government grants	1.7	63.6	18.2
Rental income	2.3	80.0	0.0
Money from friends or family (remittances)	6.5	60.5	7.0
Private pensions	2.0	15.4	0.0
Other	3.7	45.8	0.0
None	1.5	n.a.	n.a.
Total (any source of income)	98.5	84.3	4.9

Note: respondents were reminded that this question refers to the time before the coronavirus had reached Ghana. Percentages do not add to 100 as multiple answers were allowed; that is, one household may have access to multiple incomes sources.
Source: authors' estimates based on GSPS-COVID-19 survey.

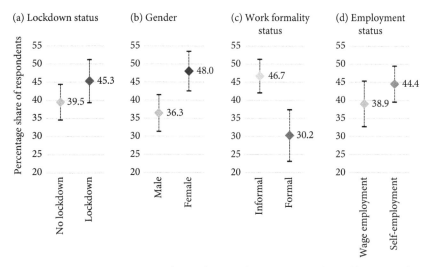

Figure 3.7 Percentage average share of respondents reporting loss of household's main source of income, by subgroup

Note: dotted lines indicate 95 per cent confidence intervals.
Source: authors' illustration based on GSPS-COVID-19 survey.

by friends or family (reported by 60.5 per cent) and in wage earnings (reported by 60.8 per cent of respondents with pre-pandemic access to this income source in their household).

By comparison, only 4.9 per cent saw an increase in at least one income source. Increases in earnings were mainly reported by respondents with pre-pandemic access to government grants, of whom 18.2 per cent experienced a top-up in benefits. In addition, 7.0 per cent reported that friends or family had scaled up the monetary support provided to the respondent's household.

Alarmingly, 41.9 per cent of respondents reported that their household had lost its main source of income since February 2020. As displayed in Figure 3.7, this loss of the main source of household income was more frequently experienced by respondents residing in districts subject to the partial lockdown (45.3 per cent) than by those residing in districts with no stringent lockdown policies in place (39.5 per cent). In addition, an above-average risk of having lost the main source of household income was reported by women (48.0 per cent), informal workers (46.7 per cent), and workers in self-employment (44.4 per cent).

Matching the reported losses in household income, 62 per cent of respondents lived in households that had run out of money to buy food in April 2020, when the strictest coronavirus confinement measures were in place (see Figure 3.8a). This presents a substantial increase of 34.6 percentage points compared to February 2020, more than doubling the incidence of food poverty in the sample. A yet higher share of 68.8 per cent reported running out of money to buy food or essential

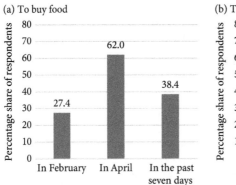

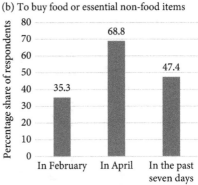

Figure 3.8 Percentage average share of respondents whose household ran out of money, by subperiod

Source: authors' illustration based on GSPS-COVID-19 survey.

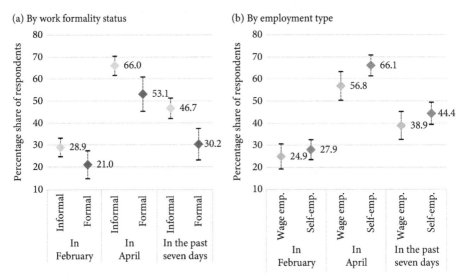

Figure 3.9 Percentage average share of respondents whose household ran out of money for food, by subperiod

Source: authors' illustration based on GSPS-COVID-19 survey.

non-food items (see Figure 3.8b). This represents an increase of 33.5 percentage points in the deprivation of basic consumption needs from February to April 2020 and must be associated with the COVID-19 pandemic and related policy measures. Workers in informal employment and self-employed workers experienced a more pronounced shock to household finances, as Figure 3.9 illustrates.

Figure 3.8 also provides evidence of a recovery in households' ability to cover basic food and non-food needs from April to August/September 2020. At the time of the interview, 38.4 per cent of respondents reported that their household had run out of money to buy food in the past seven days. This indicates a decline by 23.6 percentage points compared to April but still presents an 11 percentage point higher incidence in food poverty compared to February. Similarly, 47.4 per cent of respondents reported running out of money to buy food or essential non-food items in the past seven days prior to the interview conducted between 19 August and 17 September 2020. This indicates a decline by 21.4 percentage points compared to April but still presents a 12.1 percentage point higher level of deprivation in basic needs compared to February of the same year.

Next, respondents were asked about the coping strategies they had used to cover their household's basic needs. Figure 3.10 reports the results. Matching the observed rise in the share of households running out of money for food, 65.1 per cent reported relying on less preferred or less expensive foods, 62.3 had reduced the number or size of meals for some household members, and 29.8 per cent had borrowed food or asked for help within their social networks. With 46.3 per cent, almost half of the respondents had access to cash or bank savings that they drew on to buffer the effect of the crisis. In addition, 28 per cent reported taking on credit to cover basic needs. Only one of five respondents (21.2 per cent) reported looking for ways to earn additional money. This strategy is likely to have been hindered by the implemented confinement measures, which rendered many 'easy-access' economic activities unavailable during the early phases of the pandemic. Additionally, the slowdown in economic activities may have also limited opportunities for these households.

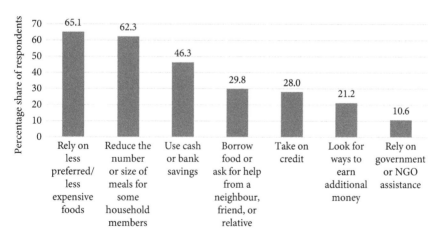

Figure 3.10 Coping strategies used since the start of the coronavirus pandemic to cover basic household needs

Note: percentages do not add to 100 as multiple answers were allowed.
Source: authors' estimates based on GSPS-COVID-19 survey.

While only 10.6 per cent of respondents mentioned relying on assistance by the government or NGOs as a main coping strategy to cover basic household needs (see Figure 3.10), 88.2 per cent reported making use of at least one of the relief measures provided by the government under the Coronavirus Alleviation Programme, when asked about these specifically. With 77.2 and 66.1 per cent, the majority had received subsidized electricity and free water supplies, respectively. In addition, 23.2 per cent had sent mobile money at reduced transaction costs or free of charge, 10.9 per cent had received free food parcels or hot meals, and 5.9 per cent reported having taken on bank credit at a reduced interest rate.

4. Labour market impact of COVID-19

A core goal of the survey was to provide a detailed assessment of the initial labour market impact of COVID-19 in Ghana. For this purpose, information was collected on respondents' labour market history and the conditions of employment in the subsequent two sections of the survey. To assess changes in labour market outcomes that occurred over the early phase of the pandemic, in this part of the report, results are presented for the subsample of 612 respondents who reported to be working—in either wage employment or self-employment—in February 2020.

About half (53.1 per cent) of the respondents who had been working in February 2020 were able to continue work throughout the month of April, while the other half (46.9 per cent) had dropped out of work at that time, when the strictest confinement measures were in place.

About four out of five respondents who had stopped work in April considered this break to be temporary rather than permanent in nature, and the vast majority (67.9 per cent) saw workplace and business closures due to government regulations as the main reason for this break in economic activity (see Figure 3.11). Interestingly, this latter finding equally applies to workers located in lockdown and no-lockdown districts.

While clearly sizeable, the immediate shock of the pandemic on Ghana's labour market did not affect all workers equally. In Figure 3.8, differences in losses of employment are accessed along three main dimensions: (a) district-level lockdown policy, (b) gender, and (c) work formality status and type of employment.

First, the immediate employment effect in April 2020 was significantly more sizable in districts affected by the lockdown. As Figure 3.12a indicates, two out of three respondents (66.7 per cent) in no-lockdown districts continued working throughout the month of April compared to one out of three respondents (34.5 per cent) in lockdown districts. In other words, workers in districts under lockdown were twice as likely to drop out of work as workers in districts with less stringent policies in place.

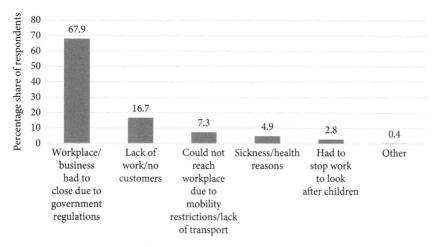

Figure 3.11 Main reason for stopping working in April 2020

Note: sample limited to respondents working in February 2020.
Source: authors' estimates based on GSPS-COVID-19 survey.

Second, across Ghana, women were more likely than men to see a (temporary) break in employment in the early phase of the pandemic, and female workers were disproportionally affected by lockdown policies. In lockdown districts, 41.7 per cent of males continued working throughout April compared to 25.4 per cent of females (see Figure 3.12b). This gender gap may be explained by a combination of two factors: (a) caring responsibilities for children and/or sick family members, which continue to fall on women, and (b) gender differences in employment stability and vulnerability as women in Ghana tend to be overrepresented in informal self-employment and underrepresented in formal wage employment.[3]

Third, interlinked with the gender gap, workers in formal wage employment had the best chances of keeping their jobs (see Figure 3.12b). These are dominantly office jobs, often in the public sector, which were among the least affected by the pandemic (see Figure 3.12c). In contrast, workers in informal self-employment were at the highest risk of having to close their businesses during the lockdown (see Figure 3.12c). These are dominantly activities that are contact-intensive (such as restaurants, tourism businesses, small retail shops, and street vending), which were particularly affected by stringent confinement policies (see Figure 3.13). Importantly, most of the informally self-employed are low-income earners with no or small savings, who need to earn a living on a daily basis (Danquah et al. 2019). Therefore, in districts with no strict lockdown policies in place, this group was the

---

[3] On average, 63.7 per cent of female workers in the sample were informally self-employed—the most vulnerable type of employment during the pandemic—compared to 40 per cent of males. At the same time, only 9.7 per cent of females were formally wage employed—the most stable type of employment during the pandemic—compared to 19.7 per cent of males (see Table A3 in the online report published by UNU-WIDER: Schotte et al. 2021).

(a) By lockdown status

(b) By lockdown status and gender

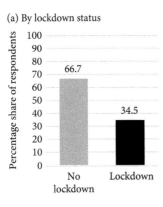
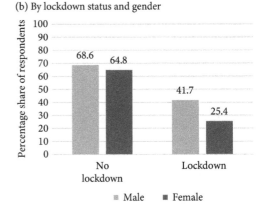

(c) By lockdown status, work formality status, and employment type in February

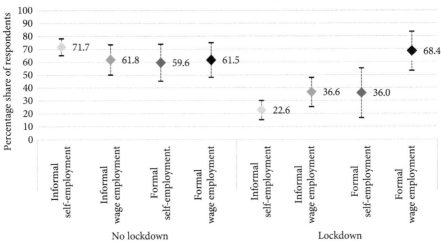

Figure 3.12 Share of respondents who were working in April 2020, by subgroup

Note: sample limited to respondents working in February 2020. Dotted lines indicate 95 per cent confidence intervals.
Source: authors' illustration based on GSPS-COVID-19 survey.

most likely to continue working, despite the danger posed by the pandemic (see Figure 3.12c and Figure 3.13).

Despite the magnitude of the initial shock, the survey data suggest that the majority of workers in Ghana were able to resume work once confinement measures had been relaxed, pointing to a strong recovery in employment over the post-lockdown period. At the time of the interview (August/September 2020), 85.3 per cent of the respondents who had been employed in February were again observed to be working, and the gap in employment rates between lockdown and no-lockdown districts had closed (see Figure 3.14). In districts that had been under lockdown, 84.1 per cent of respondents who had been working in February 2020

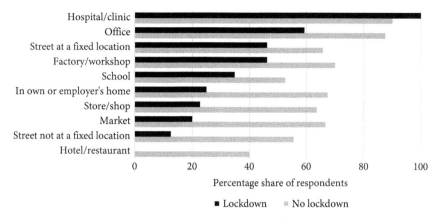

Figure 3.13 Share of respondents working in April 2020, by location of employment in February

Note: sample limited to respondents working in February 2020; responses by workers in self- and wage employment have been combined.
Source: authors' estimates based on GSPS-COVID-19 survey.

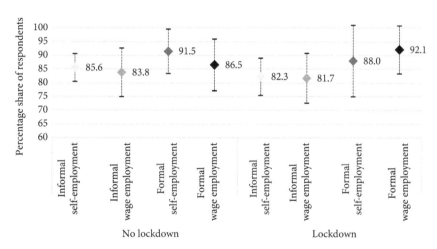

Figure 3.14 Lockdown status, work formality status, and employment type in August/September

Note: dotted lines indicate 95 per cent confidence intervals.
Source: authors' illustration based on GSPS-COVID-19 survey.

were observed to be working again compared with 86.2 per cent of respondents in no-lockdown districts.

After employment had plummeted in April 2020, this recovery is clearly remarkable. However, these figures also imply that the average employment rate in August/September 2020 across the full sample was still 14.7 percentage points lower compared to the pre-pandemic level, and specifically, 23.7 per cent of those who had stopped work in April were still out of employment four months after. Moreover, the data reveal an important gender gap in labour market recovery. In both lockdown and no-lockdown districts, females were less likely than men to have resumed work. Specifically, 18 per cent of all men and 29.1 per cent of all women who dropped out of work in April were still unemployed at the time of the interview (August/September 2020). Moreover, workers who had been informally employed pre-pandemic were less likely to have resumed work compared to workers who had been in formal self-employment or wage employment.

We further explore the job characteristics of wage-employed workers who were most severely affected by the economic disruption caused by the pandemic. The survey data suggest that the pandemic has both exposed and exacerbated pre-existing vulnerabilities in the labour market. Workers who were, *ex-ante*, in less stable forms of employment—that is, jobs that are not based on written contracts, have no social security coverage, are in the private sector, and have no labour union at the workplace—were more likely to drop out of work in April and less likely to have resumed work by August/September 2020.

Similarly, we also relate the characteristics of enterprises run by self-employed workers to the labour market impact of the pandemic. On average, informal businesses and/or own-account workers were as likely as formal businesses and/or employers to see themselves forced to stop their business activities in April 2020.[4] However, the latter were more likely to resume work once containment measures had been relaxed. Enterprises selling their products to large established businesses or the government were, on average, less affected by the crisis.

Interestingly, enterprises with access to digital technology were more likely to put their activities on hold in April but generally resumed work in the months after. This pattern is consistent across different markers of technology access—such as having a smart phone or tablet, internet access, a website or social media presence, or accepting electronic payments/mobile money. While the stronger disruption in economic activity among this group during April is surprising, it may be explained by the type of activities that these workers engage in—being concentrated in retail.

The COVID-19 pandemic and related policy measures had a lasting impact not only on job loss and unemployment but also on the working hours and earnings of workers who resumed work. The data show a decline in average weekly working hours by 13.3 per cent and weekly earnings fell by 18.2 per cent, from GH₵303 to GH₵248[5] (see Figure 3.15a). An even larger decline of 36.8 per cent is estimated when accounting for differences in the composition of employment (Schotte et al. 2021)—that is, when taking into consideration that particularly low-income earners had dropped out of work due to the pandemic shock and

---

[4] As discussed before, this average perspective masks important differences by location, as the partial lockdown had a significantly more disruptive effect on informal business activities (see Figure 3.12c).

[5] The exchange rate for the US dollar to Ghana Cedis in April 2020 was US$1 = 5.7 Gh Cedis.

(a) By period

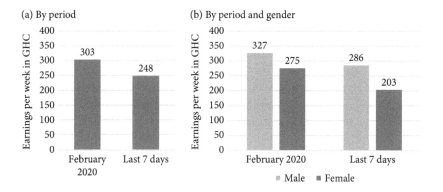

(b) By period and gender

(c) By period, work formality status,a nd employment type in February

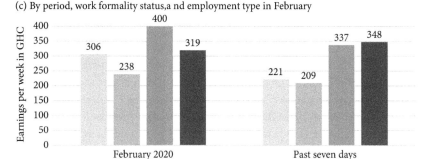

Figure 3.15 Average weekly earnings, pre- and post-COVID, by subgroup

Notes: sample limited to respondents who had been working February 2020. In each period, only employed workers with non-zero earnings are considered.
Source: authors' illustration based on GSPS-COVID-19 survey.

remained unemployed even months after closure policies had been relaxed. While the overall shock to earnings was felt by almost all workers in the sample, the consequences were especially severe and long-lasting for those in informal work, whether in wage labour or self-employment (see Figure 3.15c). Moreover, the data show an alarming increase in the gender pay gap from GH₵52 to GH₵83 (see Figure 3.15b), with the latter amounting to one-third of average weekly earnings.

5. Summary and lessons for policy

This chapter has sought to give a description of how COVID-19 has affected workers and their livelihoods in urban Ghana during the early part of the pandemic. Based on information from the GSPS-COVID Panel Survey, the chapter provides a detailed account of the economic and labour market effects of COVID-19 as well as of workers' perceptions regarding the early pandemic response measures adopted by authorities.

For policymakers around the world, navigating the response to the pandemic has been a balancing act between protecting public health and the economy. Ghana was one of the first African countries to enact strict containment policies against COVID-19. Yet, the partial lockdown of the Greater Accra and Greater Kumasi Metropolitan Areas and contiguous districts—presenting the most stringent policy response—was lifted after a period of only three weeks once the economic consequences on people's livelihoods had become visible. Results from the GSPS-COVID Panel Survey indicate that this decisive government action—in terms of both the early implementation and subsequent rollback of confinement measures—was largely backed by public support, and the majority of respondents expressed content with the way the government was handling the crisis.

Certainly, from a public health perspective, the early lifting of the partial lockdown may be considered premature. It had not lasted long enough to flatten the pandemic curve. Instead, the number of confirmed infections continued to rise during the lockdown and doubled in subsequent months (Danquah and Schotte 2020). However, results from the GSPS-COVID Panel Survey confirm that the lifting of the lockdown in Ghana was not just a choice between lives and the economy but also a choice between lives and livelihoods. The lockdown had been exerting heightened pressures on people's livelihoods, mainly through its disruptive effect of labour markets. Workers residing in districts affected by the partial lockdown were more than twice as likely to drop out of work—only one in three (34.5 per cent) continued working throughout April 2020 compared to two in three (66.7 per cent) in no-lockdown districts. Two-thirds (67.9 per cent) saw workplace and business closures due to government regulations as the main reason for this break in economic activity.

As wages and business profits were by far the most important sources of household income prior to the pandemic, this labour market effect was acutely felt—84.3 per cent of respondents reported a decline in household income since the start of the coronavirus pandemic, and an alarming 41.9 per cent said that their household had lost its main income source. Losses of the main source of income not only occurred more frequently in districts under lockdown (45.3 per cent) but were also disproportionally reported by women (48.0 per cent), informal workers (46.7 per cent), and the self-employed (44.4 per cent), thus accentuating pre-existing inequalities. In the face of this income shock, the share of respondents running out of money to buy food surged by 34.6 percentage points from February to April 2020, more than doubling the incidence of food poverty in the sample.

While labour markets witnessed a strong rebound with the gradual relaxation of confinement measures, the GSPS-COVID Panel Survey points to a partial recovery that has been slow to reach the most vulnerable. In September 2020, employment was still 14.7 percentage points lower and the incidence of food poverty 11 percentage points higher compared to the pre-pandemic level and, across the country, low-income earners in informal work and women remained more negatively affected. The persistent, nationwide effect, however, can only partly be explained by the stringency level of confinement policies. Amongst other factors, the overall economic decline (which, in the case of Ghana, has been driven by the global drop in commodity prices and external demand from the main trading partners—including China, India, the United States, and several European countries), is likely to have played a key role.

Summarizing, the findings indicate that the COVID-19 pandemic was acutely felt in Ghana's labour market. Workers who were *ex-ante* in less stable forms of employment were hit hardest by the crisis, which exposed and exacerbated pre-existing vulnerabilities. Given the subsequent higher inflation and low economic growth in Ghana, it is important for policymakers to target support to those in informal work, particularly women, in order to mitigate the needs of those at risk of being left behind as a result of the pandemic. Such measures would help avoid a backsliding in Ghana's progress on reducing poverty and inequality.

References

Asante, L.A., and R.O. Mills (2020). 'Exploring the Socio-Economic Impact of COVID-19 Pandemic in Marketplaces in Urban Ghana'. Africa Spectrum, 55(2): 170–81. https://doi.org/10.1177/0002039720943612.

Balde, R., M. Boly, and E. Avenyo (2020). 'Labour Market Effects of COVID-19 in Sub-Saharan Africa: An Informality Lens from Burkina Faso, Mali and Senegal', United Nations University-Maastricht Economic and Social Research Institute on Innovation and Technology (UNU-MERIT) Working Paper No. 22, Maastricht: UNU-MERIT.

Danquah, M., and S. Schotte (2020). 'COVID-19 and the Socioeconomic Impact in Africa: The Case of Ghana', United Nations University-World Institute for Development Economics Research (UNU-WIDER) Background Note No. 5/2020, Helsinki: UNU-WIDER. https://doi.org/10.35188/UNU-WIDER/WBN/2020-5.

Danquah, M., S. Schotte, and K. Sen (2019). 'Informal Work in Sub-Saharan Africa: Dead End or Steppingstone?', WIDER Working Paper 2019/107 Helsinki: UNU-WIDER. https://doi.org/10.35188/UNU-WIDER/2019/743-9.

Danquah, M., S. Schotte, and K. Sen (2020). 'COVID-19 and Employment: Insights from the Sub-Saharan African Experience', Indian Journal of Labour Economics, 63: 23–30. https://doi.org/10.1007/s41027-020-00251-4.

ILO (International Labour Organization) (2020a). COVID-19 and the World of Work, Updated Estimates and Analysis (2nd edn), ILO Monitor (18 March). Geneva: ILO.

ILO (2020b). COVID-19 and the World of Work, Updated Estimates and Analysis (3rd edn), ILO Monitor (29 April). Geneva: ILO.

Schotte, S., M. Danquah, R.D. Osei, and K. Sen (2021). 'The Labour Market Impact of COVID-19 Lockdowns', UNU-WIDER Working Paper No. 27/2021, Helsinki: UNU-WIDER. https://doi.org/10.35188/UNU-WIDER/2021/965-5.

4

South Africa's Informal Economy and COVID-19

Differentiated Impacts and an Uneven Recovery

Michael Rogan and Caroline Skinner

1. Introduction

Since the onset of the COVID-19 pandemic, it has been recognized that informal workers would be among the most severely affected (ILO 2020). This is a departure from the past, where it has often been assumed that the informal sector absorbs jobs which have been lost in the formal sector due to greater flexibility in the ability to respond to downturns and to make adjustments at the intensive margins (Ohnsorge and Yu 2021; Verick 2010). However, not only is the current crisis fairly unique in the way it has impacted on labour markets in particular and economies in general, but also the effects of the crisis have been experienced most acutely in the sectors of the labour market in which women, young people, and informal workers are most heavily concentrated. Together with a well-documented gendered component to the crisis (Alon et al. 2020), this has meant that informal economies in middle- and low-income countries have been left exposed and with few resources to recover. The fact that the majority of employment in these economies is informal (ILO 2018; Ohnsorge and Yu 2021) then translates into a vicious cycle of reduced demand and limited fiscal space to stimulate the economy (Mhlana et al. 2023).

However, despite these widespread a priori expectations of a crisis in informal employment, there is not necessarily a consensus on this outcome. For example, a recent World Bank publication on informal employment argued that 'the [pandemic may have induced an *increase* in informal employment] . . . that may not be unwound in the recovery' (Ohnsorge and Yu 2021: xviii, emphasis added). While the precise impact of the pandemic on labour markets is an open empirical question, it is clear that there are some expectations that the disruptions to the global economy during 2020 and 2021 will lead to a longer-term increase in informal employment in some contexts. At the time of writing, three years after the outbreak of the pandemic, data are only now becoming available to provide evidence on the impact on employment, in general Khamis et al. 2021; Lee et al.

Michael Rogan and Caroline Skinner, *South Africa's Informal Economy and COVID-19*. In: *COVID-19 and the Informal Economy*. Edited by: Martha Alter Chen, Michael Rogan, and Kunal Sen, Oxford University Press. © Michael Rogan and Caroline Skinner (2024). DOI: 10.1093/oso/9780198887041.003.0005

2020; (OECD 2021), and informal employment, in particular (Balde et al. 2020; Cueva et al. 2021; Köhler et al. 2021; Lakshmi Ratan et al. 2021).

South Africa is one context where data have allowed the monitoring of the negative and disproportionate impact of the pandemic on the informal economy from the beginning of the crisis (Rogan and Skinner 2020). This chapter now examines three years of labour force data in order to identify the differentiated impacts of the crisis on specific groups of informal workers. It draws on official nationally representative labour force surveys which are collected quarterly by South Africa's national statistical agency (Statistics South Africa). Based on an analysis of 12 quarters of labour market data (with the first quarter of 2020 as the 'pre-COVID' baseline), the chapter aims to identify the impacts of the first three waves of the pandemic and of one of the world's strictest 'lockdowns' (as it was described at the time—in April 2020). In investigating the contours of the pandemic's impact on the South African informal economy, the chapter focuses, in particular, on the different impacts by gender, sector, and status in employment.

The remainder of the chapter is structured as follows. Section 2 begins with a brief overview of South Africa's Quarterly Labour Force Surveys (QLFSs). Section 3 then provides a description of the South African informal economy and offers some context on the timelines of the pandemic and associated government restrictions and responses throughout 2020 and 2021. The definition of informal employment used throughout this chapter is based on the International Conference of Labour Statisticians (ICLS) recommendations, where informal employment includes all types of employment, both inside and outside of the informal sector, without adequate legal and social protection[1] (Hussmanns 2004; ILO 2013). Section 4 begins the empirical section of the chapter by identifying the employment impacts of the pandemic and government restrictions in 2020. Section 5 then narrows the focuses to the gender-differentiated impacts of the pandemic on employment within the informal economy. In section 6, employment changes by industry sector and status in employment are investigated. Finally, section 7 concludes with some reflections on how policy responses can mitigate the impact of the crisis on informal workers by understanding the differentiated nature of employment changes within the informal economy.

---

[1] Following the statistical guidelines set out by the 15th and 17th International Conferences of Labour Statisticians (ICLS), the 'informal sector' is defined in terms of productive activities in (typically) small unincorporated or unregistered production units. 'Informal employment' is a separate concept related to employment (both inside and outside the informal sector) which is not sufficiently covered by formal arrangements such as legal and social protection. In operationalizing these definitions, the chapter follows Statistics South Africa's measurement approach in which employment in the informal sector consists of both employees and the self-employed. Employees are identified as working in the informal sector if they work in establishments that employ less than five people and do not report income tax being deducted from their salaries. The self-employed in the informal sector includes employers, own-account workers, and persons helping unpaid in their household business who are not registered for either income tax or value-added tax. Informal employment is then identified as a broader category, which includes all persons in the informal sector (as above) and employees in the formal sector and persons employed in private households who are not entitled to a pension or medical aid and who do not have a written contract of employment (Rogan and Skinner 2021: 758).

2. Data

The data analysed in this chapter is from the national QLFSs. The QLFS is conducted by Statistics South Africa and is a nationally representative household survey which is the official source of labour market statistics in the country. Internationally, the QLFS enjoys a reputation as a high-quality labour force survey which compares favourably with household surveys from more developed countries (Bhorat et al. 2022). Prior to the pandemic, the survey was conducted face-to-face for a sample of roughly 60,000–70,000 individuals from about 30,000 households/dwelling units.

As in other contexts, the circumstances surrounding the pandemic required a drastic change in the approach to data collection. For seven consecutive quarters (from Q2 of 2020 to Q4 of 2021), the QLFS was conducted telephonically on a subsample of the QLFS for which Statistics South Africa had telephone numbers. This resulted in a substantial decrease in the QLFS sample size, which, by the end of 2021, had decreased by 41 per cent (Bhorat et al. 2022). One important consequence of this decrease in the sample size is that the precision of statistical estimates worsened substantially over the period. Bhorat et al. (2022) show how the confidence intervals for estimates of the unemployment rate widened with each consecutive quarter (as attrition rates increased) and warn that analysing subsamples is likely to result in particularly low levels of precision. A related concern is that the same sample was interviewed for all seven quarters of the period, which resulted in survey fatigue, attrition, and selection bias.

While Statistics South Africa has attempted to correct for selection bias through survey weights, the problem should not simply be ignored. This means that caution should be exercised in interpreting the results in this chapter. Nonetheless, we have taken several further measures to account for the fairly drastic change in data collection and sampling during the pandemic. First, we present standard errors in the two tables with our main results. To the extent that there has been a loss of precision during the pandemic period, we allow readers to evaluate the results alongside estimates of the survey margins of error. Second, in the graphs where we analyse trends for subgroups, we make no claims of statistically significant changes. While we are encouraged that there do not appear to be structural breaks in the longer-term trends which span the telephonic and (return to) face-to-face interviews, we urge caution in interpreting these results. In other words, we see these quarterly trends as broad indications of the direction of changes in employment rather than evidence of statistically significant shifts in employment levels. Put differently, all changes in employment estimates between 2021 and 2022 should be interpreted cautiously.

It is also possible that there could be compositional effects behind some of the trends depicted in this chapter. Typically, the QLFS samples a rotating panel, where 25 per cent of the sample is 'refreshed' each quarter (Bhorat et al. 2022). This was not possible during the pandemic and, as a result, the same households were sampled for seven consecutive quarters. Once face-to-face interviews resumed in the first quarter of 2022, new households were introduced into the sample again. As such, there is a break in the sampling approach across the period in which we analyse changes in informal employment. For the COVID-19 period, the sample was fixed such that the same households were interviewed each quarter. Thereafter, the QLFS reverted to a rotating sample which could be most easily described as a series of repeated cross-sections. We therefore present both relative and absolute changes in informal (and formal) employment in order to give a broader sense of the key changes in employment during the pandemic. We also present the results of a multinomial logit model which estimates the probabilities of transitions into the full range of employment categories (including unemployment and economic inactivity). Nonetheless, we again urge caution in interpreting the results in this chapter due to the substantial changes in both sampling and data collection between the second quarter of 2020 and the final quarter of 2021.

3. Background, progression of the pandemic, and the South African policy environment

South Africa's informal economy is smaller than its developing country counterparts, averaging around one-third of total employment over the post-apartheid period (ILO 2018; Rogan and Skinner 2021). The relatively small size of the informal economy amidst some of the highest levels of open unemployment in the world has been an enduring curiosity. Analysts point to a range of factors, including the legacy of apartheid restrictions on the economic activities of Black South Africans but also the way in which economic concentration in the formal sector constrains sales and output growth as well as employment creation in the informal sector (Philip 2018; Rogan and Skinner 2021).

While employment in the informal economy is dominated by Black South Africans (in 2019, for example, this group constituted 89 per cent of informal employment, despite accounting for only 75 per cent of total non-agricultural employment—own calculations from the Quarterly Labour Force Surveys (QLFSs)), it is heterogeneous in most other respects (Rogan and Skinner 2018). In addition, and well before the onset of the COVID-19 crisis, there were existing inequalities and fault lines within the South African informal economy (Heintz and Posel 2008; Rogan and Alfers 2019). Perhaps most notably, there has been persistent gender inequality within the informal economy, with women being over-represented in the lowest earning types of informal employment but also experiencing an earnings gap within informal occupations (Rogan and Alfers 2019).

Against this backdrop, there have been several studies, to date, which suggest that the existing vulnerabilities within the informal economy have been exacerbated by the pandemic (Benhura and Magejo 2020; Köhler et al. 2021; Rogan and Skinner 2020). Once the World Health Organization declared COVID-19 a global pandemic in early March 2020, the South African government acted swiftly, instituting some of the strictest measures to prevent the spread of the virus. Over the subsequent 18 months, the country had variously lifted restrictions and re-imposed them in response to multiple waves of infections. The country has experienced higher COVID-19 prevalence and fatalities in comparison to African and global averages, while the national vaccination programme only started in earnest in May 2021. While vaccination rates are higher than the average for Africa, they remain low in comparison to rates in the Global North, with only 36 per cent of the adult population being fully vaccinated by the end of November 2021. In 2020, the South African government instituted a range of support measures to households, employees, and employers. These included increasing existing social grants for six months, introducing the Social Relief of Distress Grant (SRDG), extending the Temporary Employer/Employee Relief Scheme (TERS), and initiating new support to small businesses. Assessments have repeatedly found, however, that informal workers have largely been missed by these impact mitigation measures (Skinner et al. 2021; WIEGO and Asiye eTafuleni 2021).

4. Employment impacts of the pandemic and government restrictions in 2020

First and foremost, the impact of the pandemic and the introduction of government restrictions to contain the spread of the virus resulted in the single greatest shock to the post-apartheid labour market. During the previous significant economic downturn, the global financial crisis in 2008/09, roughly one million jobs were lost (Verick 2010). As Table 4.1 shows, the impact of the current crisis on job losses has been substantially greater. In the second quarter of 2020, a year-on-year comparison with 2019 suggests that roughly 2.2 million jobs were lost at the outset of the crisis. This period coincided with the introduction of the severe 'lockdown' restrictions. By the fourth quarter of 2020, many of the initial government restrictions had been relaxed (although the second wave of the virus resulted in the reinstatement of some restrictions in the final weeks of the calendar year). However, the labour market still had roughly 1.4 million fewer jobs relative to the same quarter in 2019. The estimates of total employment in Table 4.1 below, therefore, depict a sharp initial shock to the labour market followed by a somewhat muted recovery throughout 2020.

Apart from the scale of job losses during the unfolding of the crisis, the other key feature from the South African context is the disproportionate number of informal jobs that were lost. Of the nearly 2.2 million net jobs lost during the second quarter

Table 4.1 Total employment in the South African labour market, 2019–20

	Quarter 1			Quarter 2			Quarter 3			Quarter 4		
	2019	2020	Absolute change	2019	2020	Absolute change	2019	2020	Absolute change	2019	2020	Absolute change
Informal employment	4,945,832 (69,326)	4,941,020 (70,934)	**-4,812**	5,085,705 (70,394)	3,620,309 (75,750)	**-1,465,396**	5,093,242 (70,639)	3,918,667 (78,234)	**-1,174,575**	4,907,311 (69,516)	4,047,667 (79,054)	**-859,644**
Formal employment	10,790,712 (102,468)	10,838,100 (105,043)	**47,388**	10,649,907 (101,922)	9,807,229 (128,052)	**-842,678**	10,673,496 (102,222)	10,223,020 (130,715)	**-450,476**	10,933,092 (103,708)	10,440,274 (130,340)	**-492,818**
Total employment	16,513,041 (119,609)	16,595,799 (123,167)	**82,758**	16,535,411 (119,900)	14,336,719 (148,151)	**-2,198,692**	16,593,818 (120,346)	14,880,503 (150,413)	**-1,713,315**	16,640,794 (120,864)	15,200,723 (149,904)	**-1,440,071**

Note: the data are weighted. Standard errors in brackets. Sample not restricted to the working-age (15–65) population. All workers aged 15 and older, including older workers, are included in the estimates in the table. The table does not reflect the category of 'Other employment', which includes observations that could not be classified as 'formal' or 'informal'. Therefore, the estimate of total employment is greater than the sum of formal and informal employment. See n 1 for the different categories of informal employment.
Source: authors' calculations from the Quarterly Labour Force Surveys (QLFSs).

of 2020, roughly 1.5 million were informal jobs. By the third quarter, 1.2 million of the 1.7 million lost jobs were informal and, during the final quarter of the year, 860,000 of the 1.4 million lost jobs were in the informal economy. Therefore, both relative and absolute job losses were greater in the informal economy, while the rate and level of 'recovery' was greater for formal employment.

Figure 4.1 allows for greater ease of comparison between informal and formal job losses by expressing labour market changes, by quarter, in relative terms. During the initial phase of the crisis (the second quarter of 2020), informal employment contracted by about 29 per cent, while formal employment decreased by 8 per cent. In other words, informal job losses were more than three times greater than formal job losses. A similar pattern is evident throughout the remainder of 2020, with the relative rate of informal job losses being far higher than formal job losses. By the end of 2020, informal job numbers were 18 per cent lower, year-on-year, while formal jobs were only about 5 per cent lower than 2019 levels.

Figure 4.2 looks more closely at these job losses by comparing employment in 2020 to the corresponding quarter in the previous year in the formal and informal sectors and in private households.[2] In the second quarter, relative job losses were far higher in the informal sector and in private households (mostly consisting of women engaged in domestic work) than in the formal sector. In quarters 2–4 of

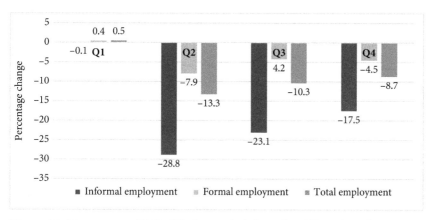

Figure 4.1 Year-on-year (2019–20) changes in informal and formal employment, by quarter

Note: the data are weighted. Sample not restricted to the working-age population.
Source: authors' calculations from the Quarterly Labour Force Surveys (QLFSs).

---

[2] Since these estimates are based on the sector of employment, there are some informal workers included under the 'formal sector', that is, those who are employed informally by formal-sector employers. This group is, however, relatively small in South Africa, and the effects of the pandemic on informal workers within the formal sector are analysed separately later in the chapter.

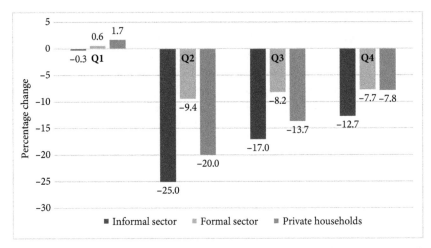

Figure 4.2 Year-on-year (2019–20) changes in the formal and informal sectors and private households

Note: the data are weighted. Sample not restricted to the working-age population.
Source: authors' calculations from the QLFSs.

2020, the largest job losses were in the informal sector, with employment losses more than double those in the formal sector in quarters 2 and 3 in comparison to the previous year. Somewhat surprisingly, employment in private households recorded a more rapid recovery than employment in the informal sector over the course of the year. Informal-sector employment made the slowest recovery following the greatest initial decrease in job numbers.

5. Gender differences in the loss of employment and earnings

One of the most distinguishing features of the current crisis, both in South Africa (Casale and Posel 2021; Casale and Shepherd 2021; Rogan and Skinner 2020) and globally (Alon et al. 2020; Collins et al. 2021), is the disproportionate job and income losses borne by women. During the first two quarters of the crisis, women's informal employment, at the extensive margin, contracted more than men's, that is, by 30 per cent in the second quarter and by 27 per cent in the third quarter. By the fourth quarter of 2020, and likely driven by the return to work of many domestic workers, both women's and men's informal employment numbers were about 17.5 per cent lower than in the same quarter of 2019. Therefore, in terms of job losses in the informal economy, women seem to have experienced a greater impact earlier in the crisis but then 'recovered' to similar levels to men by the end of the calendar year.

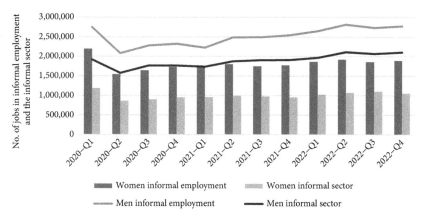

Figure 4.3 Total employment in the informal sector and in informal employment, by sex (2020–22)

Note: the data are weighted. Sample not restricted to the working-age population.
Source: authors' calculations from the QLFSs.

However, this overall picture masks important differences within the informal economy as well as gender differences in the longer-term recovery of jobs. The estimates in Figure 4.3 suggest that, among men (lines), the total number of jobs in informal employment in the fourth quarter of 2022 had returned to the same absolute level compared with the pre-crisis data point (the first quarter of 2020). Over the same period, levels of informal-sector employment actually increased slightly relative to the beginning of 2020. Among women (bars), however, both informal employment and informal-sector employment are substantially lower than the pre-crisis period. Perhaps most notably, the rate of employment recovery among women (both within and outside of the informal sector) has improved very little (if at all) since the third quarter of 2020. By the end of 2022, women's total informal employment and informal sector employment were still 13.7 per cent and 11 per cent, respectively, lower than the first quarter of 2020. In other words, the level of male informal employment was roughly the same as it was just prior to the pandemic, while women's employment in the informal economy had still not recovered to pre-pandemic levels after three years. At the same time, the number of formal jobs was still 1.7 per cent lower at the end of 2022 compared with the beginning of 2020.

Table 4.2 explores these gendered differences in losses in both informal and formal employment within the context of the broader impact of the crisis on the South African labour market. In focusing on the immediate and acute phase of the crisis, the first step was to identify the determinants of labour force status based on two multinomial logit models—one estimated before the crisis and one during the first period of pandemic job losses (2019—Q2 and 2020—Q2, respectively). The regressions control for gender, race, level of education, marital status, age (and its quadratic), and province. The regressions are first estimated with

Table 4.2 Selected average predicted probabilities of labour force status, 2019–20 (second quarters)

	Unemployed		Discouraged		Informal employment		Formal employment	
	2019—Q2	2020—Q2	2019—Q2	2020—Q2	2019—Q2	2020—Q2	2019—Q2	2020—Q2
Gender								
Women	18.3 (0.37)	10.3*** (0.33)	7.7 (0.23)	6.3*** (0.28)	11.6 (0.28)	7.0*** (0.26)	21.2 (0.38)	17.0*** (0.42)
Men	19.6 (0.40)	11.8*** (0.39)	7.4 (0.70)	6.0 (0.30)	16.8 (0.36)	10.5*** (0.36)	32.3 (0.46)	25.2*** (0.54)
Race								
African/Black	21.5 (0.33)	12.0*** (0.30)	7.7 (0.23)	6.8 (0.26)	15.2 (0.27)	9.6*** (0.27)	25.0 (0.33)	19.6*** (0.37)
Coloured	18.1 (0.91)	9.7*** (0.89)	7.4 (0.70)	7.2 (0.94)	9.6 (0.62)	6.0*** (0.70)	34.7 (1.24)	24.5*** (1.49)
Indian/Asian	8.6 (1.24)	10.6 (2.07)	2.2 (0.58)	3.1 (0.97)	12.0 (1.30)	5.0*** (0.92)	23.39 (1.83)	23.6 (2.18)
White	7.5 (0.84)	5.4 (0.81)	3.0 (0.63)	2.2 (0.58)	9.3 (0.91)	5.1*** (0.76)	32.21 (1.43)	28.7 (1.58)

Note: the data are weighted. Conditional predicted probabilities are based on the estimates from the multinomial logit model. The specified independent variable is set to a reference value, while each confounder is fixed at its mean value. Predicted probabilities for economic inactivity and 'other' employment are not displayed but were included in the regression. The sample is restricted to the working-age population. The base model included additional controls for level of education, marital status, age, and provincial fixed effects. *** indicates that the change from 2019(Q2) to 2020(Q2) is significant at the 95 per cent confidence level. Standard errors are in brackets.
Source: authors' calculations from the QLFSs.

the full working-age sample (Table 4.2) and then separately for women and men (Figure 4.5). Since the focus is on changes between the pre-crisis and crisis periods, Table 4.2 presents the results in the form of average predicted probabilities derived from the multinomial logit estimates. Accordingly, the table shows the predicted probabilities of being in strict unemployment, discouraged unemployment, informal employment, and formal employment by gender and population group.

As suggested by the results in the table, the onset of the pandemic had a substantial effect on the South African labour market. Overall, there was a large reduction in both formal and informal employment along with a substantial and significant decrease in unemployment[3] for both women and men and among the African and Coloured sample. In terms of decreases in formal and informal employment, the decreases were large and significant, particularly for informal employment. Among women, for example, the probability of informal employment decreased by 4.6 percentage points (from 11.6 per cent to 7 per cent), while the likelihood of formal employment decreased by 4.2 percentage points (from 21.2 per cent to 17 per cent). Similarly, among working-age men, there was a 6.3 percentage point drop in informal employment after the onset of the crisis and a 7.1 percentage point drop in the probability of being in formal employment. Given the lower probabilities of informal employment for both women and men (relative to formal employment), these percentage point changes denote larger relative decreases in the probability of informal employment, that is, by 39.6 per cent among women and 37.5 per cent among men.[4]

While these estimates demonstrate the large and significant decreases in the probability of informal employment during the first months of the pandemic in South Africa (after controlling for several factors), Figure 4.4 considers the labour market changes for the Black African population alone. In South Africa, the informal economy is fairly homogenous in terms of race, with roughly 90 per cent of all informal workers identifying as Black African (own calculations from the 2019 QLFS—Q2). Given the gender differences in labour force participation, the estimates in Figure 4.4 below are also based on separate regressions for women and men. The results suggest large and significant differences in the probabilities of employment and inactivity between Black African women and men. Perhaps most notably, the likelihood of labour force non-participation (inactivity) among working-age women increased from about 40 per cent for women in 2019 to nearly 60 per cent in 2020 (and from 21 per cent among men to 45 per cent).

Turning to the main categories of interest, among women, the probability of being in both informal and formal employment decreased by 4.6 percentage points between 2019 and the onset of the crisis. The relative decreases in the likelihood of being in informal employment were, therefore, considerably larger than the

[3] Given the unique features of the crisis, unemployment actually declined while economic inactivity (i.e. labour force withdrawal) increased significantly (not shown in Table 4.2).
[4] The corresponding relative declines in the probability of formal employment for women and men are 19.8 per cent and 21.9 per cent, respectively.

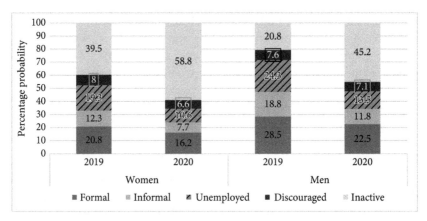

Figure 4.4 Average predicted probabilities of labour force status among Black Africans, 2019–20 (second quarters)

Note: the data are weighted. Conditional predicted probabilities are based on the estimates from separate multinomial logit estimates for women and men. The specified independent variable is set to a reference value, while each confounder is fixed at its mean value. Sample restricted to the working-age population. 'Other employment' not included. The base model included additional controls for population group, level of education, age, marital status, and provincial fixed effects. *Source:* authors' calculations from the QLFSs.

decreases in the probability of formal employment (37.4 per cent and 22.1 per cent, respectively). Among men, the relative decreases in the likelihood of informal and formal employment were 37.2 per cent and 21.1 per cent, respectively. Therefore, among both women and men, the conditional probabilities for informal employment decreased by far more than for formal employment. Complementing the descriptive analysis earlier in the chapter, the multivariate analysis suggests that a particular feature of the 'pandemic recession' is a large and disproportionate impact on informal employment.

6. Changes in informal employment by industry sector and status in employment

The informal economy consists of a diverse set of activities and employment arrangements. As such, the effects of government restrictions to contain the spread of COVID-19 are likely to vary for different groups of workers. Figure 4.5 presents 12 quarters of informal employment estimates for the 4 largest industry sectors in the informal economy: wholesale and retail trade, private households (domestic work), construction, and community and social services. Wholesale and retail trade is the single largest employer in the informal economy and includes trade in streets, markets, and from homes ('*spaza*' shops) as well as various service activities. As demonstrated by the sharp decrease in the second quarter of 2020,

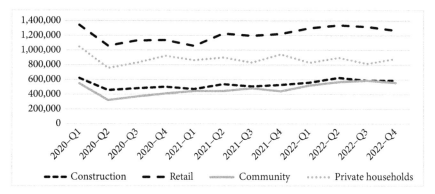

Figure 4.5 Employment in the informal economy (2020–21), by industry sector

Note: the data are weighted. Sample not restricted to the working-age population.
Source: authors' calculations from the QLFSs.

workers in this sector were impacted by the government 'lockdown' in April of that year. Restrictions on movement and all non-essential activities were stringently enforced. The severe reduction in income, consumption, and aggregate demand meant that this sector was slow to recover over the course of 2020 and into 2021 (depicted by the flat line for most of the period). Only in the second quarter of 2021 is there evidence of a recovery in employment in informal trade, but the employment numbers were still lower than pre-pandemic levels by the end of 2022 (by roughly 5 per cent).

Informal employment in private households consists of domestic workers and other types of household employment (e.g. gardeners) and is predominately a source of employment for women, at 73 per cent of total employment. The estimates in Figure 4.6 show a sharp contraction in employment in private households followed by a muted recovery. Despite a brief increase in employment numbers in domestic work at the end of 2020, the recovery across 2021 and 2022 has been somewhat flat. In contrast, informal employment in the construction sector (93 per cent men) saw a more gradual drop off in the second quarter of 2020 and then a similar (in size) recovery across 2021 and 2022. While still lower than before the pandemic, the difference in employment in this sector between the start and end of the three-year period falls within the survey margin of error. Finally, employment in community and social services, which includes informal childcare providers, hairdressers, mechanics, traditional medicine providers, and waste recyclers and is dominated by women (62 per cent), saw a large shock at the outset of the crisis followed by a slow initial recovery. These activities gradually recovered during 2020, stalled in 2021, and then returned to pre-pandemic levels by the end of 2022. Taken as a whole, the findings from Figure 4.6 demonstrate that the crisis was not felt evenly across the informal economy and that the sectors in which women are concentrated were disproportionately impacted.

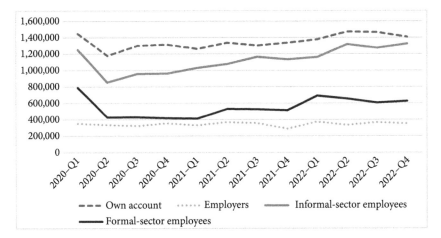

Figure 4.6 Informal employment by status in employment (2020–22)

Note: the data are weighted. Sample not restricted to the working-age population.
Source: authors' calculations from the QLFSs.

Finally, Figure 4.6 presents estimates of employment changes in the informal economy by status in employment. It includes two groups of self-employed workers (own-account workers and employers) and two types of employees (those in informal sector enterprises and those employed informally in the formal sector). Own-account work is the single largest category in the South African informal economy and is often the most visible type of informal employment as it includes street vendors, waste pickers, and other workers who operate in public spaces. At the outset of the crisis, there was an immediate and sharp drop in own-account work when access to public spaces was restricted. However, there has been a gradual recovery over the following quarters as demand for essential goods (and basic food products in particular) has increased. By the end of 2022, the recovery was still incomplete, however, with own-account employment about 3 per cent lower compared with the beginning of 2020. The other category of self-employment, employers, is a relatively small group, which is comprised predominantly of men (81 per cent) and does not seem to have been affected by the pandemic (at least in terms of employment numbers).

The two types of informal employees (those in the informal sector and those in the formal sector) recorded the largest declines in employment during the height of the crisis. The larger of the two types of employees (informal-sector employees) experienced a roughly 30 per cent reduction in employment between the first two quarters of 2020. For these employees, the recovery was relatively slow over the course of 2020 and then improved gradually until the end of 2022, when the number in employment was similar to the period prior to the pandemic. In relative terms, the group that experienced the largest decline in employment is that of employees who work informally for formal-sector firms. This type of employment has some parallels with 'precarious employment' in the broader literature but, in the South African context, includes male-dominated (62 per cent) occupations such as construction and agricultural labourers as well as taxi drivers (but also several types of restaurant, retail, and service workers). At the outset of the pandemic, these employees saw a nearly 50 per cent reduction in employment (at the extensive margin) and practically no recovery for the following three quarters. Employment numbers only increased again in the second quarter of 2021, but employment levels were still 20 per cent lower at the end of 2022 compared with early 2020. This suggests that some formal firms/industries responded[5] to the economic downturn by laying off their most vulnerable workers—that is, those that were outsourced and/or working on insecure contracts and without any type of social protection.

7. Conclusion

Analysis of official South African employment data over the 2020–22 period shows that measures to prevent the spread of COVID-19 have coincided with a disproportionate decrease in informal employment. Countering earlier World Bank predictions that the pandemic may induce an *increase* in informal employment, the South African data show that both relative and absolute job losses have been greater in the informal economy, while the rate and level of recovery have been greater for formal employment. Further, the data suggest uneven impacts within the informal economy, with women, those working in the informal sector, and those in retail and domestic work being particularly hard hit. The pandemic period has thus widened pre-existing inequalities and fault lines. In policy terms, this suggests that the informal economy should be a priority in economic recovery efforts but also that support requires differentiated approaches and a range of measures.

The COVID-19 recovery efforts provide an opportunity to address pre-existing disparities and to accelerate structural change in the economy. The crisis has highlighted both the essential services informal workers provide but also their lack of social protection. By way of example, in 2019, only 20 per cent of South Africa's 1.2 million domestic workers reported being registered for the Unemployment Insurance Fund (UIF) (QLFS, own calculations). This is despite registration being a legal requirement for the employers of domestic workers. While domestic workers are the largest group, this is also the case for other informal wage workers—farm workers, taxi drivers, waiters, and construction workers—and for employees in informal enterprises. As a result, the vast majority of informal wage workers who

---

[5] It is, of course, also possible that smaller formal firms that employed workers informally did not survive the pandemic and closed altogether.

lost their jobs in 2020 were unable to access relief from TERS. Changes underway in the social protection system (see, e.g. the Department of Social Development 2021) need to extend protections to informal wage workers—including unemployment insurance, maternity leave, occupational health and safety protections, and pensions.

The anaemic jobs recovery in the informal economy is, in part, an outcome of constrained demand. Cash transfers not only reduce poverty and inequality but are also a key mechanism to boost demand. Existing evidence suggests grant recipients often use the money to buy local goods and services but also to search for work or start their own informal enterprises (Davis et al. 2016; Fisher et al. 2017). As noted earlier in the chapter, the South African government introduced a temporary relief grant (the SRD grant) of ZAR350[6] a month per person. While the grant amount is very small (roughly the equivalent of US$22), its impact on poverty and inequality has been documented (Barnes et al. 2021), with some arguing that this should form the basis of a universal income guarantee (see, e.g. IEJ 2021). In addition, small business support should be extended to the informally self-employed. Despite stating that the informal sector is a target of support, the Department of Small Business Development's support programme has not reached informal enterprises (Skinner et al. 2021; WIEGO and Asiye eTafuleni 2021). Given the disproportionate impact of the crisis on women informal workers, they should be a particular target for both forms of support but have fallen through the gaps so far (Skinner et al. 2021; WIEGO and Asiye eTafuleni 2021). More broadly, the fact that employment levels in the informal economy are only now reaching their pre-pandemic levels for some groups of workers suggests that supporting the most vulnerable members of South Africa's workforce should be a priority for the government.

References

Alon, T., M. Doepke, J. Olmstead-Rumsey, and M. Tertilt (2020). 'The Impact of COVID-19 on Gender Equality', National Bureau of Economic Research (NBER) Working Paper No. 26947, Cambridge, MA: NBER. https://doi.org/10.3386/w26947.

Balde, R., M. Boly, and E. Avenyo (2020). 'Labour Market Effects of COVID-19 in Sub-Saharan Africa: An Informality Lens from Burkina Faso, Mali and Senegal', United Nations University-Maastricht Economic and Social Research Institute on Innovation and Technology (UNU-MERIT) Working Paper No. 2020–022, Maastricht: UNU-MERIT.

Barnes, H., G. Espi-Sanchis, M. Leibbrandt, D. McLennan, M. Noble, J. Pirttilä et al. (2021). 'Analysis of the Distributional Effects of COVID-19 and State-Led Remedial Measures in South Africa', United Nations University-World Institute for Development

---

[6] Many have noted that ZAR350 is below the food poverty line of ZAR585 (IEJ 2021:4).

Economics Research (UNU-WIDER) Working Paper No. 2021/68,. Helsinki: UNU-WIDER. https://doi.org/10.35188/UNU-WIDER/2021/006-1.

Benhura, M., and P. Magejo (2020). 'Differences between Formal and Informal Workers' Outcomes during the COVID-19 Crisis Lockdown in South Africa', National Income Dynamics Study-Coronavirus Rapid Mobile Survey (NIDS-CRAM) Policy Paper No. 2, Cape Town: NIDS-CRAM.

Bhorat, H., T. Köhler, and B. Stanwix (2022). 'Non-response Rates in the Quarterly Labour Force Survey during COVID-19: A Brief Commentary', Development Policy Research Unit (DPRU) Policy Brief No. 2022/56, Cape Town: DPRU.

Casale, D., and D. Posel (2021). 'Gender Inequality and the COVID-19 Crisis: Evidence from a Large National Survey during South Africa's Lockdown', *Research in Social Stratification and Mobility*, 71: 100569. https://doi.org/10.1016/j.rssm.2020.100569.

Casale, D., and D. Shepherd (2021). 'The Gendered Effects of the Covid-19 Crisis and Ongoing Lockdown in South Africa: Evidence from NIDS-CRAM Waves 1–5', NIDS-CRAM Working Paper No. 4, Wave 5, Cape Town: NIDS-CRAM.

Collins, C, L.C. Landivar, L. Ruppanner, and W.J. Scarborough (2021). 'COVID-19 and the Gender Gap in Work Hours', *Gender, Work and Organization*, 28(S1): 101–12. https://doi.org/10.1111/gwao.12506.

Cueva, R., X. Del Carpio, and H. Winkler (2021). 'The Impacts of COVID-19 on Informal Labor Markets: Evidence from Peru', Policy Research Working Paper No. 9675, Washington, DC: World Bank. https://doi.org/10.1596/1813-9450-9675.

Davis, B., S. Handa, N. Hypher, N. Winder Rossi, P. Winters, and J. Yablonski (2016). *From Evidence to Action: The Story of Cash Transfers and Impact Evaluation in Sub Saharan Africa*. Oxford: Oxford University Press. https://doi.org/10.1093/acprof:oso/9780198769446.001.0001.

Department of Social Development (2021). 'Green Paper on Comprehensive Social Security and Retirement Reform', Pretoria: South African National Department of Social Development.

Fisher, E., R. Attah, V. Barca, C. O'Brien, S. Brook, J. Holland et al. (2017). 'The Livelihood Impacts of Cash Transfers in Sub-Saharan Africa: Beneficiary Perspectives from Six Countries', *World Development*, 99: 299–319. https://doi.org/10.1016/j.worlddev.2017.05.020.

Heintz, J., and D. Posel (2008). 'Revisiting Informal Employment and Segmentation in the South African Labour Market', *South African Journal of Economics*, 76(1): 26–44. https://doi.org/10.1111/j.1813-6982.2008.00153.x.

Hussmanns, R. (2004). 'Measuring the Informal Economy: From Employment in the Informal Sector to Informal Employment', International Labour Organization (ILO) Working Paper No. 53, Geneva: ILO.

IEJ (Institute for Economic Justice) (2021). 'Introducing a Universal Basic Income Guarantee for South Africa, towards Income Security for All', Social Protection Series Policy Brief 1, Johannesburg: IEJ.

ILO (International Labour Organization) (2013). *Measuring Informality: A Statistical Manual on the Informal Sector and Informal Employment*. Geneva: ILO.

ILO (2018). *Women and Men in the Informal Economy: A Statistical Picture*. (3rd edn). Geneva: ILO.

ILO (2020). *ILO Monitor: COVID-19 and the World of Work* (3rd edn, 29 April). Geneva: ILO.

Khamis, M., D. Prinz, D. Newhouse, A. Palacios-Lopez, U. Pape, and M. Weber (2021). 'The Early Labor Market Impacts of COVID-19 in Developing Countries: Evidence from

High-Frequency Phone Surveys', Jobs Working Paper No. 58. Washington, DC: World Bank. https://doi.org/10.1596/35044.

Köhler, T., H. Bhorat, R. Hill, and B. Stanwix (2021). 'COVID-19 and the Labour Market: Estimating the Employment Effects of South Africa's National Lockdown', DPRU Working Paper No. 202107, Cape Town: DPRU.

Lakshmi Ratan, A., S. Roever, R. Jhabvala, and P. Sen (2021). 'Evidence Review of COVID-19 and Women's Informal Employment: A Call to Support the Most Vulnerable First in the Economic Recovery', Washington, DC: Bill & Melinda Gates Foundation.

Lee, S., D. Schmidt-Klau, and S. Verick (2020). 'The Labour Market Impacts of the COVID-19: A Global Perspective', *Indian Journal of Labour Economics*, 63: 11–15. https://doi.org/10.1007/s41027-020-00249-y.

OECD (Organisation for Economic Co-operation and Development) (2021). *OECD Employment Outlook 2021: Navigating the COVID-19 Crisis and Recovery*. Paris: OECD Publishing. https://doi.org/10.1787/19991266.

Ohnsorge, F., and S. Yu (eds) (2021). *The Long Shadow of Informality: Challenges and Policies* (advance edn). Washington, DC: World Bank. https://doi.org/10.1596/35782.

Philip, K. (2018). 'Limiting Opportunities in the Informal Sector: The Impact of the Structure of the South African Economy'. In F. Fourie (ed.), *The South African Informal Sector: Creating Jobs, Reducing Poverty*. Cape Town: Human Sciences Research Council (HSRC) Press, pp. 297–316.

Mhlana, S., R. Moussié, S. Roever, and M. Rogan (2023) Informal employment: what is missing from national economic recovery plans?. WIDER Working Paper 2023/92, Helsinki: UNU-WIDER. https://doi.org/10.35188/UNU-WIDER/2023/400-7.

Rogan, M., and L. Alfers (2019). 'Gendered Inequalities in the South African Informal Economy'. *Agenda*, 33(4): 91–102. https://doi.org/10.1080/10130950.2019.1676163.

Rogan, M., and C. Skinner (2018). 'The Size and Structure of the South African Informal Sector 2008–2014: A Labour-Force Analysis'. In F. Fourie (ed.), *The South African Informal Sector: Creating Jobs, Reducing Poverty*. Cape Town: HSRC Press, pp. 70–95.

Rogan, M., and C. Skinner (2020). 'The Covid-19 Crisis and the South African Informal Economy: "Locked out" of Livelihoods and Employment', NIDS-CRAM Working Paper 10, Cape Town: NIDS-CRAM.

Rogan, M., and C. Skinner (2021). 'The South African Informal Economy'. In A. Oqubay, F. Tregenna, and I. Valodia (eds), *The Oxford Handbook of the South African Economy*. Oxford: Oxford University Press, pp. 757–76. https://doi.org/10.1093/oxfordhb/9780192894199.013.33.

Skinner, C., J. Barrett, L. Alfers, and M. Rogan (2021). 'Informal Work in South Africa and COVID-19: Gendered Impacts and Priority Interventions', Women In Informal Employment: Globalizing and Organizing (WIEGO) Policy Brief No. 22, Manchester: WIEGO.

Verick, S. (2010). 'Unravelling the Impact of the Global Financial Crisis on the South African Labour Market', Employment Working Paper No. 48. Geneva: ILO.

WIEGO (Women in Informal Employment: Globalizing and Organizing) and Asiye eTafuleni (2021). *The COVID-19 Crisis and the Informal Economy in Durban, South Africa*. Manchester: WIEGO.

5

Impact of COVID-19 on Urban Vulnerable Livelihoods

Accounts from Residents of Cape Town's Largest Township

Simone Schotte and Rocco Zizzamia

1. Introduction

The COVID-19 lockdown in South Africa was one of the earliest and strictest in global comparison. Despite stringent early confinement policies implemented to reduce contagion, COVID-19 infections rapidly surged across the country. Cape Town, with its poor, densely populated townships, and the surrounding Western Cape province quickly emerged as hotspots in the early phases of the pandemic.

Together with Gauteng, the Western Cape is one of the two richest—and, at the same time, most unequal—provinces in the country. Many South Africans who came to the province in search of opportunities have been left at the fringes of society, often using informal, creative, and improvisatory economic strategies to earn a living on a day-to-day basis. The unequal economic impact of the pandemic and associated distancing polices were acutely felt among the urban vulnerable population, especially due to the disruption in survivalist, informal economic activities (see Rogan and Skinner, Chapter 4 in this volume, on the impact of COVID-19 on informal workers in South Africa).

Historically, pockets of chronic poverty in South Africa have persisted in the country's rural areas, especially in the Eastern Cape and KwaZulu-Natal. By contrast, transitorily poor and vulnerable households—characterized by their position at the edge of escaping from or falling into poverty—make up the peri-urban areas on the outskirts of South Africa's major cities in Gauteng and the Western Cape (Zizzamia et al. 2019). Their pre-existing vulnerability has been compounded by the pandemic.

Newly collected panel data from South Africa's National Income Dynamics Study-Coronavirus Rapid Mobile Survey (NIDS-CRAM) show that the profiles of those who came under economic distress since the onset of the COVID-19

Simone Schotte and Rocco Zizzamia, *Impact of COVID-19 on Urban Vulnerable Livelihoods*. In: *COVID-19 and the Informal Economy*. Edited by: Martha Alter Chen, Michael Rogan, and Kunal Sen, Oxford University Press. © Simone Schotte and Rocco Zizzamia (2024). DOI: 10.1093/oso/9780198887041.003.0006

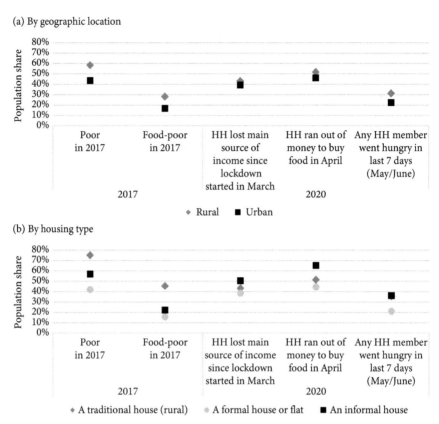

Figure 5.1 Pre-pandemic poverty rates and COVID-19 economic shock

Note: estimates for weighted NIDS-CRAM adult population. HH abbreviates household.
Source: authors' calculations using NIDS wave 5 and NIDS-CRAM wave 1.

pandemic differ in key respects from those who had experienced poverty previously (Schotte and Zizzamia 2021). While poverty has historically been substantially higher in rural compared to urban areas, this geographic gap is remarkably less pronounced in welfare outcomes measured for 2020 (see Figure 5.1a). Importantly, respondents living in informal housing, usually concentrated in urban peripheral areas, showed the highest incidence of financial distress since the start of the lockdown—with half of them reporting having lost their main source of income, two-thirds running out of money for food, and one-third going hungry during the initial lockdown (see Figure 5.1b). Moreover, while labour earnings and remittances typically shield against poverty, these income sources were at the highest risk of being lost during the crisis.

Considering these patterns, this chapter analyses the impact of the COVID-19 pandemic on urban vulnerable livelihoods, based on the accounts of 15 residents of Khayelitsha, a large and rapidly growing township situated about 30 kilometres southeast of Cape Town's city centre. In two rounds of semi-structured phone interviews conducted over a period of four months (between June and September 2020), we talked with them about their experiences during the initial lockdown and subsequent reopening and learned how it had impacted their economic and emotional well-being.

Complementing the other contributions in this section, this chapter seeks to speak to processes which remain out of reach of large, quantitative, rapid-assessment surveys—such as the interlinkages between livelihood strategies and informal support networks, the psychological experience of the pandemic, and the exacerbation of underlying vulnerabilities. The chapter shows that pre-existing markers of vulnerability map onto poverty and deprivation outcomes in the post-COVID context and may help explain heterogeneity in the experience of the shock.

The remainder of the chapter is structured as follows. Section 2 begins with a brief description of the research context, regarding Khayelitsha as a study site, the broader South African policy environment, and the data collection for this study. Section 3 focuses on the direct labour market implications of the COVID-19 pandemic, while section 4 assesses the effect on insurance mechanism, education and training, and the informal settlement landscape as three core dimensions of amplified vulnerabilities. Finally, section 5 concludes.

2. Research context

Khayelitsha was selected as a study site because it closely resembles many of the context characteristics that typically condition the livelihoods of those residing in low-income and disadvantaged communities in urban South Africa (Schotte 2019; Zizzamia 2020). On the one hand, service delivery, economic activity, and opportunities for employment are generally better in urban than in rural areas and continue to entice rural-to-urban migration (Burger et al. 2017; Schotte et al. 2018). On the other hand, rapid urbanization has left many on the fringes of society, resulting in a proliferation of informal settlements and increasingly densely populated townships. With poor access to sanitation and other infrastructure and high levels of unemployment and informal-sector activity (Turok and Visagie 2018), these communities were particularly vulnerable to the health and economic consequences of the pandemic.

This section provides a condensed overview of Khayelitsha's social and economic characteristics, as well as South Africa's COVID-19 policy landscape, and some details on the qualitative data.

2.1 Study site: Khayelitsha

Established in 1985 by the apartheid government as a site for relocations from other overcrowded African townships in Cape Town, Khayelitsha initially accommodated 30,000 people. Since then, it has grown rapidly, driven by endogenous population growth and continuing rural-to-urban migration. According to the 2011 Census, the population of Khayelitsha was 392,000—making it South Africa's second largest township after Soweto in Johannesburg. Roughly every second inhabitant is under 24 years old, and 55.8 per cent were born outside of the Western Cape, almost all of whom migrated from rural areas in the Eastern Cape. Culturally, the population structure is relatively homogenous in terms of race (98.6 per cent African) and language (90.5 per cent isiXhosa).

The township comprises old formal areas built originally by the apartheid government, which are generally wealthier, and newer areas that contain a mix of informal settlements, government-provided housing, and informal backyard dwellings. Regardless of the important extent of variation in living standards, Khayelitsha overall has high levels of income poverty and is facing serious challenges in education, crime, employment, housing, sanitation, service delivery, and substance abuse. According to 2011 Census data, around 55 per cent of residents live in informal dwellings and 29 per cent are not connected to any sewage system. Only 36 per cent of residents above the age of 20 have completed high school and only 40 per cent of the labour force is employed, of which many work in temporary or informal employment relationships (see Table 5.1).

Table 5.1 Khayelitsha descriptive statistics, 2011

Census suburb Khayelitsha	2011
Average household size	3.30
Share (%) of HHs living in informal dwellings (shack in/not in backyard)	55.4
Share (%) of HHs with piped water access (inside dwelling/yard)	61.9
Share (%) of HHs connected to sewerage system (flush toilet)	71.7
Share (%) of HHs using electricity for lighting	80.8
Share (%) of HHs with average monthly HH income of less than R3,200	73.7
Share (%) of population under 24 years old	49.6
Share (%) of population that is African	98.6
Share (%) of population that speaks isiXhosa	90.5
Share (%) of population that was born in the Eastern Cape	50.8
Share (%) of adult population (aged 20+ years) with completed secondary or higher education	35.6
Average labour force participation rate (%) among working-age (15–64 years) population	65.1
Average unemployment rate (%) among working-age (15–64 years) population	38.0

Source: authors' compilation based on City of Cape Town (2013).

2.2 COVID-19 shock and policy environment

South Africa went into a full lockdown on 27 March 2020 in response to rising infections in the country. This initial lockdown was stringent and included strict stay-at-home orders and the active involvement of the South African Defence Force in enforcing regulations. The initial lockdown was later framed by the government as 'Level 5' in a 'Risk Adjusted Strategy' to manage the spread of COVID-19. Over time, the government relaxed these lockdown regulations, with a move onto 'Level 4' coming into effect on 1 May 2020, 'Level 3' on 1 June 2020, 'Level 2' on 18 August 2020, and finally 'Level 1' on 21 September 2020 (see Figure 5.2). Level 5 entailed a complete stop to all but essential commercial activity and a severe curtailment of freedom of personal movement. In subsequent levels, the restrictions on commercial activity were gradually relaxed. Strict stay-at-home orders remained in force in Level 4, so that meaningful relaxation on the freedom of movement for the general population only began in Level 3.

As discussed by Rogan and Skinner in Chapter 4 in this volume, the economic impact of stringent distancing polices and the overall drop in demand were acutely felt in the labour market—triggering job losses, business closures, and underemployment. Employment losses were concentrated among those who were already disadvantaged prior to the pandemic—women, less-skilled workers, informal workers, low-income earners, and those with a history of unemployment (Casale and Shepherd 2020; Espi et al. 2020; Jain et al. 2020a; Ranchhod and Daniels 2020a; Rogan and Skinner 2020).

With the gradual relaxation of confinement measures to Level 4 (1 May) and Level 3 (1 June), commercial activity recommenced, and labour markets experienced a partial recovery (Jain et al. 2020b; Ranchhod and Daniels 2020b). Approximately half of the loss in active employment that occurred between February and April was recovered by June (Jain et al. 2020b), and the recovery was sustained into October (Bassier et al. 2021a).

Targeted social assistance measures introduced from May onwards also helped to cushion the blow delivered by COVID-19. In response to the crisis, on 26 March 2020, South Africa's government introduced the Temporary Employee/Employer Relief Scheme (TERS), a social insurance scheme administered through the contribution-based Unemployment Insurance Fund (UIF).[1] Approximately one month later, on 21 April 2020, a set of social assistance

---

[1] TERS is an earnings relief benefit for employers unable to pay their employees due to the COVID-19 lockdown. The minimum payment was set at R3,500 per month (US$205), equal to the national minimum wage, and the maximum payment was set at approximately R6,700 (US$394). TERS benefits were initially restricted to workers who were contributing to UIF, but on 26 May 2020, a successful legal challenge expanded the scheme to any worker who could prove an employment relationship, whether registered with UIF or not.

measures were announced, aimed at delivering relief to households not covered by employment-related insurance schemes. These consisted of (a) an increase to the Child Support Grant (CSG) of ZAR300 (US$17)[2] for one month, followed by an increase of ZAR500 (US$30) per month from June to October (but limited during the latter period to one increase per caregiver); (b) an increase to all other social grants (such as the old-age pension and the disability grant) of ZAR250 (US$15) per month until October; and (c) the introduction of a special COVID-19 Social Relief of Distress Grant (SRDG) of ZAR350 (US$21) per month, newly introduced to assist people who are unemployed and not receiving any other grant or UIF (Bassier et al. 2021b).

Despite these initial delays in the delivery of UIF-TERS and the SRDG,[3] Jain et al. (2020b) show that coverage increased remarkably between June and July/August 2020. By October, the SRDG had become a core element of South Africa's social assistance landscape and, alongside the CSG, proved most effective at reaching the poorest South Africans (Bassier et al. 2021b). While the labour market shock was inequality-enhancing (initially, poorer households were worst affected and benefited least from the partial recovery), social assistance interventions were progressively targeted, with the lowest deciles of the populations benefiting disproportionately (Jain et al. 2020b; Köhler and Bhorat 2020).

2.3 Data collection and analysis

This chapter draws on two rounds of in-depth interviews. The 15 respondents, who are identical between interview rounds, were selected from a previous qualitative study conducted in Khayelitsha in 2017.[4]

Figure 5.2 Illustrates the timing of the data collection, along with the relevant policy context. The first interview round, conducted from 11 June to 7 July 2020 (Alert Level 3), included a set of retrospective questions to establish how the participants' overall life circumstances had evolved between our last visit in 2017

---

[2] US$ calculated with an exchange rate of US$1 = ZAR17, the approximate value during the first months of the pandemic.

[3] TERS payments were initially delayed due to large backlogs of applications and infrastructure breakdowns. While eligibility for an SRDG-like grant was previously estimated at approximately 15 million South Africans, as of 11 June 2020, the South African Social Security Agency had received over 6.5 million applications but had only paid 600,000 grants.

[4] Participants of the 2017 study were drawn from a sampling frame that had been designed to capture the local socio-economic diversity, covering different neighbourhoods and welfare levels (for details, see Schotte 2019; Zizzamia 2020). For the present extension study, respondents were recontacted in early June 2020. Out of 31 original respondents, 11 could not be reached, 1 was deceased, 5 refused to be re-interviewed, and 14 agreed to participate in this research. To improve the representation of the young population in Khayelitsha and increase our sample size, one additional respondent—a young male—was added from the 2017 sampling frame.

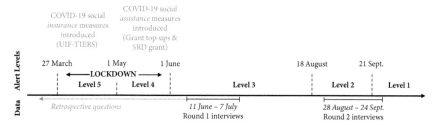

Figure 5.2 Timeline of COVID-19 government response and data collection in 2020

Source: authors' graphical presentation.

and February 2020, before the pandemic had reached South Africa. The remainder of the interviews focused on how the participants' situation had changed since the onset of the pandemic up to the time of the interview, including probing questions regarding their household's ability to buy essential goods, changes in their own and close family members' employment situation, and the schooling situation of children in the household. Respondents were also asked about their opinions regarding the implemented government containment and relief measures. The second round, conducted from 28 August to 24 September 2020 (Alert Levels 2/1), traced the changes in respondents' replies as containment measures had been gradually relaxed.

As part of the interviews, respondents were asked to rank their welfare levels in February, June, and September 2020, using the same four-level welfare scale established as part of the original research back in 2017. This allowed us to identify shifts in welfare—both in terms of the initial shock and the subsequent recovery—and relate these to the COVID-19 economic shock. Each interview round was coded and analysed using a thematic approach, following a similar methodology as proposed by Nyashanu et al. (2020).[5]

To supplement the evidence gathered, two key informant interviews were conducted after participant interviews had been completed. These were designed to provide background information on two broader changes in the township environment attributable to the pandemic, which were brought up as relevant by some of the interviewees.

---

[5] Interviews took 35 minutes on average and were conducted in respondents' native language (isiXhosa) by a skilled and experienced interviewer who had been part of the 2017 research. All interviews were audio recorded and subsequently translated and transcribed into English. The transcripts were entered into NVivo for organization and to facilitate the analysis. Transcripts were read repeatedly by both lead researchers, and pertinent sections were clustered together into themes. Within each theme, comparisons were then made across the body of interviews to identify recurring accounts as well as relevant discrepancies. Each round of interviews was first analysed independently before comparing and relating themes across the two rounds in a final step of analysis.

3. Economic losses in formal and informal employment

Overall, in our sample, the labour market shock affected a population which does not have a particularly strong attachment to the formal labour market but which, nevertheless, remains heavily reliant on labour income—often derived from labour income shared within extended support networks and from informal work.

Out of 15 participants, 14 reported a decline in household welfare between February and June 2020 (see Table 5.A1 in the Appendix).[6] Among these 14, only one (R5) saw no change in labour earnings (being a public school teacher) but instead reported a fall in rental income as her tenant had lost her job and left the city. In the remaining 13 cases, the decline in labour income was experienced either by respondents themselves, a household member, or a family member who had been supporting the household financially. Almost all (11/13) explicitly identified this negative labour market event as the driver of downward mobility between February and June 2020.

The patterns observed during the second study period from June to August 2020 are much more mixed: 4 out of 15 reported a continued but attenuated deterioration in welfare (R1–R4), 5 out of 15 perceived the situation as unchanged (R5–R9), and 6 out of 15 saw a full or partial recovery (R10–R15). This recovery was mainly facilitated by respondents being able to return to work. In line with the quantitative evidence on South Africa (Jain et al. 2020b), we find that a more robust labour market recovery was experienced by those who had maintained an active employment relationship over the lockdown—especially if this employment relationship was formal.

We observe that those in informal work were especially vulnerable to the labour market shock. Among the two respondents (R7, R12) who had been in informal wage employment prior to the pandemic, R12 was able to continue working at reduced hours during the lockdown. By September, she was still working a reduced number of days. The other, R7, had been laid off during the lockdown. Moreover, all four respondents (R2, R4, R8, R10) who had been running informal enterprises prior to the pandemic had either terminated or scaled back their activity by June, and only one (R10) had resumed operating at pre-lockdown capacity by September. Respondents mentioned three main reasons to explain this break in business activity: lockdown regulations, challenges in transportation and in procuring stock, and a fall in demand. Regarding the latter, one of our key informants emphasized the interdependence between formal- and informal-sector activities, arguing that informal businesses rely on the spending of those with incomes from the formal economy—using his example, selling snacks on trains or at stations is not possible if nobody is going to work. A recovery in

---

[6] In the only case where no decline was experienced (R9), both household members were elderly and relied exclusively on the old-age pension grant.

the informal economy will thus depend on a prior recovery in the formal labour market.

Beyond the evident vulnerability of those in informal work, our qualitative evidence provides further nuance to the formal–informal sector dichotomy. As formal-sector businesses were also affected by government regulations and the overall drop in demand, our data show that even formal jobs were not necessarily secure and, in instances, experienced a partial informalization. Out of four respondents (R5, R11, R13, R15) who had been formally employed prior to the pandemic, only one (R5) saw no change in labour earnings. As a government-employed school teacher, her salary remained unaffected. Another respondent (R11), a supermarket worker, continued working throughout the lockdown. Nonetheless, he experienced a decline in earnings due to a reduction in hours worked. The other two respondents were on unpaid leave during the lockdown. Only one of them (R15) received UIF payments (after substantial delays), while the other was ineligible because of insufficient tenure.

Even though all four formal wage employees were able to resume work in the post-lockdown period, the pandemic did not leave these jobs unaffected. For example, R15 explained that the company he was working for was experiencing severe financial difficulties since the onset of the pandemic and stated, 'I am noticing that after this coronavirus things are not stable [at the firm]. Even the bosses look weak now because there are rumours that the company may be closed.' He also reported an informalization of his previously formal employment relationship. Talking about himself and his co-workers, he said, 'We have just been de-registered from the Building Industry Bargaining Council and there won't be any deductions now. You will be given your money and save it yourself. That is what worries me now.'[7] Increased job instability left workers more vulnerable to future shocks and contributed to an overall feeling of insecurity and consequent psychological distress.

Eventually, it is worth reflecting on the implications of the COVID-19 labour market shock on how our sample members spoke about and valued informal earning opportunities. During the first phase of the project in 2017, casual work and piece jobs were often not considered valuable or dignified by respondents. They were characteristic of those who had to make ends meet, being—and considered as—'second best' options and as a way of 'making do' when times were tough. However, the lockdown exposed how important these often volatile and comparatively undesirable jobs had been in sustaining the livelihoods of those struggling to keep their heads above water. For example, one of the respondents (R3), who used to rely on financial support from her children, reported slipping into deep poverty when her daughter, who used to do piece work at a restaurant in Cape Town, was

---

[7] The Building Industry Bargaining Council negotiates the terms of employment for the industry and administers the industry pension, provident, medical aid, sick, and holiday funds.

laid off at the beginning of the lockdown. She had little hope for her daughter to resume work in the near future and also could not draw on other informal support networks, saying 'times are tough for everyone and everyone is stranded with no way to hustle'. The lesson from this is both obvious and important—while the poor do not cast a fond or aspirational gaze upon survivalist livelihood strategies, the availability of these strategies remains an essential means of survival for South Africa's poor. This view was shared by a key informant, who claimed that 'a lot of guys are in the informal sector, working piece jobs. [Now that] they don't have them, we have seen the value of [these jobs].'

4. Amplified vulnerabilities and emerging risk factors

The shock of the pandemic exposed and deepened vulnerabilities in the labour market. Going beyond these findings, our qualitative interviews highlight three additional dimensions of amplified vulnerabilities and emerging risk factors. First, households with limited assets to withstand a sudden economic loss responded to the crisis by running down savings and defaulting on insurance payments, leaving them yet more vulnerable to future economic shocks. Second, school closures posed a double burden to children from socio-economically disadvantaged backgrounds. The absence of meals provided at schools posed risks exacerbating food insecurity, and many were lacking the basic infrastructure to continue remote learning, reducing their chances of educational attainment and future upward social mobility. Third, new risk factors emerged. New informal settlements mushroomed in the shadow of the lockdown, which may exacerbate health risks and fuel social unrest. In addition, the economic downturn appears to have been accompanied by a surge in opportunistic criminality as well as organized crime. Local businesses and community institutions became targets of the latter, hampering prospects for development.

4.1 Formal and informal insurance mechanism

The success with which households were able to withstand the pandemic shock depended largely on their ability to access formal or informal systems of social protection.

In face of the COVID-19 labour market shock, government grants provided an essential, stable stream of income. At least 11 out of 15 interviewees reported living in households with access to grant income. For these households, the top-up to government grants, issued from May 2020 onwards, provided some buffer to the negative income shocks they experienced. In many cases, respondents and their households relied primarily, or even exclusively, on social grants when labour incomes collapsed, and would have been left destitute in their absence. While, in most cases, the grant income was used to cover immediate consumption needs, we also found evidence of social grants being used as strategies for accumulation and insurance. In several cases (R2, R4, R9, R14), grants were used to invest in durable assets (like housing repairs or improvements) or as start-up capital for survivalist enterprises once the economy had more fully reopened in September.

In addition to public social welfare schemes, informal insurance mechanisms can provide protection against the impact of economic shocks and earnings volatility. While the COVID-19 pandemic has delivered such a shock, at the same time, it undermined the present and future effectiveness of these mechanisms. A strong example of this effect was given by one respondent (R11), who (together with his wife) had been contributing to a stokvel—a rotating savings and credit association—prior to the pandemic. R11 was worried that his household or other members of the group would fail to pay their contributions, saying, 'Now we are not sure whether to continue [contributing] because of the current situation. There are [other stokvel members] who work at a coffee shop [. . .] so they stopped working during the lockdown. [. . .] So it is going to be difficult to fork out ZAR1,500 [semi-annual contribution].' This account reveals how informal financial instruments are often effective for managing idiosyncratic risks—affecting individuals or groups of individuals—while being less effective at dealing with large, covariate shocks—simultaneously affecting entire communities (Dercon 2002).

To buffer the loss of household income, several respondents were forced to run down savings and/or to default on insurance payments, leaving them vulnerable to future shocks—including the health risks posed by the pandemic. For example, one respondent (R10) said, 'Economically and health-wise I am worried because if anything would happen I don't know where I would go or where to start. [. . .] Like if any of my family members were to die I am not sure how I would bury them because I am not working and my policies lapsed.' In this case, the relative stability in observable living standards masks the increase in underlying economic vulnerability. Cutting back on savings and insurance to meet basic needs in the present may risk potential ruin in the future. Moreover, it may also block avenues of social upward mobility, as the example of a young male respondent (R13) illustrates. Before the pandemic hit and he was temporarily laid-off from work, he had been saving money to acquire a certificate that would enable him to work as a petrol attendant. Now that his financial situation had changed, he was no longer able to contribute to the stokvel that he had joined with the aim of using the pay-out to finance his training. As people recover economically, they will have to catch up on insurance instalments or face the risk of remaining vulnerable. The former choice would hold back the pace of the economic recovery, while the latter would increase vulnerability enduringly.

4.2 Lost chances in education and training

Higher educational attainment is an important enabling factor for improved labour market outcomes and social upward mobility. In this regard, the pandemic may not only present a temporary shock to parents' earnings but also have lasting implications for children's development and future income prospects. School closures and the constraints that poor children face in online teaching may have a negative effect on human capital formation, with potentially lasting consequences for inequality and intergenerational mobility.

The closure of schools and universities caused major disruptions to students' learning. For example, one of our respondents (R5), who is a primary school teacher, explained that schools were often unable to contact parents during the lockdown, and many children had been left behind during the period of home schooling: 'Some of them were helped by parents, but others were just left on their own. [. . .] There are those [who] have the potential to pass but I don't want to lie, many of them are struggling and will surely repeat this year.' This general concern about failing the school year was echoed by other respondents, expressing concerns about their children being left with an insecure future.

Differences in the ability to access remote learning may have exacerbated existing educational inequalities, with the children most in need of close attention belonging to those households which could not be contacted and which did not have resources to pursue remote learning under parental supervision. Among the economically vulnerable population without access to computers or tablets, having a smartphone with internet access appeared to be a key determinant of whether or not schooling could continue. While some respondents reported that their children had received school exercises (R12) and university assignments (R9) on their phones, the majority said they had not received anything. For instance, the daughter of one respondent (R7), whose phone was not equipped to receive any exercises, reported feeling disadvantaged compared to her peers, who had better phones and had received the tasks. She also did not feel supported by teachers in catching up with the material when schools reopened and reported that teachers were running through material too quickly, trying to make up for lost time. She described the situation as 'learning in a pressure situation', which caused her to feel overwhelmed and—despite having passed the trial exams in March—left her without hope of passing her upcoming final school-leaving exams.

4.3 New informal settlements and crime

Informal settlements have been a specific public health concern during the pandemic since they are densely populated and lack adequate access to sanitation and basic infrastructure. As discussed by other studies, high settlement density and small housing spaces, often shared by extended households, make it difficult, or virtually impossible, to adhere to social distancing (Nyashanu et al. 2020).

Given the lack of alternative sites to shelter-in-place and the heightened economic pressures in the wake of the pandemic, a special government gazette put a national ban on evictions of people from homes built on public land without permission for the duration of the lockdown (Department of Co-operative Governance and Traditional Affairs 2020). This decision was motivated by concerns that evictions would lead to homelessness, which would pose even higher COVID-19 health risks to the evicted. With the ban on evictions (combined with rising unemployment and economic distress that left many unable to pay rent), new informal settlements have sprung up in Cape Town's peripheries. One of these, which emerged in Khayelitsha on previously unoccupied land along the N2 highway, is reportedly referred to as 'COVID-19' by residents, being further subdivided into two sections dubbed 'Coronavirus' and 'Sanitiser'.

Compared to existing informal settlements that have been upgraded to ensure basic sanitation access, life in these newly established settlements is especially precarious. One of our study participants (R2), who, just before the lockdown, had moved from a backyard shack at his cousin's house into a shack in a recent settlement, reported, 'We have no electricity, access to running water as well as roads. The only roads we have are our makeshift roads that we make so that cars can move inside if there is someone sick, [...] so that the person does not die at home because of the lack of roads.' Another account was provided by a young male respondent (R13), who, between the first and second round of interviews, had moved out of his family home into a shack in one of the new settlements that had sprung up since the lockdown. He was concerned about the risk of being evicted from the area and told that tensions between occupants and local authorities had escalated in some areas, saying, 'There were huge problems to a point where the community ended up burning down the community hall.'

Discussions with the two key informants confirmed the link between the genesis of the new informal settlements and the economic effects of the COVID-19 crisis. They also foregrounded the increase in criminality and violence over the lockdown and cautioned that these new settlements may further contribute to these trends. Worrying trends that were mentioned included a rising prevalence of extortion from businesses by local criminal cartels (including the targeting of creches, community centres, non-governmental organizations (NGOs), and private households); a greater visibility of organized neighbourhood gangs; and an increase in opportunistic crime. These trends were mainly explained by the need for criminals to diversify their own activities as other opportunities dried up and in terms of the increased appeal of criminal livelihoods as labour market alternatives for young men deteriorated. One of the key informants also suggested that the increase in psychological distress and overall feelings of hopelessness may have eroded positive visions of a shared future in favour of a more pessimistic orientation in which the disincentives to engaging in criminal behaviour are weaker.

5. Conclusion

Studying the consequences of the COVID-19 pandemic and related policy measures for poor and vulnerable households in urban South Africa, this chapter identifies the decline in labour earnings and employment prospects as the main threat to livelihoods. While workers in both formal and informal forms of employment experienced sizable economic losses during the initial lockdown, the disruption to the informal sector seemed more profound and longer lasting. Three findings stand out in this regard: first, informal workers were most likely to see a discontinuation in employment, often leading to severe financial distress. The sudden break in economic activity not only resulted from lockdown regulation, but was also attributed to supply-chain disruptions and an overall fall in demand. Regarding the latter, the reliance of informal businesses on the spending of those with formal-sector incomes may point to a slower, lagged recovery in the informal sector. Second, our data show that despite seeing a faster recovery, even formal jobs were not necessarily secure and, in instances, experienced a partial informalization. Third, the pandemic uncovered the relevance of informal forms of employment as an essential means of survival for South Africa's poor. As South Africa's informal economy is small compared to other sub-Saharan African countries, the important role played by these jobs often goes unseen.

Importantly, the economic vulnerability caused by the lapse of survivalist livelihood strategies was intensified by the covariate nature of the shock, rendering social networks and informal insurance mechanisms ineffective means of assistance. These combined factors have led to an increased reliance on government grants—the expansions to which during the crisis have been an indispensable element in the livelihood portfolios of the poor.

Beyond the immediate economic consequences, our findings give rise to concerns that the COVID-19 pandemic may not only present a temporary income shock but also have lasting implications for poverty rates in South Africa through its effects on people's health, education, and employment prospects as well as potential knock-on effects from increasing rates of crime and domestic abuse. It may compromise household income-generating activities in the longer term as the labour market recovery has been incomplete and households have turned to liquidating their small savings and defaulting on insurance payments in the absence of alternative coping strategies. In addition, school closures and the constraints that poor children faced in online teaching may have negative long-term impacts on human capital formation and thus on employment prospects and earnings, thereby deepening existing inequalities and constraining social upward mobility. While social grants have played an indispensable role in sustaining a basic standard of living in the short term, for the millions of vulnerable South Africans whose livelihoods hang in the balance, an ambitious commitment by the state to confront mid- and long-term challenges will remain imperative.

References

Bassier, I., J. Budlender, and R. Zizzamia (2021a). 'The Labour Market Impact of COVID-19 in South Africa: An Update with NIDS-CRAM Wave 3', National Income Dynamics Study-Coronavirus Rapid Mobile Survey (NIDS-CRAM) Working Paper No. 2, Wave 3, Cape Town: NIDS-CRAM.

Bassier, I., J. Budlender, and R. Zizzamia, M. Leibbrandt, and V. Ranchhod (2021b). 'Locked Down and Locked Out: Repurposing Social Assistance as Emergency Relief to Informal Workers', *World Development*, 139: 105271. https://doi.org/10.1016/j.worlddev.2020.105271.

Burger, R., S. van der Berg, S. van der Walt, and D. Yu (2017). 'The Long Walk: Considering the Enduring Spatial and Racial Dimensions of Deprivation Two Decades after the Fall of Apartheid', *Social Indicators Research*, 130(3): 1101–23.

Casale, D., and D. Shepherd (2020). 'The Gendered Effects of the Ongoing Lockdown and School Closures in South Africa: Evidence from NIDS-CRAM Waves 1 and 2', NIDS-CRAM Working Paper No. 5, Wave 2, Cape Town: NIDS-CRAM.

City of Cape Town (2013). '2011 Census Suburb Khayelitsha', compiled by Strategic Development Information and GIS Department, Census data supplied by Statistics South Africa, available at: https://resource.capetown.gov.za/documentcentre/Documents/Maps%20and%20statistics/2011_Census_CT_Suburb_Khayelitsha_Profile.pdf (accessed December 2021).

Department of Co-operative Governance and Traditional Affairs (2020). 'Directions Issues in Terms of Regulation 10 of the Regulations under the Disaster Management Act, 2002', Notice No. 418 of 2020, Pretoria: Republic of South Africa, available at: www.gov.za/sites/default/files/gcis_document/202003/43167reg11066418.pdf (accessed March 2021).

Dercon, S. (2002). 'Income Risk, Coping Strategies, and Safety Nets', *World Bank Research Observer*, 17(2): 141–66. https://doi.org/10.1093/wbro/17.2.141.

Espi, G., Ranchhod, V., and Leibbrandt, M. (2020). 'The Relationship between Employment History and COVID19 Employment Outcomes in South Africa', NIDS-CRAM Working Paper No. 6, Wave 2,Cape Town: NIDS-CRAM.

Jain, R., Budlender, J., Zizzamia, R., and Bassier, I. (2020a). 'The Labor Market and Poverty Impacts of COVID-19 in South Africa', Centre for the Study of African Economics (CSAE) Working Paper No. WPS/2020-14, Oxford: CSAE.

Jain, R., J. Budlender, R. Zizzamia, and I Bassier (2020b). 'The Labour Market and Poverty Impacts of COVID19 in South Africa: An Update with NIDS-CRAM Wave 2', SALDRU Working Paper No. 272, Cape Town: Southern Africa Labour and Development Research Unit (SALDRU), University of Cape Town (UCT).

Köhler, T., and H. Bhorat (2020). 'Social Assistance during South Africa's National Lockdown: Examining the COVID-19 Grant, Changes to the Child Support Grant, and Post-October Policy Options', Development Policy Research Unit (DPRU) Working Paper No. 2020/09, Cape Town: DPRU, UCT.

NIDS (National Income Dynamics Study) (2017). 'National Income Dynamics Study 2017, Wave 5', Data set (Version 1.0.0); Pretoria: Department of Planning, Monitoring, and Evaluation (funding agency), Cape Town: SALDRU (implementer); DataFirst (distributor). https://doi.org/10.25828/fw3h-v708.

NIDS-CRAM (National Income Dynamics Study-Coronavirus Rapid Mobile Survey) (2020). 'National Income Dynamics Study-Coronavirus Rapid Mobile Survey (NIDSCRAM), Wave 1', Data set (Version 1.0.0), Cape Town: Allan Gray Orbis Foundation (funding agency); SALDRU (implementer); DataFirst (distributor). https://doi.org/10.25828/7tn9-1998.

Nyashanu, M., P. Simbanegavi, and L. Gibson (2020). 'Exploring the Impact of COVID-19 Pandemic Lockdown on Informal Settlements in Tshwane Gauteng Province, South Africa', Global Public Health, 15(10): 1443–53. https://doi.org/10.1080/17441692.2020.1805787.

Ranchhod, V., and R. Daniels (2020a). 'Labour Market Dynamics in the Time of COVID-19 in South Africa: Evidence from the NIDS-CRAM Survey', NIDS-CRAM Working Paper No. 9, Wave 1, Cape Town: NIDS-CRAM.

Ranchhod, V., and R. Daniels (2020b). 'Labour Market Dynamics in the Time of COVID-19 in South Africa: Evidence from Waves 1 and 2 of the NIDS-CRAM Survey', NIDS-CRAM Working Paper No. 13, Wave 2, Cape Town: NIDS-CRAM.

Rogan, M., and C. Skinner (2020). 'The COVID-19 Crisis and the South African Informal Economy: "Locked Out" of Livelihoods and Employment', NIDS-CRAM Working Paper No. 10, Wave 1, Cape Town: NIDS-CRAM.

Schotte, S. (2019). 'Structural Poverty Dynamics in Urban South Africa: A Mixed-Methods Investigation', United Nations University-World Institute for Development Economics Research (UNU-WIDER) Working Paper No. 2019/100, Helsinki: UNU-WIDER. https://doi.org/10.35188/UNUWIDER/2019/736-1.

Schotte, S. and R. Zizzamia (2021) 'The Livelihood Impacts of COVID-19 in Urban South Africa: A View from Below', UNU-WIDER Working Paper No. 2021/56, Helsinki: UNU-WIDER. https://doi.org/10.35188/UNU-WIDER/2021/994-5.

Schotte, S., R. Zizzamia, and M. Leibbrandt (2018). 'A Poverty Dynamics Approach to Social Stratification: The South African Case', World Development, 110: 88–103. https://doi.org/10.1016/j.worlddev.2018.05.024.figu

Turok, I., and J. Visagie (2018). 'Does Moving to a City Mean a Better Life? New Evidence', Econ3x3, available at: www.econ3x3.org (accessed December 2019).

Zizzamia, R. (2020). 'Is Employment a Panacea for Poverty? A Mixed-Methods Investigation of Employment Decisions in South Africa', World Development, 130: 104938. https://doi.org/10.1016/j.worlddev.2020.104938.

Zizzamia, R., S. Schotte, and M Leibbrandt (2019). 'Snakes and Ladders and Loaded Dice: Poverty Dynamics and Inequality in South Africa, 2008–2017', UNU-WIDER Working Paper No. 2019/25, Helsinki: UNU-WIDER. https://doi.org/10.35188/UNU-WIDER/2019/659-3.

Appendix

Table 5.A1 Respondent characteristics

					2017					2020			
ID	Gender	Age	Education	Birthplace	PPI score	Estimated likelihood of poverty (UBPL), %	HH size	Access to grant incl. in HH	Labour market attachment in February	HH welfare change February–June	Associated event February–June	HH welfare change June–September	Associated event June–September
R1	Female	62	Secondary incomplete	Cape Town	48	54	Three	OAP	Pensioneer, living with adult children doing odd jobs	Fall	Loss of labour income within family/household	Fall	Increased distress due to economic stagnation
R2	Male	59	Primary incomplete	Eastern Cape	36	77	Three	CSG	Self-employed (street food)	Fall	Reduction in self-employment activities	Fall	Increased distress due to economic stagnation

Continued

Table 5.A1 *Continued*

					2017					2020		
ID	Gender	Age	Education	Birth-place	PPI score	Estimated likelihood of poverty (UBPL), %	HH size	Access to grant incl. in HH	Labour market attachment in February	HH welfare change February–June	Associated event February–June	HH welfare change June–September	Associated event June–September
R3	Female	54	No Schooling	Eastern Cape	17	99	Seven or more	CSG	Unemployed, supported by daughter (work at restaurant)	Fall	Loss of labour income within family/household	Fall	Increased distress due to economic stagnation
R4	Female	61	Primary complete	Eastern Cape	40	74	Four	CSG/OAP	Pensioner, with self-employed side activity (street food)	Fall	Break in self-employment activity	Fall	Increased distress due to economic stagnation
R5	Female	58	Secondary complete (Matric)	Cape Town	57	24	Five	No	Formal wage employed (primary school teacher)	Fall	No change in formal wage employment but loss of rental income	Stable	No change
R6	Male	62	Secondary incomplete	Eastern Cape	41	74	Two	OAP	Doing temporary (piece) jobs	Fall	Loss of temporary (piece) jobs	Stable	Did not resume economic activity

R7	Female	44	Secondary incomplete	Eastern Cape	12	100	Seven or more	CSG	Informal wage employment (not registered for UIF)	Fall	Laid off from wage job (waiting to resume)	Stable	Did not resume economic activity
R8	Male	36	Secondary incomplete	Cape Town	49	54	Four	No	Self-employed (irregular)	Fall	Reduction in self-employment activities	Stable	Did not resume economic activity
R9	Male	72	Secondary incomplete	Eastern Cape	24	97	Six	OAP	Pensioneer household	Stable	No prior reliance on labour market income, only two pensions in the household	Stable	No change
R10	Male	61	Secondary incomplete	Elsewhere in South Africa	53	28	Five	No	Self-employed (home restaurant)	Fall	Reduction in self-employment activities	Rise	Resumption of self-employed activity

Continued

Table 5.A1 *Continued*

ID	Gender	Age	Education	Birth-place	2017		HH size	Access to grant incl. in HH	Labour market attachment in February	HH welfare change February–June	2020	HH welfare change June–September	Associated event June–September
					PPI score	Estimated likelihood of poverty (UBPL), %					Associated event February–June		
R11	Male	42	Secondary incomplete	Eastern Cape	36	77	Three	CSG	Formal wage employed (grocery store)	Fall	Reduction in hours of formal wage job	Rise	Resumption of full-time wage work
R12	Female	43	Secondary incomplete	Eastern Cape	40	74	Four	CSG	Part-time wage employed (domestic worker)	Fall	Reduction in hours of wage job	Rise	
R13	Male	30	Secondary complete (Matric)	Cape Town	49	54	Four	CSG	Formal wage employed (liquor store)	Fall	Reduction in hours of formal wage job	Rise	Resumption of full-time wage work

| R14 | Male | 60 | Primary incomplete | Eastern Cape | 30 | 93 | Seven or more | CSG/OAP | Unemployed, supported by wife (domestic worker) and daughter (work at restaurant) | Fall | Loss of labour income within family/household | Rise | Started to receive old-age pension |
| R15 | Male | 52 | Secondary incomplete | Eastern Cape | 64 | 11 | Two | CSG | Formal wage employed (painter) | Fall | Laid off from formal wage job (waiting to resume) | Rise | Received UIF/TERS with delay, resumed full-time wage work, and rented out shack in backyard |

Notes: the Progress out of Poverty Index (PPI) is calculated based on information collected in the sampling survey. It draws on 15 household-level indicators—including demographics, education, employment, housing, assets, and sanitation—following the scorecard for South Africa. The score is used to evaluate the likelihood of the household falling below the national cost-of-basic-needs upper-bound poverty line (UBPL).
Source: authors' compilation.

6

Recovery with Distress

Unpacking COVID-19 Impact on Livelihoods and Poverty in Rural Areas and Urban Low-Income Settlements of Bangladesh*

Hossain Zillur Rahman, Atiya Rahman, Md Saiful Islam, Avinno Faruk, Imran Matin, Mohammad Abdul Wazed, and Umama Zillur

1. Impact of COVID-19 and the imperative of 'finding out fast'

COVID-19 created a global economic upheaval and poorer people have taken its brunt, both because of the nature of their jobs and because of their limited ability to cope with the financial shock. While developed countries, with established social security systems and deeper pockets, could better support their vulnerable population, in developing countries like Bangladesh, economically vulnerable people were left with deep uncertainties and largely to fend for themselves. On the question of the livelihood and poverty impact of COVID-19, the pandemic created not only a challenge in terms of effective policy response but also a research challenge of 'finding out fast' (Rahman et al. 2021) in order to inform policy-makers grappling with the multiple fallouts of the pandemic. The situation called for research leadership and innovative methodologies as well as impactful dissemination. The Power and Participation Research Centre (PPRC) and the BRAC Institute of Governance and Development (BIGD) at BRAC University, two Bangladeshi social research centres, formed an emergency partnership to launch the PPRC-BIGD Rapid Response Panel Research initiative (Rahman et al. 2021), which became a flagship national research response to unpacking the livelihood and poverty impact of the unfolding crisis (PPRC-BIGD 2021).

The first phase of our survey, conducted in April 2020, delved into the pandemic-induced economic shock faced by poor and economically vulnerable people and their coping mechanisms in rural areas and urban slums. The second phase, conducted in June 2020, studied the impact of the pandemic on the same demographic groups immediately after the end of the first lockdown. In March

* The authors are indebted to the Power and Participation Research Centre, the BRAC Institute of Governance and Development, the Bangladesh Bureau of Statistics, the World Food Programme, and the Foreign, Commonwealth & Development Office.

Hossain Zillur Rahman et al., *Recovery with Distress*. In: *COVID-19 and the Informal Economy*. Edited by: Martha Alter Chen, Michael Rogan, and Kunal Sen, Oxford University Press. © Hossain Zillur Rahman et al. (2024).
DOI: 10.1093/oso/9780198887041.003.0007

2021, PPRC-BIGD carried out the third phase of the study, trying to identify trends and assess the nature of the recovery. The fourth phase of the study was conducted in August 2021 to examine the extent to which the second lockdown had disrupted the recovery process and to assess the longer-term impact of COVID-19 on the livelihoods of the population in rural areas and urban slums. The fifth phase—the most recent round of this survey, conducted in May 2022—assessed the longer-term impacts of this pandemic on the livelihood, coping, and recovery trends among rural and urban slum households. Here, we focus on trends in income, employment, food security, migration, and poverty to gain a clearer picture of the current state of the poor and economically vulnerable population of Bangladesh.[1]

2. Chapter structure

Section 3 provides a brief description of the methodology, and section 4 provides the basic demographic information of the sample surveyed in Phase V. Section 5 compares the impact of the first (April–May 2020) and second lockdowns (April–May 2021). Section 6 analyses the trends and vulnerabilities over the 18 months of the COVID-19 crisis, section 7 examines the poverty dynamics, and finally, section 8 discusses the key takeaways and policy messages.

3. Methodology

3.1 Survey mode

Speed, reliability, and being up to date were high priorities in this partnership because of the fast-evolving, high-impact nature of the crisis. A telephone survey, in preference to face-to-face interviews, was identified as the most practical way of reaching a large number of people cost-effectively and in a short time, while ensuring the safety of the enumerators by limiting their physical proximity to other people.

3.2 Sampling

The sample was mainly drawn from the following data sets (benchmark surveys):

1. BIGD's census, conducted from October 2016 to January 2017, of 24,283 households (HHs) in 35 slums (randomly chosen from the 150 slums of

---

[1] The World Food Programme (WFP) provided support for the execution of the second and third phases of the study. The last phase of the study was also supported by the Foreign, Commonwealth & Development Office (FCDO) of the United Kingdom through the Civic Leadership Education and Research (CLEAR) research initiative managed by the Institute of Development Studies (IDS), Sussex.

BRAC's Urban Development Programme) across 9 districts of 5 divisions: Dhaka, Chattogram, Khulna, Barishal, and Rangpur;
2. BIGD's nationally representative survey of 26,925 rural households across 64 districts of all 8 divisions, conducted from October 2017 to January 2018.

Due to the nature of these existing data sets, the chosen sample was *poor-biased*, with a preponderance of people in informal occupations. The sample was thus not reflective of the national distribution of incomes, but this bias was minimized by assigning a weight to each income group[2] and thus reducing the effect of over-represented income groups on our findings. Weights were similarly used in each of the following phases of the study.

The Phase I survey in April 2020 included a sample of 12,000 HHs, half of which were randomly selected from the urban database and the rest from the rural database. The urban sample was drawn from BIGD's census of 24,283 HHs. The rural sample was drawn from BIGD's nationally representative survey of 26,925 rural HHs. Of the total, 5,471 HHs were successfully interviewed over the phone.

For Phase II of the survey in June 2020, an additional 6,200 HHs were drawn from the same data sets—4,000 from the urban data set, 2,000 from the rural, and 200 from hard-to-reach areas, that is, the Chattogram Hill Tracts (CHT) region. A larger urban sample was selected to facilitate disaggregated analysis of the urban centres. Of the total sample of 11,671 HHS (the previously interviewed 5,471 HHs and the new 6,200 new HHs), 7,638 were successfully interviewed.

Phase III of the survey was conducted between 11 and 31 March 2021 to examine the recovery effects. The 7,638 HHs that were interviewed during Phase II were resurveyed, of which 6,099 HHs (81 per cent) were successfully interviewed. Out of these 6,099 HHs, 3,549 were surveyed in all three phases, while 2,550 were surveyed in Phases II and III only.

Phase IV of the survey was conducted between 21 August and 8 September 2021 to study the aftermath of the second lockdown. The 6,099 HHs interviewed during Phase III were resurveyed, of which 4,872 HHs (80 per cent) were successfully interviewed. Of these, 2,875 HHs were surveyed in all four phases of the study. Each contact number was tried three times via mobile phone to increase the success rate.

The last round, Phase V, was executed between 12 and 23 May 2022 in order to understand the longer-term effect of COVID-19 two years later. In this round, the sample of 6,099 HHs from Phase III was used rather than that of the round immediately before, out of concerns of attrition, and the success rate

---

[2] The weights were the ratios between a nationally representative sample of BIGD (mentioned in the section on sampling) and our surveyed samples—rural and urban.

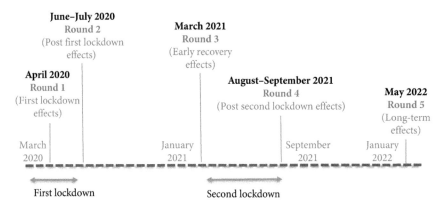

Figure 6.1 Survey overview
Source: authors' construction.

was 64 per cent (3,910 HHs). The higher attrition rate can be largely attributed to the timing of the survey, which was conducted at a time when the economy had fully resumed, unlike previous rounds. In the final successful sample, 2,017 HHs were present in all 5 rounds and 3,380 HHs in four rounds, that is, excluding the first phase. Figure 6.1 provides an overview of the phased panel surveys.

3.3 Survey instrument

A quantitative, close-ended questionnaire was used in each phase of the survey. Senior and junior researchers from PPRC-BIGD intensively brainstormed and debated the scope of the questionnaire and the wording of each question and of the response options. As it was a telephone survey, researchers paid special attention to ensuring that each question and the associated answer options were essential, clear, and brief. The questionnaire was pretested to confirm the reliability and validity of the survey questions and to estimate the time required to complete a survey.

The main segments of the questionnaire were on the impact of the COVID-19 crisis on an HH's livelihoods, coping mechanisms, food security, food and non-food expenditures, financial capacity, and social protection as well as on their related perceptions. Additionally, in Phase V, the survey had dual objectives: assessing the long-term trends of the economic recovery from COVID and the effects of the ongoing inflation crisis on the HHs. To achieve this, alongside the data for May, recall data was collected for January

2022 across several dimensions, including employment, income, food security, food and non-food expenditure, and market prices of several major food items.

4. Respondents' profile

4.1 Demographics

Of the 3,910 HHs interviewed in Phase V, 54 per cent were from urban slums across city corporations and municipalities in the districts from which the urban sample was drawn, and 45 per cent were from rural Bangladesh, with a small CHT sample of 0.5 per cent.

The average HH size of the sample was 4.87, and the average number of income earners in an HH was 1.37. Twelve per cent of the HHs were female-headed, which is close to the national proportion (13 per cent). The HH head was the primary respondent in the survey. If the HH head was not available, the secondary decision-maker or income-earner of the HH was interviewed.

4.2 Income and occupational categories

The respondents were classified into four income categories on the basis of reported per capita income for February 2020, that is, pre-COVID incomes. The inflation-adjusted divisional urban–rural upper poverty lines presented in the Household Income and Expenditure Survey (HIES) 2016 report were used for the categorization:

1. *Extreme poor*: HHs with per capita monthly income below, or equal to, the lower poverty line were categorized as extreme poor.
2. *Moderate poor*: HHs with per capita monthly income above the lower poverty line and below, or equal to, the upper poverty line were categorized as moderate poor.
3. *Vulnerable non-poor*: since there is no official classification for this category, the parameter for this vulnerability band was fixed as the range between the upper poverty line and the inflation-adjusted median income, established in consultation with the Bangladesh Bureau of Statistics (BBS).
4. *Non-poor*: the households with per capita monthly income above the median income were categorized as non-poor.

Table 6.1 below lists the occupational categories as defined in the study.

Table 6.1 Occupational categories

Broad occupational category	Corresponding occupations
Skilled labourers	Cook/restaurant worker, tailor, hairdresser, singer/musician, deed writer, salon/beauty parlour worker, cleaner/sweeper, electrician, mechanic
Unskilled labourers	Construction worker, day labourer, agricultural labourer, shop/restaurant assistant, hotel boy, *Bhangari* (collection and recycling of scrap items) worker, cobbler
Transport workers	Boatman, transport driver, transport labourer
Factory workers	RMG worker, Other factory worker
Housemaids	Housemaid
Agricultural workers	Farmer, fisherman, livestock rearer, poultry farmer
Salaried workers	Teacher/home tutor, private service holder (other salaried employees working in the private sector), security guard, professional (doctor/lawyer), employee of religious institution, office assistant, UP member/chairman (elected local government officials), pensioner
Micro-entrepreneurs	Small business owner, vendor, handicraft worker
Rickshaw pullers	Rickshaw puller
Not in income-generating activities	Beggar, person living on government or other assistance, person living on savings, person with no income source

Source: authors' construction.

5. Short-term effects: Impact of first and second lockdowns

The income shock of the second lockdown in mid-2021 was less acute than that of the first one in mid-2020.[3] One year down the line, everyone had learned, to various degrees, how to live with the new reality. With more information and experience, fear of the virus reduced significantly between 2021 and 2020. Forty-four per cent of respondents said that they were less afraid than before, while 20 per cent said they were more afraid. The government, too, perhaps used learning from the past year in estimating the future progression of the virus and the economic costs of a lockdown and thus was reportedly more lenient in applying the lockdown measures the second time. Yet, the second lockdown was not inconsequential: though 40 per cent of respondents thought that this lockdown was less stringently enforced than the last one, 46 per cent believed that it was more stringently enforced. The imposition of a second, several-weeks-long lockdown when the citizens were still recovering from the negative impact of the first lockdown seriously hampered recovery.

---

[3] We did this comparison using data from phases II and IV.

From February to June 2020, per capita daily income of HHs across all income groups—extreme poor, moderate poor, vulnerable non-poor, and non-poor—fell drastically with the onset of the pandemic and the subsequent lockdown. This was followed by a period of steady recovery until March 2021, when incomes were below, but close to, pre-COVID levels. But due to rising infections, the country went into the second lockdown from 23 July until 10 August 2021, causing a serious disruption in income recovery.

In a period of just a few months, between March and August 2021, across all income groups (extreme poor, moderate poor, vulnerable non-poor, and non-poor), incomes fell, on average, by 19 per cent. Since the second lockdown was lifted in August 2021, average daily HH per capita daily income had been on the rise: it rose by 27 per cent from BDT83 to BDT105 (in constant February 2020 prices) as of January 2022. Between January and May 2022, however, there was a disruption in real income recovery; average income fell by 6 per cent to BDT99.

Compared with rural HHs, urban slum HHs experienced a more drastic 'income shock' due to both lockdowns. Between March and August 2021, income dropped by 21 per cent for urban slum HHs and by 19 per cent for rural HHs (Figure 6.2). In Figure 6.2, we see that the real income fall in urban slums (8 per cent) was much sharper than in rural regions (3 per cent) during the inflationary period. Average real income in rural areas is also now higher than in urban slums, which is a reversal of the pre-COVID scenario.

The majority of survey respondents in August 2021 said that they did not get enough or the expected level of work in the preceding month.[4] This dissatisfaction was higher among respondents with lower education, with lower incomes, and in lower-skill occupations. Respondents cited the lockdown and unavailability of

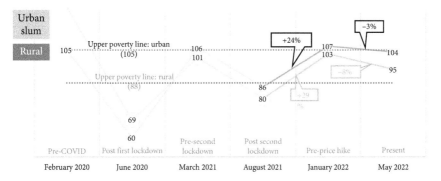

Figure 6.2 Per capita daily income in February 2020, constant BDT, at different points in time

Source: authors' construction.

---

[4] In the phase IV survey, we collected the information on whether the respondents were getting enough work or expected level of work and if not, what the reasons were.

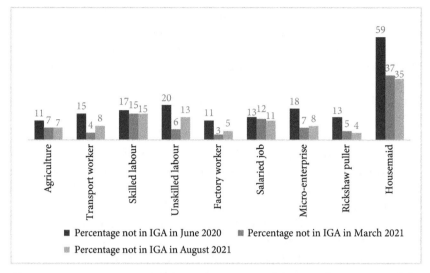

Figure 6.3 Percentage not in IGA in June 2020, March 2021, and August 2021 (of those employed in February 2020; excl. 'Others')

Source: authors' construction.

work as the principal reasons behind not getting enough or the expected amount of work.

Figure 6.3 shows the percentage of those who were engaged in any income-generating activity (IGA) before the pandemic that were also engaged in an IGA at different points in time since the pandemic.[5] This estimate can be used as a proxy for employment. The most volatile change in employment status is observed among unskilled labourers, factory workers, and transport workers—sectors whose demand is sensitive to economic lockdowns, which have an informal dimension to their work, or both. The exception is the figure for housemaids: starting with the highest overall rate of unemployment, the sector has seen a steady rise in employment. This can probably be explained by the decline in the fear factor, as mentioned above, as well as early vaccination drives in urban areas. Yet, the unemployment rate among housemaids remains higher than any other occupational groups by a large margin.

In terms of nutrition, the percentage of HHs skipping at least one meal the day preceding the interview increased significantly between March and August 2021, especially in the urban slums and the CHT.[6] On average, the situation regressed almost to the level of June 2020 right after the first lockdown (Figure 6.4).

---

[5] We did this analysis using phases I–IV. Since the attrition was higher in phase V, we did not do occupational disaggregated analysis because of lack of sample power.

[6] We could not compare phase V with the previous surveys in terms of this variable because inflation was a major concern during the survey period of phase V (between August 2021 and May 2022).

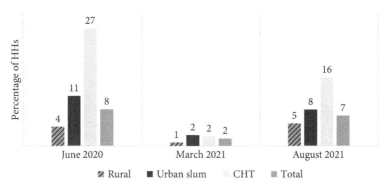

Figure 6.4 Percentage of HHs skipping a meal the day before interview
Source: authors' construction.

When asked about how the HHs were coping with the crisis (i.e. how they were meeting their daily dietary needs), the majority (91 per cent) mentioned their own income. This rate is greater than the situation after the first lockdown in April 2020, when the economic shock was much deeper. A comparison of the aftermath of the first lockdown with that of the second lockdown in mid-2021 shows that use of savings had gone down from 15 per cent to 3 per cent, but at the same time, the use of loans and shopkeepers' credit had gone up, which has implications for longer-term financial capacity, as discussed below. Help from friends and relatives had also gone up from 7 per cent to 17 per cent. These figures also indicate a significant disruption in income recovery caused by the second lockdown.

Yet, the number of HHs that received any kind of support from the government or other sources went down considerably from the first lockdown, particularly in urban slums (Figure 6.5), although the monetary value of the support among HHs that received it increased from an estimated BDT1,282 to BDT1,874, on average.

However, the fall in borrowing indicated above does not necessarily reflect the demand for credit. In order to gauge it, as well as link it with creditworthiness, we posed a question to our respondents whether they needed any new loan in addition to their existing ones if they had any (see Figure 6.6). When asked, overall, 38 per cent said they needed another loan but could not take it or did not get it. When asked why, they gave one or more of the following reasons: they already had too much loan (34 per cent), were already falling behind on existing loan payments (49 per cent), or were uncertain about their ability to make a payment (47 per cent). This is extremely important for designing financial interventions and innovations in microfinance. To rejuvenate the underlying economic structure and support the vulnerable population, a combination of grant and loan may be needed. There seems to be an ongoing erosion in creditworthiness which may limit the access to credit for many who genuinely need it.

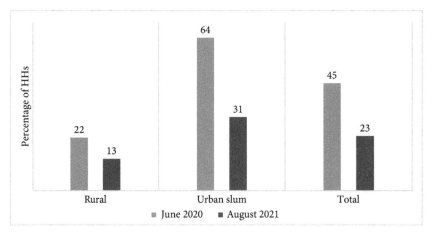

Figure 6.5 Percentage of HHs that received any kind of support

Source: authors' construction.

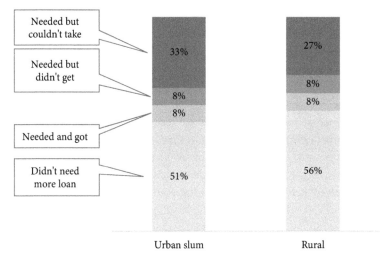

Figure 6.6 Demand for credit

Source: authors' construction.

6. Longer-term effects: Recovery with distress

The PPRC-BIGD panel surveys over 18 months of the COVID-19 crisis provide an overview of both the economic shocks induced by the pandemic and the recovery process.

6.1 Income dynamics

After the first lockdown, income for HHs in urban slums and rural areas and across income groups declined drastically, but thereafter it improved steadily and almost reached pre-COVID levels by June 2021, on average. But because of the second lockdown, income took another hit. Though the impact of the second lockdown was not as sharp as that of the first, it was still substantial. Consequently, 18 months after the start of the pandemic, per capita daily income among the surveyed HHs remained 23 per cent lower than its pre-COVID level. In constant prices of February 2020, this is BDT88 (US$1.04) per capita per day, which also happens to be the rural upper poverty line. Overall, it was found that income is still much below the pre-COVID level, even after two years of the pandemic-induced initial and most intense economic shock. Average household per capita daily income for the entire sample stood at BDT99 (in constant February 2020 prices) as of May 2022, which was still 15 per cent below pre-COVID levels. The recovery process was first disrupted by the second lockdown and again by inflation.

When disaggregated by income groups based on pre-COVID incomes, it is noticeable that those below the upper poverty line (i.e. the extreme poor and moderate poor) appear to be faring somewhat well, with either having almost reached pre-COVID level or having already reached it (see Figure 6.7). They may have opted for more labour-intensive jobs or taken on multiple jobs with lower pay to compensate for the COVID-induced setback. The ones above the poverty line (the non-poor and the vulnerable non-poor), however, have borne the larger brunt of the pandemic and have been less successful in recovering the lost earnings. This could be because, unlike those below the poverty line, non-poor who were financially struggling due to COVID were less adaptive to labour-intensive jobs, which are often deemed undignified by the society. They might be looking for workplaces with relatively higher pay or better working conditions—the opportunities for which might still be limited. Non-poor HHs took the greatest hit. Their per capita daily income before COVID was BDT216 (US$2.46). Eighteen months into the crisis, in August 2021, their per capita daily income stood at BDT135 (US$1.47); 37.5 per cent lower than the pre-COVID level. For the vulnerable non-poor and moderate poor HHs, incomes were 10.5 per cent per cent and 11.7 per cent lower than pre-COVID levels, respectively. Only among the extreme poor HHs were incomes higher (by 16 per cent) than their pre-COVID level. However, further research is needed to understand the underlying mechanisms leading to this undesirable convergence—not because the poor are getting richer but because the non-poor are getting poorer.

The inflation-adjusted upper poverty line is BDT88 (US$1.04) for rural areas and BDT105 (US$1.24) for urban areas. There is a persistent difference in the

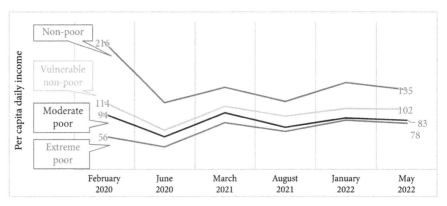

Figure 6.7 Per capita daily income in February 2020, constant BDT, across income groups

Source: authors' construction.

recovery rate between the urban slum and rural HHs. Urban slum HHs are in a disproportionately harder time in terms of long-term income recovery, and the urban disadvantage prevails beyond the inflation period. Before COVID-19, urban slum HHs had higher per capita income than the rural HHs. But as of May 2022, rural real-income recovery almost reached its pre-pandemic levels (only 1 per cent below) after two years and urban slum income was still 25 per cent below pre-COVID levels. Moreover, since March 2021, the average income in the urban slum has consistently been less than the rural average, which is a complete reversal of the status quo before the pandemic hit. Thus, in line with previous rounds, the urban distress is a constant area of concern.

The gaps in per capita daily incomes among the surveyed urban slum and rural HHs shrank considerably between February 2020 and August 2021. But while rural incomes had rebounded to just above the rural upper poverty line in August 2021, incomes in urban slums were still languishing well below the urban upper poverty line.

Urban slum dwellers experienced a much deeper livelihood impact from the first lockdown. Though their rate of recovery, until March 2020, was slightly better than their rural counterparts, the second lockdown again caused a sharper decline in their income (Figure 6.2). As a result, per capita daily income in August 2021 in urban slums was lower than that in rural areas, although the opposite was true before COVID. Given the higher cost of living in cities compared with the cost in villages, these figures indicate a persistent decline in the quality of life and erosion of financial capabilities in urban slums.

When we consider the income effects on the different occupation groups, we observe that formal salaried workers, including factory workers, have shown a

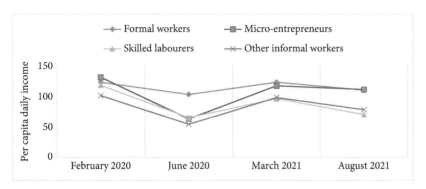

Figure 6.8 Per capita daily income in February 2020, constant BDT, across aggregate pre-COVID occupational groups

Note: 'Others' and 'Not in IGA' are excluded. 'Formal workers' comprise salaried workers and factory workers and 'Other informal workers' consist of the remaining occupation groups except for micro-entrepreneurs and skilled labourers.
Source: authors' construction.

more stable pattern. Informal workers, including skilled labourers, are far worse off than pre-COVID (Figure 6.8). While self-employed micro-entrepreneurs took a large hit after the first lockdown in 2020, they recovered fast, and the second lockdown had a minimal effect on them. A more disaggregated chart is available in Appendix Figure 6.A1.

6.2 Labour market dynamics and vulnerable shifts

In both rural areas and urban slums, many people who were involved in IGAs before COVID were yet to find work as of August 2021. Unemployment soared after the first lockdown, everywhere. In the case of rural areas, the rate came down to pre-COVID levels by March 2021 before increasing again after the second lockdown. But in the case of urban slums, unemployment remained persistently high. Although it declined from 24 per cent in June 2020 to 13 per cent in March 2021, it was still almost twice as high as pre-COVID and had increased further by August 2021 (Figure 6.9).

When we look at the shifts in employment pattern among those who were involved in IGAs before COVID, two insights emerge. Many occupational groups who are vulnerable in general have been affected disproportionately. For example, 35 per cent of housemaids and 13 per cent of unskilled labourers (e.g. day labourers) remained out of work in August 2020. On the other hand, we can also find an indication of vulnerable shifts for relatively skilled and secure occupations: many previously skilled workers now worked as unskilled labours (17 per cent) or were out of work (15 per cent), and only 54 per cent of salaried employees had held on

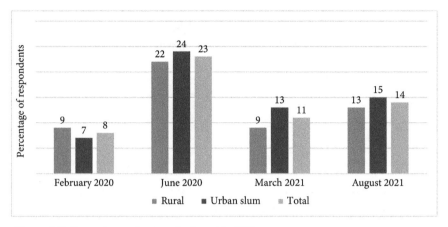

Figure 6.9 Percentage of respondents not in IGAs
Source: authors' construction.

to their jobs, the rest moving to less secure, more vulnerable occupations, including unskilled labouring (8 per cent) and rickshaw pulling (4 per cent), and 11 per cent of them remaining out of work as of August 2021.

6.3 Expenditure dynamics

In both urban slum and rural HHs, food and nutrition expenditure had been slowly recovering since the sharp drop observed in June 2020, but the recovery has slowed and flattened since March 2021. Consequently, food and nutrition expenditure in August 2021 was 16 per cent lower in urban slums and 12 per cent lower in rural areas than pre-COVID levels. As caloric demands are often prioritized over the nutritional demands of the body in times of economic crisis (Laran and Salerno 2013), many HHs are likely to reduce their consumption of nutritious food and increase consumption of cheaper, high-calorie food like rice and potatoes. Indeed, we find that the majority of the surveyed HHs did not have any meat or milk throughout the pandemic, and fruit intake has declined consistently since June 2020 (Figure 6.10).

Long-term lack of critical food items like milk, fruits, and meat may be particularly damaging to the physical and mental growth of children, which may have long-term welfare consequences for them.

Because of the drastic reduction in income during the first lockdown, rent and utility payments were deferred, particularly for many urban HHs. And because all educational institutions were closed, educational expenses were also deferred. To cope with the financial crunch, non-emergency medical costs were also likely to

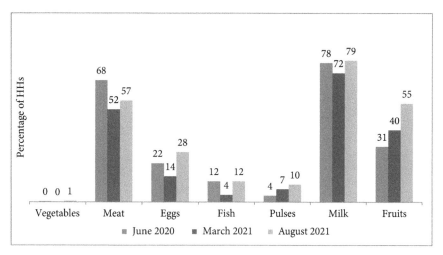

Figure 6.10   Percentage of HHs that did not have certain types of food in the past seven days

Source: authors' construction.

be put off. So non-food expenditure was found to be low in the June 2020 survey. But these expenditures can be deferred only for so long. Unpaid bills pile up and untreated medical conditions often become more expensive to treat over time. As a result, households' total monthly per capita non-food expenditure burden continued to increase after the initial shock.

In urban slums, per capital expenditure was almost twice as high as that of June 2020, the increase being driven by the rise in rent, utility, and medical expenditure. In rural areas, monthly per capita non-food expenditure almost tripled between June 2020 and August 2021, mainly driven by increases in medical and educational expenditure. But non-food expenditure in urban slums (BDT964 per month per capita) remained much higher than that of rural areas (BDT777 per month per capita). Combined with lower income, as discussed earlier, high non-food expenditure in urban areas caused greater hardship among urban slum residents.

6.4 Financial capacity dynamics

Savings were depleted considerably during the first lockdown across all the income groups. Since then, savings, as a percentage of annual HH income in 2020, based on monthly income in February 2020, have been increasing gradually for all but the vulnerable non-poor. Even for the other income groups, savings are yet to reach pre-COVID levels.

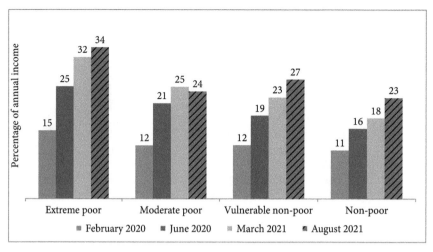

Figure 6.11 Outstanding loan as a percentage of annual income
Source: authors' construction.

On the other hand, we observed a consistent rise in outstanding loans in each phase of the survey. Between February 2020 and August 2021, outstanding loans as a percentage of annual income (2020), based on monthly income in February 2020, more than doubled for each income group—extreme poor, moderate poor, vulnerable non-poor, and non-poor (Figure 6.11).

The gradual erosion of financial capacity was also ubiquitous among urban slums and rural HHs, though, as a percentage of annual income, outstanding loans were 10 percentage points higher in rural areas (33 per cent) than in urban areas (23 per cent) as of August 2021.

We observed that the majority of HHs borrowed from shopkeepers (61 per cent), non-governmental organizations (NGOs) (49 per cent), and neighbours or relatives (38 per cent). Another 11 per cent borrowed from moneylenders. The majority of the HHs were borrowing to cover either daily consumption expenses or medical bills. Around one-fifth were borrowing to invest in business, and a similar proportion were repaying loans.

6.5 Migration

Over one-quarter (28 per cent) of respondents and their families migrated from urban slum areas at some point during the course of the pandemic. Eighteen per cent had returned by the time of the fourth-round survey in August 2021. The remaining 10 per cent have remained, which is the present rate of net reverse migration nationally. However, many of those who stayed migrated later during the pandemic. Whether their migration is longer term cannot be said with the present data.

This is the first time in the history of Bangladesh that we have observed such a large-scale urban-to-rural migration. Since the 1960s, people have moved from villages to urban centres in large numbers in search of better economic opportunities. Now, COVID-induced income shock, combined with higher expenditures in cities, is pushing many people back to rural or less urban areas. Many have subsequently returned to urban areas, but many others may not. Migration is expensive and involves uncertainties. Thus, people—particularly those who are economically vulnerable—may not migrate, even when it offers clear economic advantages. Personal preferences, aspirations, employment, and income opportunities will influence the decision of return migrants to migrate again or stay in their rural communities (ILO 2021). Whether most of the slum dwellers who migrated to other places will return and how the economic lives of those who do not return will evolve are important policy questions.

7. Poverty dynamics and the new poor

Fifty-five per cent of the sample HHs, both in urban slums and in rural areas, lived below the inflation-adjusted upper poverty line just before COVID. The rate skyrocketed right after the first lockdown and then gradually went down to close to the pre-COVID level by March 2021 before shooting up again to 72 per cent by August 2021. The rate remained at 64 per cent as of May 2022. And the impact is not equally distributed across different groups.

The impact has been most severe in urban areas. Poverty, as of May 2022, in the rural sample remains the same as pre-COVID levels, whereas in urban slums, it increased by 17 percentage points. People whose income falls around the poverty line often oscillate above and below the line. But it is safe to assume that the increase in the poverty rates observed in this survey cannot be explained by the regular phenomenon of transitional poverty. The point will be clearer if we look at the change in poverty status among the vulnerable non-poor and poor HHs in our study. Among the HHs that were vulnerable non-poor before COVID-19, with income above the income-adjusted upper poverty line and below median income, 35 per cent were found to be below the poverty line in all three survey rounds between June 2020 and August 2021, and 34 per cent were found to be under the poverty line any two out of the three survey rounds.[7]

After the first round of the survey, we found that most of the HHs that were vulnerable non-poor as of February 2020 fell below the poverty line by April; these we identified as the 'new poor'—vulnerable non-poor people made poor by the

[7] The transition analysis was not done for phase V because of higher attrition rate.

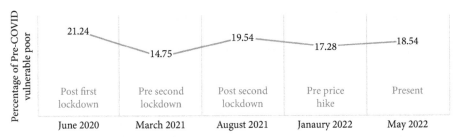

Figure 6.12 Percentage of pre-COVID vulnerable non-poor below the poverty line
Source: authors' construction.

pandemic. Though a large number of sample non-poor HHs—those above the median income—also fell below the poverty line in April 2020, considering their possible better coping capabilities, we concentrated only on the vulnerable non-poor to estimate the percentage of 'new poor' in the national population. We found the percentage of the national population that were vulnerable non-poor before the pandemic and multiplied the rate by the weight-adjusted percentage of the same group in our sample that fell below the poverty line.

According to this estimate, 21 per cent of the national population fell into the 'new poor' category, which went down over time but jumped back to 20 per cent after the second lockdown. Even in March 2021, when the recovery situation was at its best, 15 per cent of the national population was estimated to be 'new poor' (Figure 6.12). After two years, it has fallen by only 2.7 percentage points.

Additionally, when we look at the near-term scenario, we also see a reversal during the inflation period: the proportion of new poor has risen from January 2022 to May 2022 by 1.26 percentage points. The overall recovery trends do not demonstrate the perils of the large segment of vulnerable non-poor people.

Vulnerable non-poor, by definition, are vulnerable; they are less likely to have the solid financial buffers—properties, savings, strong social networks—necessary to weather the income shock for such a long time and spring back out of poverty. Many of the new poor, particularly those who could not get out of poverty throughout the pandemic, may be stuck in poverty without external support.

8. Key takeaways and policy messages

Two lockdowns and 18 months into a global pandemic, key takeaways from the panel study findings are:

Disrupted recovery: not only has recovery been fragile but also the second lockdown in April 2021 underscored the continuing threat and reality of disruptions in the recovery process due to new waves of COVID-19 infection and how they are managed. Income recovery reversed, and after 18 months, average income among the surveyed HHs in August 2021 was 23 per cent below pre-COVID levels. Employment recovery, too, was disrupted; unemployment rose by three percentage points between March and August 2021. The percentage of HHs that had skipped a meal the previous day went up from 2 per cent in March 2021 to 7 per cent in August 2021.

Transient poverty versus emerging poverty traps: the onset of recovery after the initial shock of the COVID-19 crisis led some to view the phenomenon of the 'new poor' as a transient problem. Eighteen months into the crisis, the reversal of recovery after the second lockdown has, however, only deepened the problem. In June 2020, the national estimate of the new poor was 21.24 per cent. This declined to 14.75 per cent in March 2021, but the latest estimate, in August 2021, is 19.54 per cent—or a total of 32.4 million people when extrapolated to the entire population of the country.

Persistently high number of the new poor: despite substantial increase in overall income over the past two years, the proportion of vulnerable non-poor remaining below the poverty line remains stubbornly high, further worsened by the inflation. The estimated proportion of 'new poor' in the national population stands at 18.54 per cent as of May 2022, which translates to a staggering 30.9 million. The trend has grave implications for national poverty reduction.

Distress resilience: resilience has been, and continues to be, a defining characteristic of people's response to adversity. But the pandemic has brought to the fore a different facet of resilience as an unfair bargain in a vicious cycle—higher deployment of family labour put into vulnerable and lower-income occupations, rising expenditure burdens, eroding financial capacity, and token social support or protection, if any. Between June 2020 and March 2021, recovery among the surveyed extreme poor HHs took place on the back of an increase in the average number of earners per HH from 1.25 to 1.46. From the education module of the same survey, we find that about 8 per cent of school-going boys were engaged in IGAs, both in March and in August 2021. Food expenditures have had to be kept in check, forgoing nutrition, while the non-food expenditure burden doubled, and debt climbed to nearly one-third of average annual incomes.

Depleted coping capacity: another important finding was the depleted coping capacity of the households, which is a worrying sign for the future. The most important statistic supporting this is the stated inability to borrow despite need: 38 per cent of the HHs needing the loan either did not apply for it—to avoid further indebtedness or fear of not being able to pay—or they did not get it due to loss of creditworthiness. The government has adopted many credit-based stimulus packages during COVID-19, and the finding goes on to partially explain why the take-up among the poor and vulnerable has been low—they cannot advance towards those with eroding creditworthiness and financial capacity.

Additionally, social support from family, neighbour and friends, as well as institutional support from the government and NGOs in the form of aid or grants, has decreased from about a year ago. There has, instead, been a move towards market-based, subsidized social support such as Trading Corporation of Bangladesh (TCB) now. Hence, creating opportunities is not enough if the poor and vulnerable lack the capacity to take them on; we might possibly have to move towards mixed support schemes, such as a credit plus grant-based approach, for these segments of the population.

Continuing disproportionate impact on the urban poor: compared with rural HHs, unemployment was 2 percentage points lower in urban slums in the pre-COVID period. But by August 2021, the scenario had reversed, with unemployment in urban slums now 2 percentage points higher than in rural areas. Moreover, income drop due to the second lockdown was 18 per cent in urban slums compared with 15 per cent in rural areas.

A new sociology of new poor and reverse migration: 28 per cent of the urban HHs surveyed had involuntarily migrated during the 18 months of the ongoing pandemic. Eighteen per cent have returned, while the remaining 10 per cent have not—and might not—return. These reverse migrants, who are mostly part of the 'new poor', represent a novel socio-economic group not only for Bangladeshi society as a whole but also for the poverty alleviation paradigms of governments and NGOs alike. Though these reverse migrants are likely to be in distress, their motivations and aspirations do not necessarily conform to those of the pre-existing rural poor. Effective policy responses to the needs of this group will depend on overcoming a critical knowledge gap.

8.1 Policy messages

Living-with-COVID approach

Eighteen months into the COVID-19 crisis, the rapid and widespread disruptions to recovery caused by the second lockdown have underscored the urgency of a shift in mindset. Health-care response to the infection, administrative response to lockdown-like measures to contain new outbreaks, and economic policy response to support recovery: these three essential pillars of a holistic pandemic management policy cannot produce the desired results if pursued as isolated policy streams. Bangladesh has rightly refrained from embracing a zero-COVID policy built on prolonged lockdowns. But a clear and effective approach to the alternative that is 'living with COVID' has also been missing. A credible integration of the three essential policy strands—health, administrative, and economic—is imperative if disrupted recovery is to be avoided.

A question of social justice

The COVID-19 response is also fundamentally a question of social justice. While the pandemic has affected all social and economic classes, the PPRC-BIGD research findings underscore an unfair burden of distress resilience that the poorer sections of society, including the new poor, appear to have been left to deal with. The following policy imperatives demand immediate attention:

- jump-starting a scaled-up and fit-for-purpose urban social protection programme portfolio to address both the new poor and the old poor;
- preparing a budgetary action plan for a comprehensive recovery and development strategy for cottage, micro, small, and medium enterprises (CMSME) encompassing both rural and urban sectors;
- preparing a priority lesson-learning report through a national consultative process on previous lockdown experiences for the purpose of minimizing recovery disruptions due to possible future infection waves;
- continuing and strengthening vaccination drives and community awareness programmes for mask-wearing and handwashing.

Addressing cost drivers and expenditure burdens of the poor

The four cost drivers that have contributed to the expenditure burdens of the poor and lower-income groups are all related to macroeconomic policy: health care, education, transportation, and utilities. The COVID-19 crisis has created a compelling policy window to review reform measures that can address these critical cost drivers for the poor. If the entrenched roadblocks to governance reforms can be confronted, leading to rationalization of such expenditure burdens, the impact on the well-being of the poor and middle-income classes alike will be as great as—if not greater than—the welfare from social protection measures alone.

Scaling up the policy focus on urban social protection

The PPRC-BIGD panel surveys have brought out the continuing disproportionate vulnerability of the urban poor. Over the years, poverty has been indelibly associated with the 'rural' in the policy mindset. However, this reality is rapidly being overtaken by growing urbanization and burgeoning urban slums. The economic impact of COVID has underscored the urgency of addressing the predicaments of the urban poor. Social protection programming for the rural poor may not often be the right response in the case of the urban poor. The challenge is a twofold one:

a shift in policy mindset towards acceptance of the urban poor as a priority focus for social protection and innovations in programming that can address the specific needs of the urban poor.

References

ILO (International Labour Organization) (2021). *Reverse Migration to Rural Areas of Origin in the Context of the COVID-19 Pandemic.* Geneva: ILO.

Laran, J., and A. Salerno (2013). 'Life-History Strategy, Food Choice, and Caloric Consumption', *Psychological Science*, 24(2): 167–73. https://doi.org/10.1177/0956797612450033.

PPRC-BIGD (Power and Participation Research Centre-BRAC Institute of Governance and Development) (2021). 'Livelihoods, Coping and Recovery during COVID-19 Crisis', Dhaka: PPRC-BIGD, available at: https://bigd.bracu.ac.bd/publications/livelihoods-coping-and-recovery-during-covid-19-crisis-2/.

Rahman, H.Z., I. Matin, N. Banks, and D. Hulme (2021). 'Finding Out Fast about the Impact of COVID-19: The Need for Policy-Relevant Methodological Innovation', *World Development*, 140: 105380. https://doi.org/10.1016/j.worlddev.2020.105380.

Appendix

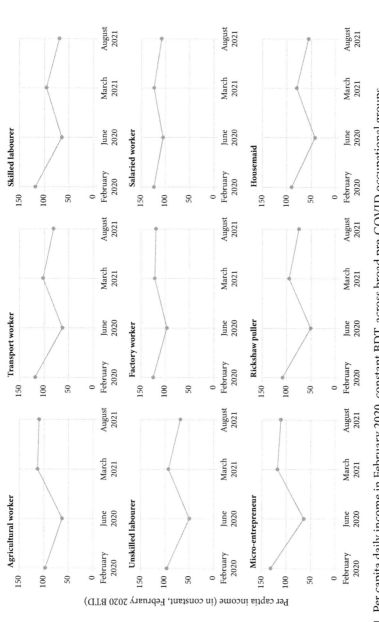

Figure 6A.1 Per capita daily income in February 2020, constant BDT, across broad pre-COVID occupational groups

Source: authors' construction.

7

The COVID-19 Pandemic and Intra-household Bargaining

A Case of Domestic Workers in Delhi

*Deepita Chakravarty and Nandini Nayak**

1. Introduction

Studies on the impact of the COVID-19 pandemic have demonstrated that the poor in general, and poor women in particular, are the worst sufferers in terms of pay cuts and job losses caused by the economic fallout of the pandemic (Alon et al. 2020; Deshpande 2020). Women are also the hardest hit at the household level and have had to bear the brunt of the reduction in household budgets. Studies also point out the increasing levels of domestic violence against women during the long and uncertain spells of pandemic-induced lockdowns, when men stayed at home for much longer periods of time than usual (Agarwal 2021). This study on the gender impact of the pandemic and the consequent lockdowns and curfews in the city of Delhi, India, seeks to explore whether women who have gained some agency from their work are less likely to face household-level discrimination. We also try to understand whether the extent, severity, and nature of discrimination within the household may change if women have better chances than men to retain or get back their jobs.

We use two overarching concepts to inform the analysis of our data. A key concern in this chapter is to understand the implications of the economic fallout of the pandemic on intra-household dynamics. The impact of any calamity is usually analysed holding the household as a unit. The implicit assumption here is that families are essentially 'harmonious' units maximizing a 'single/joint utility function' (Becker 1981: 33). Closer and detailed empirical observations contradict the concept of harmony: the division of resources within a household often turns

* We are grateful to Kunal Sen, Martha Chen, Ishita Chakravarty, Nalini Nayak, Pulin B. Nayak for discussions and comments. We thank our students Anjali Sharma, Raj Shekhar Singh, Elizabeth Alexander, and Bharati Kondipodi for helping us conduct the primary survey and Deepali Singh Gautam and Ambiya Bibi for helping us to set up the survey and establish contacts. Finally, we thank all domestic workers who agreed to talk to us, sometimes more than once, despite their extremely busy schedules and difficult conditions of lockdown and near-lockdown situations in the city of Delhi. Without their support this chapter would not have been possible at all.

Deepita Chakravarty and Nandini Nayak, *The COVID-19 Pandemic and Intra-household Bargaining*. In: *COVID-19 and the Informal Economy*. Edited by: Martha Alter Chen, Michael Rogan, and Kunal Sen, Oxford University Press. © Deepita Chakravarty and Nandini Nayak (2024). DOI: 10.1093/oso/9780198887041.003.0008 out to be discriminatory against women in general and girl children in particular in poor South Asian economies. This is likely to be even more acute at times of hardships induced by calamities of different kinds, such as a pandemic. Therefore, we draw on Amartya Sen's (1987) seminal work on cooperative conflicts within households, conceptualizing households as bargaining units in which household members cooperate as long as it is beneficial to each of them. Importantly, Sen (1987) also highlights that personal perceptions are crucial for determining the manner in which family members negotiate intra-household relationships. Situations of conflict among family members also arise. The final outcome depends on the differential bargaining powers of the household members. Agarwal (2008: 162) argues that 'family breakup and female victimization can thus be seen as outcomes of shifts in relative male–female entitlements and fall-back positions, and so in their relative bargaining strengths within the family'. In the backdrop of overall precarity in households, and the informal nature of domestic work, we discuss the implications of this work for the fall-back positions of our respondent workers. We are also interested in how respondents perceive their interests, work, and contribution to their household. The nature of domestic work may be seen as 'reflective of', 'traditional within household divisions' (Sen 1987: 14); however, we consider whether this understanding of domestic work is challenged by women workers themselves, implicitly or explicitly. Is it the case, then, that women domestic workers view their paid work as important and as clearly separate from their personal domestic work? Intra-household dynamics and bargaining are also significantly affected by a range of 'extra-household environmental parameters' (Agarwal 1997; McElroy 1990), including, for instance, community initiatives and social protection interventions by government agencies. In the present chapter, we are also interested in the implications of extra-household factors on intra-household dynamics reported by our respondents.

To explore cooperative conflicts within the household, we are interested in how women workers exercise agency. Sen (1987, 1990) suggests that an individual's 'agency role' may be understood as being 'overshadowed by social rules', while *also* contributing to a person's 'well-being' (Sen 1987: 45). Keeping in mind the social inequity of intra-household dynamics, we draw on Sen's view that to understand intra-household relationships, reflecting on agency and perceptions is important for understanding women's well-being. We also draw on Kabeer's (1999) framing of agency and empowerment as we have an interest in reflecting on *how* those who might not have previously made strategic personal decisions acquire such an ability. Thus, we are interested in a processual understanding of how agency is negotiated. This includes how one's exercising of agency comes about and, indeed, how the capacity to exercise agency, once gained, may also falter or otherwise be modified, with consequent implications for intra-household bargaining. We are therefore interested in the circumstances and context that affect a person's agency. Specifically, we consider whether domestic work itself, despite its precarity, proves to be a source of somewhat 'stable' employment for these women workers, particularly in the context of the pandemic. We consider how our respondent women workers view the significance of their work for helping them cope with the pandemic.

We focus on domestic workers because of the significance of this category of work for women workers in urban areas. The latest quinquennial survey of the National Sample Survey (2011–12) shows that domestic service has emerged as one of the most important occupations for women in urban areas.[1] More importantly, Delhi stands at the second position in the country when we consider the number of households with domestic work as the main source of income. Primary surveys suggest that most domestic workers inDelhi are migrants. The settled, city-dwelling domestic workers often migrate with their husbands. Researchers, however, have also mentioned cases of single adult women's migration for domestic service, sometimes through recruiting agencies and sometimes through personal contacts in the city (Jain 2016). Girl children migrate singly as well, through agencies and family networks, as full-time workers in middle-class city homes (Chakravarty and Chakravarty 2015). In the case of the last two categories, women usually do not settle down in the city unless their families join them at some point. Research based on primary data has also documented that, in a substantial number of cases, urban domestic workers have turned out to be the main breadwinners for their families (Chakravarty and Chakravarty 2015; Neetha 2004, 2013).

In this chapter, we draw on interviews with 31 part-time female domestic workers who have been working in Delhi for varying periods of time (Chakravarty and Nayak 2022: Table B1). Interviews were conducted inperson, keeping in mind COVID-19 protocols such as wearing face masks and physical distancing. However, the fieldwork was delayed and postponed several times when fears of infection were particularly acute in Delhi. Some follow-up clarifications were sought by telephone, although, for these too, we did our best to carry out face-to-face meetings.

The primary survey was conducted in different parts of Delhi in two phases: during February–March 2021 and in July–August 2021. Because of its informal nature, there is no ready list of domestic workers available on the basis of which one can think of drawing a proper sample of any kind. In any case, the aim of this

---

[1] It is worth noting that home-based manufacturing, taken as a whole, engages more women urban informal workers than domestic work alone (19 per cent of total female urban informal employment is in home-based manufacturing, taken as a whole, compared with 11.7 per cent of the same in domestic work—Chen and Raveendran 2014). However, home-based employment can be disaggregated into several distinct types of work, that is, garment work, kite-making, bidi-rolling, basket- and rope-making, etc., which are all quite distinct. Domestic work, on the other hand, mainly refers to work done by carers for children and older adults, cooks, and maids.

study, and hence the methodology adopted, consists of exploring the possibilities of different gender outcomes of the pandemic when women have already achieved some agency rather than the production of statistically generalizable findings. We thus decided to stick to a carefully chosen small sample of women with whom we could have detailed discussions. We decided to concentrate only on settled, city-dwelling adult domestic workers who have been based in Delhi for some time with their families. All of our respondents work on a part-time basis in one or more households, doing primarily cleaning, cooking, and (in some cases) adult or childcare work beyond these tasks.

The locations of the slums we visited were solely determined by our ability to establish a contact through whom we could approach others. We visited four slums in the city; two were in southwest Delhi and the other two in north Delhi. Many workers had simply refused to talk to us; those who agreed to talk often did not have the patience or the time to answer the minute details we needed to understand household dynamics in the context of the pandemic, and therefore we needed to make repeated visits. As most of these women's husbands were unemployed during the months when fieldwork was conducted, they were often found to be at home interfering in the interview process. Thus, we tried to speak with our respondent workers either during their free hours in a nearby park or on the way to their workplaces and, in some cases, when they were at work. This made the whole process even more challenging, especially given the pandemic situation in the city. We could collect detailed and insightful data only from a few women among the 31 respondents that could really capture the nuances of the household dynamics during the hard-hit days of the pandemic. We could not get data for the period during the second wave and its aftermath for many of the women with whom we interacted during the first wave as several of them could not be contacted later, even by telephone. It is worth noting that the reduction in mobile phone connections in the period during and after the pandemic has been documented in the Indian context, and this is viewed as indicative of economic hardship. Owing to the above-mentioned factors, our findings are mostly indicative in nature.

This chapter has five sections. In section 2, we briefly touch upon the hardships faced by the poor due to the pandemic on the basis of existing literature. Section 3 discusses the significance of domestic service in creating a relatively stronger fall-back position and, in turn, agency in working women. With reference to our survey data, this section also discusses some broad manifestations of such agency at the workplace during the difficult months of the pandemic. In section 4, we further elaborate on the question of emergence of agency through domestic work and its implications for intra-household negotiations during the pandemic, focusing on three detailed case studies. Section 5 concludes.

2. Hardships due to the pandemic

In a global context, India witnessed one of the most stringent national lockdowns spread over the months of March–May 2020 (Vyas 2020). This was followed by continuing lockdown-like conditions for several more months in 2020, from June 2020 onwards (Chakravarty and Nayak 2022: Table A1). Later, state and local-level lockdowns and curfews were imposed again during the exceptionally devastating second wave of the pandemic from April to July 2021. Curfews and various restrictions were also imposed from December 2021 to January 2022, as a public health measure to manage the pandemic. The lockdowns themselves were poorly planned and reflected ignorance of the living conditions of the working poor, where there is typically little or nothing to fall back on by way of social protection and where regular access to a livelihood is crucial. While the stringency and the period of lockdowns and curfews varied between states to some extent, the overall effect of these measures for the economy was devastating. The lockdowns also had a significant human cost. A 'migrant crisis', primarily of informal-sector workers walking from urban to rural areas, started immediately after the first lockdown was announced in March 2020 (Stranded Workers Action Network 2020). On the basis of the Centre for Monitoring Indian Economy's Consumer Pyramids Household Survey (CPHS) data, Vyas (2020) showed that the unemployment rate in India during April–May 2020 was more than 23 per cent, which is three times higher than what had been experienced in 2019. The brunt was mainly borne by workers who are informally employed without any employment security (also see Chen et al. 2021). The crisis continued well after the national lockdown was eased in early June 2020 because of the drastic decline in the purchasing power of a large section of people, with continued restrictions in several areas (Drèze and Somanchi 2021).

Drèze and Somanchi (2021) highlight that different public services that help sustain the poor got disrupted badly as a result of the lockdowns. These included nutrition-related services, such as midday meals. They argue that the relief measures that were extended by the government could only partially handle hunger-related deprivation. The Hunger Watch Surveys conducted by the Right to Food campaign in October–November 2020 and in December 2021–January 2022 also document in detail the hunger experienced by vulnerable populations as a direct consequence of the pandemic (Raghunathan et al. 2022; Sinha 2022). The situation got even worse during the second wave of the pandemic, beginning in late March 2021, and the consequent near complete lockdown in several parts of the country. Official statistics and macroeconomic aggregates do not shed much light on the livelihood crisis caused by the pandemic, although the adverse implications of the pandemic on specific categories of workers, including domestic workers in the Indian context, has been documented (for instance, see Banerjee 2021; Bhan et al. 2021). It is worth noting that, in Delhi, while specific categories of workers, such as transport workers and construction workers, were provided some cash transfers by the government for COVID-19 relief, no such payments were made available for domestic workers.

In 2020, when the pandemic first struck, there was some recovery in the economy from June 2020 onwards, when the lockdown was gradually relaxed, but hardship persisted well beyond that. The recurring crises of early and late 2021 added to the distress already suffered. Drèze and Somanchi (2021: 9) also point out that relief measures helped, but they were patchy and their effective reach was uncertain. On the basis of carefully collected and scrutinized data, mainly from media reports, Aman et al. (2021) conclude that there is a gross denial by the Indian state that a large number of people died as a result of lockdown-induced distress and losses in income leading to acute hunger.

In sections 3 and 4, we document and analyse our interactions with some women domestic workers who often had to negotiate with these hardships of the pandemic, which influenced their intra-household dynamics in different ways.

3. The pandemic, women domestic workers, and their source of agency

In our study, we have concentrated on adult, settled, city-dwelling domestic workers living with their families because we are trying to understand the consequences of the pandemic for poor women in the context of their households. As mentioned, we conducted detailed interviews with 31 women using semi-structured questionnaires.[2] In most of the cases, these women are migrants and live in rented, one-room accommodation. Most of these families used to be landless labourers, share-croppers, or marginal farmers before migration. Increasing family size and the lack of a viable agrarian or non-agrarian income from rural areas causing a lack of work in the villages pushed them to the city. When they came to the city, they often had limited or no assets and very little to fall back on in their native places.

The majority of the domestic workers we talked with were married before 18 years of age and had not worked for pay before marriage. But often they were party, together with their husbands, to the decision of moving to the city. They knew that both of them would have to work for a living. They also knew that domestic work would be the most viable avenue of employment for poor,

---

[2] All interviews for this study were conducted in Hindi or Bangla and have been translated here into English by the authors.

migrant women in the city. Some of our respondents mentioned that, even before migrating, they had an idea about the nature of work and wages for different kinds of domestic services from the women who had migrated earlier from their villages. In fact, some of them took an important role in the decision-making process of migration to the city on the basis that domestic work would be readily available through their own networks. This finding is supported by a larger primary survey conducted several years ago (Neetha, 2004). According to Neetha (2004: 1,684), 'domestic work for women is found to be the immediate resort for family survival, after migration. Availability of employment for women was found not only central to the family's decision to migrate but also gave women a considerable role in the decisions.' During our survey, we found a whole slum where the majority of residents are from the same village in northern West Bengal. Women from this squatter settlement work as domestic workers in the nearby apartment complexes. These women not only facilitate their family and friends to move to the city but also see to it that the women among them get enough jobs to survive through their own networks with employers.

Husbands of our respondents, on the contrary, often had some paid work experience, mainly in the fields or in some petty trade and manufacturing, before migration. In the case of most of our respondents, their husbands do not possess any particular skill that could have enabled them to get a somewhat better job in the city to improve their fall-back positions. We found that, in most cases, husbands and wives both had minimal formal education. The husbands of our respondents typically worked as waste pickers, vegetable or fruit vendors, shop attendants, watchmen, delivery staff, and security guards. Their earnings were sometimes less than what our respondent domestic worker women earned before the COVID-19 pandemic struck. Only a few of the husbands were found to be working in relatively more skilled jobs such as drivers, plumbers, or electricians. Their incomes were, in some cases, substantial but often uncertain unless they worked under a contract with a household or an organization.

We found that even if the husbands earned substantially, in most cases, their personal expenditures were significant. A little over one-third of our respondents reported that their husbands spend a significant amount of money on alcohol. Particularly, these respondents reported domestic violence of varying degrees. Their husbands often failed to contribute to the household budget substantially, and this led our respondent female domestic workers to emerge as breadwinners of their families. In other cases, sheer poverty led to our respondents seeking paid work. A majority of our respondents view the husband as the head of the family, but in reality, they had developed distinct traces of agency through working and earning, and they took most of their crucial decisions themselves.

Demand for domestic service (particularly for part-time, live-out domestic workers who we were interviewing) was severely affected during the lockdown, as pointed out by all our respondents. This trend is also borne out in a Women in

Informal Employment: Globalizing and Organizing (WIEGO) study of informal economy workers in 11 cities (see Chen et al., Chapter 1 in this volume). Given the nature of domestic service, almost all employers asked our respondents not to come for work once the lockdown was announced. Hardly any of the employers gave them full salaries during the two months of the lockdown in 2020, irrespective of the employer's job status and earnings. A similar finding has been reported by Banerjee (2021) on the basis of a much larger sample.

Employers did start calling domestic workers back for work after the first lockdown was partially lifted in June 2020 as this is considered an 'essential' service, especially for middle-class working women and for households of persons in need of care. On the basis of large-scale macrodata, research suggests a close relationship between the increased participation in paid employment of relatively affluent city women and increasing demand for domestic help (Chakravarty and Chakravarty 2008). The 'essential' nature of domestic service in the urban Indian context also becomes obvious from our informal discussions with resident welfare associations (RWAs) of large apartment complexes in Southwest Delhi, as discussed below. By late 2020, most of our respondents had got back some work, whereas most of their husbands were still looking for some stability in income.

However, several of our respondents reported that employers were now offering less money as they wanted them to work for fewer hours to do only some tasks. Such evidence is also prevalent in many large-scale surveys of domestic workers (e.g. Bhan et al. 2021). Some respondents reported active efforts by employer households to squeeze them by paying less money than earlier for a larger number of tasks, which were often surreptitiously added to their work.

Some respondent workers reported being harassed by RWAs as they were repeatedly stopped at the gates of residential complexes by security guards employed by RWAs. However, it seems that RWAs started getting calls from some residents to allow their domestic workers to enter residential areas during the lockdown periods. These residents were extremely worried as they were completely dependent on different kinds of personal services performed by domestic workers. From our discussions, we also noticed an increase in the incidence of engaging full-time, live-in workers, who would stay with their employer's family. One of our respondents, in fact, was offered such work but refused to give up her part-time status since this would mean losing her personal freedom.

Other anecdotal evidence suggests that a notable number of middle-class employers living in different housing societies in Delhi accompanied their domestic workers to paid vaccination centres for inoculation.[3] In many cases, where the housing societies conducted vaccination camps in their premises from the middle

---

[3] Reference is being made here to the period before July 2021 when free vaccinations at government centres were not commonly available. The government had deployed a policy of encouraging paid vaccinations, the prices of which were not regulated until June 2021 (The Hindu 2021).

of June 2021, this included domestic workers, often assisted by their employers. In the context of a discussion about who pays the charges for vaccination when the inoculation takes place in the camps organized by the RWAs, one respondent replied,

> Why should I pay from my pocket? True, I need the jobs but it's also true that my employers need my services as well. One Didi[4] used to keep calling me often and she arranged for a gate pass for me. When other employers saw me coming to one house, they all started calling me and took the initiative to get the clearance from the RWA. I hardly earned anything for the last few months. I have no money to pay for the vaccine.

Let us remember that the burden of household work falls disproportionately on women across the classes (Deshpande and Kabeer 2019). It has been pointed out that during the pandemic the burden of household work on women increased significantly. Initially, it was shared by men to some extent, but data show that this help from men tapered off with time (Deshpande 2020). In some cases, our respondents mentioned that they did not go back to the households that employed them before the lockdown, despite being called back by them, because they were not paid anything at all during the lock down. Despite their vulnerability, these respondent workers were in a position to exercise agency and reject work in cases where they felt they had not been fairly treated during the lockdown period. They were confident of getting alternative jobs with some effort and time.

Another instance where domestic workers were seen as having a strong foothold in work can be seen in the following example related to care work for older persons. Rekha has been working as a carer in a household of an elderly couple. She has been looking after a man who is unable to walk. While she lost jobs in all other households during consecutive lockdowns in 2020 and 2021, in this household, the employers simply could not manage without her services, and she kept working through the lockdowns. Demand for care work for older adults, a relatively more skilled job within domestic work, is increasing in the cities with the increase in average life expectancy of the better-off classes. This demand is high, especially in nuclear families, where older adults live by themselves or where younger women from the household are engaged in paid work outside the home, where traditionally they have been expected to stay home and care for older persons in the family. We argue that these particular features of domestic work, on the one hand, and the fact that this work is almost completely feminized (relatively few men are found in this segment of work), on the other, have helped strengthen the fall-back position of women domestic workers significantly. This, in turn, strengthened their ability to exercise personal agency.

---

[4] This is a colloquial Bangla and Hindi term used in Delhi for a woman employer.

We argue, therefore, that the relative strengthening of women's fall-back position and emerging agency of women domestic workers in the household decision-making processes is the result of two factors. First, the husband does not have any fall-back position except his often precarious informal job and has substantial personal expenses. The precarity of informal jobs has been on the rise ever since demonetization in India in 2016, followed by the introduction of the goods and services tax (GST) in 2017 (Sinha 2022). Informal jobs, such as street vending and daily-wage work, were especially severely affected. Let us remember that a large number of men are engaged in these informal occupations disproportionately. Interestingly, these policies of demonetization and the introduction of GST are unlikely to have had any effect on domestic service. A crucial second factor strengthening women's fall-back position is their engagement in domestic service, a livelihood option that has emerged as one of the most important occupations for poor women in the urban areas of India, especially in Delhi. Although this livelihood option suffers equally from the precarity of other informal work, it has specific features that have made it distinctively different, as discussed above. (We will discuss these features of paid domestic service again in section 4.) These women workers cannot be considered as passive agents in any way, even though they may not be in a position to bargain at the workplace explicitly on a regular basis, as often they are not unionized as such. But when time is opportune, they do exercise their agency and bargaining power at the workplace as well.

In section 4, we will document how this strengthening of fall-back position and achievement of agency by our respondents has influenced intrafamily outcomes due to pandemic-induced economic hardships, including significant loss of income in many instances. To present a nuanced understanding, we have divided our respondents' families into three categories on the basis of the family's status before the lockdowns began: Category 1: husband having a regular income, more than that of the wife; Category 2: husband having a regular income but significantly less than that of the wife; and Category 3: husband with irregular earnings and irregular contributions to the household budget. The reason behind such a classification is to highlight the significance of women's involvement in paid domestic service in achieving an independent fall-back position and also agency that turned out to be crucial in the context of the recent pandemic, irrespective of their husband's status of earning before the pandemic. As 'agency' is a highly complex concept, we have not attempted to compare the strength of agency in different cases. Rather, we have only tried to trace agency, personal perceptions of work, and intra-household dynamics in its different forms through the life stories of three women workers. We present one case study each from Categories 1, 2, and 3.[5]

---

[5] All names in case studies have been changed.

4. Intra-household bargaining and the pandemic: Life stories of three women

4.1 Category 1

Ameena

Ameena, a 24-year-old Muslim woman, belongs to the first category of households in our classification. She migrated six years ago, with her husband, from the Cooch Behar district of West Bengal. Back in the village, both she and her husband used to work in their family fields. The family has about five acres of land, and the household was just able to manage two square meals a day. The couple left for Delhi as they had some relatives in the city who assured help in settling down. Upon reaching Delhi, both Ameena and her husband started searching for work. She could have joined rag picking or construction work. Earning in rag picking is uncertain. Moreover, rag picking is dominated by men; women work as helpers. Working in the construction sector does not ensure a fixed or regular income either. Also, when there is work, one has to work for the whole day. Ameena had two very young children at the time they migrated. Part-time domestic service, with its assured pay structure, thus turned out to be the best option. In 5hours a day, she could earn more than half of what her husband did in 12 hours as a delivery staff in a large department store. Over the years, Ameena started working in more households, and before the lockdown of 2020, she was earning about 11,000 rupees per month from four households, whereas her husband was earning about 13,000 rupees.

As their children grew older, Ameena decided it would be best for the children to live with their maternal grandparents as she thought their education and well-being would be better taken care of in the village. Ameena had to send 4,000 rupees per month to her parents for looking after the children. Ameena's husband was not very keen about this arrangement as he felt the expenditure was excessive. But Ameena argued and started working for longer hours in one household and picked up work in a new household to earn more money and convinced her husband. Back in her natal village, their son goes to a government school, but their daughter goes to a madrassa (an educational institution run by a mosque). When asked why she has decided to put her daughter in a madrassa, Ameena said that she wanted her daughter to learn Urdu so that she can read and explain the Qur'an Shareef in the mosque to illiterate women in return for some remuneration. She said she has seen a woman earning in this manner in the locality where she lives in Delhi.

It was clear that even though Ameena was not the main breadwinner of the family, she had assumed a crucial role in the decision-making process of the household. In this particular case, Ameena's ability to play an important role here is not only because she earns a stable income—almost as much as her husband—but also because her natal family gives her significant support. Her unmarried brother, who works in Delhi, lives with them and contributes substantially to household expenditure.[6] Ameena also mentions that her husband shouts at her often but never physically abuses her because of the presence of her brother and the brother's contribution to the family's budget.

In normal times, Ameena is able to save 4,000–5,000 rupees per month as the household expenditure is shared by the three of them and they do not have to pay house rent because there is a court case going on between the owner of the *jhuggi* (squatter settlement) and the residents. She keeps this money in her brother's account and has managed to buy a small plot of land back in her natal village, which she jointly owns with her husband. Ameena's father looks after this land in their absence. Ameena feels that all this has been possible because of a more or less regular and stable income that she earns from domestic service.

During the lockdown of 2020, Ameena lost all her jobs. One household paid Ameena her full salary and another paid her half her salary, and altogether she was earning around 3,000 rupees. Her husband was able to earn around 4,000 rupees only, that too for just one month. Ameena's brother continued to earn his full salary and assumed major responsibility of running the household. Ameena managed to send about 2,000 rupees to her children and could not save anything during this period. Because all of them were earning, they did not have to rely on cooked food supplied by individuals and organizations in their locality. After the lockdown, Ameena was called back by three (of the four) households where she had worked earlier. But two of these households offered a reduced salary. On top of this, it took quite some time for her to get one more job as the fourth household did not call her back. At the time of the survey, Ameena was earning only 9,000 rupees from four households. Her husband's salary also did not return to the pre-pandemic level as the department store was not getting enough customers and online purchases increased dramatically during the pandemic: he was now paid 8,000 rupees only.

The picture changed significantly during April 2021, with restrictions imposed for the devastating second wave of the pandemic. Ameena's husband was not called for work and did not have any income for more than two months. However, Ameena managed to earn 4,000 rupees from two households where she was working. They had a very difficult time during the second wave and had to spend some of their savings, although her brother continued to support the household. Ameena was called back soon after the second-wave restrictions were eased in early June 2021 as employer households started negotiating with the RWAs, as mentioned earlier, but her husband was not called back, even in August 2021. In fact, he was thinking of going back to the village to work on their land and wanted Ameena to accompany him. But Ameena decided that, as long as she had the jobs,

---

[6] Agarwal (1997) discusses the crucial role of natal family support in strengthening the fall-back position of women.

she would stay in Delhi, alone if necessary. She feels that the land they have is not enough for all four of them. Ameena's husband even threatened to give her *talaq* (divorce) if she did not move back with him. When asked what her reaction to this threat was, Ameena responded,

> My husband cannot divorce me as the land we have is in joint title and my parents and brothers will make sure that he cannot do any mischief in this regard. I am sure the situation in Delhi will change soon, at least for domestic servants as my employers got in touch with me themselves after the second lockdown. This wasn't the case after the first lockdown (in 2020). I have already got four households to work again. My neighbours in my *jhuggi* are getting back their jobs as well. [. . .] In some cases the domestic workers are asked to stay with their employers as full-time employees. But we all have families and nobody (in my neighbourhood) agreed to this demand of the employers yet. If my husband goes away to the village, I will take up a 24-hour job and will earn much more than I do right now.

From Ameena's account, two things become clear. First, she has already acquired confidence and a position of authority in her family through her paid employment, so much so that she simply did not care whether her husband took care of her. Yet, she cares for her husband and family. The strength of her fall-back position mainly increases from the nature of her informal job in the city, the asset she jointly owns in her natal village, and from natal family support. Second, the strength of Ameena's husband's fall-back position decreases because of his loss of an informal but regular job and because he does not have single ownership of the land in the village. Family dissolution in such situations is unlikely because women, owing to strong cultural reasons, will try their best to keep the family intact unless circumstances are unbearable for them. Also, as the relative strength of men's fall-back position is declining with respect to women's fall-back position, men will not gain by abandoning their wives. It is interesting to note that both Ameena's perception about her own contribution towards the family and the importance of her paid work for the well-being of the family, as well as to a certain extent for herself, especially in the context of the pandemic, become quite explicit here.

4.2   Category 2

Deeksha

Deeksha, a 29-year-old Hindu woman from a slum in southwest Delhi, worked mainly as a cook before the 2020 lockdown. A migrant from the Sundarbans, West Bengal, Deeksha was sent by her uncle to Delhi when she was only nine years old, to work as a full-time domestic worker in the home of a Punjabi family. Her parents died when she was very young. She had no education and worked for this family for ten years until her uncle got her married to a man from eastern Uttar Pradesh who was more than twice her age.[7] This was Deeksha's husband's second marriage. He had a son from his first marriage who was nine years old when he married Deeksha. After the marriage, they stayed in the village where Deeksha's in-laws had some land. The father-in-law and all six of his sons used to work in the fields. Women were not allowed to work outside the home. After her father-in-law died, the land was divided between the sons, and Deeksha and her husband moved to Delhi as it was difficult to manage in the village because of the paltry amount of land that they got. In fact, Deeksha convinced her husband to move to Delhi as she knew, from her earlier experience of the city, that she would easily get jobs as a maid. With the help of a relative, Deeksha's husband managed to find a job as a security guard and the family moved to Delhi. Soon after, Deeksha managed to get a job at the residence of a professor's family who lived inside a university campus. During this time, Deeksha got in touch with a non-governmental organization (NGO) that helped her to start studying and achieve basic literacy, but she could not continue her studies after the birth of her first child. Deeksha's husband had reservations about her association with the NGO and her decision to continue her studies. He had been drinking and abusing her on a regular basis all these years. He was also extremely suspicious and jealous of Deeksha as she was much younger than him and a very friendly and capable woman, liked by all.

As her children grew older, Deeksha started working in more households. Seeing her ability to manage things, the NGO offered Deeksha some work in a creche run by them. In the meantime, Deeksha was introduced to a local church and started going there quite often. She also started doing cleaning work for this church to earn more money. Before the 2020 lockdown, Deeksha used to earn about 26,000 rupees per month: 15,000 from domestic work and another 11,000 from the church and the NGO. Her husband used to earn 12,000 rupees per month. Though Deeksha never revealed to her husband her income from the church and the NGO, he could guess that she was earning well. In revenge, he started to contribute only 5,000 rupees towards the house rent. Even after taking care of all other expenditures, Deeksha managed to save substantially. She opened three bank accounts: two in the names of her two children and one in her own name. Her husband managed to get hold of Deeksha's bank account details and often withdrew money from it. So, Deeksha started keeping only small amounts in this account and shifted her main savings to the accounts of her children. She also started keeping some money for emergencies with one of her employers. In addition, Deeksha joined a women's committee, an informal self-help group for saving money, quite popular among poor, slum-dwelling women in Delhi. She developed a very good network

---

[7] It is quite possible that the uncle sold Deeksha to this older widowed man. For a discussion on related cases, see Chakravarty and Chakravarty (2015) and Roy (2008).

among her neighbours, most of whom were also domestic workers and committee members and most of whose husbands also have irregular incomes, are abusive, and have drinking habits. The women have developed a bond among themselves, helping each other out in times of need. This networking was of great help during the pandemic recession.

During the first lockdown in 2020, Deeksha lost all her jobs in the university campus, and not a single employer paid Deeksha her salary for the months of April and May. Her husband also lost his job. Deeksha continued working with the NGO, and they offered her a full salary. There was extra work in the NGO from pandemic-related relief work and Deeksha volunteered as a relief worker. The church paid Deeksha half her salary and gave her a substantial amount of dry food rations. One of her employers also gave her about 15 days' dry rations. Deeksha's family has a ration card as well.[8] So, altogether, she could manage without touching her savings. In fact, her family received excess dry rations, so Deeksha distributed the surplus among her needy neighbours. Since her husband was at home all day, he soon found out about Deeksha's involvement with the NGO and the church and opposed it vehemently. Deeksha said, 'my husband was not earning anything during the three months of lockdown. But he must be having some savings as he was getting his drinks quite regularly and used to enjoy with his friends. He did not contribute a paisa for household expenditure during this time.'

After the 2020 lockdown, initially, Deeksha could not get back any of her previous domestic jobs. Later, she managed to get some work, but her income from domestic services was half of what she earned before the pandemic. Her husband, with some effort, got his job back after three months. Deeksha informed us that most domestic workers have got back some jobs after the lockdown, and the situation is improving slowly. She sounded quite confident that her job situation would improve in the near future.

During the lockdown-like situation in early 2021, Deeksha's husband lost his job again, but she was able to retain most of her jobs, except for one case, where the university student who employed her as a cook returned home after completing her studies. Deeksha found it difficult to make ends meet during the second wave in early 2021 as her supplementary income from the church and the NGO also decreased significantly. She had to spend money from her savings. By August 2021, she had taken the first dose of the COVID-19 vaccine and hoped to get back a sufficient number of jobs after the second dose. Deeksha's husband was still jobless, and he started threatening her that he would go back to his extended family with their children. Deeksha said she did not really care about her husband leaving her alone in Delhi as she had a fairly good network and she would easily manage on her own, especially when there was every hope that the job market would revive soon.

---

[8] As a central government relief measure, rations for existing PDS card holders were doubled and were provided free of cost at this point.

However, she would never let him take their children. Deeksha was confident that if he tried to take their children with him, her neighbours and friends, including other domestic workers she knew, would stand with her in solidarity.

In this case, we see the possibility of a family breaking down in the context of the pandemic. But this is not a case of a woman being abandoned in the sense noted by Mahalanobis (1946) and discussed by Greenough (1980) in the context of the Bengal Famine of 1943. Agarwal (2008) conceives this issue of family dissolution during the Bengal Famine of 1943 as one pertaining to cooperative conflicts in the household, where women have limited or no capacity to exercise their agency due to lack of control over material resources. However, Deeksha has achieved a certain kind of agency from her experience and labour, and she is in no way dependent on her husband's support.

4.3 Category 3

Marjina

Marjina Bivi is a 40-year-old Muslim woman who used to live in a village in Lower Assam before migrating to Delhi. Married at 12 years of age, Marjina had to work as an agricultural labourer in the village in Assam as her marital family had a very small plot of land not sufficient for subsistence. She studied until the eighth standard and had her first child at the age of 14 years. Her husband, who used to be a labourer as well, was never very responsible towards the family. He went away to Delhi alone, leaving the family behind and came back only after three years. Marjina was working in the fields and raising their two children with little support from her in-laws. It was difficult to get regular wage work in the village because there were hardly any large-hold farmers who would hire wage labour throughout the year. Wage rates were also quite low. Marjina heard about the possibility of getting jobs as a domestic worker in Delhi, where a friend of hers had moved with her family. When her husband finally came home, Marjina insisted that he should take the family with him to the city. Marjina moved to Delhi 15 years ago. They initially lived with a friend and then got a shelter in the *masjid* (mosque) in a slum in Southwest Delhi, where they later got a small place to live. Marjina's husband started working as a waste collector in the nearby apartments. Initially, the husband fed the family, but Marjina soon started to search for work with the help of the neighbours in the *jhuggi*. Her children were grown up, to some extent, and Marjina managed to work in five households. Just before the 2020 lockdown, she was earning about 15,000 rupees per month. Soon after Marjina started working, her husband lost his job because he was very irregular. Afterwards, he tried to sell vegetables and fruit for some time. But nothing worked for him as [Marjina told us] he 'has bad habits: he goes to a woman and spends whatever he earns on her'; he also spends on alcohol. Marjina tried to counsel him with the help of the Imam of the *masjid*, because everyone in the slum listens to him. But nothing worked for Marjina's husband. He used to shout at her and beat her quite often. Domestic violence, however, became less frequent as the children grew older and became an important source of support for Marjina.

Because her husband never contributed regularly to the family budget, Marjina's role became crucial and she assumed the role of the breadwinner in the family. She educated her children to the extent possible and got her daughter married to a *thelawala* (mobile vendor of different goods), who earns regularly and looks after her daughter. With great satisfaction, Marjina mentioned that her son-in-law does not allow her daughter to work outside the home. However, Marjina still regards her husband as the head of the family, despite taking all major decisions on her own, often going against her husband's will. Marjina started saving as much as she could after she started working and was able to hide these savings from her drunken and abusive husband.

In this case, again, we see that the woman of the household cannot be considered dependent in any way, even before she moved to the city. Marjina's role in the family is not just important but pivotal. She is well aware of this fact. She repeatedly mentioned that forcing her husband to move to the city was the right decision. They would have starved if they had stayed back in the village. (Marjina's exact expression in Bangla was '*khiderchotemoreijitaam*'—'we would have died of hunger'.)

Marjina lost all her jobs during the first lockdown in March 2020. None of her employers paid her, except in March. During April and May 2020, nobody in her family had any income. They were primarily managing with the dry ration provided by the government and the cooked food offered by a rich man. Marjina managed not to touch her savings so long as dole was available.

After the first lockdown, only three of five employer households re-employed Marjina. And in her post-lockdown terms of contract, both her workload and hours of work, as well as her salary, were reduced. She managed to earn only 4,000 rupees a month. As neither her husband nor son were able to get their jobs back, Marjina suggested they start a small eatery on a portable van, selling onion and potato *pakorey* (deep-fried snacks). She invested almost all her savings to set up this business. The family somehow survived on this business from mid-2020 to mid-2021. As her husband does not have any independent income, he stays home most of the time. Marjina had to be vigilant that her husband did not abscond with any money to spend on drinks and other habits. They fought over this almost every day, but Marjina somehow ensured that no money was wasted. During the second wave of the pandemic in April–May 2021, the situation became even worse. Marjina lost all her jobs once again. They survived on the little income from their eatery and the meagre savings that Marjina still had. But even before the second-wave curfew was called off, Marjina started getting calls from her employers. As mentioned earlier, the employers started negotiating with the RWAs to let Marjina and other domestic maids enter the premises. Marjina started getting back her jobs slowly, but she was worried about her small business because, in her absence, things could go wrong very easily.

Marjina and her husband had no assets when they came to the city. Apart from some social and religious networks, they did not have anything or anyone else to fallback on. But the relative stability of income from domestic service and Marjina's own effort to save as much as possible over the years helped her develop a stronger fall-back position, not only for herself but also for the family. This significantly influenced the family's ability to cope with the food insecurity and uncertainty of the pandemic recession. However, even though Marjina achieved a significant level of agency through her work, she was still highly influenced by the *perception* that she needs to keep the family together. In this case, Marjina is actually in a position to abandon her husband, but she will never do that as the family is extremely important to her. If she could step away from these social perceptions, she could enjoy a much higher level of well-being, more so in the context of the pandemic.

In each of the above-mentioned cases, the women domestic workers appreciate the significance of their more or less secure independent income from paid domestic service, irrespective of their husbands' income status. The significance of domestic service in strengthening fall-back positions and also agency roles of these women turned out to be even more crucial in the context of the pandemic. Taking a cue from Sen's idea of cooperative conflicts, Agarwal (2008) explained the phenomenon of large-scale abandonment of women and children leading to family dissolution during the Bengal Famine of 1943 as an outcome of women's very weak or absent fall-back positions in the wake of the famine compared with men. Our findings during another calamity, induced by the recent COVID-19 pandemic in the context of poor urban families of women domestic workers, offer a sharp contrast. In all the three case studies discussed above, women have achieved an independent fall-back position, not only for themselves but also often for the family as a whole, because of their engagement in paid domestic service. This is juxtaposed with husbands who have faced a decline in their fall-back positions for different reasons induced by the pandemic. Consequently, intra-household outcomes of the pandemic turn out to be significantly different from those of the Bengal Famine of 1943.

5. Conclusion

Domestic workers, including those whose case studies are described in this chapter, come from circumstances of meagre personal resources. Among our respondents, bar none, land assets in the village were too limited to serve as a viable source of livelihood. It was marriage or difficult economic circumstances that led them to move to the city and, later, to take on domestic work, a commonly resorted to type of work for women in urban areas in India, especially after the 1990s liberalized macroeconomic regime.

Domestic work provides a relatively stable income compared with the other precarious jobs in the informal economy. At the very least, our respondents suggested they were optimistic about getting back work, even in cases where work had been lost due to the pandemic. In the case of most of the women we interacted with, domestic service was a significant contributor in the family budget before the lockdown of 2020. There is sufficient data to show that these women not only do not depend on their husbands but also often take the principal responsibility of providing food and shelter for the family. In some cases, these domestic worker women could also manage to save substantially from their regular incomes. During the lockdown, these women too lost jobs and income, like their husbands. But given the specific nature of demand for domestic service, in most of the cases, our respondents not only got back a substantial number of jobs immediately after the lockdowns or curfews ended but also were hopeful that they would reach previous levels of income in the coming months. As such, even though the nature of domestic work may be seen as 'reflective of', 'traditional within household divisions' (Sen 1987: 14), we suggest that these workers do, indeed, explicitly see their work as separate from their personal domestic care work and as significant in contributing in some measure to their economic security.

When reflecting on intra-household dynamics, particularly in the context of the pandemic, we observe the following. The agency these slum-dwelling women have acquired through domestic service, along with the husbands' fall-back positions often being even less secure than their own, has led them to exercise significant decision-making power, allowing them to challenge their context and thereby the outcome of unemployment that they experienced. A crucial aspect of the pandemic-induced unemployment for these domestic workers has been that the duration of their unemployment has tended to be shorter than that for several categories of work in which their husbands are engaged. As discussed, this is due to the nature of domestic work itself. However, socially ingrained perceptions about their well-being related to keeping the family together, and the relatively indifferent importance they attribute to their contributions towards their family, do often keep working explicitly or implicitly to determine the ultimate outcome of interpersonal dynamics at the household level. This has significant implications for a processual understanding of empowerment.

None of the above is stated, however, to deny the backdrop of virtually permanent precarity that domestic workers negotiate. It is also the case that as a category of workers, despite being large in number, domestic workers have been overlooked by governments for pandemic relief cash transfers of the kind offered to construction workers in several states in India and to transport workers in Delhi. The non-payment of these cash transfers to domestic workers highlights the wilful invisibilization of these workers by the state. A key excuse for non-payment has been that a reliable, state-recognized record of domestic workers did not exist in 2020. But this was hardly a tenable justification. The central or state governments need only to have demonstrated some political will and commitment to using the provisions of the Unorganised Workers Social Security Act, 2008 after it was passed, rather than waiting for a calamity to strike. The new e-Shram portal of the Ministry of Labour and Employment (Government of India 2021) attempts to address this lacuna, but the nature of cash transfers that may be initiated via this database remains to be seen. Both the central and state governments also performed poorly on other elementary forms of social protection, such as food transfers, particularly to those who did not already hold public distribution system (PDS) ration cards under the National Food Security Act, 2013 (Nayak 2022). Some food rations were provided to non-PDS card holders but in a manner that can at best be described as miserly. Administrative mechanisms should have been found to make more generous free food rations available to domestic workers who did not already have a ration card before 2020.

It should also be noted that domestic workers as a category are workers in whom the state invests absolutely nothing. No training or infrastructure is demanded by this category of workers. They are self-trained and self-sufficient. Yet, this category of workers is treated poorly. The new Labour Code initiated by the Government of India also offers them little recognition and no specific protections. At present, then, their fall-back positions are strengthened by dint of their own agency alone.

References

Agarwal, B. (1997). '"Bargaining" and Gender Relations: Within and Beyond the Household', *Feminist Economics*, 3(1): 1–51. https://doi.org/10.1080/135457097338799.

Agarwal, B. (2008). 'Engaging with Sen on Gender Relations: Cooperative-Conflicts, False Perceptions and Relative Capabilities'. In R.Kanbur and K.Basu (eds), *Essays in Honor of Amartya Sen*. Oxford: Oxford University Press, pp. 157–77. https://doi.org/10.1093/acprof:oso/9780199239979.003.0010.

Agarwal, B. (2021). 'Livelihoods in COVID Times: Gendered Perils and New Pathways in India', *World Development*, 139: Article105312. https://doi.org/10.1016/j.worlddev.2020.105312.

Alon, T., M.Doepke, J.Olmstead-Rumsey, and M.Tertilt (2020). 'The Impact of COVID-19 on Gender Equality', National Bureau of Economic Research (NBER) Working Paper No. w26947, Cambridge, MA: NBER. https://doi.org/10.3386/w26947.

Aman, G., N. Thejesh, K.Ranaware, and K.Sharma (2021). 'Deaths due to India's COVID-19 National Lockdown: Of Denial and Data', *Economic and Political Weekly*, 56(23), available at: www.epw.in/journal/2021/23/insight/denial-and-data.html.

Banerjee, M. (2021). 'Emerging from the Lockdown: Insights from Women Domestic Workers' Lives in Delhi', New Delhi: Institute of Social Studies Trust, available at: https://papers.ssrn.com/sol3/papers.cfm?abstract_id=3971572.

Becker, G.S. (1981). *A Treatise on the Family*. Cambridge: Cambridge University Press.

Bhan, G., A.Rai Chowdhury, and R.Mehra (2021). 'State of Occupational Safety and Health Practices at Workplace for Domestic Workers in COVID-19 and Possibilities for Action', International Labour Organization (ILO) Report (July), available at: www.ilo.org/wcmsp5/groups/public/—asia/—ro-bangkok/—sro-new_delhi/documents/publication/wcms_813644.pdf (accessed July 2022).

Chakravarty, D., and I.Chakravarty (2008). 'Girl Children in the Care Economy: Domestics in West Bengal', *Economic and Political Weekly*, 43(48): 93–100, available at: www.epw.in/journal/2008/48/special-articles/girl-children-care-economy-domestics-west-bengal.html (accessed July 2022).

Chakravarty, D., and I.Chakravarty (2015). *Women, Labour and the Economy in India: From Migrant Menservants to Uprooted Girl Children Maids*. London and New York: Routledge. https://doi.org/10.4324/9781315668994.

Chakravarty, D., and N.Nayak (2022). 'The COVID-19 Pandemic and Poor Women's Agency', United Nations University-World Institute for Development Economics Research (UNU-WIDER) Working Paper No.109/2022, Helsinki: UNU-WIDER.

Chen, M.A., and G.Raveendran (2014). 'Urban Employment in India: Recent Trends and Patterns', WIEGO Working Paper No. 7, Manchester: WIEGO (January), available at: www.wiego.org/publications/urban-employment-india-recent-trends-and-patterns (accessed July 2022).

Chen, M.A., E.Grapsa, G.Ismail, S.Orleans Reed, M.Rogan, and M.Valdivia (2021). 'COVID-19 and Informal Work: Distinct Pathways of Impact and Recovery in 11 Cities around the World', Women in Informal Employment: Globalizing and Organizing (WIEGO) Working Paper No. 42, Manchester: WIEGO (May), available at https://www.wiego.org/publications/covid-19-and-informal-work-distinct-pathways-impact-and-recovery-11-cities-around (accessed July 2022).

Deshpande, A. (2020). 'Early Effects of Lockdown in India: Gender Gaps in Job Losses and Domestic Work', *Indian Journal of Labour Economics*, 63(1): 87–90. https://doi.org/10.1007/s41027-020-00261-2.

Deshpande, A., and N.Kabeer (2019). '(In)visibility, Care and Cultural Barriers: The Size and Shape of Women's Work in India'. Discussion Paper Series in Economics No. 04/2019, Haryana, India: Asoka University.

Drèze, J., and A.Somanchi (2021). 'The Covid-19 Crisis and People's Right to Food', SocArXiv. https://doi.org/10.31235/osf.io/ybrmg.

Government of India (2021). 'e-Shram: National Database of Unorganised Workers', Delhi: Ministry of Labour & Employment, available at: https://eshram.gov.in (accessed July 2022).

Greenough, P.R. (1980). 'Indian Famines and Peasant Victims: The Case of Bengal in 1943–44', *Modern Asian Studies*, 14(2): 205–35. https://doi.org/10.1017/S0026749X00007319.

Jain, S. (2016). 'Employment Relations for Female Domestic Workers in the National Capital Region', unpublished MPhil dissertation, Centre for Development Studies, Trivandrum.

Kabeer, N. (1999). 'Resources, Agency, Achievements: Reflections on the Measurement of Women's Empowerment', *Development and Change*, 30(3): 435–64. https://doi.org/10.1111/1467-7660.00125.

Mahalanobis, P.C. (1946). *Bengal Famine: The Background and Basic Facts*. Calcutta: Indian Statistical Institute.

McElroy, M.B. (1990). 'The Empirical Content of Nash-Bargained Household Behavior', *Journal of Human Resources*, 25(4): 559–83. https://doi.org/10.2307/145667.

Nayak, N. (2022). 'Hunger in India Likely to Grow Again', 360info (4 April), available at: https://360info.org/hunger-in-india-likely-to-grow-again (accessed May 2022). https://doi.org/10.54377/595b-043d.

Neetha, N. (2004). 'Making of Female Breadwinners: Migration and Social Networking of Women Domestics in Delhi', *Economic and Political Weekly*, 39(17): 1681–88.

Neetha, N. (2013). 'Paid Domestic Work: Making Sense of the Jigsaw Puzzle', *Economic and Political Weekly*, 48(43): 35–38.

Raghunathan, K. D. Sinha, and R.Narayanan (2022). 'The Worsening Hunger Problem of India's Poor', Indian Express (25 March), available at: https://indianexpress.com/article/opinion/columns/the-worsening-hunger-problem-of-indias-poor-7835064 (accessed July 2022).

Roy, A. (2008). *Kolkata Requiem: Gender and the Politics of Poverty*. India: Pearson Longman.

Sen, A. (1987). 'Gender and Cooperative Conflicts', UNU-WIDER Working Papers (1986–2000) No. 1987/018, Helsinki: UNU WIDER, available at: www.wider.unu.edu/publication/gender-and-cooperative-conflicts (accessed July 2022).

Sen, A. (1990). 'Gender and Cooperative Conflicts'. In I.Tinker (ed.), *'Persistent Inequalities'. Women and World Development*. Oxford: Oxford University Press, pp. 123–48.

Sinha, D. (2022). 'Persistence of Food Insecurity and Malnutrition', The India Forum (9 March), available at: www.theindiaforum.in/article/persistence-food-insecurity-malnutrition (accessed July 2022).

Stranded Workers Action Network (2020). '21 Days and Counting: Covid-19 Lockdown, Migrant Workers, and the Inadequacy of Welfare Measures in India', People's Archive of Rural India (PARI), available at: https://ruralindiaonline.org/en/library/resource/21-days-and-counting-covid-19-lockdown-migrant-workers-and-the-inadequacy-of-welfare-measures-in-india (accessed July 2022).

The Hindu (2021). 'Government Caps Prices of COVID-19 Vaccines at Private Hospitals', *The Hindu* (9 June), available at: www.thehindu.com/news/national/high-cost-of-vaccination-at-private-hospitals-unacceptable-paul/article34763106.ece (accessed July 2022).

Vyas, M. (2020). 'Impact of Lockdown on Labour in India', *Indian Journal of Labour Economics*, 63(Suppl. 1): S73–S77. https://doi.org/10.1007/s41027-020-00259-w.

PART II
RECOVERY

8

The Uneven Path to Recovery

The Sub-Saharan African Experience

Michael Danquah, Amina Ebrahim, and Maureen Were

1. Introduction

The COVID-19 pandemic caused a major disruption to economic activity across the world. In sub–Saharan Africa (SSA), the containment measures, particularly the severe lockdowns, contributed to a significant economic downturn in many countries across the region, with subsequent major impacts on unemployment, poverty, and food insecurity. A global drop in commodity prices and demand from the main trading partners (including China, India, the United States, and several European countries), alongside stringent government response measures, had a devastating impact on the incomes of workers and their dependents. While the longer-term socio-economic impacts of the pandemic remain unclear, the pandemic's impact on the labour market is a major issue of global concern.

In SSA, workplace and market closures, restrictions on mobility, the suspension of some activities, and the associated reduction in demand for goods and services resulted in a slowdown in production and caused a reduction in working hours and labour earnings. In some countries in the region, lockdown measures reduced business activity by more than half (Lakuma and Sunday 2020). This especially affected workers in the large informal sector, which accounts for 80 per cent of all non-agricultural employment in the region (ILO 2018). Real-time survey data collected in Senegal, Mali, and Burkina Faso suggests that, on average, by the end of April 2020, one out of four workers had lost their jobs and one out of two workers had experienced a decline in earnings. These findings furthermore indicate that informal workers were at higher risk as they generally rely on daily sales for their earnings, lack mechanisms for collective bargaining, and tend to be in activities that are contact-intensive and, thus, were most affected—particularly livelihood sources such as restaurants, tourism, small retail shops, hairdressers, and taxi drivers (Balde et al. 2020).

The policy measures taken to combat the adverse economic effects of the pandemic and respond to the economic crisis by SSA governments included a combination of measures to stabilize the economy via support to businesses and households (tax breaks, lowering of bank rates, loans to micro, small, and

Michael Danquah, Amina Ebrahim, and Maureen Were, *The Uneven Path to Recovery*. In: *COVID-19 and the Informal Economy*. Edited by: Martha Alter Chen, Michael Rogan, and Kunal Sen, Oxford University Press. © Michael Danquah, Amina Ebrahim, and Maureen Were (2024). DOI: 10.1093/oso/9780198887041.003.0009 medium enterprises, MSMEs), cash and in-kind transfers to support households, and 'moderate' economic stimulus programmes. A notable challenge faced by SSA governments is that informal workers, who constitute a large proportion of the workforce on the continent, are often outside the reach of the state, making it difficult to enact the furlough schemes that Western governments undertook. While the spread of COVID-19 in SSA has been more limited compared to other developing regions, so far, the effectiveness of these policy responses in stimulating recovery in many SSA countries is uncertain.

In this chapter, we discuss the evolution of the pandemic, the subsequent policy responses, and the effectiveness of these early interventions in three SSA countries—Ghana, Kenya, and South Africa. The relief and stimulus packages in these countries, in particular, are of interest because the three countries rolled out very similar policies in different economies and labour markets. For instance, Ghana and Kenya have very high numbers of informal workers compared to South Africa (ILO 2018). The detailed country case studies for Ghana, Kenya, and South Africa are discussed in sections 2, 3, and 4, respectively. The conclusions are presented in section 5.

2. Ghana

2.1 Evolution of the pandemic and containment measures

The first two cases of COVID-19 were reported in Ghana on 12 March 2020 by the health ministry. As a first response, on 15 March, all public gatherings were banned and all schools and universities were closed, and on 23 March, all of the country's borders were closed. In the interest of public safety, a partial lockdown was introduced on 30 March in Accra, Tema, Kasoa, and Kumasi, which have been identified by the Ghana Health Service as 'hotspot' areas. This was lifted on 19 April. When lifting the partial lockdown, the President cited the country's current capacity to trace, test, isolate and quarantine, and treat victims of the disease as one of the reasons for the decision. Mask-wearing was made mandatory for all.

The second phase of re-opening started on 1 August, lifting restrictions on the number of people in public gatherings and opening tourist sites. However, beaches, pubs, cinemas, and nightclubs remained closed. International flights resumed from 1 September, subject to enhanced COVID-19 protocols. Land and sea borders remained closed to human traffic. Figure 8.1 illustrates the stringency of policy measures that were in place in Ghana between January and November 2020 in response to the COVID-19 pandemic (see also Chen and Vanek, Chapter 2 in this volume). The stringency index shows the response level in the national subregion with the strictest policies (districts subject to lockdown regulations),

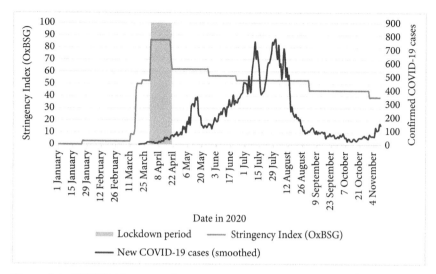

Figure 8.1 COVID-19 cases and government response stringency index in Ghana

Note: the stringency index shows the response level in the national subregion with the strictest policies (districts subject to lockdown regulations), and the grey shaded area indicates the lockdown period from 30 March to 19 April. The stringency index is a composite measure based on nine response indicators including school closures, workplace closures, and travel bans, rescaled to a value from 0 to 100 (strictest); it shows the pandemic response level in the districts subject to the strictest lockdown measures.

Source: authors' illustration based on data from Hale et al. (2020) and Roser et al. (2020).

and the grey shaded area indicates the lockdown period. The stringency index in November largely remained in place throughout 2021.

Considering the evolution of newly confirmed COVID-19 cases (see Figure 8.1), the Ghanaian government was quick to implement stringent measures when case numbers were still relatively low. The number of confirmed COVID-19 infections continued to escalate during the lockdown and increased exponentially after restrictions were lifted, reaching peak levels only in late July or early August 2020, after which the pandemic curve of the first infection wave flattened. The decision to lift the partial lockdown was largely influenced by mounting concerns regarding the severe economic burden that the restrictions posed, especially on the livelihoods of the urban poor, many of whom had, by that time, run out of money to buy food, due both to the hike in food prices and to the restricted possibilities to earn a living (Asante and Mills 2020).

As at the end of March 2023, the number of confirmed COVID-19 infections had risen to 171,412, whilst COVID-related deaths stood at 1,462. Accordingly, as of 25 March 2023, a total of 22,384,226 doses of COVID vaccines had been administered, representing 72 per cent of total doses administered per 100 population (WHO 2023).

2.2 Economic policy response

The policy measures taken by the government of Ghana to combat the adverse economic effects of the pandemic are representative of what other SSA governments have also done in responding to the economic crisis—a combination of stimulus packages, cash and in-kind transfers, tax breaks, and loans to MSMEs. The government of Ghana rolled out the Coronavirus Alleviation Programme (CAP) to address the disruption in economic activities and the hardship of the people, and to rescue and revitalize industries. Some of these measures included:

1. an extension of the tax filing date from April to June;
2. a 2 per cent reduction of interest rates by banks, effective 1 April 2020;
3. the granting by the banks of a six-month moratorium of principal repayments to entities in the airline and hospitality industries (i.e. hotels, restaurants, car rentals, food vendors, taxis, and uber operators);
4. the ability of mobile money users to send up to GH¢100 for free and a 100–300 per cent increase in daily transaction limits for mobile money transactions;
5. the establishment of a COVID-19 fund, to be managed by an independent board of trustees and to receive contributions and donations from the public, to assist in the welfare of the needy and the vulnerable;
6. a three-month tax holiday for health workers at the beginning of April 2020 and an amount of GH¢80 million to pay a special allowance for frontline health workers;
7. fumigation of public places, including markets and schools;
8. a directive to the ministries of gender, children, and social protection; local government and rural development; and the National Disaster Management Organization (NADMO), working with metropolitan, municipal district chief executives (MMDCEs) and faith-based organizations, to provide food for up to 400,000 individuals and homes in the affected areas of the restrictions;
9. a doubling of payments to the beneficiaries of the Livelihood Empowerment against Poverty (LEAP) programme;
10. absorption by the government of the water bills for all Ghanaians for the three months of April, May, and June;
11. full absorption by the government of electricity bills for the poorest of the poor, defined as lifeline consumers who consume between zero and 50 kilowatt hours a month for this period. For all other consumers, residential and commercial, government absorbed half of the cost of electricity bills for this period;
12. a 1.5 per cent decrease in the policy rate and a 2 per cent decrease in the reserve requirement by the Bank of Ghana to help improve credit

to businesses. Commercial banks were to respond to these measures by the regulator and provide a GH₵3 billion facility to support industry—especially in the pharmaceutical, hospitality, service, and manufacturing sectors;

13. implementation of the flagship CAP business support scheme. An amount of GH₵1.2 billion was earmarked for the CAP business support scheme to be made available to businesses, particularly small and medium-scale enterprises (SMEs).

Among these measures, the flagship CAP business support scheme was the major intervention mitigating the negative impact of COVID-19 on households and livelihoods and providing support to MSMEs. Out of the GH₵1.2 billion earmarked for this programme, GH₵600 million was to be disbursed as soft loans to SMEs, with up to a one-year moratorium and a two-year repayment period. The rate of interest on this facility was 3 per cent. Additionally, selected participating banks provided negotiated counterpart funding to the tune of GH₵400 million, making the facility worth, in all, GH₵1 billion for disbursement under this business support scheme, with the entire scheme initially expected to attract some 180,000 beneficiaries across the country. The funds were managed by the National Board for Small Scale Industries (NBSSI) and supervised by a loan committee. The NBSSI reports that more than 450,000 applicants, representing MSMEs, registered for the fund, with 66 per cent of the applicants being female and 34 per cent male. All applicants were required to register for a tax identification number (TIN) with the Ghana Revenue Authority to enable them to access the COVID-19 Relief Fund. The beneficiary sectors included agribusinesses, manufacturing, water and sanitation, tourism and hospitality, education, food and beverages, technology, transportation, commerce and trade, health care and pharmaceuticals, and textiles and garments.

2.3 Effectiveness of policy responses

Although the rate of infections of COVID-19 in Ghana has been low compared to other countries, the policy responses rolled out by the Ghanaian government have had some effects on employment and incomes and seem to have put the country on a path of partial recovery in economic growth. For instance, Ghana's economy grew by 5.4 per cent in 2021; this was a significant increase from the 0.4 per cent growth rate recorded in the full year of 2020 (GSS 2021).However, growth slowed to 3.2 per cent in 2022, and it is projected to slow further to 1.6 per cent in 2023. The agriculture and services sectors experienced slower growth, especially in 2022, than before. Higher inflation and interest rates depressed private consumption and investment, thereby slowing down employment. The policies targeted at reducing the hardships on households, such as reduction in cost of mobile money services, free food for individuals and households, and the free utility services (water and electricity), allowed many households and individuals who lost jobs and incomes to survive during the period. The COVID Relief Fund made various donations to communities to help them build back, especially when the lockdown was lifted.

The flagship CAP business support scheme implemented by the NBSSI seems to have revitalized many MSMEs across the country. It supported many SMEs, both formal and informal enterprises, including petty traders and hairdressers, among many others, and most importantly, sectors like tourism and hospitality, which were hit badly by the pandemic. An additional emergency programme, funded by the MasterCard foundation and administered by NBSSI, also effectively supported:

- MSMEs who needed support to survive the COVID-19 pandemic;
- businesses in growth sectors where the employment of young people, especially young women, was negatively impacted as a result of business operation disruptions, supply-chain challenges, liquidity shortages, declining sales and profits, and business closures;
- businesses providing services that were in demand during the pandemic and that have the potential to grow and positively impact communities affected by COVID-19;
- businesses that focused on digitization to support MSMEs.

The nature of the partial lockdown and the swift implementation of CAP business support seems to have had some impact on the recovery in the labour market in Ghana. The country saw some green shoots in the labour market, given that many Ghanaians in the business sector were able to receive adequate support and capital to start working again. The recovery in employment up to August/September 2020 was strong, albeit uneven. As at September 2020, about 85.3 per cent of workers who had been employed in February 2020 were again observed to be working, and more importantly, the gap in employment rates between lockdown and no-lockdown districts had closed. The slower growth in 2022, coupled with high inflation (up from 10 per cent in 2021 to 31.5 in 2022), interest rate, and weakened government demand due to lack of access to capital markets and high debt service obligations resulted in decline in employment, a 0.05 per cent decrease from 2020. However, there was a concerning gender gap in employment recovery. Specifically, women were less likely than men to have resumed work, whilst workers who had been informally employed pre-pandemic were less likely to have resumed work compared to workers who had been in formal employment (see also Chen and Vanek, Chapter 2 in this volume). The argument is that these initial gains in August/September 2020 can be attributed to the policies adopted by the Ghanaian government, such as the timely lifting of the partial lockdown and the swift support to households and businesses. As of early 2023, gains in employment and earnings have remained partial and uneven, and the economic burden of the pandemic continues to fall on the most vulnerable (i.e. low-income earners in informal work and women), who were more likely to drop out of work in the early phases of the pandemic and saw a slower recovery in both employment and earnings (see details in Chen and Vanek, Chapter 2 in this volume). The current situation of high inflation and public debt crisis, and its attendant effect on retarding employment and incomes, indicate the need for protective measures that prevent the most vulnerable workers from being left behind in the crisis.

3. Kenya

3.1 Evolution of the pandemic and containment measures

Kenya reported its first COVID-19 case on 13 March 2020. The country experienced four key waves of COVID-19 infections that peaked during the second and fourth quarters of 2020, around March–April 2021, and the third quarter of 2021 (Figure 8.2).

Following confirmation of the first case, the government moved swiftly to curb the spread of the pandemic. The starting point included standard measures such as

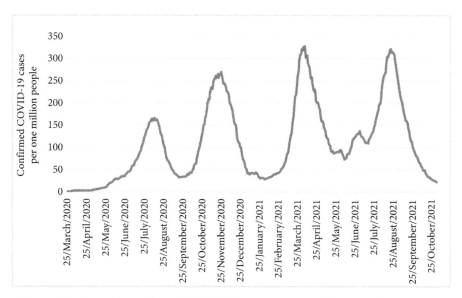

Figure 8.2 Bi-weekly confirmed COVID-19 cases per one million people

Source: Our World in Data; reproduced here under Creative Commons BY license.

encouraging regular hand washing, social distancing, suspension of public gatherings and events, the closure of learning institutions, and travel restrictions limiting entry to citizens and foreigners. International passenger flights were suspended effective 25 March 2020. Government offices and businesses were asked to allow staff to work from home, with the exception of employees working in critical or essential services.

As the number of confirmed cases increased, the suspension of public gatherings was extended to churches, mosques, and other religious gatherings. Bars and restaurants were directed to close. On 27 March, the President instituted a countrywide curfew from 7 p.m. to 5 a.m., excepting only critical and essential service providers. Furthermore, the wearing of face masks in public places was made mandatory. In addition, the government began to recruit additional health workers to combat the COVID-19 pandemic. To limit intracommunity transmission from urban to rural areas, the government imposed a temporary ban on movement in and out of the Nairobi metropolitan area and the most affected counties.[1]

Over time, the intensification of containment measures was largely determined by the rate of spread and severity of infections. For instance, in June 2021, the infections started edging up again, mainly driven by an upsurge of cases in the Western Kenya region, attributable to the Delta variant. In response, 13 counties in the region were placed under partial lockdown up to 31 July 2021. The national curfew remained in force for over a year until 20 October 2021, with variations in curfew hours. Most of the containment measures were, however, done away with over time following the easing of infection rates.

As of the end of November 2021, total confirmed cases were 255,164, while the number of recorded fatalities stood at 5,335. A total of 2,839,918 tests had been conducted. Although the government launched a vaccination programme in March 2021, like most African countries, Kenya is still lagging behind in COVID-19 inoculations. This is partly attributable to the limited supply of vaccines, particularly during the first phase, coupled with the sluggish uptake. As of 30 November 2021, the number of people who had been vaccinated at least once stood at 7,175,590.[2] However, the majority (61.5 per cent) had only received the first jab. Only 2,759,827 people—about 5.6 per cent of the population—had been fully vaccinated. Total vaccines administered increased to 10,100,993 as of end of December 2021, while the number of people fully vaccinated increased to 4,206,106—8.5 per cent of the population. As of the end of December 2022, the number of confirmed cases was 342,499, while fatalities stood at 5,688.

---

[1] Mombasa, Kilifi, Kwale, and Mandera.
[2] Daily press statement on COVID-19, update by the Ministry of Health, Kenya.

3.2 Economic policy response

At the onset of the COVID-19 pandemic in the country, various policy response measures were undertaken by the government to protect incomes and cushion the economy from the adverse effects of the pandemic. On 25 March 2020, the President announced fiscal policy measures consisting of tax relief and other measures:

1. 100 per cent relief for persons earning gross monthly income of up to KES24,000 (about US$235);[3]
2. reduction of income tax rate (pay-as-you-earn) from 30 per cent to 25 per cent and resident income tax (corporation tax) from 30 per cent to 25 per cent;
3. reduction of the turnover tax rate from 3 per cent to 1 per cent for all MSMEs;
4. appropriation of an additional KES10 billion to the elderly, orphans, and other vulnerable members of society through cash transfers;
5. reduction of the value-added tax (VAT) from 16 per cent to 14 per cent effective 1 April 2020;
6. payment of at least of KES13 billion of the verified pending bills and all verified VAT refund claims amounting to KES10 billion, or alternatively, allowing for offsetting of withholding VAT, in order to improve cash flows for businesses, and a voluntary reduction in the salaries of the senior ranks of the National Executive.

In addition, a COVID-19 Emergency Response Fund was established to receive donations from well-wishers, and the National Treasury was directed to utilize KES2 billion of recovered corruption proceeds and reallocate the travel budgets of state agencies to support the most vulnerable. Other measures included presidential directives to develop a welfare package for health-care professionals, an allocation of KES5 billion to support county governments, inauguration of a weekly support stipend to needy households in Nairobi on a pilot basis, and release of KES500 million that were in arrears to persons with severe disabilities.

With regard to monetary policy, the CBK lowered the central bank rate (CBR) from 8.25 per cent to 7.25 per cent and the cash reserve ratio (CRR) from 5.25 per cent to 4.25 per cent, thus effectively adopting an accommodative monetary policy stance to support the economy. The CBR was further lowered to 7 per cent. The maximum tenor of repurchase agreements (REPOs) was extended from 28

---

[3] Based on the exchange rate at the time.

to 91 days to allow flexibility on liquidity management.[4] By lowering the CRR, an additional liquidity of KES35 billion was made available to commercial banks to loan out to borrowers. Additionally, the CBK outlined commercial banks' loans restructuring emergency measures in March 2020 to provide relief to borrowers, based on their individual circumstances arising from the pandemic. Furthermore, in a bid to facilitate increased use of mobile money transactions and curb the spread of the virus through cash handling, charges for mobile transactions up to Ksh.1,000 (about US$9) were waived, while transaction amounts and daily limits for mobile transactions were revised upwards. The CBK also revised the minimum threshold for submitting negative credit information on borrowers to credit reference bureaus and delisted borrowers previously blacklisted for loans of less than KES1,000. These types of small loans are mainly accessed by the low-income segments of the population when hard pressed to meet various needs.

In May 2020, the government unveiled an eight-point economic stimulus programme with an allocation of KES56.6 billion (US$540 million) in the 2020/21 financial year and a further KES23.1 billion (US$220 million) in 2021/22. The programme aimed to cushion vulnerable citizens and businesses, particularly those affected by the pandemic. The key sectors covered included the following:

1. *Infrastructure*: rehabilitation of access roads and footbridges to optimize the use of local labour and materials, and employment creation for the youth through 'Kazi Mtaani Programme'. The programme targeted unemployed youth in the major cities and urban settlements, under which they were to be engaged in menial urban civil works and activities aimed at improving public hygiene;
2. *Education*: recruitment of unemployed teachers, construction of classrooms, ICT interns to support digital learning in public schools, etc.;
3. *Enhancing liquidity to businesses*: a credit guarantee scheme (CGS) aimed at de-risking lending to MSMEs in order to increase credit uptake, especially by the vulnerable SMEs. The government allocated KES3 billion in 2020/21 as seed capital and an additional KES2 billion in 2021/22 financial year. The scheme became operational in October 2020. By the end of April 2021, seven approved banks had started lending under the scheme;
4. *Health*: recruitment of health workers and establishment of modern, walk-through sanitizers at border points and main hospitals across the country;
5. *Agriculture*: subsidization of the supply of farm inputs, expanded community irrigation, and assistance to flower and horticultural farmers to access international markets;

---

[4] REPO rate is the rate at which the central bank lends short-term money to commercial banks against securities.

6. *Tourism*: temporary lifting of the ban to hold meetings in private hotels by government agencies, waiving of landing and parking fees at airports to facilitate movement of cargo in and out of Kenya, supporting hotel refurbishment and business restructuring through soft loans, among others;

7. *Manufacturing*: promoting 'Buy Kenya build Kenya' policy through purchase of locally assembled motor vehicles and provision of credit targeting MSMEs in the sector;

8. *Improving environment, water, and sanitation facilities*: through flood control, rehabilitation of wells, and underground tanks, especially in arid areas.

The informal sector accounts for slightly over 80 per cent of total employment in Kenya. Following the adverse impacts of COVID containment measures, workers in the informal sector, casual labourers, and poor households were hard hit. Hence, there was need to provide some quick support to the socially and economically vulnerable households, particularly in densely populated settlements. This was implemented through the multi-agency COVID-19 cash transfer initiative, under which vulnerable households received a stipend of KES4,000 (US$37) per month to help them cope with the adverse effects of the pandemic. Support was prioritized for households in informal settlements with a high poverty index, where the head or breadwinner had a physical disability, was widowed, a minor (orphan or child-headed households), had pre-existing medical conditions such as cancer or HIV, had a mental health condition, and was not benefiting from other government support. The programme ran from April to November 2020 and, in its first phase, targeted 85,300 households in four counties—Nairobi, Mombasa, Kilifi, and Kwale—before being rolled out to more counties. However, there has been quite limited public documentation on the implementation and impact of the government COVID-19 cash transfer initiative.

The government's multi-agency COVID-19 cash transfer initiative was complimented by emergency cash transfer programmes provided by non-governmental organizations (NGOs) and some development partners in a bid to reach out to more vulnerable households. Between June and December 2020, a total of KES590,292,000 (about US$5.5 million) is reported to have been transferred by a consortium of NGOs[5] to 29,400 families in Nairobi and Mombasa informal settlements (Oxfam International 2020). Compared to the government's regular cash transfer programme, the NGO's safety net programme covered slightly

---

[5] Comprised of Oxfam in Kenya, The Kenya Red Cross Society, Concern Worldwide, the Agency for Technical Cooperation and Development (ACTED), IMPACT Initiatives, the Centre for Rights Education and Awareness (CREAW), and the Wangu Kanja Foundation.

more needs and provided top-up payments to beneficiaries of the regular *Inua Jamii*[6] to enable them to adequately cover basic needs in light of COVID-19 challenges.

3.3 Effectiveness of policy responses

The fiscal stimulus and social protection measures were severely constrained by the limited fiscal space and fell short of the huge stimulus packages unveiled by many developed countries. The containment measures and subdued economic activities adversely affected revenue performance amidst elevated COVID-19-related expenditures, ballooning public debt, a high wage bill, and budgetary allocations to the 47 county governments. Consequently, the fiscal space needed to provide a generous economic stimulus package and safety nets for the poor and vulnerable were limited. Moreover, most of the key policy response measures were short-lived. Not only were tax relief measures reversed in January 2021, but also some taxes were later adjusted upwards or subsequently introduced. The waiver of charges on the low-value mobile money transactions expired on 31 December 2020, while loan-restructuring measures expired in March 2021. In the absence of comprehensive information and data regarding the specific socio-economic outcomes, it is difficult to measure the effectiveness of the policy responses, particularly at the household level. Overall, while the supportive policy response and relief measures helped boost resilience and economic recovery, they remained limited in scope, coverage, and focus.

The Kenyan economy contracted by 0.3 per cent in 2020 following the adverse impact of the pandemic. The sectors that were most affected include the services sectors (especially education, wholesale, and retail trade) and accommodation and restaurants. However, following the lifting of the various COVID containment measures, the economy recovered strongly and recorded a growth of 7.5 per cent in 2021. Growth was largely supported by the recovery of the manufacturing and services sectors. The agriculture sector recorded a contraction of 0.2 per cent, largely due to adverse weather conditions. Some services sectors (such as education, information and communication, transport and storage, and finance and insurance) recovered relatively faster than others, such as the tourism sector—especially international tourism. Economic growth normalized at 5.5 per cent in the first quarter of 2022. However, the performance of the agriculture sector remained subdued owing to prolonged drought. Although total employment recovered from a contraction of 4.1 per cent in 2020 to a growth of 5.3 per cent in 2021, the rate of recovery was relatively higher for modern wage employment

---

[6] This is a government cash transfer programme that targets the most vulnerable, that is, the elderly, children, and persons with disabilities.

(6 per cent) compared with the estimated informal-sector employment (5.2 per cent).

Some of the financial-sector COVID response measures undertaken by the CBK, such as loan restructuring, were instrumental in facilitating continuity of business activities and aiding enterprises to remain afloat, particularly the MSMEs, which ordinarily tend to experience credit constraints. Besides helping to curb the spread of COVID infections, the emergency measures instituted to facilitate mobile money transactions led to a notable increase in mobile money usage, thus further boosting the country's fairly advanced mobile financial services and the drive towards a cashless society. The use of mobile money saw an increase of 2.8 million additional customers. Most of the micro and informal activities are bound to have equally benefited, especially from the waiver of charges on low-value mobile money transactions and the increased digitization. Additionally, the introduction of CGS to de-risk lending benefited some of the MSMEs—a total of KES604.6 million (about US$6 million) had been disbursed by June 2021, with a guaranteed amount of KES151.2 million (CBK 2021).

The multi-agency COVID-19 cash transfer initiative was quite limited in coverage. According to a report by the Human Rights Watch (2021), the initiative provided support to less than 5 per cent of the socio-economically vulnerable families in Nairobi, and an even smaller percentage across the country. The report indicated a lack of transparency, awareness, and involvement of politicians that made the implementation process vulnerable to cronyism. Some of the beneficiaries reported receiving cash for only one or two months. The majority of the vulnerable households meeting the criteria did not benefit from the COVID-19 cash transfer programme. In the absence of a social registry with data on beneficiaries, the need to undertake new registration, targeting, and enrolment undermined the timeliness and efficient implementation of the social protection response (Wyatt and Guest 2021). By August 2020, the cash transfers made had not reached the caseload target. This is in spite of the convenience of using mobile money to effect the cash transfers, which also helped minimize physical mobility and contact.

In terms of comprehensiveness, the COVID-19 cash transfer programmes were generally limited to subsistence support, with no linkage to interventions that address additional risks that vulnerable households might face (Wyatt and Guest 2021). However, to the few beneficiaries, the social protection initiatives helped meet basic daily needs such as ability to buy food or increase the number of meals per day. Most of the recipients reported to have spent the money on food, with approximately 51 per cent of the grant provided being used to meet daily food needs. Similarly, 98 per cent of the respondents reported having spent part of the cash received to buy food (Human Rights Watch 2021).

Although the 'Kazi Mtaani' (urban public works programme) targeting the youth in urban informal settlements might have provided some reprieve, the coverage was quite limited in relation to the high unemployment among.[7] Over 100,000 job opportunities are reported to have been created during the first year.[8]

Overall, the COVID-19 policy response and measures, though helpful in aiding economic recovery, were limited in scope, amount, and coverage and, hence, unlikely to have effectively addressed the more serious impacts on the lowest-income households and vulnerabilities of informal workers. The pandemic has provided key lessons, including the need to develop a robust social protection system. Additionally, safety net and economic stimulus packages during such crises should be gender-sensitive and well targeted to ensure they benefit the most affected. There is the need to maintain an updated comprehensive database of information and statistics that is vital for planning and identification of beneficiaries for targeted social protection.

4. South Africa

4.1 Evolution of the pandemic and containment measures

The first COVID-19 positive case in South Africa was confirmed on 5 March 2020. Three weeks later, the government declared a national state of disaster and initiated one of the most severe lockdowns seen around the world (see also Rogan and Skinner, Chapter 4 in this volume). The adopted measures to mitigate and supress the spread of the virus included limiting contact between persons (social distancing), a travel ban on foreign nationals travelling from countries classified as 'high risk', quarantine for citizens returning from high-risk countries, health surveillance at ports of entry, and school closures. During the lockdown, movement was only permitted by health-care and essential-service workers. Wide-scale testing and tracing, with quarantine of confirmed cases, was put in place in an attempt to control the outbreak in the early phase of the pandemic.

In order to balance between the public health and economic crises brought about by the pandemic, the government initiated five alert levels, with varying levels of restrictions to be used in various waves of the pandemic. This ranged from Level 1 (no restrictions on economic activity and limited curfew) to Level 5 (all businesses closed except for essential services and no movement permitted without permission).

The alert levels were used in the country as cases surged or declined but ended in April 2022. Figure 8.3 shows a COVID-19 stringency index for South Africa with

---

[7] Unemployment rates of the age groups 20–24 years and 25–29 years increased from 12.7 per cent and 7.4 per cent in 2020—Q1, to 22.8 per cent and 21.7 per cent in 2020—Q2, respectively.
[8] Based on the budget statement for 2021/2022.

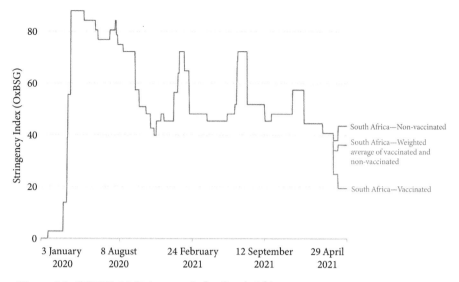

Figure 8.3 COVID-19 Stringency Index South Africa

Note: the graph shows a COVID-19 stringency index from 0 to 100 (strictest). Where policies are implemented at the provincial level, the index shows the response in the strictest region. Indicators such as school and workplace closures, as well as travel limitations, are used to calculate the index.
Source: data from Oxford COVID-19 Government Response Tracker (Hale et al. 2021) and OurWorldInData.org/coronavirus (Roser et al. 2020); reproduced here under Creative Commons BY license.

the various escalations and phasedowns of the alert levels. The index is a composite measure from various indicators, including school or workplace closure and travel restrictions (Hale et al. 2021).

Sixteen months after the first case in South Africa, the country reached 2.45 million confirmed cases, translating to 40,762 cases per million people (Ritchie et al. 2020). At the end of July 2021, the country had reached 75,000 coronavirus-related deaths and an estimated number of 227,000 excess deaths (Bradshaw et al. 2021; NICD 2021). A total of 360,000 COVID-19 hospital admissions have been recorded, with only 36 per cent of the adult population being fully vaccinated by the end of November 2021 (NICD 2021).

4.2 Economic policy response

Lockdown was largely viewed as necessary to respond to the public health crisis. Beyond the very high levels of inequality and large numbers of poor, the South African population has a large number of people with suppressed immunity due to HIV, tuberculosis, and malnutrition. At the same time, it was acknowledged that the economic impact for the poor and most vulnerable would be devastating.

Bassier et al. (2020) predicted that the extreme poverty rate among vulnerable households would almost triple without any intervention. The paper by Bassier et al. (2020) also showed that the extension of the existing child support grant would be an effective way to reach informal workers, who were otherwise largely out of reach of government support mechanisms.

As an immediate response, the government put in place several measures to reduce the economic impact when the lockdown was announced. Some measures were clearly articulated, while promises were made to create additional measures. Most of the measures were concentrated in the formal economy (see Ramaphosa 2020 for a full list of measures).

Price ceilings were introduced on many essential items and regulations put in place to prohibit unjustified price hikes and stockpiling by individuals. Several complaints of price gouging had been lodged and the police were asked to investigate cases across the country. To support the poor and vulnerable, the government set up a solidarity fund, which had ZAR3 billion in funds committed by the middle of 2021. The aim of the fund was to support the government's response to combat the spread of the virus by assisting existing programmes and initiatives. In the early weeks of the lockdown period, the fund supported emergency food relief to distressed households across the country and other similar initiatives.

The government made existing social grants available a few days earlier than usual to alleviate congestion and maintain social distancing during collection of grants by recipients. This measure also provided recipients with an extended period to access their funds. Several measures were put in place to support businesses in distress. This included tax relief, funding support to SMEs, and extending the wage subsidy programme, allowing firms to retain a larger number of workers.

A secondary response to the pandemic was aimed at stabilizing the economy through supporting businesses and households to resume economic activity. In April, the president announced a social and economic support package amounting to 10 per cent of gross domestic product (GDP) or ZAR500 billion. The funds were to be allocated in three areas: health, households, and businesses. Additional cash in the hands of poor individuals is critical to protect the poor and vulnerable in South Africa. The first measure was to use the country's well-established, extensive social grant system to distribute additional support to households in need. The increase in the grants was intended to be temporary, lasting for a period of seven months.

Another measure was the creation of the COVID-19 Social Relief of Distress (COVID grant). This new support mechanism was a temporary provision of assistance intended for individuals that were unable to meet their families' most basic needs. The relief came in the form of food parcels, food vouchers, or cash. The relief was only intended for a short period of time but was extended through April 2021 and was recently reinstated after severe riots took place in the country. In order to support South African households, unemployment insurance via the Unemployment Insurance Fund (UIF) was expanded. Employers were able to claim from the COVID-19 Temporary Employee/Employer Relief Scheme (TERS) and continue supporting workers' wages. The COVID-TERS benefits were intended to be temporary but were extended until January 2021 and then further extended until April 2021.

A tertiary response to the pandemic has aimed to drive the recovery of the economy. Measures to stimulate demand and supply through interventions such as infrastructure-building programmes, the implementation of economic reforms, and other actions have been discussed to kickstart inclusive economic growth. While considering and implementing the broader economic recovery, initial interventions, such as the food parcel distribution, was increased. In early 2021, funds were made available to the tourism industry, and an official loan guarantee scheme was introduced to provide government-guaranteed bank loans to assist eligible businesses with operational expenses. The loan scheme was extended until July 2021 as there were several challenges to economic recovery.

The pandemic presented a distinct challenge to policymakers with respect to support for informal workers. Informal workers, and the households they support, were placed in a particularly severe situation during the initial, most stringent part of the lockdown, when informal food vendors were excluded from the essential services workforce. This informal workforce is often the only source of income for many households, ensuring that they stay above the poverty line. Furthermore, 70 per cent of households in townships usually source food from informal vendors (PLAAS 2020). The very nature of informality makes it difficult for governments to provide appropriate and timely relief. Close to 3 million people were working in the informal sector (around 18 per cent of total employment) in the months before the pandemic struck South Africa (see Rogan and Skinner, Chapter 4 in this volume). The COVID grant was intended to cover those not already included in the safety net of social grants and unemployment insurance, such as those in the informal sector. The COVID grant, in addition to the top up offered via the social grant system, was arguably the only protection provided to informal-sector workers.

4.3 Effectiveness of policy responses

It is perhaps too early, and challenging, to conclusively answer the question whether the particular mitigation strategies used in South Africa have resulted in lower infection rates, or fewer deaths, or boosted the paths to recovery. The emergence of new strains of the virus and delayed rollout of the vaccinations in South

Africa are also understood to have affected the severity of the subsequent waves of the pandemic.

Several studies have been able to examine the effectiveness of the social protection policies enacted during the pandemic (see Benhura and Magejo 2020; Bridgman et al. 2020; Jain et al. 2020; Köhler et al. 2021). The general consensus from the evidence is that the policies were well intentioned, but many workers and household still fell through the safety net, pointing to inadequacy of the policies both in terms of scale and targeting. It is known that the safety net provided by pre-pandemic social policies did not reach all those that needed support. The pandemic makes clear the large holes in the social security safety net, and several research projects have been able to point to very specific groups of individuals who received very little or no support (see Köhler et al. 2021 for a detailed analysis).

Food insecurity and adult and child hunger increased alarmingly in the early stages of the pandemic, reversing the improvements from the past 20 years (Bridgman et al. 2020). No single policy is found to be responsible for reducing food insecurity during the pandemic; rather, a combination of the COVID-TERS, individuals returning to work, the COVID grant, return to the National Schools Nutrition Programme in July 2020, and public and private food assistance all played a role. Further research shows that, for 10 per cent of South African households, the only government grant received by the household was the COVID grant (Jain et al. 2020). The civil unrest in July 2021 in South Africa is testament to the serious hunger crisis faced by the vulnerable since much of the social support was suspended in April 2021.

Employment losses were most significant among women, those with lower levels of education, those in manual occupations, informal workers, and the poor (Jain et al. 2020). Wage decreases were seen for formally and informally employed workers, whereas informally employed men and urban area workers faced larger decreases. There have been large decreases in hours worked for both men and women in urban informal employment relative to formal employment (Benhura and Magejo 2020). Early in the pandemic, it was evident that informal workers had been locked out of the economy and that interventions needed to be scaled up and better targeted to informal workers (Rogan and Skinner 2020). Evidence shows that a small share of TERS recipients were informally employed (Köhler and Hill 2021). The programme targeted workers registered for UIF, typically in the formal sector. The evidence suggests that the TERS programme supported informal workers disproportionately affected by the lockdown. At the end of 2020, only one-third of jobs lost in the informal sector had been recovered (Köhler et al. 2021). At the same time, the government faced a challenging budget situation. The unemployment rate remained high, at 32.7 per cent, at the end of 2022. Efforts will need to continue until there is consistent evidence of economic recovery and stabilization in households.

5. Conclusion

This chapter discussed the evolution of the pandemic and containment measures and the policy responses as well as the effectiveness of the policies in Ghana, Kenya, and South Africa. All these countries confirmed the first COVID case in March 2020 and initiated more or less similar restriction measures such as lockdowns, travel restrictions, closure of schools, and curfews, among others, to contain the spread of the disease. The countries also came up with several policy measures to reduce the economic impact, especially when the lockdowns were introduced. Some initiatives were put in place to help highly vulnerable households and informal workers who dominate the labour market, particularly in Ghana and Kenya. To stabilize the economy, policies were initiated to support enterprises and businesses, particularly MSMEs. Some of the policies, particularly the economic stimulus packages, were also aimed at aiding the recovery of the economy.

Although, it is still too early to ascertain the effectiveness of these policies, it is clear from these case studies that there seems to be a strong but uneven recovery in employment and incomes following the relaxation of the stringent measures and support from policy interventions. In Ghana, although there was a rebound in economic growth in the third quarter of 2021, the recovery in employment is stronger for formal employment, whilst females and informal workers were less likely to resume work. In Kenya, the supportive policy and relief interventions helped to boost economic recovery, as demonstrated by the strong growth of 7.5 per cent in 2021, largely supported by services sectors. Growth normalized to 5.5 per cent in the first quarter of 2022. However, the employment and income effects of the pandemic are still being felt, especially among the youth, women, and workers in the informal sector. In South Africa, the recovery has been uneven: economic growth decreased by 1.3 per cent in the last quarter of 2022, following an increase in the third quarter. The economy only grew by 0.3 per cent from the pre-pandemic period, lagging behind the 3.5 per cent population growth over the same period. Whilst the rate and level of recovery in employment have been greater for formal employment, it has been very sluggish and uneven for informal workers, particularly women.

The employment situation in all three countries suggests a slow and uneven recovery for informal workers, particularly women, given lack of access to the cash transfers and other relief packages available during the pandemic. The Ghanaian case showed that informal workers were less likely to start work compared to workers who had been in formal employment. There is also a gender gap in the labour market recovery, where more men are able to start work compared to women. In Kenya, the limitation in scope, amount, and coverage of policy interventions and safety nets had adverse impacts on informal workers, including the youth. Although at the aggregate level employment recovered in 2021, the effects still linger, though they are difficult to quantify at the micro level, given limited detailed data on informal-sector employment. In South Africa, the rate of informal employment is still significantly lower than the pre-pandemic period. Particularly, the recovery in employment among women has only improved slightly since the third quarter of 2020. Within these countries, there is unevenness in the recovery of informal employment. It is also likely that the recovery of informal employment between these countries differs as the size of the informal sector and recovery measures differ across these countries.

The experiences from these countries show the difficulty in attempting to achieve the balance between protecting lives and sustaining livelihoods. It also highlights the challenge of designing targeted policies that ensure the most vulnerable are not being left behind. The pandemic has provided key lessons, including the need to develop a robust social protection system. Additionally, safety net and economic stimulus packages during such pandemics should be gender-sensitive and well coordinated to ensure that they benefit the most affected. Containment measures must be complemented by adequate relief to the poor and vulnerable in a quick, safe, and effective manner. In order to restore income and preserve livelihoods, income support, in the form of direct cash payments to those in need, are crucial. But more needs to be done to mitigate the impact of the pandemic on informal workers, particularly women. It is important for countries to develop measures to support workers in this segment of employment. Maintaining an updated comprehensive database of information and statistics is vital for planning and identification of beneficiaries for targeted social protection. There is, therefore, the need to build capacities across all the countries to deal with future shocks and pandemics.

The pandemic is not over yet, and hence, access to vaccines to boost herd immunity remains central to stronger recovery. Furthermore, the emergence of other global shocks, including the Russia–Ukraine war in 2022 and elevated inflation in advanced economies, has slowed recovery. It is time for the world to continue showing solidarity with the needy and most affected since pandemics know no boundaries.

References

Asante, L.A., and R.O. Mills (2020). 'Exploring the Socio-economic Impact of COVID-19 Pandemic in Marketplaces in Urban Ghana', *Africa Spectrum*, 55(2): 170–81. https://doi.org/10.1177/0002039720943612.

Balde, R., M. Boly, and E. Avenyo (2020). 'Labour Market Effects of COVID-19 in Sub-Saharan Africa: An Informality Lens from Burkina Faso, Mali and Senegal', United

Nations University-Maastricht Economic and Social Research Institute on Innovation and Technology (UNI-MERIT) Working Paper No. 22, Maastricht: UNU-MERIT, available at: www.merit.unu.edu/publications/working-papers/abstract/?id=8514 (accessed October 2023).

Bassier, I., J. Budlender, M. Leibbrandt, R. Zizzamia, and V. Ranchhod (2020). 'South Africa Can—and Should—Top Up Child Support Grants to Avoid a Humanitarian Crisis', *The Conversation Africa* (31 March), available at: https://theconversation.com/south-africa-can-and-should-top-up-child-support-grants-to-avoid-a-humanitarian-crisis-135222 (accessed April 2020).

Benhura, M., and P. Magejo. (2020). 'Differences between Formal and Informal Workers' Outcomes during the COVID-19 Crisis Lockdown in South Africa', National Income Dynamics Study-Coronavirus Rapid Mobile Survey (NIDS-CRAM) Working Paper No. 2, Wave 2, Cape Town: NIDS-CRAM.

Bradshaw, D., R. Laubscher, R. Dorrington, P. Groenwald, and T. Moultrie. (2021) 'Report on Weekly Deaths in South Africa', research report, Cape Town: Burden of Disease Research Unit and South African Medical Research Council, available at: www.samrc.ac.za/sites/default/files/files/2021-09-15/weekly11Sep2021.pdf (accessed September 2021).

Bridgeman, G., S. van der Berg, and L. Patel. (2020). 'Hunger in South Africa during 2020: Results from Wave 2 of NIDS-CRAM', NIDS-CRAM Working Paper No. 2, Wave 3, Cape Town: NIDS-CRAM.

CBK (Central Bank of Kenya) (2021). '2020 Survey Report on MSME Access to Bank Credit', Nairobi: CBK.

Ghana Statistical Service (2021). 'Quarterly GDP Newsletters', available at: https://www.statsghana.gov.gh/gssmain/fileUpload/National%20Accounts/Newsletter%20quarterly%20GDP%202021%20_Q3_December%202021%20Edition.pdf (accessed on March 2023).

Hale, T., A. Petherick, T. Phillips, and S. Webster (2020). 'Oxford COVID-19 Government Response Tracker (OxCGRT)', last updated 10 November 2020, 08:30 (London time). Available at: https://ourworldindata.org/coronavirus (accessed 10 November 2020).

Hale, T., N. Angrist, R. Goldszmidt, B. Kira, A. Petherick, T. Phillips et al. (2021). 'A Global Panel Database of Pandemic Policies (Oxford COVID-19 Government Response Tracker)', *Nature Human Behaviour*, 5: 529–38. https://doi.org/10.1038/s41562-021-01079-8.

Human Rights Watch (2021). 'We Are All Vulnerable Here: Kenya's Pandemic Cash Transfer Program Riddled with Irregularities', report by Human Rights Watch, available at: https://www.hrw.org/report/2021/07/20/we-are-all-vulnerable-here/kenyas-pandemic-cash-transfer-program-riddled (accessed in March 2023).

ILO (International Labour Organization) (2018). *Women and Men in the Informal Economy: A Statistical Picture* (3rd edn). Geneva: ILO, available at: www.ilo.org/global/publications/books/WCMS_626831/lang—en/index.htm (accessed October 2023).

Jain, R., J. Budlender, R. Zizzamia, and I. Bassier. (2020). 'The Labour Market and Poverty Impacts of COVID-19 in South Africa', NIDS-CRAM Working Paper No. 1, Wave 5, Cape Town: NIDS-CRAM.

Köhler T., and R. Hill. (2021). 'The Distribution and Dynamics of South Africa's TERS Policy: Results from NIDS-CRAM Waves 1 to 5', NIDS-CRAM Working Paper No. 5, Wave 7, Cape Town: NIDS-CRAM.

Köhler, T., H. Bhorat, R. Hill, and B. Stanwix (2021). 'COVID-19 and the Labour Market: Estimating the Employment Effects of South Africa's National Lockdown', Development Policy Research Unit (DPRU) Working Paper No. 202107, Cape Town: DPRU, University of Cape Town.

Lakuma, C.P., and N. Sunday (2020). 'Africa in Focus: Impact of COVID-19 on Micro, Small, and Medium Businesses in Uganda', available at: www.brookings.edu/blog/africa-infocus/2020/05/19/impact-of-covid-19-on-micro-small-and-medium-businesses-in-uganda (accessed October 2023).

NICD (National Institute for Communicable Diseases) (2021). 'Weekly Hospital Surveillance (DATCOV) Update. Johannesburg: Division of the National Health Laboratory Service', available at: www.nicd.ac.za/diseases-a-z-index/disease-index-covid-19/surveillance-reports/weekly-hospital-surveillance-datcov-update (accessed August 2021)

Oxfam International (2020). 'COVID-19 and Vulnerable, Hardworking Kenyans Why It's Time for a Strong Social Protection Plan', Oxfam Briefing Paper, Oxford: Oxfam GB for Oxfam International, available at: https://reliefweb.int/sites/reliefweb.int/files/resources/bp-kenya-social-protection-101120-en.pdf (accessed October 2023).

PLAAS (Institute for Poverty, Land and Agrarian Studies) (2020). 'Food in the Time of the Coronavirus: Why We Should Be Very, Very Afraid', Cape Town: PLAAS, available at: www.plaas.org.za/food-in-the-time-of-the-coronavirus-why-we-should-be-very-very-afraid (accessed August 2021).

Ramaphosa, C. (2020). 'Statement by President Cyril Ramaphosa on Escalation of Measures to Combat the Covid-19 Epidemic', Pretoria: The Presidency (24 March), available at: www.thepresidency.gov.za/speeches/statement-president-cyril-ramaphosa-escalation-measures-combat-covid-19-epidemic%2C-union (accessed August 2021).

Ritchie, H., E. Ortiz-Ospina, D. Beltekian, E. Mathieu, J. Hasell, B. Macdonald et al. (2020). 'Coronavirus Pandemic (COVID-19)', *OurWorldInData.org*, available at: https://ourworldindata.org/coronavirus (accessed August 2021).

Rogan, M., and C. Skinner. (2020). 'The Covid-19 Crisis and the South African Informal Economy', NIDS-CRAM Working Paper No. 1, Wave 10, Cape Town: NIDS-CRAM.

Roser, M., H. Ritchie, E. Ortiz-Ospina, and J. Hasell (2020). 'Coronavirus Pandemic (COVID-19)', Our World Data file, available at: https://ourworldindata.org/coronavirus (accessed 10 November 2020).

Schotte, S., M. Danquah, R. Darko Osei, and K. Sen (2021). 'How Covid-19 Is Affecting Workers and Their Livelihoods In Urban Ghana: Results from the GSPS-Covid Panel Survey', Helsinki: United Nations University-World Institute for Development Economics Research (UNU-WIDER).

The Presidency, Republic of Ghana (2020). 'Briefing Room: Speeches', available at: http://presidency.gov.gh/index.php/briefing-room/speeches (accessed May 2020).

World Health Organisation (2023). 'WHO Coronavirus (COVID-19) Dashboard', available at: https://covid19.who.int/region/afro/country/gh (accessed March 2023).

Wyatt, A., and M. Guest (2021). 'Towards Shock-Responsive Social Protection: Lessons from the COVID-19 Response in Kenya', Policy Brief, Oxford: Oxford Policy Management.

9

Informal Employment and an Inclusive Recovery

What Is Missing from National Economic Recovery Plans?

Siviwe Mhlana, Rachel Moussié, Sally Roever, and Michael Rogan

1. Introduction

At the outset of the COVID-19 pandemic in the first half of 2020, there was near-universal acknowledgement that employment losses, globally, would be borne disproportionately by vulnerable workers, in general, and informal workers, in particular (ILO 2020a). Of the world's 2.2 billion informal workers, it was estimated that 1.6 billion would be among the most severely affected by job losses and reduced working hours (ILO 2020b). The result of this impact has been the reversal of decades of progress in human development. For example, the number of people living in extreme poverty in emerging markets and developing economies was expected to increase by 100 million by the end of 2021 (World Bank 2021a). Similarly, the gendered burden of job losses has threatened progress towards gender equality, as evidenced by the highly uneven recovery of employment between women and men throughout 2021 (ILO 2021a).

Country-level data on job losses provides support for the International Labour Organization's (ILO) initial projections about the vulnerability of informal workers to the global 'pandemic recession'. Most informal workers in the world are located in low- and middle-income countries and are in self-employment. Data from ILOSTAT shows that working hours in lower-income countries in 2021 were about 7 per cent below their pre-COVID (2019) levels, while the corresponding decrease was only about 4 per cent in high-income countries (ILO 2021c). Data from Peru in 2020 suggests that the difference in the decrease in labour income between employees and the self-employed (who are largely in the informal sector) was 21 percentage points (ILO 2021b; see also Chen and Vanek, Chapter 2 in this volume). Following these unprecedented losses in global employment in 2020, and their accompanying impact on development progress, the ILO described 2021 as a year of stalled global recovery. This is particularly the case for low- and

Siviwe Mhlana et al., *Informal Employment and an Inclusive Recovery*. In: *COVID-19 and the Informal Economy*. Edited by: Martha Alter Chen, Michael Rogan, and Kunal Sen, Oxford University Press. © Siviwe Mhlana et al. (2024). DOI: 10.1093/oso/9780198887041.003.0010 middle-income countries, where employment, output, and growth remain below their pre-COVID levels (World Bank 2021a).

By the first quarter of 2022, the economic downturn was compounded by a cost-of-living crisis precipitated by global supply-chain constraints and the onset of war between Russia and Ukraine. The United Nations' Food and Agriculture Organization's food price index reached an all-time high (159.3 points) in March 2022, while ILOSTAT data estimated global inflation to be 9.2 per cent between 2021 and 2022. Throughout 2022, the situation was markedly worse in emerging market and developing economies, where inflation was more persistent, having reached 10.1 per cent in the second quarter of 2022 and 11 per cent in the third (IMF 2022). In other words, the countries that were impacted the most during the pandemic then experienced some of the highest rates of inflation and food price increases.

Notwithstanding the stalled progress in job recovery and the ongoing cost-of-living crisis, there has been a renewed focus on medium-term recovery at both the global and national levels. Throughout 2021, fiscal stimulus packages were introduced to jump-start the economic recovery process. However, as with the uneven impact of the pandemic on job and earnings losses, the roll-out of stimulus packages was also imbalanced. According to the October (2021) International Monetary Fund (IMF) Fiscal Monitor, the global stimulus amounted to roughly US$16.9 trillion but with only 13.8 and 0.4 per cent of this amount allocated to emerging and developing countries, respectively (IMF 2021). In addition, fiscal support in emerging and developing economies was concentrated on relief measures in 2020, while developed country stimulus packages were more focused on the medium-term recovery (World Bank 2021a).

While calls for economic recovery packages that promise to 'build back better' (or 'build forward better') have come from many directions, the under-allocation of recovery resources to countries that have borne the brunt of job losses threatens the recovery of livelihoods for the majority of the world's workforce. Not only has the quantum of stimulus packages been allocated disproportionately to advanced economies, but there is also no clear roadmap for an economic recovery that addresses the large losses of informal jobs and stagnating demand in emerging and developing economies. At the same time, the cost-of-living crisis has peaked at precisely the time that many middle- and low-income countries have reduced fiscal support for vulnerable groups, including informal workers, that were impacted by the pandemic (IMF 2022). Households in these countries are often supported by the earnings of informal workers and are particularly vulnerable to food price increases. The IMF (2022) estimates that up to half of household consumption expenditure is on food in these contexts, which means that food price inflation will likely have detrimental impacts on human development.

The remainder of this chapter is structured as follows. Section 2 summarizes what is known about the impact of the crisis on informal workers through 2020–21. In section 3, we analyse the national recovery plans from two middle-income and two low-income countries. This section aims to highlight the diversity of economic responses against the backdrop of the pandemic's impact on informal workers in the selected countries. Section 4 then assesses these national recovery packages in terms of the extent to which they appear to target, or align with, the structure of employment in each country. The chapter concludes with a reflection on possible pathways toward making national-level economic recovery packages more relevant to the livelihoods of the majority of workers in emerging and developing countries.

2. Impact of crisis on informal workers globally

Several assessments of the impact of the pandemic on employment globally focus on job losses, one of the most visible early indicators of the crisis in 2020. Domestic workers were especially vulnerable to job loss (see Chakravarty and Nayak, Chapter 7 in this volume), particularly those who did not live in their employers' homes when the pandemic began. Eight out of ten domestic workers globally are informally employed and therefore lack labour protections, which translated into job losses that were systematically higher than for other employees in the second quarter of 2020 (ILO 2021d). Live-out domestic workers were more likely to lose their jobs than live-in domestic workers due to employers' fears of virus transmission, whereas live-in domestic workers experienced deteriorating working conditions due to higher workloads in 2020 (WIEGO 2021).

However, for self-employed informal workers, who represent the majority of informal workers globally (ILO 2018b), job loss has proven to be less relevant than other more nuanced forms of impact. For example, despite returning to their income-generating activities after lockdowns eased, weak demand meant that many self-employed workers in informal employment had to pawn or sell off their assets, deplete their meagre savings, and take out new loans to purchase food and basic necessities in order to survive in 2020 and 2021. Many also postponed their payments (often with compounding interest) for rent, utility bills, and school fees during the initial lockdown in 2020, leading to accumulated expenses once restrictions eased (Chen et al. 2021). Survey findings from 2021 show that workers were still struggling to repay these debts and few were benefiting from rent, utility, or tuition fee cancellations and temporary deferrals (Orleans Reed et al. 2021).

The disproportionate impact of the crisis on women in informal employment is well documented (Lakshmi Ratan et al. 2021), and a significant contributor to this disproportionate impact is unpaid care work. In one study of 38 countries, for example, a higher proportion of women than men reported increases in time spent on unpaid care responsibilities and a higher intensity of that work because of the pandemic (UN Women 2020). These increases posed a particular challenge for women workers. Earnings of women in informal employment in April 2020 were substantially lower among those who reported an increase in care responsibilities due to a combination of lacking childcare support, working in public space with children present, the need to give attention to home schooling, and caring for sick and elderly family members (Ogando et al. 2022). Moreover, women and men informal workers who noted an increase in care responsibilities due to COVID-19 restrictions in 2020 were more likely than other workers to sell their assets, draw down their savings, and take out loans (Ogando et al. 2022). Access to government relief was limited for informal workers—an important factor when considering the relevance of government recovery plans to the informal workforce.

3. Key pillars of national economic recovery plans

This section examines the national economic recovery approaches of four governments in response to the social and economic crises presented by the COVID-19 pandemic. Our analysis reviews the recovery plans from two low-income countries (Bangladesh and Kenya) and two middle-income countries (South Africa and Thailand) in a context of growing reliance on the IMF for concessional loans. For the period from 2020 to 2021, Bangladesh, Kenya, and South Africa received emergency financing from the IMF of US$732 million, US$3,086.35 million, and US$4,300 million, respectively. These IMF programmes include conditionalities aimed at fiscal consolidation, fostering private investment, and contractionary macroeconomic policies (IMF 2021).

The review in this chapter focuses on five key areas that are, for the most part, common across the national economic recovery approaches and are aimed at stimulating economic development. These are financing economic recovery; developing local value chains; facilitating international trade; boosting public investment; and supporting micro, small, and medium enterprises (MSMEs). These are areas that would theoretically have a bearing on the activities and income security of informal workers in the long run. The aim of this section is to distil what the plans say with regard to measures that are likely to have implications for employment, in general, and informal employment, in particular. It is based on a reading of published development plans and secondary literature conducted between August 2020 and September 2022. For all four countries, the review included both long-term strategies formulated before the COVID-19 pandemic and crisis response plans developed in response to the pandemic.

3.1 Financing economic recovery

As governments tried to mitigate the social and economic impacts early in the pandemic, the need for greater government spending to support firms and households increased. The recovery approaches in all four countries therefore include measures to address the impact of the crisis on poor households. These measures focus primarily on cash and food support schemes and enhanced health care. To balance these measures, the plans indicate an effort to strengthen macroeconomic policies in order to increase revenues and decrease debt in this context.

The four governments' approaches to creating fiscal space vary to some extent, but in all four cases, they are linked to strategies to recover jobs and stimulate economic activity. In the case of Bangladesh, the eighth five-year development plan is centred on accelerating gross domestic product (GDP) growth through export-orientated, manufacturing-led growth in the garment, processed food, leather and footwear, light engineering, and pharmaceutical sectors, along with interventions in agriculture, services, and information and communication technologies (ICTs). The pathway to growth envisioned in the plan is to increase foreign direct investment inflows by improving the investment climate, delivering quick and efficient services to investors, and reducing ICT taxes and regulatory barriers (Government of the People of Bangladesh 2020). Accelerated GDP growth is the foundation of the plan.[1] It is understood to increase demand for labour, in turn increasing the labour share of income, with the main impediment being a lack of skills and education among those employed in the informal sector (Government of the People of Bangladesh 2020: 44). The centrepiece of the COVID-19 recovery approach is a US$1.05 billion World Bank package combining three projects to attract private investment to the ICT sector and modernize government institutions.

The Kenyan government's approach to creating fiscal space is likewise linked to its longer-term development strategy—Vision 2030. The fundamental pillar of its economic recovery strategy is a sound macroeconomic framework, and the strategy is centred around accelerated growth in private-sector investment, strengthened health-care systems, MSME growth, upscaled investment in ICT and digital infrastructure, and other growth-orientated measures (Republic of Kenya 2021). Following an economic stimulus programme focused mainly on cash support and jobs for youth early in the pandemic, its 2021 budget policy statement commits to a fiscal consolidation path over the medium term, alongside increasing efficiency in public investment, reversing tax cuts, and introducing new taxes and other revenue recovery measures. Priority pro-growth policy measures include improving business regulations and fast-tracking critical infrastructure alongside improved security and reduced corruption. As of 2020, the total World Bank portfolio in Kenya stood at US$7.8 billion and focused on investments in the transport and energy and extractives sectors (World Bank 2022).

Thailand's five-year development plan, in place from 2017 and aligned with its 20-year development strategy, differs substantially from those of Bangladesh and Kenya in that it foregrounds ethics and values, economic and social security, fair access to resources and quality social services, strengthening the grassroots

---

[1] The word 'growth' is mentioned 1,178 times in the 780-page plan.

economy, and preserving and restoring natural resources and environmental quality (Office of the National Economic and Social Development Board 2017). The
only mention of growth among the plan's seven objectives is to support green
growth alongside quality of life. To ensure fiscal space, the 2017 Thai plan committed to increase competitiveness sector by sector, through increased industrial
and innovative capacity, and to strengthen budgeting, revenue collection, and
state-owned enterprises. By 2021, the government had recommitted to stimulating exports and private investment to help promote recovery, but its restructuring
policy aimed to balance competitiveness with improving income distribution and
moving towards a low-carbon society (Office of the National Economic and Social
Development Board 2022).

Finally, South Africa's 'Economic Reconstruction and Recovery Plan' of October 2020 is aligned with its longer-term development strategy, the 'National
Development Plan 2030', launched in 2012. The National Development Plan commits to faster economic growth through an expansion of exports, alongside a
developmental role for the state and recognition of the need for the benefits of
growth to be more equitably distributed (Republic of South Africa 2012). The pandemic response plan created in 2020 recognizes the vulnerabilities in the economy
already present due to low growth and 'revenue leakages' when the pandemic hit,
and it commits to resource mobilization by enabling private-sector investment,
reducing the cost of doing business, and intensifying anti-corruption measures
(Republic of South Africa 2020a).

3.2 Developing local value chains

Developing local value chains can be an important strategy for creating jobs and
building resilient economies in the long run. For all four countries, this includes
support and investment in agricultural supply chains and promoting growth
through greater investment in traditional sectors such as manufacturing, retail,
and high-productivity service sectors. Each plan reflects sectoral choices for priority public and private investment linked to a particular vision of growth and
employment.

For Bangladesh, the emphasis of the five-year plan is centred primarily on global
value chains. Its approaches for supporting agricultural supply chains include
improvements in farm productivity, price policy support, water supply, and farm
credit and marketing support as well as agricultural diversification. The plan also
commits to the expansion of the ready-made garment (RMG) industry, while also
promoting non-RMG manufacturing diversification in food, leather, footwear,
light engineering, pharmaceuticals, and service exports such as those related to
international shipping (Government of the People of Bangladesh 2020). These
sectoral choices reflect an intent to shift the growth strategy towards more job

creation (relative to the previous five-year plan) alongside social assistance to reduce extreme poverty.

Kenya's recovery plan similarly focuses on value chains in agriculture but, unlike Bangladesh, it explicitly focuses on deepening domestic production in order to reduce exposure to risks associated with dependence on imports. It envisions the revival and restoration of major cash crops through agro-processing, greater investment in warehousing, expansion of irrigation schemes, support for the large-scale production of staples, and an economic stimulus programme to subsidize small-scale farmers for the supply of farm inputs. The plan also prioritizes the establishment of special economic zones, which would boost manufacturing employment, and the streamlining of the motor assembly industry (National Treasury and Planning 2020). The Kenyan 'Building Back Better' pandemic response plan briefly mentions employment creation as a goal across many sectors, while envisioning a reduction in public-sector employment to reduce the wage bill (Republic of Kenya 2021).

Thailand's plan envisions the introduction of innovation and creativity at all stages of value chains in order to boost product-and-service standards as well as economic opportunities. The plan has a significant focus on agriculture and agro-industry but also places importance on innovation and the commercialization of high-tech products and services which affect people's quality of life and well-being. Infrastructure development and logistics development are also expected to increase the country's competitiveness by facilitating Thai outward investment and promoting the involvement of Thai entrepreneurs in business activities abroad. The plan makes reference to deepening local, regional, and global value chains (Office of the National Economic and Social Development Board 2017).

South Africa's 'National Development Plan 2030' (Republic of South Africa 2012) makes a more explicit link between sectoral investment and employment through domestic value chains than other national plans. In recognizing the country's significant challenge with unemployment in particular, the plan notes that

> Employment scenarios prepared by the Commission suggest that most new jobs are likely to be sourced in domestic-orientated businesses, and in growing small- and medium-sized firms. While most jobs are not created directly in exporting firms, the sectors that are globally traded tend to have more potential to stimulate domestic spin-offs. Given South Africa's low savings rate and the need to invest at a higher rate, it is important to grow exports and expand output in those sectors.

The plan focuses on sectors where South Africa already has endowments and comparative advantage, such as mining, construction, mid-skill manufacturing, agriculture and agro-processing, higher education, tourism, and business services

(Republic of South Africa 2012: 39). The pandemic 'Economic Reconstruction and Recovery Plan 2020' also commits to 'employment-oriented strategic localization, reindustrialization and export promotion', retaining the link between employment and value chain development while adding a mass public employment dimension. It envisions strengthening small and medium-sized supply chain inclusion, working with private-sector firms to localize their supply chains, and 'decisively' shifting state procurement to local procurement (Republic of South Africa 2020a: 11–13).

3.3 Facilitating international trade

Bangladesh's long-term national development vision is centred on export-led growth with ambitious growth targets. Both the five-year development plan issued in 2017 and the 20-year plan launched in March 2021 commit to improving the incentives for manufacturing exports. The vision is for the bulk of job creation to be in a diversified manufacturing sector that extends the model of low-cost labour as a source of competitiveness beyond the RMG sector into other manufacturing sectors (Bangladesh Planning Commission (General Economics Division) 2020: viii). Thus, the strategic framework envisions accelerated growth in manufacturing associated with a transfer of surplus labour from the informal economy into low-cost manufacturing jobs during the first ten years, while quality of employment would become more of a concern during the next ten years (Bangladesh Planning Commission (General Economics Division) 2020: X). In essence, the plan defers concerns about working poverty to the post-2030 period.

Kenya's approach to international trade, as articulated in its third medium-term plan for 2018–22 (Republic of Kenya 2018), is likewise linked to ambitious growth targets. The approach aims to raise the manufacturing share of GDP to accelerate growth and create jobs and to guarantee food security by expanding food production and supply as part of its 'Big Four' priorities (including universal health care and more housing, in addition to boosting manufacturing and food security). The trade strategy is linked to state involvement in the formation of special economic zones and industrial parks and an increased commitment to take advantage of various trade agreements, such as the East African Community and the African Continental Free Trade Area (National Treasury and Planning 2020). Textiles, agro-processing, and leather are among the sectors mentioned in the 'Build Back Better' plan as priorities for spurring manufacturing activity linked to exports (Republic of Kenya 2021). Kenya's strategy documents mention the need for employment creation without an explicit vision of how that may happen through trade or value-chain development.

For Thailand, improving trade facilitation practices and supporting deeper subregional and regional integration through trade are part of the five-year development plan launched in 2017. That plan sees Thailand establishing itself as a major trade and investment base in the subregion through increasing competitiveness in transportation and supply-chain logistics. The five-year plan mentions jobs only in the context of enhancing opportunities for the 40 per cent of the population with the lowest incomes and fostering the self-reliance of communities based on the 'sufficiency economy philosophy'—a development theory that prioritizes moderation, self-reliance, and human capital (Mongsawad 2010).

South Africa's long-term development strategy envisions more robust regional trade with partners in Southern Africa through improvements in regional trade infrastructure and cooperation. The emphasis on regional trade reflects an expectation that more vibrant growth will take place in emerging economies (Republic of South Africa 2012). The country's Reconstruction and Recovery Plan reaffirms this orientation. A priority intervention is 'industrialization through localization', where special measures to support local industries (e.g. through working capital loans at 0–2 per cent interest to MSMEs) would be linked to investments in infrastructure, which would lead to reduced dependence on imported finished goods and more competitive export sectors. Alongside shifting state procurement to local producers and enacting mass public employment interventions, this approach is understood to be one which will generate jobs by building MSME participation in the manufacturing value chain.

3.4 Public investment

The Bangladeshi five-year plan explicitly places private investment at the forefront of the country's development strategy, making the creation of a private, investment-friendly environment the government's primary role. The five-year plan released in July 2020 envisions public investment primarily in improving health infrastructure, rebuilding the social protection system, addressing infrastructure constraints, and strengthening water management (Bangladesh Planning Commission (General Economics Division) 2020: 115–16). Other areas targeted for public investment include education, skill development programmes, ICT training, and infrastructure projects.

Similarly, Kenya has prioritized investment in digital infrastructure and ICT services to facilitate e-commerce and the efficient delivery of public services. In particular, the Kenyan government will focus on bridging digital gaps; developing appropriate content; skills development,; and enhancing the affordability, accessibility, and reliability of digital infrastructure. Investing in infrastructure is expected to stimulate consumer demand, in turn further increasing public and private investment. Deepening public financial management reform, including consolidating public investment project data into a centralized system for analysis, is envisioned as a way to reprioritize and rationalize spending so as to attain fiscal consolidation.

While there is consensus across the four countries that public investment in education, public health, and infrastructure is necessary for economic growth and the creation of jobs in the recovery, the national economic policy plans of middle-income countries also include labour market interventions such as investment in skills development programmes and the implementation of labour policies to boost employment, improve labour productivity, and increase wages. Thailand's approach, for example, envisions human capital development via improved access to social protection and quality social services, including education, public health, infrastructure, and social welfare, alongside workforce skills development.

Similarly, the 'South African National Economic Reconstruction and Recovery Plan' (Republic of South Africa 2020b) is concerned with the creation of jobs through public employment programmes, infrastructure investment and delivery, and achieving gender equality and economic inclusion of women and youth. Based on this approach, mass employment opportunities will be created through social employment programmes, supporting the learning environment, as well as through initiatives that support and expand small producers producing food for their own consumption and for local informal markets. In addition, linked to the public employment programme, the South African government has proposed initiatives for employment protection and stimulation, such as fast-tracking measures that provide relief to industries, embracing digitalization for retraining retrenched workers, and promoting health and safety in the workplace, alongside exploration of reasonable alternatives to retrenchments for affected firms.

3.5 Supporting MSMEs

Finally, a review of the national economic recovery policy plans indicates greater prioritization of policies targeted at MSMEs in order to boost employment, rebuild supply chains, and establish new pathways for economic growth. For Bangladesh, this will be achieved through the provision of low-cost loans through the banking sector. Likewise, the Kenyan government will initiate innovative financial products to increase credit to MSMEs. According to its 2021 Budget Policy Statement, the provision of credit to MSMEs is critical for fostering macroeconomic stability and ensuring inclusive growth. Moreover, expanding access to credit to MSMEs is envisioned to result in an increase in credit to the private sector and a decrease in the risk of lending by commercial banks (National Treasury and Planning 2020).

The expansion of grassroots economic development is identified as a priority intervention for covering a large number of communities in Thailand (Office of the National Economic and Social Development Board 2017). Furthermore, according to the 'Twelfth National Economic and Social Development Plan (2017–2021)', production sectors such as farming, community enterprises, and MSMEs will be linked to research and education institutes with the aim of ensuring access to research for commercialization and nurturing competent entrepreneurs.

As noted above, through its 'industrialization through localization' strategy, the South African government will provide low-interest working capital loans to assist firms during the start-up phase, fast-track the involvement of township and rural enterprises in the economy, and facilitate the participation of MSMEs in key sectors such as agriculture, infrastructure development, manufacturing, retail, and tourism. In addition, critical interventions in South Africa's green economy strategy include support for MSMEs and cooperatives to take advantage of opportunities in the green economy, support for small-scale farmers through public–private partnerships in forestry, and the integration of waste pickers in the public waste management system.

4. Gap analysis

The chapter now considers the relationship between the economic recovery approaches outlined in section 3 and the composition and characteristics of the employment structure in the four countries analysed. The objective is to assess the extent to which the plans do or do not make a connection, whether explicit or implicit, between the existing employment structure and the recovery approach. This 'gap analysis', in turn, identifies questions for further research which could shed light on future evaluations of the recovery approaches.

4.1 Creating new jobs versus supporting existing jobs

One notable characteristic of all four countries' recovery approaches is that they each have a vision for job creation based on investments in targeted sectors. While all four address the quantity of employment, none explicitly addresses the quality of employment—either the quality of existing employment (e.g. through measures that would address working poverty) or the quality of future employment to be created through the envisioned investments. The Thai plan comes the closest through its mention of supporting grassroots economic development, increasing wages, and investing in human capital development. However, none of the four plans centres working poverty as a relevant factor to be considered in developing economic recovery approaches.

Yet, working poverty is widespread, and the negative impact of the pandemic on working poverty has been well documented. Globally, working poverty rates increased for the first time in 20 years in 2020 and 2021 (ILOSTAT 2022). Moreover, in many developing and middle-income countries, poverty is not necessarily associated with unemployment but with low-quality work (Rogan and Reynolds

2019). This is particularly the case in contexts where a large segment of the workforce is in informal employment. According to recent ILOSTAT estimates, over half (54 per cent) of the work force in Kenya is either in extreme or moderate poverty. Similarly, an estimated 19 per cent of the South African workforce and 26 per cent of Bangladesh's workers are below an accepted poverty line (ILOSTAT 2022).

Implicit in the national recovery plans is an emphasis on short-term relief measures, such as emergency cash grants that are not linked to employment, combined with long-term growth and structural reform measures. In all cases, the vision of job creation is one that would only be realized over many years. Interventions that could theoretically assist those in working poverty in the short-to-medium term—such as low-cost loans and skills training—are not explicitly linked to decent work deficits related to employment relationships. Rather, they locate the deficits in the workers themselves, without an analysis of the structural environment in which they work.

There is no mention, for example, of the potential role of digital platform employment in degrading the quality of existing or future jobs. Yet, many people who access work through digital platform employment have no way to access social protection or labour rights because the platform is designed precisely to avoid creating an employment relationship that would obligate employers to make social contributions. Instead of addressing the potential negative consequences of digital platform employment on job quality, the plans exclusively point to the potential for digital infrastructure of any kind to create jobs. Likewise, there is no mention of a government role in ensuring even basic standards of decent work or in protecting existing jobs. Put differently, the plans have much to say about potential job creation and nothing to say about potential job destruction or degradation.

Also implicit in the plans is a view of women's employment that privileges women's labour force participation over improving the quality of women's employment. The plans say little about the over-representation of women in low-quality jobs, the barriers women face in accessing formal employment and decent work, and the effects of women's exclusion from employment-based social protection. All of these factors affect not just women workers but also their households and communities—but they are not explicitly addressed in the plans.

4.2 Addressing employment versus addressing informal employment

The plans' treatment of informal employment is similar, to some extent, to their treatment of working poverty. They make little explicit reference to the prevalence of informal employment in the country, the links between informality and poverty, or the impact of the COVID-19 pandemic on informal workers. Rather, the plans assume the creation of wage employment through firm growth, without explicit attention to potential transitions from informality to formality among informal workers. To the extent that any approach to formalization is implicit in the plans, none of them reflect the principles embedded in ILO Recommendation 204 on Formalizing the Informal Economy.

Yet, in all four countries, informal employment accounts for a significant proportion of the workforce and is crucial to economic recovery. Informal employment accounts for 89 per cent of total employment in Bangladesh, 83 per cent of total employment in Kenya, 64 per cent of total employment in Thailand, and 34 per cent of total employment in South Africa (ILO 2018b; Kenya National Bureau of Statistics 2020). Although informal employment is a relatively low share of total employment in South Africa, earnings from informal employment are particularly important in reducing poverty in low-income households (Rogan and Cichello 2020). In Kenya, the most recent data suggests that the informal economy continues to grow and accounted for 90.7 per cent of new jobs in 2019 (Kenya National Bureau of Statistics 2020).

By definition, workers in informal employment lack access to institutional buffers against risk, such as social protection and a range of labour protections. In the two low-income countries, where more than eight in ten workers are informally employed, there is considerable scope for governments to stimulate recovery at the grassroots level by directing productive resources towards informally employed workers and creating a more enabling environment for income generation, asset accumulation, and the formalization of employment conditions. This potential is generally not addressed in the four country approaches to economic recovery, nor is there a vision of the role that formalizing the informal economy could play in the country's overall economic trajectory.

4.3   Employment in households versus formal sector units versus informal sector units

The plans do have in common a clear emphasis on creating wage employment through private-sector development in targeted sectors, alongside support for the self-employed through low-cost loans and skills development. The plans have an implicit focus on wage employment in private-sector firms, without mention of whether the envisioned wage employment would be formal or informal. While there is some mention of wage employment in the public sector, there is no mention of wage employment in households. Self-employment is implicitly viewed through the lens of entrepreneurship and interventions designed to support enterprise growth among MSMEs.

However, the plans generally do not address the distinctions between formal and informal wage employment in different types of economic units. For example, there is no mention of informal wage employment at all, and no mention of informal wage employment in firms (whether formal or informal) or in households. Yet, this diversity within the employment structure is relevant to the recovery approaches. A brief comparison of the structure of employment in Bangladesh and South Africa shows the relevance of these categories.

First, in Bangladesh, more than one-quarter of informal employment is located in households, whereas in South Africa around 7 per cent are employed by households (Table 9.1). Given that informal employment accounts for roughly nine out of ten workers in Bangladesh, and one-quarter of those are employed by households, recovery efforts would have broad reach if they considered workers in households. Yet, the plans make no mention of this significant segment of the workforce. Domestic workers in Bangladesh identify low wages, irregular payments, lack of leave provisions, numerous occupational health and safety hazards, lack of bargaining power, and lack of affordable housing as characteristics of their work and areas where government interventions could support recovery (WIEGO 2020).

As Table 9.1 shows, Bangladesh also has nearly three times as many informal workers in the formal sector compared to South Africa. Informal workers in the formal sector would include, for example, those working in garment factories, where they have an employment relationship with a formal-sector employer but lack any form of social or labour protection through their work. Again, the recovery of these workers is not a factor in the recovery plan. Like workers employed by households, workers in informal employment arrangements with formal-sector firms lack bargaining power to negotiate better working conditions.

The modal category of informal employment in both countries is employment in informal-sector units, representing nearly half of total informal employment. This is the segment of the workforce where interventions supporting the self-employed in small and microenterprises have potential to support recovery. Yet, the plans focus much more heavily on the creation of new jobs through private-sector investment, where those new jobs are likely to be informal, and say little about the recovery of self-employed workers in small and microenterprises aside from references to loans and skills training.

Table 9.1 Share of informal employment in total employment by status in employment

| | Total informal employment (%) | | | |
	Total	In the informal sector	In the formal sector	In households
Bangladesh	89.0	48.9	13.5	26.7
South Africa	34.0	21.8	4.8	7.4

Source: ILO 2018a: Table B.3.

4.4 Informal employment versus status in employment

The orientation in the plans towards entrepreneurship through investments in financial inclusion and skills training assume some degree of growth potential for operators of microenterprises. Yet, statistics describing the existing employment structure in the four countries, especially in the low-income countries, suggest natural limits on the extent to which growth-orientated interventions may help. In fact, there are very few operators within the informal economy who employ others. Globally, employers—those whose enterprises are productive enough for the operator to employ at least one other person—account for only 2 per cent of all informal employment.

Again, a comparison between low-income and middle-income countries is instructive. In Bangladesh, for example, employers account for less than 1 per cent of total informal employment (Table 9.2). By contrast, own-account workers— those who are not employed by others and also do not employ others—account for over 36 per cent. Contributing family workers, who work in family enterprises but do not have autonomy or authority within the family enterprise, account for over 20 per cent. South Africa also has more than four times as many own-account workers than employers, although there are more employers than in Bangladesh. Though comparable national estimates do not exist in Kenya, the MSME survey estimates that 79 per cent of microenterprises are owned by a sole proprietor and 16 per cent operate as a family business (Kenya National Bureau of Statistics 2017), suggesting a similarly low portion of employers.

4.5 Men versus women in informal employment

The concentration of workers in the categories of own-account work and contributing family work is even more noticeable among women in informal employment. As Table 9.3 shows, more than half of all women in informal employment in Bangladesh are contributing family workers, reflecting gender norms that restrict women's economic autonomy in that country. In both Bangladesh

Table 9.2 Distribution of workers in informal employment by employment status

	Total informal employment (%)			
	Employees	Employers	Own-account workers	Contributing family workers
Bangladesh	41.6	0.7	36.4	21.3
South Africa	70.2	5.8	23.2	0.8

Source: ILO 2018a: Table B.5.

Table 9.3 Distribution of workers in informal employment by employment status and sex

	Total informal employment (%)							
	Men				Women			
	Employees	Employers	Own- account workers	Contributing family workers	Employees	Employers	Own-account workers	Contributing family workers
Bangladesh	43.8	1.1	50.0	5.2	37.6	0.1	12.0	50.3
South Africa	66.9	9.0	23.4	0.7	74.2	2.0	22.9	1.0

Source: ILO 2018a: Table B.5.

and South Africa, a far higher share of men than women are employees. This suggests that interventions aimed at employers who operate enterprises with one or more employees have little chance of reaching a significant number of women.

Among women in informal employment in South Africa, a large proportion—nearly three-quarters—are employees of either households or firms. The fact that so many women are in employment relationships that lack social protection reflects their lack of bargaining power. It should be noted that domestic workers would fall into this category, and quarterly labour force data shows a significant drop in employment among domestic workers due to the pandemic from a little over 1 million domestic workers employed between January and March 2020 to only 848,000 domestic workers employed over the same period in 2021 (see Chakravarty and Nayak, Chapter 7 in this volume). This reflects both a loss of employment and a greater likelihood of poverty and hunger in these workers' households. Here again, improving the terms of employment—such as written contracts with protections against arbitrary dismissal—could have a significant impact on recovery, but such measures do not appear in the recovery plans.

5. An economic recovery for the informal economy?

Where expanding economic activities create employment opportunities, the economic recovery plans are largely silent on how these can contribute to a transition from the informal to the formal economy and support the livelihoods of informal workers. In particular, the top-down approach taken in all four national economic recovery plans fails to examine the sectors of work within the informal economy that could benefit from more favourable integration into local and global supply chains. This suggests limited recognition of the way the formal economy—workers, employers, and government—rely on the cheaper goods and services offered by the informal economy for their productive activities and social reproduction (Agarwala 2009: 315–42).

A useful example can be drawn from the case of Bangladesh. As noted above, Bangladesh plans to expand the RMG sector to generate jobs and replenish foreign exchange reserves as it accounts for 83 per cent of the country's exports (ILO and UN Women 2020). The sector was hit hard by the pandemic as raw materials became difficult to procure, payments were delayed, and orders cancelled, with over one million workers fired or furloughed by March 2020 (Anner 2020). Within the RMG sector, women outnumber men as factory workers and homeworkers (ILO and UN Women 2020). Factory workers are in either informal or formal waged employment, while homeworkers are dependent contractors in the informal economy. The latter work from their homes and have contractual arrangements of a commercial nature (but not a contract of employment) and are dependent on that unit for access to the market (ILO 2018a). Far from curtailing growth or diminishing productivity, women homeworkers in the informal economy subsidize the production costs of formal firms in the RMG sector. They enable factories to shift over the costs of production to workers operating from their homes (Chen 2014) and allow Bangladesh to fend off fierce competition in the global market.

However, there is no mention of homeworkers in the planned investments to expand the RMG sector. A more nuanced recovery policy would acknowledge the role of homeworkers in Bangladesh's largest export industry. There are, moreover, a number of easily implementable policy interventions which could support informal livelihoods in a crucial sector. Key support measures could include work guarantee schemes linked to the garment industry, supply-chain relief for selected subsectors, incentives for firms to provide work orders to home-based workers, the promotion of extended producer responsibility schemes, and the extension of social protection to homeworkers.

The South African context offers similar lessons. On the one hand, economic recovery plans continue to privilege existing private-sector firms in the agro-business sector through the Comprehensive Land and Agrarian Strategy, which calls on firms to create 317,000 new jobs in the fruit and other high-value crops. The inconsistencies in South Africa's approach to food production and distribution suggest that there will be no significant redistribution of profits between large agro-business companies and smallholder farmers, waged informal agricultural workers, or street vendors and market traders. In response, some informal worker organizations are calling for more significant shifts in economic recovery plans to redistribute profits more equitably across local and national supply chains.

On other hand, the South African government's social employment programmes will be targeted at the unemployed and directed at recycling and waste collection and supporting smaller food producers to produce for their own consumption and for local informal markets. This may reflect lessons learned from South Africa's first lockdown in 2020, when the government initially banned informal trade, privileging the sale of food in supermarkets. Faced with immediate backlash, the government was pushed by informal traders' organizations to designate informal food vending in markets, streets, and home shops as an essential service, given their critical role in food security in low-income areas (Bamu and Marchiori 2020). Such recognition is, therefore, an example of how recovery policies can be used to promote the integration of informal workers into supply chains.

Middle-income countries such as South Africa and Thailand could also consider extending and expanding their social assistance programmes as a complementary form of support to own-account workers and contributing family workers. Recent evidence from countries such as Brazil and South Africa suggests that social assistance through cash and in-kind transfers directed at informal workers can alleviate poverty by reducing pressure on household finances for food and basic commodities (Köhler and Bhorat 2021; Lustig et al. 2020). The scope for public investment is greater in middle-income countries, but even this remains limited, given the pressure imposed by international financial institutions for fiscal consolidation. A review of recent IMF loan arrangements suggests that 83 countries will experience fiscal contraction by 2023. This will be most pronounced in middle-income countries, while low-income countries will maintain low and stagnating social spending levels (Kentikelenis and Stubbs 2021).

Finally, a promising proposal to integrate self-employed and waged workers in the informal economy into supply chains is to support worker collectives. National economic recovery plans mention support to cooperatives in South Africa and 'community enterprises' in Thailand. In these two countries, the intention is to support workers who often face discrimination within the labour market. Evidence shows that women own-account operators organized into collectives, such as cooperatives or producer groups, will have greater capacity to create and sustain market linkages (Chen and Roever 2016; ILO and SEWA 2018). They can also help to formalize the economic activities of own-account workers through registration, allowing them to gain access to credit, business development support, and new markets. By reducing the transaction costs, collective organizations can create economies of scale in terms of both backward and forward linkages. They also serve as aggregators by providing information on markets and supporting members to adapt to new risks and constraints brought on by the pandemic (ILO 2020c).

For cooperatives and collectives to access and compete in local and global supply chains, tailored policies are needed. National economic recovery plans in South Africa propose to reduce time frames for relevant licences and permits, making it easier to register, while focusing on integration in specific sectors—retail, agriculture and agro-processing, financial services, manufacturing, and infrastructure. However, these measures are unlikely to level the playing field between cooperatives owned and managed by informal workers and larger corporations in the sectors. In India, the Self Employed Women's Association—the largest trade union of women informal workers—is calling for specific measures to reverse the disadvantages faced by women-owned cooperatives by instituting procurement policies that privilege women-run cooperatives and collectives, expanded access to digital technology through improved infrastructure and simplification of online platforms and representation of women-owned cooperatives in national and international policy spaces pertaining to the cooperative movement (SEWA 2020).

6. Conclusion

When reviewed against the composition of their respective labour markets, the four national economic recovery plans reviewed in this chapter reveal a number of common gaps. The national plans place great emphasis on the formal private sector to generate employment, with little regard to the terms of waged employment in the formal and informal economy or the reliance of private firms and public services on the goods and services produced by self-employed informal workers.

Across all four countries, the MSME policies suggest a lack of awareness of the constraints faced by own-account workers and contributing family workers to national economic output and household incomes. The policies are unlikely to reach these workers and are aimed more at entrepreneurs in small and medium enterprises, who will more likely be men. The intersection of gender and class biases in this approach risks penalizing women self-employed workers most acutely. Where South Africa and Thailand recognize the need to specifically target 'vulnerable workers', including women, older persons, and people living with disabilities, in order to improve their access to markets, this remains in line with the World Bank's approach to 'target and streamline'. Given the size of the informal economy, even in these middle-income countries, this is a wholly inadequate approach to protect informal workers from adverse integration in the labour market and ensure they have more equitable access to productive resources and higher earnings.

The emphasis placed on formal private-sector firms creates an inherent disadvantage in the recovery packages for informal workers and enterprises. The omission of explicit policies aimed at self-employed informal workers will likely exclude the vast majority of the labour force in Bangladesh, Kenya, and Thailand from an inclusive and equitable recovery. As a result, these imbalances in the national economic recovery plans are likely to deepen inequalities and entrench the increase in poverty experienced by women and men in the informal economy as countries attempt to recover from the pandemic and ongoing cost-of-living crisis.

References

Agarwala, R. (2009). 'An Economic Sociology of Informal Work: The Case of India'. In N. Bandelj (ed.), *Economic Sociology of Work (Research in the Sociology of Work)*, Vol. 18. Bingley: Emerald Group Publishing Limited. https://doi.org/10.1108/S0277-2833(2009)0000018015.

Anner, M. (2020). 'Abandoned? The Impact of Covid-19 on Workers and Businesses at the Bottom of Global Garment Supply Chains', research report, University Park, PA: Center for Global Workers' Rights, pp. 315–342.

Bamu, P., and T. Marchiori (2020). *The Recognition and Protection of Informal Traders in COVID-19 Laws: Lessons from Africa*. Manchester: Women in Informal Employment: Globalizing and Organizing (WIEGO).

Bangladesh Planning Commission (General Economics Division) (2020). 'Making Vision 2041 a Reality: Perspective Plan of Bangladesh 2021–2041' (March), available at: http://oldweb.lged.gov.bd/uploadeddocument/unitpublication/1/1049/vision%202021-2041.pdf (accessed October 2022).

Chen, M. (2014). *Informal Economy Monitoring Study Sector Report: Home*-Based Workers. Cambridge, MA: WIEGO.

Chen, M., and S. Roever (2016). 'Enhancing the Productivity of Own Account Enterprises from the Perspective of Women in the Informal Economy', a Policy Brief for the UN Secretary General's High-Level Panel on Women's Economic Empowerment, Manchester, UK.

Chen, M., E. Grapsa, G. Ismail, M. Rogan, M. Valdivia, L. Alfers et al. (2021). 'COVID-19 and Informal Work: Distinct Pathways of Impact and Recovery in 11 Cities around the World', WIEGO Working Paper No. 42, Manchester: WIEGO (May), available at: www.wiego.org/publications/covid-19-and-informal-work-distinct-pathways-impact-and-recovery-11-cities-around (accessed October 2023).

Government of the People of Bangladesh (2020). 'Eighth Five Year Plan (2020–2025)', available at: https://gedkp.gov.bd/knowledge-archive/five-year-plans/plan-documents/?cn=five-year-plans-plan-documents (accessed June 2023).

ILO (International Labour Organization) (2018a) 'Resolution Concerning Statistics on Work Relationships', 20th International Conference of Labour Statisticians (ICLS), Geneva: ILO.

ILO (2018b). *Women and Men in the Informal Economy: A Statistical Picture* (3rd edn). Geneva: ILO.

ILO (2020a). *COVID-19 and the World of Work: Impact and Policy Responses* (1st edn), ILO Monitor. Geneva: ILO.

ILO (2020b). *COVID-19 and the World of Work: Updated Analysis and Estimates* (3rd edn), ILO Monitor. Geneva: ILO.

ILO (2020c). *Interventions to Support Enterprises during the COVID-19 Pandemic and Recovery*. Geneva: ILO.

ILO (2021a). 'Building Forward Fairer: Women's Rights to Work and at Work at the Core of the COVID-19 Recovery', ILO Brief, Geneva: ILO.

ILO (2021b). *COVID-19 and the World of Work: Updated Analysis and Estimates* (7th edn), ILO Monitor. Geneva: ILO.

ILO (2021c). *COVID-19 and the World of Work: Updated Analysis and Estimates* (8th edn), ILO Monitor. Geneva: ILO.

ILO (2021d). 'Making Decent Work a Reality for Domestic Workers: Progress and Prospects Ten Years after the Adoption of the Domestic Workers Convention, 2011', No. 189, Geneva: ILO.

ILO and SEWA (2018). *Advancing Cooperation among Women Workers in the Informal Economy: The SEWA Way*. Geneva: ILO.

ILO and UN Women (2020). *Understanding the Gender Composition and Experience of Ready-Made Garment (RMG) Workers in Bangladesh*. Geneva: ILO.

ILOSTAT (2022). 'Inflation More Than Doubled between March 2021 and March 2022' (10 May), available at: https://ilostat.ilo.org/inflation-more-than-doubled-between-march-2021-and-march-2022 (accessed June 2023).

IMF (International Monetary Fund) (2021). *Fiscal Monitor: Strengthening the Credibility of Public Finances*. Washington DC: IMF.

IMF (2022). 'World Economic Outlook: October', Washington, DC: IMF.

Kentikelenis, A., and T. Stubbs. (2021). 'Austerity Redux: The Post-Pandemic Wave of Budget Cuts and the Future of Global Public Health', *Global Policy*, 13(1): 5–17. https://doi.org/10.1111/1758-5899.13028.

KNBS (Kenya National Bureau of Statistics) (2017). 'Micro, Small, Medium Establishments: Basic Report 2016', Nairobi: KNBS.

KNBS (2020). 'Economic Survey 2020', Nairobi: KNBS.

Köhler, T., and H. Bhorat (2021). 'Can Cash Transfers Aid Labour Market Recovery? Evidence from South Africa's Special COVID-19 Grant', Development Policy Research Unit (DPRU) Working Paper No. 202108, Cape Town: University of Cape Town.

Lakshmi Ratan, A., S. Roever, R. Jhabvala, and P. Sen (2021). 'Evidence Review of COVID-19 and Women's Informal Employment: A Call to Support the Most Vulnerable First in the Economic Recovery', Bill & Melinda Gates Foundation, available at: https://docs.gatesfoundation.org/documents/evidence_review_covid-19_and_women's_informal_employment_a_call_to_support_the_most_vulnerable_first_in_the_economic_recovery.pdf.

Lustig, N., V. Martin, S. Orleans Reed, M. Rogan, E. Grapsa, G. Ismail et al. (2020). 'The Impact of COVID-19 Lockdowns and Expanded Social Assistance on Inequality, Poverty and Mobility in Argentina, Brazil, Colombia and Mexico', Center for Global Development (CGD) Working Paper No. 556, Washington, DC: CGD.

Mongsawad, P. (2010). 'The Philosophy of the Sufficiency Economy: A Contribution to the Theory of Development', *Asia-Pacific Development Journal*, 17(1): 123–43. https://doi.org/10.18356/02bd5fb3-en.

National Treasury and Planning (2020). 'Republic of Kenya 2021 Budget Policy Statement. Nairobi: Budget Policy Statement' (February), available at: www.treasury.go.ke/wp-content/uploads/2021/03/2021-Budget-Policy-Statement.pdf (accessed August 2021).

Office of the National Economic and Social Development Board (2017). 'The Twelfth National Economic and Social Development Plan (2017–2021)', Bangkok: Office of the Prime Minister, available at: www.nesdc.go.th/nesdb_en/ewt_dl_link.php?nid=4345 (accessed August 2021).

Office of the National Economic and Social Development Board (2022). 'The Thirteenth National Economic and Social Development Plan (2023–2027)', Bangkok: Office of the Prime Minister, available at: www.nesdc.go.th/nesdb_en/main.php?filename=develop_issue (accessed June 2023)

Ogando, A.C., M. Rogan, and R. Moussié (2022). 'Impacts of the Covid-19 Pandemic and Unpaid Care Work on Informal Workers' Livelihoods', *International Labour Review*, 161(2): 171–94. https://doi.org/10.1111/ilr.12332.

Orleans Reed, S., M. Rogan, E. Grapsa, G. Ismail, and M. Valdivia (2021). 'The Crisis Is Far from Over for Informal Workers: We Need an Inclusive Recovery for the Majority of the World's Workforce', Policy Insights No. 8, Manchester: WIEGO.

Republic of Kenya (2018). 'Third Medium-Term Plan 2018–2022', available at: https://vision2030.go.ke/publication/third-medium-term-plan-2018-2022/#:~:text=Our%20country's%20long%20term%20development,five%2Dyear%20medium%20term%20plans.

Republic of Kenya (2021). 'Budget Policy Statement' (February), available at: www.treasury.go.ke/wp-content/uploads/2021/03/2021-Budget-Policy-Statement.pdf (accessed September 2022).

Republic of South Africa (2012). 'National Development Plan 2030', available at: www.gov.
za/sites/default/files/gcis_document/201409/ndp-2030-our-future-make-it-workr.pdf
(accessed September 2022).

Republic of South Africa (2020a). 'Economic Reconstruction and Recovery Plan 2020',
available at: www.gov.za/sites/default/files/gcis_document/202010/south-african-
economic-reconstruction-and-recovery-plan.pdf (accessed September 2022).

Republic of South Africa (2020b). 'The South African Economic Reconstruction and Recovery Plan', available at: www.gov.za/sites/default/files/gcis_document/202010/south-
african-economic-reconstruction-and-recovery-plan.pdf (accessed August 2020).

Rogan, M., and P. Cichello (2020). '(Re)Conceptualising Poverty and Informal Employment'. In M. Chen and F. Carré (eds), *The Informal Economy Revisited: Examining the
Past, Envisioning the Future.* London: Routledge, pp. 98–102. https://doi.org/10.4324/
9780429200724-15

Rogan, M., and J. Reynolds (2019). 'Trends in the Working Poverty Rate (WPR) in Post-
Apartheid South Africa, 1997–2012', *Development Southern Africa*, 36(5): 699–715.
https://doi.org/10.1080/0376835X.2019.1590181.

SEWA (2020). *Women's Cooperatives and COVID-19: Learnings and the Way Forward.*
Ahmedabad: SEWA Cooperative Federation.

UN Women (2020). 'Whose Time to Care? Unpaid Care and Domestic Work during
Covid', New York: UN Women (25 November), available at: https://data.unwomen.org/
publications/whose-time-care-unpaid-care-and-domestic-work-during-covid-19#:~:
text=To%20answer%20this%20question%2C%20UN,still%20doing%20the%20lion's%
20share (accessed July 2023).

WIEGO (Women in Informal Employment: Globalizing and Organizing) (2020). 'The
Costs of Insecurity: Domestic Workers' Access to Social Protection and Services in
Dhaka, Bangladesh', WIEGO Policy Brief 19, Manchester: WIEGO (October), avail-
able at: www.wiego.org/sites/default/files/publications/file/WIEGO_PolicyBrief_N19_
Bangladesh%20for%20Web.pdf (accessed June 2023).

WIEGO (2021). 'COVID-19 Crisis and the Informal Economy: Round 1 Global Summary', Manchester: WIEGO, available at: www.wiego.org/covid-19-crisis-and-informal-
economy-study-global-findings (accessed July 2023).

World Bank (2021a). *Global Economic Prospects.* Washington, DC: World Bank.

World Bank (2022). 'The World Bank in Kenya', Washington, DC: World Bank, available
at: www.worldbank.org/en/country/kenya/overview#2 (accessed September 2022).

PART III

THE FUTURE

10

Social Protection, the COVID-19 Crisis, and the Informal Economy

Lessons from Relief for Comprehensive Social Protection

Laura Alfers and Florian Juergens-Grant

1. Introduction

One of the overarching lessons from the COVID-19 crisis has been the need for universal social protection; social protection which covers everyone, including the so-called 'missing majority' of workers in the informal economy. What was clear from the hard lockdowns of 2020 was that the lack of adequate social protection coverage exacerbated the economic fallout of the crisis, with many informal workers—over 60 per cent of those sampled in the first round of Women in Informal Employment: Globalizing and Organizing's (WIEGO's) COVID-19 and the Informal Economy Impact Study—unable to access even the most basic relief measures extended by governments whilst earning little to no income.

Despite these limitations in access, however, governments were rolling out relief measures at an unprecedented rate, often attempting to reach the informal workers who were largely invisible to the state. By January 2022, the World Bank had recorded a total of 3,856 social protection and labour market measures aimed at relieving the impacts of the COVID-19 crisis (Gentilini et al. 2022). As Dafuleya (2020) points out, short-term, emergency relief measures should not be confused with social protection, which should be understood as longer-term, institutionalized forms of protection. Nevertheless, the fact that many of the relief measures—particularly those rolled out in 2020—leveraged existing social protection systems and programmes and, in several cases, made a first attempt at reaching informal workers means that there are lessons to reflect on for the longer-term comprehensive extension of social protection to informal workers.

This chapter considers the implications of COVID-19 relief measures for the building and extension of comprehensive and universal social protection systems. It begins with a synthesis of existing literature, which has reflected on the lessons from relief for social protection more generally, using this to situate and contextualize the findings of WIEGO's COVID-19 Informal Economy Impact Study as well as other reflections on the COVID-19 relief response and social protection

Laura Alfers and Florian Juergens-Grant, *Social Protection, the COVID-19 Crisis, and the Informal Economy*. In: *COVID-19 and the Informal Economy*. Edited by: Martha Alter Chen, Michael Rogan, and Kunal Sen, Oxford University Press.
© Laura Alfers and Florian Juergens-Grant (2024). DOI: 10.1093/oso/9780198887041.003.0011

from within the wider WIEGO network. It then examines three key areas that were highlighted by the crisis and are likely to impact the shape of social protection systems moving forwards. These include the contested meaning of universality, the digitization of social protection systems, and the possibilities for informal workers' participation in building a more inclusive social protection. In doing so, the chapter argues that the terrain of the social protection debate is shifting—it is increasingly uncontroversial that universal social protection is needed and that the state must play a role. However, the more nuanced debates that are emerging across the three areas identified above will shape the terrain of whether the form of universal social protection that remains after COVID-19 is a positive and supportive form of inclusion.

2. Learning from the COVID-19 relief response: A review of the literature

Over the course of 2021 and 2022, multiple papers and commentaries emerged which summarized and analysed the evidence on the roll-out of relief measures in 2020 and reflected on what had been learned for social protection more widely. The following sections present key lessons learned from the global social protection response to the COVID-19 pandemic, organized by key themes.

2.1 Pre-crisis social protection shaped relief measures

If there is one consensus amongst analysts of COVID-19 relief measures, it is that the characteristics of pre-crisis social protection systems and programmes significantly shaped the crisis response. Analysing the timeliness and adequacy (extent of coverage and quality of benefits) of relief responses across 53 low- and middle-income countries, Beazley et al. (2021) found that the fastest and most adequate responses tended to be in countries where existing systems and programmes already covered all or most of the intended recipients. Drawing on a series of in-depth case studies to look at the coverage, adequacy, and timeliness of relief in selected low-and middle-income countries, Bastagli and Lowe (2021) similarly observe that effective responses were enabled by the quality and scope of the underlying social protection infrastructure, including identification systems, widespread financial service provision, and mobile phone ownership as well as robust internet and data networks. Focusing on relief measures in Africa, a key learning for Devereux (2021: 442) was that countries with 'comprehensive, well-functioning and well-funded social protection systems' were in a better position to quickly and effectively respond to COVID-19. Kidd and Sibun (2020) likewise pointed to the superior performance of universal social protection systems during the crisis, compared to those that relied primarily on narrowly poverty-targeted programmes, where there was a struggle to quickly identify, enrol, and reach previously excluded groups. For these reasons, the International Labour Organization (ILO 2021: 29, 65) argues that the pandemic has 'made the case for universal social protection irrefutable', while making the weakness of limited safety net approaches 'glaringly apparent' as countries without comprehensive coverage needed to rapidly fill gaps in their system 'under duress, sometimes with a fair amount of improvisation and teething problems'.

2.2 Data and digital technologies were pivotal

Most observers, moreover, agree on the critical role that data systems and digital technologies played in the provision of COVID-19 relief. Critical to the success of relief efforts were the presence of information systems and databases to identify potential recipients of support and the electronic transfer of benefits. As many pre-crises social protection systems had large coverage gaps, countries sought to quickly identify and enrol new recipients at the onset of the pandemic. In identifying new recipients, governments mainly relied on existing databases and on-demand registration. Bastagli and Lowe (2021) and Beazley et al. (2021) both agree that the existence of up-to-date data and inclusive information systems were key enablers of an effective response. However, this was only the case for databases that had sufficiently wide coverage and had been updated; in cases where databases were not updated, the effectiveness of the response was undermined.

It is noteworthy that *social registries* (databases of potential recipients for social protection, often identified on the basis of poverty indicators), which are promoted by the World Bank as a key enabler for achieving universal coverage, did 'not appear to be strongly associated with faster implementation of any type of expansion. Indeed, it appears to be associated with slower expansion), especially coverage expansion' (Beazley et al. 2021: 14). This is mainly due to limited coverage of such registries and quickly outdated information. Looking at 38 countries with data on social registries and COVID-19 cash transfers, Gentilini et al. (2021: 13) find only a 'mild relationship'[1] between the two.

While in use in more a limited way before COVID-19, the widespread adoption of electronic payment modalities, such as e-wallets and digital transfers, may be amongst the most important legacies of the pandemic. On the positive side, electronic payments appear to have facilitated a faster response. Analysing national cash transfers in 53 low- and middle-income countries, Beazley et al. (2021) find that, on average, those using electronic systems delivered their first payment a month before comparable programmes relying on manual or mixed

---

[1] An R^2 of 0.0113.

mechanisms. This advantage was particularly pronounced in contexts with high levels of digital and financial inclusion. Gentilini et al. (2022: 16), however, find that digital payments were 'faster, but not by a significant amount of time—i.e., 21 versus 23 days, respectively'. Moving beyond timeliness and towards questions of inclusion, authors of a number of World Bank publications have also expressed their expectation that direct payments to women through accounts in their name may enhance financial inclusion and autonomy (Demirgüç-Kunt et al. 2022; Zimmerman et al. 2020).

Others, however, caution that the 'use of digital technology in making social assistance payments can be a double-edged sword for marginalised and vulnerable groups' (Roelen and Carter 2022: 14). In many contexts, women and vulnerable groups tend to have lower access to identification documents, mobile phones, and bank or mobile accounts, which can heighten the risks of exclusion from digital payments (Beazley et al. 2021; Roelen and Carter 2022). Data from 2021 shows that despite progress (financial account ownership globally increased by 50 per cent in the past decade), gender gaps in access to digital and financial services remain. Worldwide, women are six percentage points less likely to have a financial account, whether at a bank or through a mobile money service (Demirgüç-Kunt et al. 2022). In low- and middle-income countries, 234 million fewer women than men have access to the internet on their mobile phones (UN Women and UN DESA 2021). During COVID-19, these disparities meant that digitally enabled social protection interventions often failed to reach the most marginalized women (Staab et al. 2022).

2.3 Universal social protection requires inclusive design and implementation

The pandemic has once more highlighted that universal access and the inclusion of marginalized groups in social protection cannot be assumed but rather is the result of concerted efforts based on nuanced understanding of exclusion risks. This was recognized early into the pandemic by the Social Protection Inter-Agency Cooperation Board (SPIAC-B), chaired jointly by the World Bank and the ILO, which issued a call for the inclusion of previously excluded groups, including workers in the informal economy, for sustained efforts to increase financing and to ensure participation from all affected stakeholders in programme design, implementation, and monitoring and evaluation (SPIAC-B 2020a).

Such statements notwithstanding, social protection systems—including their pandemic-driven expansions—often failed to adequately support those most affected by the crisis. Exclusion can be the result of insufficient attention being paid to the characteristics and needs of excluded groups at the design stage. For instance, only 32 per cent of the 4,968 crisis measures by governments recorded by

UNDP and UN Women (2022) between March 2020 and August 2021 took gender into account (Staab et al. 2022). Similar blind spots are evident in the pre-crisis design of social protection systems, which largely excluded informal workers from both poverty-targeted social assistance and employment social insurance (Barca and Alfers 2021). This lack of consideration of informal workers has constrained systems' abilities to rapidly ensure comprehensive coverage during COVID-19. According to WIEGO's longitudinal impact study on COVID-19 conducted in 12 global cities, just over 40 per cent of informal workers reported access to a cash grant (41 per cent) and food aid (42 per cent) in mid-2020 (Chen et al. 2021). The study found that access to relief differed widely depending on the strength and inclusiveness of the existing social protection infrastructure. In places such as Bangkok (Thailand) and Tiruppur (India), comparatively high levels of access to relief were the result of relatively developed social protection infrastructure as well as the efforts of organizations of informal workers, who supported their members to overcome barriers (Chen et al. 2021).

Lack of consideration to informal workers also extends to choices made by governments in the administration of relief. WIEGO's longitudinal COVID-19 study points to persistent challenges that informal workers faced in accessing social protection across the 12 study locations. Key barriers include the lack of data on informal workers and complicated administrative procedures involved in the application process as well as limited access to digital technologies and low levels of digital literacy (Chen et al. 2021). Invisibility in government databases that acted as gatekeepers to eligibility for relief was a particularly important issue. In Lima, Peru, for instance, the most important barrier to access was not being listed in the country's incomplete social registry. The exclusion of non-citizens and documentation requirements were the main reasons for respondents reporting not receiving relief in Bangkok (Thailand), and Durban (South Africa). In Bangkok, this contributed to the widespread exclusion of migrant domestic workers, while in Durban, these requirements made it difficult for waste pickers to access support (Alfers et al. 2022).

Despite challenges and blind spots, it is worth reflecting on the important innovations developed by governments in their sometimes first ever efforts to extend at least basic protection to informal workers. Particularly noteworthy are the introductions of cash transfers explicitly—although not always exclusively—designed for informal workers, such as Togo's Novissi, Brazil's Auxílio Emergencial, Madagascar's Tosika Fameno, Sri Lanka's emergency cash transfers, and Peru's Bono Familiar Universal (Bastagli and Lowe 2021). While these schemes were temporary, they may serve as a 'proof of concept', potentially convincing policymakers in the feasibility and legitimacy of direct income support to people in need, including to informal workers (Gentilini 2021).

At the same time, the crisis highlighted that cash assistance is rarely enough, prompting renewed efforts in many low- and middle-income countries (such as

Togo, Laos, Tanzania, and Cambodia) to extend contributory social insurance to informal workers (Barca and Alfers 2021). Barca and Alfers (2021: 5) suggest that, post-COVID, there is a 'political opportunity to engage with scheme financing, design and implementation to make them more accessible to informal workers'. On the implementation side, reforms are needed to make registration more accessible, for instance, by adapting registration processes to the working patterns and location of informal workers, ensuring the participation of workers' organizations, simplifying procedures and required documentation, and linking registration for social insurance with social assistance schemes. Payments can be simplified into a single annual payment or by introducing more flexibility: by allowing mobile phone payments or enabling workers to contribute whenever they have sufficient income (Barca and Alfers 2021).

From a policy perspective, key questions are whether social insurance should be voluntary or mandatory, whether informal workers will be integrated into mainstream schemes or segmented into stand-alone ones, and the extent to which the system will be based on 'solidarity financing'. In the absence of employers' contributions, informal workers must often contribute an unaffordably high share of their income, which creates barriers to accessing social insurance. Barca and Alfers (2021) argue that without full or partial subsidization of insurance premiums, contributory schemes will be unlikely to reach large-scale coverage. To enable low-income groups to join social insurance schemes, governments should consider lowering or removing contributions and institute matching contributions from the state as well as top-up systems and care credits for those with irregular contributions due to care responsibilities (Barca and Alfers 2021).

2.4 An effective response requires readily available financing

Conversative estimates[2] suggest that countries spend an extra USD3 trillion on social protection during COVID-19. This additional spending represented 2.1 per cent of gross domestic product (GDP) in high-income countries, 2.5 per cent in upper-middle-income countries, 1.7 per cent in lower-middle-income countries, and 1.3 per cent in low-income countries (Gentilini et al. 2022). Governments that were able to source the necessary financing domestically or had established contribution agreements and contingency financing mechanisms before the crisis were able to respond quicker than those who needed to go through the bureaucracy of raising funds through external sources (Bastagli and Lowe 2021; Beazley et al. 2021). As a result, government-funded interventions were, on average, faster than those that relied fully or partially on external donor financing (Beazley et al. 2021).

---

[2] This is a conservative estimate since spending data is available for about 23 per cent of social protection measures in the database maintained by Gentilini et al. (2022).

2.5 Perspectives of informal workers

The learnings presented in the previous sections are very much 'from above'—from international institutions, researchers, and social protection policy experts. What has been learned by organizations of informal workers themselves about social protection? Amongst other reflections, WIEGO's *Covid-19 and the Informal Economy* impact study provides a grounded complement to the reflections discussed above (Chen et al. 2021).

First, there has been a shift in perspective from organizations of informal workers on the elements which make up comprehensive social protection systems. When WIEGO first developed its social protection programme over 20 years ago, its constituent membership-based organizations (MBOs) had identified health care, income security in old age, and childcare as key issues. As Moussié and Alfers (2022) note, this led to a strong focus on public services for WIEGO. However, with the greater visibility that relief responses brought to income protection measures, as well as the opening of political space, MBOs have started to make much stronger demands for income protection in the form of both social insurance and social assistance, including protection against income losses as the result of unemployment and underemployment, work injury, and older age. To this effect, delegations of informal workers to the International Labour Conference (ILC) in 2021 made demands for greater public financing for social protection, for ensuring employer contributions where possible, and for the state subsidization of informal workers' contributions to contributory social protection schemes (WIEGO 2021a).

Second, while the advances with digital systems during the COVID-19 relief response were met with great excitement within the broader social protection community, from the perspective of MBOs, what stands out is the critical role they themselves played in expanding the reach of relief measures to the ground. In the most successful cases, this facilitation role built on long-standing relationships with the state so that a degree of trust and communication already existed. For example, both HomeNet Thailand and the Anuhatham Union drew on their existing relationship with state actors to provide 'last-mile' services, ensuring that their members were able to overcome major barriers to access, including those created by the use of digital systems and platforms (Alfers 2021; Alfers et al. 2021). This emphasizes the importance of grassroots organizations as active participants in the public sphere and the very real need for their inclusion across social protection systems, from governance to delivery.

Third, the issue of the relative inadequacy of relief measures on offer to informal workers has arisen. The WIEGO study findings suggest that while cash grants and food rations did help to keep food on the table, they were largely inadequate to serve their original intention—to enable informal workers and their families to stay at home and protect their health (Alfers et al. 2020; Reed et al. 2021). Moreover, the amount they received in comparison to the billions spent on economic stimulus measures aimed at large corporations was paltry. As a street vendor from Lima, Peru put it, 'The bono [cash grant] is an insult to the dignity of human beings, they should have given us an economic incentive to generate income to be able to work. But with 600 Soles [USD 160] what are you going to do? On the other hand, large companies got billions' (Alfers et al. 2022: 31).

3. Moving forwards: Implications for comprehensive social protection systems inclusive of informal workers

What are the overarching considerations or issues that can be taken forwards arising out of the analyses discussed above? There are five areas which suggest themselves immediately:

- Social protection systems need to be expanded beyond formal workers to cover workers in the informal economy. Certainly, the COVID-19 crisis has resulted in a greater consensus than ever that *universal social protection systems*—systems which cover the entire population—are needed both to provide more effective crisis responses and to ensure protection from more everyday life-cycle risks. Critically, linked to this is the need to mobilize *sources of financing* for social protection to ensure that provision can be extended to previously uncovered groups but also to improve the adequacy of the benefits so that they are able to make a meaningful difference in people's lives.
- The design of social protection programmes does matter; *how* systems are designed and *how* programmes are implemented has real consequences for inclusion. Evaluations of programme design abound with respect to social assistance (and particularly cash transfers), but there remains a gap in understanding how design impacts on the inclusion of (informal) workers as a specific population group. Moreover, much less work has been done to evaluate the impact of design on this group in other parts of the social protection system, for example social insurance.
- While the arrival of the so-called digital welfare state is not linked solely to the COVID-19 crisis, the crisis has sped up its reach and implementation, with some benefits, but also posing real challenges to those informal workers on the wrong side of the digital divide. This means that issues such as *digital and financial inclusion* are likely to become increasingly important as informal workers and their organizations increasingly engage in the social protection policy space.
- The importance of making space for *participation* in the design and governance of social protection systems has also been emphasized through the

relative successes of relief efforts which were able to build off existing relationships between the state and organizations of informal workers. Here, the challenge is to ensure that informal workers and their organizations are viewed as not only passive recipients of social protection but also active agents in the building of social protection systems.

This section elaborates on three of the issues that we feel are particularly up for contestation as the battle for universal and comprehensive social protection moves forwards.

3.1   Universalism

As noted above, the extension of 'universal social protection' has become increasingly accepted as an important policy goal, signed up to by both the leading international agencies working on the issue—the World Bank and the ILO.[3] The reality is, however, that there are different interpretations of what universalism means in practice. The ILO advocates for what could be termed a social democratic model, combining social assistance to different categories of people (children, unemployed people, the disabled, older people) with public social insurance, funded by a combination of contributions from the state, workers, and employers. Furthermore, the ILO favours defined benefit (DB) schemes that guarantee benefit levels and allow for redistribution between earners of higher and lower incomes. In this model, adapting to a world of work which is largely informal requires bolstering the social protection floor, formalizing employment relationships where possible, and adapting social insurance for large numbers of self-employed workers (ILO 2021).

The World Bank, in its white paper on social protection, proposes a radically different model of universalism. At the centre of it is a tax-funded 'guaranteed minimum' to protect against 'poverty and catastrophic losses'.[4] This scheme will be funded by general taxes and replace existing minimum guarantees in contributory systems and tax incentives to contribute. To ensure a 'minimum adequate level of consumption smoothing', the model envisions mandatory and individually financed public insurance schemes, which should be either defined contribution (DC) schemes—where contributions are directly linked to individual accounts and benefits—or 'actuarially fair' defined benefit schemes. By 'actuarially fair', the World Bank means not redistributing between poorer and richer members of insurance schemes. Indeed, a central principle of the World Bank's

---

[3] See the Global Partnership for Universal Social Protection (USP 2030) platform, available at: https://usp2030.org (accessed November 2023).
[4] In the World Development Report (2019) this is discussed as a 'progressively universal' basic income.

proposal—and departure from the ILO's model—is to pursue 'poverty-prevention and redistribution objectives' purely through tax-financed instruments, with statutory contributions limited to consumption smoothing and insurance (Packard et al. 2019: 10). These basic schemes are complemented by higher layers of voluntary and individually financed insurance schemes with a limited regulatory and behavioural 'nudging' role for the state to encourage savings.

There is a lot to unpack in this high-level overview of the differences in models of universalism, and not all can be discussed here. Centrally important for informal workers, however, are the differences in the proposals around insurance because this is where their coverage as working people is most likely to be located. It is also an area of social protection and development policy that receives relatively little attention in comparison to the much-discussed questions of social assistance.

Both models see a role for insurance, but there are important differences in how that insurance is financed, whether it remains under the purview of the state or is privatized (or hybridized), and whether those insurances remain within the realm of labour regulation or not. For the World Bank, the adapted social democratic model is not well suited to the modern world of work for several reasons. First, while attaching social security to employment was logical during the era of industrial revolution when state capacity was weak, governments now are much better equipped to pool risks through taxation and provide many forms of social protection themselves. Second, asking employers to contribute directly to the financing of social security establishes a 'tax' on formal employment which is not equalized out by the perceived benefits of social security for workers or employers. This 'tax wedge' distorts the labour market and drives up levels of unemployment and informality as workers and employers seek to evade additional payments for which they see little benefit. Third, while informality means that incomes are often not visible to the state and therefore hard to tax, spending on consumption is increasingly visible through digital transactions. Therefore, consumption taxes are an important way to expand fiscal space for social protection and have the added benefit of a less distortionary impact on the labour market than taxes attached to income (Packard et al. 2019).

From the perspective of many informal workers, particularly the self-employed, this vision of universalism does have pragmatic elements. The proposed expansion of cash transfers and income-targeted subsidies to access publicly managed schemes providing basic income protection that are not reliant on an employment relationship lines up well with demands from organizations of informal workers for governments to take more responsibility for the subsidization of contributory schemes (WIEGO Network 2021).

At the same time, however, proposals for the expansion of fiscal space through the imposition of taxes on consumption, whilst reducing contributions through income taxes, are not completely straightforward. Certainly, governments such as Ghana have created fiscal space through increases in value-added tax (VAT), ensuring that exemptions limit regressivity (Bastagli 2015). At the same time, such increases may not be able to continue infinitely, and recent research from the International Trade Union Confederation (ITUC) suggests that, in general, indirect taxes on consumption cause an 'additional rise in output prices and overall consumer prices, thereby lowering real income and crowding out consumption and investment, which offset any positive impact from social protection transfers' (ITUC 2022). The recent imposition of an e-levy on electronic money transactions in that same country in an attempt to expand the domestic tax base was felt by already struggling informal workers and failed to generate more than 10 per cent of the US$900 million it was intended to raise as people curtailed electronic payments (MENAFN-AFP 2022). This example does raise questions about the capacity of consumption taxes to adequately replace taxes on income as a financing method; as various United Nations (UN) agencies have argued, the expansion of employer contributions to the social protection financing mix is critical to ensuring that fiscal space is opened up for social assistance and to potentially subsidize the self-employed (Ortiz et al. 2019).

The problem with not having sufficient financing for the full package proposed in the white paper is that what results is a somewhat disappointing recommendation to institute minimalist 'social safety nets' complemented by voluntary individual savings accounts to cover the 'missing middle', as seen in a subsequent World Bank report on social protection and informality (Guven et al. 2021). As Juergens-Grant (2022) points out, for informal workers already suffering the impacts of the economic crisis attached to COVID-19, it will be a challenge, to say the least, for individual savings to provide adequate protections. Neither has there been much reflection on how individual savings accounts have historically failed to provide adequate social protection in regions like Latin America (Ortiz et al. 2018).

If we are going to argue for the withdrawal of one type of financing for a policy area as critical (and as generally underfunded) as social protection, it is important to examine the theoretical and empirical robustness of the arguments against employer contributions. Certainly, the state can be a more efficient provider of certain protections than employers, but as Behrendt and Nguyen (2018) point out, this is not necessarily an argument against direct employer contributions into a public insurance scheme. Here, the state still operates the insurance fund, with employer contributions as one of the income streams. What is really at issue, then, is whether this financing stream does, in fact, have the 'damaging' distortionary effects on the labour market it is claimed to have.

Although the argument for the distortionary impacts of labour market regulation (including social insurance) has achieved the status of an orthodoxy, neither the theoretical nor empirical evidence for it are uncontested. Theoretically, Heintz

(2008) points out that arguments for the removal of labour market regulation are based on neoclassical models of the perfectly competitive labour market, where any interference from the state distorts functioning and leads to misallocation of productive resources. Yet, as he argues, the idea of the perfectly functioning labour market is 'theoretical make-believe'; in the real world, labour markets do not function perfectly—they are already distorted, not least by the power relations which are implicit within them. Heintz suggests that understanding labour markets as imperfect from the start provides an opportunity to understand how social protection—'even those that directly affect labour market dynamics'—may have the potential to enhance rather than undermine welfare. This is not to mention that no dominant macroeconomic theory has even started to theorize the functioning of labour markets dominated by self-employment (Heintz 2008). The empirical evidence is itself contested. There is both evidence to show that labour market regulation may impact levels of formality and unemployment (Levy 2008; Bosch and Campos-Vazquez 2014), while alternative evidence has shown that taxation and labour market regulation have no effect on informality (Williams and Kedir 2017). Moreover, the assumption that informal workers have a choice in their formality status is also problematic—there are multiple drivers of informality which may differ in impact according to status in employment. Not least amongst them is the inability of economies to generate sufficient formal employment (Chacaltana et al. 2022).

Why is this important for informal workers? If we are to see meaningful extensions of social protection to this group, it is critical that financing solutions are found—the proceeds from general taxation are unlikely to be sufficient. However, if one important stream of financing—financing from those who profit from the work of informal workers—is precluded, universal social protection is likely to remain highly constrained and probably not very universal. And yet, models for deriving contributions from those who profit from the work of informal workers but are not formal employers do exist. India's sectoral workers welfare boards, for example, have been around since the 1950s. The boards function differently across sectors, but some have very useful financing models—the Building and Other Construction Workers Board levies a 1 per cent tax on the building industry to finance benefits. The Headload Porters Welfare Board charges an additional levy when a headload porter is hired to finance welfare benefits (Kannan 2002; Sankaran 2019). While the boards are not without their problems and their existence is currently threatened by changes in India's labour and social security laws, they do establish the possibility of models of financing which draw on the economic relationships in which informal workers are situated. In this way, they expand the realm of the possible—but are only likely to have a real chance of implementation if there is greater clarity and consensus of the role of social protection as labour regulation.

3.2 Digitization

The central role that digital technology has played in most responses to COVID-19 has further sped up the digital transformation of social protection. From the start of the crisis, 'Big Tech has quickly (in partnership with governments) established itself as our (new) infrastructure for everything from health to education to work' (Dencik and Kaun 2020: 1). As a result, over 60 per cent of all cash transfers with available information were paid digitally, reaching 763 million people (Gentilini 2022).

Alston (2019a) insists that the neutral-sounding term 'digital transformation' 'should not be permitted to conceal the revolutionary, politically driven, character of many such innovations' (Alston 2019a: 4). Dencik and Kaun (2020) similarly emphasize that the 'datafication' of the welfare state is not 'simply a matter of efficiency or a quantitative shift: more information, shared faster' but rather a qualitative change that is inherently political in nature (Dencik and Kaun 2020: 3).

Already, digital technologies have changed the administration, governance, and substance of social protection. Decisions that previously required professional judgement have been supplemented or replaced by digital decision-making systems (Henman 2022). These changes have also provided the basis for a *different kind* of policy. Henman (2022) observes a shift towards social policy that is more codified and, at the same time, increasingly 'differentiated, individualised, personalised—for example, creating different payment rates for different subpopulations, geographical areas, or risk/need profiles' (Henman 2022: 539). There is also a greater emphasis on conditionality by 'making eligibility to certain services and benefits conditional on circumstances or behaviours evidenced in digital databases' (Henman 2022: 539).

Below, we discuss some of the key issues which are likely to become areas of contention in the near-to-mid-term. While these will impact everyone, informal workers will likely be particularly exposed to new developments as digitization can be expected to become central to inclusion efforts. Indeed, connecting informal workers to formal economic and protection systems is a central objective of digitized social policy. Meagher (2021: 732) notes that although such 'formal–informal linkages are conventionally portrayed as conduits of resources, skills, jobs, rights and services in support of marginalized populations', inclusion does not always increase rights and opportunities for informal workers but can also 'increase rather than reduce precarity'. The notion of 'adverse incorporation' captures these concerns and highlights the importance of critically examining the terms of inclusion for informal workers (Barrientos et al. 2013; Meagher and Lindell 2013; Meagher et al. 2016). The digitization of these 'infrastructures of inclusion' raises additional questions as to whether informal workers' inclusion in formal economic and protection systems is empowering or not.

First, arguments in favour of digitizing social policy often promise gains in cost-effectiveness and efficiency. Despite this strong motivation, it is not clear to what extent digitization reduces administration costs, at least in the medium term. Wagner and Ferro (2020) caution that although new technologies have the potential to simplify processes, reduce some costs, and increase efficiencies, they can be costly themselves due to their high technological cost, required investments into different skill sets for administrative staff, and the need to regularly update data (Wagner and Ferro (2020). Reflecting on the role of electronic payments during COVID-19, as well as their potential for 'better, quicker' transfers, Gelb et al. (2020) likewise stress that transitioning to electronic systems requires 'enormous' increases in state capacity (Gelb et al. 2020: 3rd paragraph).

While costs may be significant, it is important also to recognize their potential, which Togo's experience of paying electronic cash transfers to informal workers during COVID-19 shows. It took just ten days to set up a new digital platform for enrolment and payments via mobile phones. One week after the Novissi programme was launched, 450,000 beneficiaries had already received their first payment (Gentilini 2022).

Second, for programmes to meet their objectives they need to be accessible. However, numerous studies suggest that the reliance of data in delivering public services can create barriers that prevent people from accessing their entitlements, one that will particularly impact those from lower socio-economic status groups such as informal workers (Larsson 2021; Lindgren et al. 2019). While digital technology may reduce some barriers (such as the need to travel long distances to register or receive payments, which can reduce the time informal workers may have to spend away from their work), new barriers will be established. Masiero and Das (2019) identify three types of data injustices—legal, informational, and design-related—in digital social protection. Legal injustice relates to shifts from social protection being a fundamental right to being conditional on registration in digital systems like India's Aadhaar or Uganda's *Ndaga Muntu* digital identification systems (Cioffi et al. 2022). Informational injustice refers to actors not appropriately informing individuals about the use of their data. These include 'black-box' approaches such as proxy-means tests in poverty-targeting and algorithmic decision-making processes. Finally, design-related injustices arise when technologically enabled changes fail to reflect people's concerns or realities. This can be an overriding focus on 'inclusion errors' when people are mainly worried about exclusion.

Many informal workers are currently facing versions or combinations of these digital injustices, and trends towards the digitization of social protection will likely exacerbate their consequences. For informal workers, who often face exclusion from government databases due to lack of documentation, limited information and inaccessible processes, the move towards digital systems that are gatekeepers not just to specific programmes but also prerequisites to participation in much of public policy is concerning. As digitization of social protection is often framed around the reduction of 'leakage and inclusion errors' (Bastagli and Lowe 2021), informal workers will likely continue to face significant administrative and documentation-related barriers in registering.

Third, the greater emphasis on differentiation and conditionality that accompanies digitization increases complexity and can further complicate access and accountability. On the positive side, digitization relies on clearly codified entitlements and procedures that can be traced, potentially enhancing accountability. Digitization may also increase informal workers' access to social protection by reducing certain types of overt discrimination by government officials. Online systems that are 'open 24/7' may also make it easier for working people to access services compared to more restricted office hours of traditional bureaucracies.

However, accessing social protection will fundamentally depend on digital access and literacy, with devastating consequences for those without these capabilities. Digitization also tends to increase the distance between administrators and potential recipients of social protection (Henman 2022). A scaling back of bricks-and-mortar offices and removing opportunities for in-person engagement with programme officials can make it harder for people to understand and claim their entitlements, challenge decisions made by implementers, and seek to work out solutions to problems. A reliance on difficult-to-understand automated decisions that are constructed as objective will likely make it harder to challenge decisions. As Henman (2022: 540) argues, 'cultural attitudes that "the computer is correct", a lack of administrative openness, and the complexity of algorithms [...] can undermine administrative justice processes and outcomes'. This is precisely what Afshar (2021) is concerned about regarding the replacement of Brazil's Bolsa Família cash transfer programme, which was based on frontline workers tasked with addressing recipients' multidimensional needs and issues, with a programme called Auxílio Brasil that enrols people through automated digital processes. In the new system, the relationship between citizens and the state is mediated through apps rather than human beings. Following a visit to the United Kingdom, Alston (2019b: 13) raised the alarm that the 'welfare state is gradually disappearing behind a webpage and an algorithm'.

Finally, digitization often goes hand in hand with the full or partial privatization of implementation structures. Both hold the potential to further reduce accountability while also creating the potential for conflicts between public and private interests and risks to data safety as well as enhanced surveillance (Alston 2019a). While rights to privacy and data protection are well recognized in domestic and international law, they are not consistently followed in social protection (Sepulveda 2018). In 2020, only 24 African countries had privacy laws in place (Privacy International 2020).

Social protection programmes have always required significant amounts of often sensitive data, for instance on assets, health status, and disabilities. However, systems based on biometrics collect both more and more sensitive data. Digital management information systems also make it easier to share sensitive data with public and private actors (Sepulveda 2018). The ability of different public and private entities to access databases is a key argument advanced by proponents of digital social protection as it allows for conditionalities and complementarities, for instance by linking social protection and education. Yet, such data sharing also raises the risks of data misuse, in particular by private actors (Wagner and Ferro 2020). Private-sector actors may face financial incentives to misuse the data they have access to as implementers. In particular, the 'issuance and administration of electronic cards to private companies has led to problems such as users being encouraged to pay for commercial financial products and the imposition of user fees' (Alston 2019a: 10). This can trap recipients of social protection in credit and debt (Lavinas 2018), as was the case with the privatized payment of South Africa's social grants (Black Sash 2019; Castel-Branco 2021).

Governments may use the vast amounts of intimate data on social protection recipients, as well as new abilities to exclude people from much of public policy, for repressive and exclusionary purposes. This is concerning as social protection often focuses on 'disadvantaged or marginal peoples within a historical system of negative social valorisation and state control' (Henman 2022: 540). Informal workers, who are often regarded by governments as less than desirable economic actors, may face particular risks.

How these changes will impact informal workers will depend considerably on contexts and choices made in digitizing systems as well as the abilities of informal workers to shape and navigate them. In terms of policy, it is worth reflecting on Henman's (2022) prognosis that governments are moving away from 'one-size-fits-all' programmes towards more differentiated approaches (Henman 2022). In most cases, the former have not been designed with informal workers in mind and rarely served them well. More context-specific and evidence-informed approaches to, for instance, the setting of social insurance contributions rates or the design of childcare services could be beneficial. Digital technology may also make social protection more affordable and responsive, at least for those with sufficient digital access and literacy. Yet, inherent to digitizing social protection is the potential to further reduce access and accountability for those already marginalized while significantly increasing the risk of surveillance and data misuse by governments and private-sector implementers for all involved. Context-specific analysis, centred on listening to informal workers' experiences, is essential to understanding the extent to which developments will result in empowering inclusion into rights-based social protection systems or adverse incorporation into exploitative economic systems.

3.3 Participation

The nature and scale of COVID-19, and the limited reach of social protection measures to informal workers, meant that attempts to reach this same group were often reliant on collaborations between the government and civil society and, in particular, grassroots organizations of the urban and working poor (de Hoop et al. 2020; WIEGO 2021a). These collaborations took different forms, depending on context and need. There was consultation and dialogue to guide the emergency response. In Argentina, for example, an Emergency Social Committee (ESC) was formed to consult a wide variety of stakeholders in order to guide its crisis response, with a focus on food, income, and job security. The ESC included representatives from different levels of government, churches, civil society, and formal and informal worker organizations (Devenish and Afshar 2020).

Organizations of informal workers are provided assistance with selection and identification. Information from grassroots organizations has been used in the identification of beneficiaries, particularly in contexts where informal workers are completely absent from state databases. For example, in Sierra Leone, lists from government and trader associations were used in the second step of the selection and identification process to identify households with informal workers. Data from business associations, small and medium-scale enterprises (SMEs), and other groups were also used in Nigeria to supplement the identification and selection process for the scale-up of the country's safety net programme (Gentilini et al. 2021). As mentioned earlier in this chapter, the provision of 'last-mile' support, ensuring connections between benefits and beneficiaries, was another important role for organizations of informal workers. Organizations worked to establish more effective connections between their constituencies and the state benefits on offer, thereby facilitating access to relief measures. In Thailand, for example, grassroots organizations raised awareness of the cash benefit provided by the government and assisted members with online registrations. In India, organizations of informal workers raised awareness of food benefits and worked with their members to overcome documentation barriers to access (WIEGO 2021a/2021b). Organizations also provided essential services to their members, thereby supplementing the crisis response. For example, in parts of India, self-help groups have worked to establish community kitchens (de Hoop et al. 2020), and to provide psycho-social support, public health information, access to testing and health care, and personal protective equipment (Kala 2020).

While the involvement of organizations of informal workers was important, questions have also been raised as to whether this type of involvement can always be seen in a positive light. Gentilini et al. (2021), for example, argue that the use of grassroots organizations in selection and identification comes 'at a cost financially' and may ultimately undermine the building of state capacity in the provision of social protection. Alternatively, it has also been argued that the reliance on grassroots organizations has sometimes unfairly shifted responsibility onto under-resourced organizations of the poor (Devenish and Afshar 2021). In Zambia, attempts to draw on organizations of informal workers in selection and identi-fication encountered the problem of how to ensure that benefits would also go to more vulnerable, unorganized informal workers (SPACE 2020). Such criticisms raise the question of the conditions under which such state–society collaborations are optimal—both in terms of the impacts they produce and the way in which the relationship is structured. As de Hoop et al. (2020) point out in relation to the role of women's groups during the pandemic, the evidence base on this topic is thin.

Nevertheless, beyond this crisis response, there are literatures which provide clues. For example, Benequista and Gaventa's (2012) review of citizen action and development outcomes suggests a number of factors which influence the trajectory of such collaborations. These include the institutional and political environment in which the relationship is situated, the capabilities held by citizens and their organi-zations, the strength and influence of officials who are committed to working with grassroots organizations, the history and style of prior engagements between the state and these organizations, the nature of the issue, and the location of power and decision-making. In relation to selection and identification for social protection specifically, lessons may also be drawn from the literature on community-based targeting. McCord (2013) notes that the relative success of community-based tar-geting is dependent on the nature of the task given to communities—whether they are being given autonomy to select beneficiaries or whether selection is externally imposed, the nature of the community itself (evidence suggests that a participa-tory, democratic, relatively stable group in a spatially defined area is likely to have more successful outcomes), and the nature of the transfer (is the transfer coverage and adequacy enough to meet the need?). The 'localization' agenda within human-itarian responses also suggests a number of conditions under which state–society relationships may be strengthened during a crisis response, including involving civil society organizations in all stages of the response, adopting measures to miti-gate the potential bias and reinforcement of power dynamics that may accompany community-based selection and identification (e.g. layering multiple sources of information, instituting robust grievance mechanisms, working with coalitions), and working to establish longer-term relationships between the state and civil society groups (Cabot Venton and Sammon 2020).

Drawing from all the above, a simple analytical device may be to ask the four questions: When? Who? What? How? When are grassroots organizations being involved in the crisis response? The evidence cited above suggests this is likely to be most effective when these organizations are included from the start rather than being engaged after the design of the programme. Who is involved—what types of organization are being involved? As with the communities discussed by McCord (2013), it is also likely that democratic, participatory organizations who are accountable to their membership may be more reliable partners than those who are not. What are grassroots organizations being asked to do? As already discussed, grassroots organizations should be involved in all stages of the response, but different parts of the response may require additional inputs and resources. For example, if organizations are providing support for selection and identification, this has implications for measures to mitigate bias and ensure inclusion (Cabot Venton and Sammon 2020). How are grassroots organizations being involved in the response? Is this being done in a way which envisions a longer-term state–society relationship and which provides an enabling environment for citizen agency or is it simply a shifting of responsibility from the state onto civil society? Often, this is not a clear-cut yes or no answer, but an indication of the type of relationship may be whether or not a longstanding relationship between the state and the organization already exists.

4. Concluding remarks

The COVID-19 pandemic has forcefully highlighted both the inadequacy of social protection systems and the urgency of developing more inclusive systems. The failure of most social protection systems to provide timely and effective protection to previously excluded people, as well as a growing awareness amongst policymakers of the importance of developing systems that can protect against future shocks and crises, is expected to keep efforts to achieve universal social protection high on the political agenda and open political windows of opportunity for reforms. However, while there is a consensus that social protection is at an inflection point and that more inclusive social protection systems are needed, considerable disagreement exists regarding their design, financing, and implementation, with different lessons being drawn from experiences and innovations developed during the pandemic. Questions on how to include informal workers in social protection systems will be at the forefront of these debates and, to a significant degree, determine the shape of future systems. These questions require further debate and investigation.

A key question is where the financing for expanded social protection coverage, including to informal workers, should come from. What are the financing models that are available in the context of pervasive informality? What potential do they hold in raising the required resources for social protection, and how would they impact workers and employers across the income distribution? In particular, what would the revenue potential and distributional impacts be of proposals to rely more heavily on consumption taxes as opposed to taxes on capital and labour?

There are also questions to be answered about optimal system and programme design. We have some clues from the COVID-19 expansions, but there is still work to be done to think through and test design features of comprehensive social protection systems in an informal world of work. Answering such questions requires the active tracking and monitoring of new models, understanding impacts on both informal workers and wider society. It also—as Meagher (2021) and others have pointed out—requires taking a critical approach to inclusion, identifying where 'infrastructures of inclusion' are being built on progressive terms and where there is potential for adverse incorporation. Considering the rapid digitization of social protection systems since the pandemic, this is a key area for analysis, as is worker participation and the extent to which systems are genuinely opening up space for active involvement and ownership by those they intend to reach.

To date, much of the global debate about models of comprehensive social protection has largely remained in the realm of theory and assumption. In this moment of crisis and its aftermath, we are likely to see many more attempts by governments to expand social protection to informal workers. This is the opportunity to move away from the abstract and towards the concrete and the empirical—to document, to monitor, to evaluate, and to hear from workers themselves about what works to provide universal social protection.

References

Afshar, C. (2021). 'Bolsa Família: Past and Future of the Brazilian Cash-Grant Programme', Women in Informal Employment: Globalizing and Organizing (WIEGO) Social Protection Briefing Note No. 3, Manchester: WIEGO, available at: www.wiego.org/publications/social-protection-informal-workers-trends-and-changes-social-protection-briefing-note (accessed November 2023).

Alfers, L. (2021). 'A Digital Bridge to Social Support', Project Syndicate, Culture and Society (16 June), available at: www.project-syndicate.org/commentary/social-programs-for-informal-workers-must-bridge-digital-divide-by-laura-alfers-2021-06 (accessed November 2023).

Alfers, L., G. Ismail, and M. Valdivia. (2020). 'Informal Workers and the Social Protection Response to COVID-19: Who Got Relief? How? And Did It Make a Difference?', Policy Insights No. 2. COVID-19 Crisis and the Informal Economy, Manchester: WIEGO.

Alfers, L., F. Galvani, E. Grapsa, F. Juergens-Grant, and A. Sevilla. (2021). 'Older Informal Workers in the COVID-19 Crisis', Policy Insights No. 5, COVID-19 Crisis and the Informal Economy, Manchester: WIEGO.

Alfers, L., C. Braham, M. Chen, E. Grapsa, J. Harvey, G. Ismail et al. (2022). 'COVID-19 and Informal Work in 11 Cities: Recovery Pathways amidst Continued Crisis', WIEGO Working Paper No. 43, Manchester: WIEGO.

Alston, P. (2019a). 'Digital Welfare States and Human Rights: Report of the Special Rapporteur on Extreme Poverty and Human Rights', Special Rapporteur on Extreme Poverty and Human Rights. Thematic Report No. A/74/493, New York: Office of the High Commissioner on Human Rights (OHCHR).

Alston, P. (2019b). 'Visit to the United Kingdom of Great Britain and Northern Ireland: Report of the Special Rapporteur on Extreme Poverty and Human Rights', Special Rapporteur on Extreme Poverty and Human Rights, New York: OHCHR.

Barca, V., and L. Alfers. (2021). 'Including Informal Workers within Social Protection Systems—A Summary of Options', Social Protection Approaches to COVID-19 Expert Advice Service (SPACE), London: DAI Global UK Ltd.

Barrientos, S., U. Kothari, and N. Phillips (2013). 'Dynamics of Unfree Labour in the Contemporary Global Economy', *Journal of Development Studies*, 49(8): 1037–41.

Bastagli, F. (2015). 'Bringing Taxation into Social Protection Analysis and Planning', Overseas Development Institute (ODI) Working Paper No. 421, London: ODI.

Bastagli, F., and C. Lowe. (2021). 'Social Protection Response to Covid-19 and Beyond: Emerging Evidence and Learning for Future Crises', ODI Working Paper No. 614, London: ODI.

Beazley, R., M. Marzi, and R. Steller. (2021). 'Drivers of Timely and Large-Scale Cash Responses to COVID-19: What Does the Data Say?', SPACE, London: DAI Global UK Ltd.

Behrendt, C., and Q.A. Nguyen (2018). *Innovative Approaches for Ensuring Universal Social Protection for the Future of Work*. Geneva: International Labour Organization (ILO).

Benequista N. and J. Gaventa (2012). 'What We Now Know about Citizen Action and Development

Outcomes'. Gouvernance en révolution(s). Chroniques de la gouvernance (2012). Institute for Research and Debate on Governance. Paris: Charles Léopold Mayer Publishing House, available at: http://www2.institut-gouvernance.org/docs/what_we_now_know_about_citizen_action_and_development_outcomes.pdf.

Black Sash (2019). 'Black Sash Submission in General Assembly on Digital Technology, Social Protection and Human Rights', available at: https://www.ohchr.org/sites/default/files/Documents/Issues/Poverty/DigitalTechnology/BlackSash.pdf.

Bosch, M., and R.M. Campos-Vazquez (2014). 'The Trade-Offs of Welfare Policies in Labor Markets with Informal Jobs: The Case of the "Seguro Popular" Program in Mexico'. *American Economic Journal: Economic Policy*, 6 (4): 71–99, available at: https://www.aeaweb.org/articles?id=10.1257/pol.6.4.71.

Cabot Venton, C., E. Sammon, and input from experts on SPACE—Social Protection Approaches to COVID-19: Expert Advice Helpline (2020). 'Programming Guidance: Embedding Localisation in the Response to COVID-19', CALP Network: Choice and Dignity for People in Crisis, available at: https://www.calpnetwork.org/publication/programming-guidance-embedding-localisation-in-the-response-to-covid-19/.

Castel-Branco, R. (2021). 'Improvising an E-state: The Struggle for Cash Transfer Digitalization in Mozambique', *Development and Change*, 52(4): 756–79. https://doi.org/10.1111/dech.12665.

Chacaltana, J., F. Bonnet, and J.M. Garcia (2022). 'Growth, Economic Structure and Informality' ILO Working Paper No. 69. International Labour Organization: Geneva, availbale at: https://www.ilo.org/wcmsp5/groups/public/---ed_emp/documents/genericdocument/wcms_849574.pdf.

Chen, M., E. Grapsa, G. Ismail, M. Rogan, M. Valdivia, L. Alfers et al. (2021). 'COVID-19 and Informal Work: Distinct Pathways of Impact and Recovery in 11 Cities around the World', Working Paper No. 42, Manchester: WIEGO.

Cioffi, K., V. Adelmant, and C. van Veen (2022). 'Paving a Digital Road to Hell? A Primer on the Role of the World Bank and Global Networks in Promoting Digital ID', Center for Human Rights and Global Justice, New York: New York University (NYU) School of Law, available at: https://chrgj.org/wp-content/uploads/2022/06/Report_Paving-a-Digital-Road-to-Hell.pdf (accessed November 2023).

Dafuleya, G. (2020). 'Social and Emergency Assistance Ex-Ante and during COVID-19 in the SADC Region', *International Journal of Community and Social Development*, 2: 251–68.

de Hoop, T., S. Desai, G. Siwach, C. Holla, Y. Belyakova, S. Paul, and R.J. Singh (2020). 'Women's groups and COVID-19: Challenges, engagement, and opportunities', brief, Evidence Consortium on Women's Groups, available at: https://knowledgecommons. popcouncil.org/departments_sbsr-pgy/1067/.

Demirgüç-Kunt, A., L. Klapper, D. Singer, and S. Ansar. (2022). 'The Global Findex Database 2021: Financial Inclusion, Digital Payments, and Resilience in the Age of COVID-19', Washington, DC: World Bank, available at: www.worldbank.org/en/ publication/globalfindex (accessed November 2023).

Dencik, L., and A. Kaun. (2020). 'Datafication and the Welfare State', *Global Perspectives*, 1(1). https://doi.org/10.1525/gp.2020.12912.

Devenish, A., and C. Afshar (2020). 'Social Protection Responses to COVID-19: Informal Workers and Dialogue for Social Protection'. WIEGO Social Protection Briefing Note Issue 3. Manchester: WIEGO, available at: https://www.wiego.org/social-protection-responses-covid-19.

Devereux, S. (2021). 'Social Protection Responses to COVID-19 in Africa', *Global Social Policy*, 21(3): 421–47. https://doi.org/10.1177/14680181211021260.

Gelb, A., A. Mukherjee, and K. Navis. (2020). 'How Can Digital ID and Payments Improve State Capacity and Effectiveness?', Washington, D.C.: Center for Global Development.

Gentilini, U. (2021). 'A Game Changer for Social Protection? Six Reflections on COVID-19 and the Future of Cash Transfers', *Let's Talk Development*, Washington, DC: World Bank (11 January), available at: https://blogs.worldbank.org/developmenttalk/game-changer-social-protection-six-reflections-covid-19-and-future-cash-transfers (accessed November 2023).

Gentilini, U. (2022). *Cash Transfers in Pandemic Times: Evidence, Practices, and Implications from the Largest Scale Up in History*. Washington, DC: World Bank.

Gentilini, U., M. Almenfi, J. Blomquist, P. Dale, L. De la Flor Giuffra, V. Desai et al. (2021). 'Social Protection and Jobs Responses to COVID-19: A Real-Time Review of Country Measures'. Living Paper Version No. 15, Washington, DC: World Bank (2 February), available at: https://openknowledge.worldbank.org/handle/10986/33635 (accessed November 2023).

Gentilini, U., M.B.A. Almenfi, T.M.M. Iyengar, Y. Okamura, J.A. Downes, P. Dale et al. (2022). 'Social Protection and Jobs Responses to COVID-19: A Real-Time Review of Country Measures', Living Paper Version No. 16, Washington, DC: World Bank (2 February), available at: https://openknowledge.worldbank.org/handle/10986/33635 (accessed November 2023).

Guven, M., H. Jain, and C. Joubert (2021). *Social Protection for the Informal Economy: Operational Lessons for Developing Countries in Africa and Beyond*. Washington, DC: World Bank.

Heintz, J. 2008. 'Revisiting Labour Markets: Implications for Macroeconomics and Social Protection', *IDS Bulletin*, 39.

Henman, P.W.F. (2022). 'Digital Social Policy: Past, Present, Future', *Journal of Social Policy*, 51(3): 535–50. https://doi.org/10.1017/S0047279422000162.

ILO (International Labour Organization) (2021). 'World Social Protection Report 2020–22: Social Protection at the Crossroads—in Pursuit of a Better Future', Geneva: ILO, available at: https://www.ilo.org/global/publications/books/WCMS_817572/lang--en/index.htm.

ITUC (2022). 'Investments in Social Protection and Their Impacts on Economic Growth: Tax Financing Options', Belgium: ITUC, available at: https://www.ituc-csi.org/IMG/pdf/ituc_tax_financing_options_en.pdf.

Juergens-Grant, F. (2022). *World Bank's Push for Individual Savings Provides Little Protection for Crisis-Hit Workers*. Manchester: WIEGO, UK.

Kala, S. (2020). 'Impact of COVID-19 on Women Home-Based Workers in South Asia', Delhi: HomeNet International, available at: https://www.homenetinternational.org/about/resources/publications/.

Kannan, K.P. (2002). 'The Welfare Fund Model of Social Security for Informal Sector Workers: The Kerala Experience', Working Paper No. 332. Thiruvananthapuram: Institute of Development Studies (IDS).

Kidd, S., and D. Sibun. (2020). 'What Has the COVID-19 Crisis Taught Us about Social Protection?', Issue No. 29. Pathways' Perspectives on Social Policy in International Development. Development Pathways, Sidcup, UK.

Larsson, K.K. (2021). 'Digitization or Equality: When Government Automation Covers Some, But Not All Citizens', *Government Information Quarterly*, 38(1): 101547. https://doi.org/10.1016/j.giq.2020.101547.

Lavinas, L. (2018). 'The Collateralization of Social Policy under Financialized Capitalism', *Development and Change*, 49(2): 502–17. https://doi.org/10.1111/dech.12370.

Levy, S., (2008). *Good intentions, bad outcomes: Social policy, informality, and economic growth in Mexico*. Brookings Institution Press. Available at: https://www.brookings.edu/books/good-intentions-bad-outcomes/.

Lindgren, I., C.Ø. Madsen, S. Hofmann, and U. Melin (2019). 'Close Encounters of the Digital Kind: A Research Agenda for the Digitalization of Public Services', *Government Information Quarterly*, 36(3): 427–36. https://doi.org/10.1016/j.giq.2019.03.002.

Lowe, C. (2022). 'The Digitalisation of Social Protection Before and Since the Onset of COVID-19: Opportunities, Challenges and Lessons', Working paper, London: ODI.

Masiero, S., and S. Das (2019). 'Datafying Anti-poverty Programmes: Implications for Data Justice', *Information, Communication and Society*, 22(7): 916–33. https://doi.org/10.1080/1369118X.2019.1575448.

Meagher, K. (2021). 'Informality and the Infrastructures of Inclusion: An Introduction', *Development and Change*, 52: 729–55. https://doi.org/10.1111/dech.12672.

Meagher, K., and I. Lindell (2013). 'ASR Forum: Engaging with African Informal Economies: Social Inclusion or Adverse Incorporation?', *African Studies Review*, 56(3): 57–76.

Meagher, K., L. Mann, and M. Bolt (2016). 'Introduction: Global Economic Inclusion and African Workers', *Journal of Development Studies*, 52(4): 471–82.

MENAFN-AFP (Middle East North Africa Financial Network-Agence France Presse) (2022). 'Ghana IMF Loan Outcry Pressures Government over Economy', MENAFN.

Moussié, R., and L. Alfers (2022). 'Pandemic, Informality and Women's Work: Redefining Social Protection Priorities at WIEGO', *Global Social Policy*, 22(1): 190–5. https://doi.org/10.1177/14680181221079089.

Oritz, I., F. Duran-Valverde, S. Urban, and V. Wodsak (2018). *Reversing Pension Privatizations: Rebuilding Public Pension Systems in Eastern Europe and Latin America*. Geneva: ILO.

Ortiz, I., A. Chowdhury, F. Duran-Valverde, T. Muzaffer, and S. Urban (2019). *Fiscal Space for Social Protection: A Handbook for Assessing Financing Options*. Geneva and New York: ILO and UN Women.

Packard, T., U. Gentilini, M. Grosh, P. O'Keefe, D. Robalino, and I. Santos (2019). *Protecting All: Risk Sharing for a Diverse and Diversifying World of Work*. Washington, DC: World Bank.

Privacy International (2020). '2020 Is a Crucial Year to Fight for Data Protection in Africa', http://privacyinternational.org/long-read/3390/2020-crucial-year-fight-data-protection-africa (accessed November 2023).

Reed, S.O., M. Rogan, E. Grapsa, G. Ismail, and M.A. Valdivia (2021). 'The Crisis Is Far from Over for Informal Workers—We Need an Inclusive Recovery for the Majority of the World's Workforce', Policy Insights No. 8, COVID-19 Crisis and the Informal Economy, Manchester: WIEGO.

Roelen, K., and B. Carter. (2022). 'Social Assistance in Response to Covid-19: Reaching the Furthest Behind First?', Thiruvananthapuram: IDS. https://doi.org/10.19088/IDS.2022.007.

Sankaran, K. (2019). 'Realising Employer Liability for Informal Workers: Lessons from in India'. In M. Chen and F. Carré (eds), *The Informal Economy Revisited: Examining the Past, Envisioning the Future*. London: Routledge. https://www.taylorfrancis.com/chapters/oa-edit/10.4324/9780429200724-40/realising-employer-liability-informal-workers-kamala-sankaran.

Sepulveda, M. (2018). 'Is Biometric Technology in Social Protection Programmes Illegal or Arbitrary? An Analysis of Privacy and Data Protection', Working Paper No. 59, Extension of Social Security (ESS), Geneva: ILO.

SPIAC-B (Social Protection Inter-Agency Cooperation Board) (2020a). 'A Joint Statement on the Role of Social Protection in Responding to the COVID-19 Pandemic', SPIAC-B.

SPIAC-B (2020b). 'COVID-19, Social Protection and Gender Equality: A Call to Action', SPIAC-B, available at: https://socialprotection.org/discover/publications/covid-19-social-protection-and-gender-equality-call-action (accessed November 2023).

Staab, S., L. Williams, C. Tabbush, C. Arza, E. Dugarova, J. Hill et al. (2022). 'Government Responses to COVID-19: Lessons on Gender Equality for a World in Turmoil', New York: UN Women, available at: www.unwomen.org/sites/default/files/2022-06/Government-responses-to-COVID-19-Lessons-on-gender-equality-for-a-world-in-turmoil-en.pdf (accessed November 2023).

UN Women and UN DESA (United Nations Department of Economic and Social Affairs) (2021). 'Progress on the Sustainable Development Goals: The Gender Snapshot 2021', available at: www.unwomen.org/en/digital-library/publications/2021/09/progress-on-the-sustainable-development-goals-the-gender-snapshot-2021 (accessed November 2023).

UNDP (United Nations Development Programme) and UN Women (2022). 'COVID-19 Global Gender Response Tracker', New York: UNDP and UN Women, available at: https://data.undp.org/gendertracker (accessed November 2023).

Wagner, B., and C. Ferro. (2020). 'Data Protection for Social Protection: Key Issues for Low- and Middle-Income Countries', Bonn, Germany: Deutsche Gesellschaft für Internationale Zusammenarbeit (GIZ) GmbH, available at: https://socialprotection.org/sites/default/files/publications_files/GIZ_Data_Protection_For_Social_Protection.pdf (accessed November 2023).

WIEGO (2021). 'Workers Take Fight for Social Protection to ILC', Global Alliance of Waste Pickers, HomeNet International, International Domestic Workers Federation; StreetNet International, Self-Employed Women's Association, Manchester: WIEGO (August), available at: www.wiego.org/publications/workers-take-fight-social-protection-ilc (accessed November 2023).

WIEGO (2021b). 'COVID-19 Crisis and the Informal Economy in Tiruppur, India: Lasting Impacts and an Agenda for Recovery', Manchester: WIEGO, available at: https://www.wiego.org/resources/covid-19-crisis-and-informal-economy-tiruppur-india-lasting-impacts-and-agenda-recovery.

WIEGO Network (2021). 'Position Paper on Extending Social Protection to Women and Men in the Informal Economy: ILC 109th Session, General Discussion on Social Protection', Manchester: WIEGO.

Williams, C.C., and A. Kedir (2017). 'Explaining Cross-National Variations in the Prevalence of Informal Sector Entrepreneurship: Lessons from a Survey of 142 Countries', *Journal of Developmental Entrepreneurship*, 23(1): 1–22. https://ideas.repec.org/a/wsi/jdexxx/v23y2018i01ns108494671850005x.html.

World Bank (2019). *World Development Report 2019: The Changing Nature of Work*. Washington DC: World Bank. https://www.worldbank.org/en/publication/wdr2019.

Zimmerman, J., M. May, E. Kellison, and J. Klugman. (2020). 'Digital Cash Transfers in Times of COVID-19: Opportunities and Considerations for Women's Inclusion and Empowerment', Working Paper No. 151472, Washington, DC: World Bank (1 August), available at: https://documents.worldbank.org/en/publication/documents-reports/documentdetail/378931596643390083/Digital-Cash-Transfers-in-Times-of-COVID-19-Opportunities-and-Considerations-for-Womens-Inclusion-and-Empowerment (accessed November 2023).

11

A New Social Contract Inclusive of Informal Workers

Martha Alter Chen, Sophie Plagerson, and Laura Alfers

1. Introduction: A new social contract

When countries experience fundamental changes to their economy and society, there is often a call for a new social contract—a new bargain—between the state, capital, society, and labour.[1] The public health and economic crises brought on by the COVID-19 pandemic has exposed and exacerbated the inequality between, and within, countries around the world. It has also exposed that, in many countries, the social contracts of the mid-twentieth century were never firmly in place and, in others, have broken down or are in serious crisis: both the social contracts between states and society (e.g. the welfare state) and between capital and labour (e.g. minimum-wage and collective-bargaining agreements).

There is growing consensus that new social contracts for the twenty-first century are needed which take into account both new and old political, social, and economic realities, including in the world of work. International institutions of various political stripes are calling for a new social contract: from the International Labour Organization (ILO), to the Organisation for Economic Co-operation and Development (OECD), to the World Bank. Also, in some countries, business associations are calling for corporations to take care of and share value with their employees, customers, suppliers, and communities, not just their shareholders. But these proposals for a new social contract vary significantly, with different degrees of recognition of informal workers and different consequences for them (Alfers et al. 2022b).

The calls for a new social contract between capital and labour tend to focus on wage employment and the employer–employee relationship—as did previous formulations of the social contract, particularly in most high-income and several middle-income countries. However, nearly half (44 per cent) of the global workforce and nearly three-quarters (72 per cent) of the workforce in developing

---

[1] In this chapter, the state refers to government at all levels: national, state/provincial, and local. Capital refers to the owners of capital, not just employers per se. In the case of informal self-employed, the owners of capital may be suppliers, buyers, and/or competitors. Labour refers to both formal and informal workers, to self-employed, wage employed, and contracted labour.

Martha Alter Chen, Sophie Plagerson, and Laura Alfers, *A New Social Contract Inclusive of Informal Workers*. In: *COVID-19 and the Informal Economy*. Edited by: Martha Alter Chen, Michael Rogan, and Kunal Sen, Oxford University Press.
© Martha Alter Chen, Sophie Plagerson, and Laura Alfers (2024). DOI: 10.1093/oso/9780198887041.003.0012

countries are self-employed; and among informal workers globally, 79 per cent are self-employed (Bonnet et al. 2019; ILO 2018c). Also, some existing and emerging forms of employment fall in between fully independent self-employment and fully dependent wage employment.

This chapter seeks to provide new concepts and insights, based on the knowledge and experience of the Women in Informal Employment: Globalizing and Organizing (WIEGO) network, to inform and motivate a new social contract that is inclusive of informal workers.[2] We are motivated by the following premises. First, there is growing inequality and injustice in the world of work and the state has a role to play in regulating the relationship between capital and labour as well as its own relationship with labour (especially with the self-employed). Second, there are significant power asymmetries between state, capital, and labour, as well as significant wealth inequality between capital and labour, which make it impossible for all parties concerned to enter a voluntary rational agreement. Third, a new social contract, which includes informal workers, would provide a key pathway to reducing income inequality and economic injustice.

While informal employment has always been the norm in the Global South, the fact that it is re-emerging in the Global North offers a window to rethink social contracts on a global scale. But dominant narratives about the informal economy, largely from the Global North, have justified its systematic exclusion from social contract formulations by stigmatizing informal workers/enterprises as noncompliant, non-productive, illegal, and associated with urban crime and grime. The COVID-19 pandemic recession has exposed and exacerbated pre-existing fault lines of the injustices and inequalities faced by informal workers by reason of what they do and who they are (their class, race/ethnicity/caste, and gender).

This chapter seeks to highlight the mismatch between the lived realities of informal work and mainstream approaches to social contracts to make the case for a new social contract that includes informal workers as a key party to the contract. This section describes the size, composition, and characteristics of informal employment and the global movement of organizations and networks of informal workers. Section 2 summarizes different schools of thought on the informal economy, including what drives it, and how these schools relate to current debates on social contracts. Section 3 outlines what a new social contract that includes informal workers should consist of in terms of negotiating parties, overarching principles, and substantive dimensions as well as what processes are necessary to negotiating such a contract. Section 4 presents three possible post-COVID-19 scenarios for informal workers: the bad old deal, a worse new deal, and a better new deal. The chapter concludes with reflections on the way forwards.

---

[2] The authors of this chapter recently co-edited a volume entitled *Social Contracts and Informal Workers in the Global South*, published by Elgar in 2022. This chapter is based on that volume, particularly the Introduction and Conclusion, which, in turn, are based largely on 25 years of joint knowledge generation and advocacy with organizations of informal workers by the WIEGO network.

1.1 Informal workers and informal worker organizations

In today's globalized economy, 61 per cent of workers worldwide (aged 15 and above) are informally employed: a total of 2 billion informal workers (ILO 2018c). Informal employment exists in all countries (developed, emerging, and developing), though the prevalence varies from 90 per cent in developing countries, to 67 per cent in emerging economies, to 18 per cent in developed economies. The prevalence of informal employment also varies across geographical regions: from around 90 per cent in sub-Saharan Africa and South Asia, to 77 per cent in East and Southeast Asia (excluding China), to 68 per cent in the Middle East and North Africa, to 54 per cent in Latin America and the Caribbean, to 37 per cent in Eastern Europe and Central Asia (ILO 2018c).

Informal employment includes a range of self-employed persons who work in unincorporated, unregistered, and often small enterprises; of wage workers who are employed without employer contributions to social protection (or paid sick leave) by formal firms, informal enterprises, and households; and of dependent contractors who work for supply chains or digital platforms (Chen 2012). They vary by occupation, including construction workers, domestic workers, home-based workers, street vendors, transport workers, and waste pickers in urban areas; agricultural day labourers, agro-processors, artisans, fisherfolk, forest gatherers, pastoralists, and smallholder farmers in rural areas. The lower tiers of global supply chains often include a broad range of home-based workers and subcontracted workers and enterprises (ILO 2018a). Many on-demand or gig economy jobs, mediated via digital platforms, share characteristics of informal work, including limited regulation and low levels of labour and social protection (Berg et al. 2018).

Most informal workers are from poor households; and informal workers face a greater risk of poverty than formal workers. Their working lives are regularly characterized by uncertainty of continued employment and by income insecurity. They are more likely than formal workers to face deficits in the four pillars of decent work: economic opportunities, legal rights, social protection, and collective voice and representation (ILO 2002). They frequently lack access to social assistance and (more so) social insurance as well as to public services, such as basic infrastructure and transport services, and have low-quality and unequal access to many state-provided social services (such as health care, childcare, or education) (Agarwala 2018; Alfers et al. 2018; Behrendt et al. 2019).

Most people do not enter the informal economy voluntarily. Many do so because they have no other means of livelihood as there are limited job opportunities in the formal economy (ILO 2018c). Some are carrying on hereditary occupations, passed on by their parents or community. Compared to their male counterparts, women in the informal economy tend to be over-represented in the lower tiers of the informal economy by status in employment (e.g. dependent contractors and contributing family workers) and in the least visible and most vulnerable occupations, notably as domestic workers and home-based workers (Chen et al. 2005).

Although informal workers represent the majority of workers in many countries and are deeply embedded in global, national, and local economies, they tend to remain at the margins of negotiation and collective-bargaining platforms. Informal worker organizations are often not recognized as equal partners within tripartite state—capital—labour structures: either excluded altogether or represented indirectly through affiliation to a trade union of formal workers. Yet frequently, trade unions are not suited for, or amenable to, articulating the demands of informal workers (Alfers and Moussié 2019).

Fortunately, there is a growing social movement of international networks of organizations of informal workers from specific sectors—HomeNet International, International Federation of Domestic Workers, StreetNet International, Global Alliance of Waste Pickers—with over 230 affiliated organizations in 94 countries and a total membership of over 4 million informal workers (Bonner and Carré 2013; Bonner et al. 2018; Carré et al. 2018; Chen et al. 2015). These broad-based networks bring together different types of organizations of informal workers with similar interests, such as trade unions, cooperatives, producer groups, trade associations, and other membership-based organizations (Agarwala 2018; Behrendt et al. 2019). This movement is embedded in the daily realities of informal workers and aims to empower informal workers to voice demands for economic and social justice (Biesecker and von Winterfeld 2018). These networks and their affiliates are actively struggling, with some success, for new social dialogue platforms, in which the interests of informal workers can be represented alongside those of government, national, and multinational companies and formal wage workers.

2. Schools of thought on the informal economy

There is growing consensus among international institutions that the current system of social contracts is broken and needs to be fixed. But what they prescribe varies: notably, by whether they are calling for repairing existing social contracts or envisioning a new contract. Also, within and between these institutions, there is still a great deal of debate and misconception about the informal economy.

Historically, there have been four quite distinct schools of thought on the nature and composition of the informal economy, its origins, its relationship to formal regulations and the formal economy, and its ideal trajectory going forwards (as detailed in Chen 2012) which resonate with different strands of social contract theory.

Dualists see the informal sector of the economy as marginal, distinct, and with few linkages to the formal sector in a segmented labour market. The informal economy is viewed as providing income for low-income, self-employed workers and a safety net in times of crisis. The dualist perspective calls for the creation of more formal jobs and the provision of credit and business development services to informal operators as well as basic infrastructure and social services to their families. Otherwise, dualists would see informal workers as marginal to social contracts.

Legalists highlight the agency and entrepreneurship of informal operators, who cannot afford or negotiate the costs, time, and effort of formal registration in a hostile legal system. They argue that governments should introduce simplified bureaucratic procedures, encourage informal enterprises to register, and extend legal property rights for their assets. Legalists would also see informal workers as marginal to social contracts.

Voluntarists view informal workers as entrepreneurs who deliberately seek to avoid regulations and taxation for personal gain. The proposed solution is to regulate and tax informal enterprises. Delinking social protection from employment is also proposed to avoid creating perverse incentives for firms and workers to operate informally through targeted interventions. This school of thought aligns with a Hobbesian, interest-based, contractarian view, which prioritizes freedom and would frame informal workers as autonomous and self-reliant agents who trade their goods and/or labour, who (in an efficient market system) are paid what they are worth, and whose 'active citizenship' arguably decreases their dependence on public welfare provisions (Dean 2013).

Structuralists regard informal and formal economies as intrinsically and inequitably linked and argue that capitalist development actually fosters or perpetuates informality by coercing microenterprises and workers to provide cheap goods and services and to work for low wages, by opposing the power of organized labour and state regulation of the economy, and by supporting global processes of industrialization such as offshore industries, subcontracting chains, and flexible specialization. They call for regulating the relationships of production, not the informal economy. The structuralist view is more aligned with a Rousseaun/Rawlsian, rights-based, egalitarian approach and a social justice approach, which takes account of informal workers as agents of change and calls for a radical restructuring of current political, economic, and social institutions to allow informal workers to have a seat at the table and to reshape institutions and the terms of the social contract (Rawls 1971).[3]

Each school of thought applies to one or more segments of the informal economy, not the whole. In promoting a social contract that is inclusive of informal workers, it is important to know the relative size of each segment of the

---

[3] This is not the time and space to go into the scholarly literature and debates on the informal economy since these four schools of thought emerged. For an early rethinking of the dualist school, see Singer (1970). For an important variation on the voluntarist school by Maloney and others, see Perry et al. (2007: 1–20). For a persuasive structuralist argument, see Sanyal 2007. For evidence from India which shows that the informal economy, given its size and heterogeneity, is a means of both exploitation and accumulation, see Maiti and Sen (2010).

informal economy in different countries or contexts: survivalist operators; plucky entrepreneurs; regular or casual wage workers; dependent workers, contractors, and enterprises. And it is important to diagnose which school of thought regarding the informal economy is espoused by the different proponents of a new social contract.

But more centrally, negotiating a new inclusive social contract will require engaging with the core values of equity and justice; envisioning new roles of—and relationships between—the state, capital, and labour; and a more equitable distribution of rights, responsibilities, and power between them. Further, and most importantly, the negotiations around a new social contract, inclusive of informal workers, should be informed by their perspectives and be prepared to re-envision and reinvent social contracts. Informal workers, through their organizations, challenge the simplistic idea that the current situation represents the unravelling of what was a good social contract that needs to be revived and repaired. Rather, they highlight that current (and past) contracts are inadequate, irrelevant, or unjust and that radically new conceptualizations of not only state–society and capital–labour relations but also state–labour and state–capital relations are required.

3. A new social contract, inclusive of informal workers

In this section, we summarize the actors, substantive content, and processes necessary to realizing a new social contract for informal workers, informed by WIEGO's research and engagement with organizations of informal workers over 25 years.

3.1 Necessary actors, jurisdictions, and relationships

The main actors in a better new contract for informal workers include an accountable state (local and national), responsible capital (employers of informal workers and those who profit from the work of informal workers, and formal labour and (recognized) informal labour. But other actors are also needed: organizations and networks of informal workers; social movements which fight for human rights, including those of informal workers; non-governmental organizations that support informal workers and their organizations; academics, statisticians, and data analysts who promote improved statistics and policy-relevant research on informal workers, units, and activities; and lawyers and legal resource centres that support the legal struggles of organizations of informal workers.

Accountable state
In regard to the informal economy, it is necessary to acknowledge the often hostile attitude of local and national government towards informal workers and their

economic activities. Indeed, state actors often penalize informal workers, abuse their authority to extract bribes and confiscate goods from informal workers, and periodically evict them from their workplaces and/or residences. Instead of an adversarial or coercive state, informal worker organizations are calling for fair relationships characterized by recognition, responsiveness, and reciprocity; and for a balanced vision of shared rights and responsibilities (Roever and Ogando 2022). These organizations seek to hold the state accountable for contributing to decent and dignified work, especially of the self-employed, who are directly impacted by government policies, plans, and practices.

Responsible capital

The owners of capital need to be held accountable by the state 'for contributing to decent and dignified work' (Breman and van der Linden 2014, in Meagher 2018). Since the mid-twentieth century, there has been a shift in the power balance between capital and labour and between the globalized private sector and the state. In the process, the balance of political and economic power across national and international contexts has shifted in favour of the owners of capital, who have found new ways to avoid regulations, including their obligations as employers; and the employment relationship has become increasingly individualized, fragmented, de-localized, and de-materialized, opening up new forms of vulnerability for workers (Daguerre 2014). The globalization of the economy has accelerated and accentuated this imbalance of capital–labour relations, given the high level of transnational globalization of capital and the increasingly stringent limits on the globalization of labour (Uzbay Pirili and Pifpirili 2015).

Responsive formal labour

The old social contract between capital and labour was premised on a recognized employer–employee relationship. But today, just under one-third of all workers globally (as low as 7 per cent in developing countries) are formal wage or salaried workers in a recognized employer–employee relationship. Nearly one-quarter of all workers globally are informal wage workers or dependent contractors, outside a formal employer–employee relationship. Forty-four per cent of all workers globally and two-thirds to three-quarters of workers in emerging and developing economies are self-employed (Bonnet et al. 2019; ILO 2018c). Trade unions which represent formal workers are being called upon by membership-based organizations of informal workers, including trade unions, cooperatives, and associations, to join hands in their negotiations and struggles for a new social contract.

Recognized informal labour

Pre-COVID, as informality re-emerged in the Global North, and in global supply chains across North–South divides, informal work, as well as its omission from social contract models, became more visible. The COVID-19 pandemic recession further exposed and exacerbated the exclusion and vulnerabilities of informal workers. Fortunately, as noted earlier, there is a growing global movement of informal worker networks and organizations actively engaged in making local, national, and transnational demands—both sector-specific and more generally—for informal workers.

In an increasingly urbanized world and globalized economy, there is a need for 'plural, overlapping social contracts at different levels' with a broader set of actors to deal with different jurisdictions: local, national, and transnational (von Broembsen 2022). Because many urban workers are informally employed, there is a need for a social contract between city governments, urban authorities, and urban informal workers. But who will hold local governments accountable? Under administrative law, local organizations of informal workers can hold local governments accountable for transparency and fair treatment but need support from activist academics, lawyers, and journalists. Because many informal workers and enterprises are inserted into global supply chains, there is a need for a social contract at not only national but also transnational level. In large part, this is because national governments are simply not willing or able to regulate employment in global supply chains; and transnational corporations tend to turn a blind eye to the employment and contracting arrangements in their supply chains. There is a need for a broader set of actors, including global union federations and social movements, to negotiate transnational employment relations and a transnational social contract.

In sum, a broad spectrum of actors needs to negotiate and a broad set of relationships needs to be negotiated in envisioning a new social contract that includes informal workers and that is relevant to contemporary urbanization and globalization, including state–society and capital–labour but also state–capital and state–informal labour. Finally, it is important to acknowledge that all negotiating parties are not equal to each other and do not have an equal seat at the negotiating table; and to ask who is at the negotiating table, who is missing, and who has the power to shape dialogue and who does not. Often, the negotiation is only between those 'who count': in the past, when it came to labour as a negotiating party, formal workers were far more likely to be 'counted' than informal workers. Moreover, when informal workers are included, there are power imbalances between not only capital and labour but also formal and informal labour.

3.2 Key principles and dimensions

Re-envisioning the social contract to include informal workers affects the actual substance of the contract: its guiding principles and key substantive dimensions. What follows are the guiding principles and substantive dimensions of a new social contract as articulated by informal workers and organizations in the WIEGO network, over the past 25 years and especially during the COVID-19 pandemic recession.

Key principles
Through the qualitative component of the WIEGO-led COVID-crisis study in 11 cities around the world, consisting of open-ended survey questions and in-depth interviews, informal workers, their organizers, and leaders, articulated three principles of a new social contract (Roever and Ogando 2022):

1. recognition: of the role they play in sustaining households, communities, cities, and the economy;
2. responsiveness: to their needs—as not only workers but also members of society;
3. reciprocity: so that the value that informal workers create for households, communities, cities, and the economy is met with some corresponding value—and benefits—from the state and owners of capital.

Fundamental to a fair social contract is the critical need to recognize informal workers as 'workers'—as legitimate economic agents—and to include them in relevant social dialogue platforms as well as policymaking and rule-setting processes. Informal workers seek recognition of themselves as workers, of their work and working conditions, and of the roles they play in economic and social life: by state entities at all levels, by private-sector firms who supply or buy goods to/from them, by their employers (if wage employed or dependent contractors), and by the general public (Roever and Ogando 2022). Ideally, informal workers seek *legal* recognition and identification of themselves as workers and of their organizations as representative labour organizations. This recognition and the need to call out the 'wrongness' of demeaning and stigmatizing policies and practice is also an important dimension of a normative framework.

Essential rights
The essential rights that informal workers demand and struggle for, and which should form the substantive dimensions of a new social contract, are summarized below:

- *universal social protection*: social protection that includes social insurance as well as social assistance for informal workers and that provides work-related protections and benefits that informal workers need, including childcare services (Alfers and Moussié 2022);
- *access to public space, public services, and public procurement*: regulated access to public space in order to pursue their livelihoods (especially for street vendors but also waste pickers), basic infrastructure and transport services at their worksites (including the homes of home-based workers), and public

procurement (e.g. municipal solid waste management contracts for waste picker cooperatives, government procurement of masks and uniforms made by home-based workers) (Chen 2022);

- *fair terms of employment and of trade*: minimum wages, social protection contributions, and worker benefits, including paid annual leave and sick leave, for informal wage workers and dependent contractors, including homeworkers/industrial outworkers who work from, in, or around their own homes for domestic and global supply chains and gig workers who work for digital platforms (Carré 2022; von Broembsen 2022) and fair terms of trade for informal self-employed, including fair prices for the supplies/stock they buy and the goods/services they sell;
- *just, progressive taxation*: taxation systems and tax reforms which recognize that the earnings of most informal workers fall below the threshold for corporate or personal income tax; that many informal workers pay taxes, including VAT on supplies and stock as well as operating fees; and that informal workers are willing to pay taxes and operating fees if they receive some benefits in exchange, that is, the principle of reciprocity (Rogan 2022). Informal workers also want the right to be free from harassment, bribes, confiscation of goods, and evictions by government authorities and the police (Chen 2022); and, perhaps most fundamentally, the right not to be stigmatized as non-compliant and non-productive, even undesirable and illegal;
- *freedom from harassment and penalization*: freedom from harassment, bribes, confiscation of goods, destruction of worksites, and evictions by local authorities and police (Chen 2022);
- *freedom from stigmatization*: freedom from the negative stigmatization of *what they do* as their work is associated with non-compliance, low productivity, crime, or grime by policymakers, local authorities, the police, and the general public; and of *who they are* as many informal workers are from disadvantaged racial, ethnic, caste, or religious groups or are migrants.

Finally, informal workers are also demanding that these rights—these substantive dimensions—should be considered as *reciprocal* to the contributions they make to taxes, the economy, and society. But state and capital are not likely to respond reciprocally unless, and until, informal workers are invited—and institutionally guaranteed the right—to negotiate as equals.

3.3 Necessary processes

But 'how to get there?' The actual struggles and several successes by informal worker organizations suggest the possibility of—and a road map for—realizing this vision for a better social contract. Building on knowledge generated and solidarity built over decades, informal worker networks and organizations have been able to negotiate effectively and secure legal and policy victories. They have done so by demanding, and being offered, a seat at the policy table and with support from activist academics and lawyers and non-governmental organizations, including WIEGO.

For the past 25 years, the WIEGO network has worked closely with organizations of informal workers to expose and address the exclusion of informal workers from legal recognition, from policy discourses, from negotiation platforms, from economic and urban planning, and from legal and social protection. The punitive and violent practices against informal workers by the state or by capital (allowed by the state) reveals that exclusion is not because informal workers are outside the reach of the state but because they are branded as undesirable for what they do (informal work) and for who they are (from races/ethnicities/castes that the elite and powerful choose to look down upon) as a deliberate state–capital policy. In short, in many countries, informal workers are deliberately kept outside the protective arm of the state but inside its punitive arm.

Importantly, membership-based organizations of informal workers, often with support from WIEGO, have been able to open up spaces for policy and social dialogue for informal workers which illustrate the possibility of an inclusive, participatory approach to negotiating a new social contract at national level. In some cases, this has involved alliances with the formal trade union movement, which, although providing an avenue for the voices of informal workers to feed into institutionalized processes, has also revealed the tensions and power imbalances which exist in such alliances. Nevertheless, such experiments in inclusion hold important lessons for formal social dialogue processes if they are to maintain relevance in a rapidly informalizing world of work (Alfers and Moussié 2022).

In the global waste sector, there has been a significant increase in recent years of extended producer responsibility (EPR) policies and systems, in which producers are responsible for the waste their production and products generate. Attempts to integrate informal waste pickers into these EPR systems on fair terms illustrate the power imbalance between capital and labour and the struggles required to shift this relationship to more favourable terms for informal workers, including the need for new lines of accountability. A global working group of several waste-picker organizations and researchers around the world is actively discussing and planning new, more equitable, systems through which EPR can help integrate waste pickers into more formal waste management systems on favourable terms (Cass Talbott 2022).

In the global garment sector, there is a movement by labour lawyers and activities for a transnational social contract for garment workers. The European Union, through its 'mandatory human rights due diligence' legislative framework, which draws from and is aligned with the UN Guiding Principles on Business and Human Rights (UNGPs). seeks to hold corporations accountable for labour rights violations in their supply chains. This framework, institutionalized through human rights rather than labour law, performs several functions: its transnational character addresses labour law's jurisdictional limitation to the nation state; its human rights framing extends protection to all workers, not just employees; and it recognizes other actors besides the state–capital–formal labour triad, including informal worker organizations, as legitimate participants in social contracting processes (von Broembsen 2022).

These examples illustrate both the desirability and the feasibility of plural, overlapping social contracts for informal workers at city, national, regional, and global levels.

4. Three possible future scenarios

At this critical inflection moment, the global community is still coming to terms with the reality that the multi-wave pandemic lingers, causing ripple effects that will last for decades. Tragically, it has become apparent that many social and economic impacts are not yet receding and may get worse. Against this sobering backdrop, it is important to highlight the real risks of simply slipping back to the 'bad old' contract or, even more ominously, of regressing to an 'even worse' contract. However, the stories of new patterns of emerging solidarities and of hard-won legal victories also pave the way for deeply rooted, politically savvy, tested yet pioneering paths towards a 'better new' social contract.

While successive waves of the virus and related restrictions continue around the world, there is an urgency to draw lessons from the pandemic recession which can serve to actively contest predatory forces and direct the course of recovery towards a better new social contract for informal workers. Below, we map three possible trajectories for the social contract and informal workers. The first scenario is a return to the status quo, which we term the 'bad old contract'. The second trajectory sees a worsening of the situation into what we term the 'even worse contract'. A third possibility is more optimistic, building on the vision for a fairer economy and society as articulated by informal workers—one which we term the 'better new contract'.

4.1 The bad old contract

There is ample evidence to show how the prevailing political economy and policy environment are unfair, exploitative, and discriminatory towards informal workers, confirming that the pre-pandemic state quo was bad for informal workers. The disparity between the reality of informal workers and the abstract unrealistic notion of the 'universal' worker on which mainstream social contracts are based is startling and has enormous implications for informal workers. What we call the 'bad old' contract can be summarized most simply by stating that while informal workers tend to be excluded from the protective arm of the state, they are regularly exposed to its punitive arm. More specifically, this includes (as detailed before) lack of legal and substantive recognition, stigmatization and penalization, and lack of institutionalized space for collective representation.

What are the drivers of this 'bad old contract'? WIEGO research and experience suggest that the fault lies with a combination of misconceptions about informality which intersect with a political economy that rewards powerful interest groups and entrenches economic disadvantage. The first misconception is the idea that informal work is an abnormality. However, both historically and today, informal work is the most consistent and dominant form of labour globally. This links to a second misconception, namely, the idea that the employer–employee relationship should be central to social contracts. A third misconception is the assumption that informal workers do not pay tax. It is true that informal workers may pay little or no personal or corporate income tax (the forms of taxation that are often understood as the instrument through which the social contract is negotiated) since their earnings usually fall below national income tax thresholds. However, empirical work in Ghana shows that informal workers are subject to a range of fees, licences, and market levies, often levied at local government level: meaning that they are far from 'tax evaders' (Rogan 2022).

A final—and very prevalent misconception—is the idea that informal work falls outside the reach of the state. This is simply not the case. The reality of the situation is that while informal workers fall outside the protective arm of the state, they are often adversely incorporated under the punitive arm of state regulation. In order to recognize this, it is critical to move beyond the idea of the state as a monolith and as either 'good' or 'bad'.

It is equally important to acknowledge that while misconceptions are significant drivers of the 'bad old contract', this status quo also benefits many powerful economic actors. In sectors such as the export garment industry, the relationship between capital and labour has yielded to complex global supply chains which transcend national boundaries, undermining the power of national law to regulate working conditions (von Broembsen 2022). This situation has not evolved by accident—it has arisen out of a drive for increased profits as brands exercise their coercive market power to download costs and risks onto poorer workers in places far removed from their home base (von Broembsen 2022).

What this means is that any move towards a more inclusive social contract for informal workers must address not only the misconceptions about the informal economy but also the underlying political economy which exacerbates the situation of informal workers. What this also means is that the new social contract must be negotiated not only by the traditional parties—state and society, capital and labour—but also by parties in other key relationships: state and informal labour, capital and informal labour, and state and capital. Without addressing these multiple relationships, and the all-too-frequent collusion between state and capital, there is a good chance that the 'bad old contract' will, in time, transform into the 'even worse' social contract described below.

4.2 The 'even worse' contract

There is growing evidence of several plausible trajectories for an even worse contract post-COVID-19, based on what has transpired during the successive waves of the pandemic recession in both 2020 and 2021.

Predatory capitalism

Beneath the unpredictable waves of the pandemic recession, glimpses of callous and calculated forces of predatory capitalism, which intentionally seek to counter efforts to institutionalize relief, recovery, and solidarity for informal workers, have become visible. In the process, a regressive solidarity can form between the state and capital, as we see in the way that national governments in Asia have capitulated to the demands of global brands for lower prices by unilaterally amending labour laws to increase working hours and engage in union busting. This even after brands refused to compensate millions of garment workers for cancelled orders during the COVID-19 crisis (von Broembsen 2022).

State overreach

There are examples where governments have, and are using, the COVID-19 crisis as an opportunity to further entrench repressive measures against informal workers in the name of public health or economic recovery. During the early months of the crisis in 2020, many law enforcement practices went beyond simply stopping workers from pursuing their livelihoods and actively harmed them at a time of intense economic desperation. The WIEGO-led crisis study identified confiscations and destruction of street-vendor goods and equipment in multiple cities, while street vendors in India reported enduring daily beatings from local government officials for the crime of selling vegetables. Alarmingly, some of the actions which took advantage of the 'distraction' provided by the pandemic will threaten incomes well into the future, as is the case for waste pickers in Accra, Ghana, where the Kpone landfill site was suddenly decommissioned in response to the World Bank's Greater Accra Resilient and Integrated Development Programme (Reed 2022) and for street vendors and market traders in Dakar, Senegal, where the largest popular 'African' market was destroyed by the government, in the name of public health, to be replaced by a mall that the government had long planned.

Overt punitive actions such as evictions, confiscations, and destruction of workers' worksites or productive assets are stark examples of how different levels or branches of the state act in ways that are mutually counterproductive. While national governments were trying to provide cash or food aid to informal workers to help smooth incomes over the crisis, local governments, or specific parts of national governments, were implementing actions which further undermined those incomes. Here again, the punitive arm of the state may ally with capital in a regressive solidarity to privatize space or commodities, ultimately dispossessing informal workers of their livelihoods (Reed 2022).

Inappropriate application of social contract ideas

A final component of the 'even worse' contract is the possibility that arguably well-intentioned new social contract architects, including international institutions and national governments, apply elements of a new social contract to informal workers in an inappropriate manner. This would include, for example, the application of the type of formalization focused on registration and the levying of taxes without any reciprocal benefits (Cass Talbott 2022; Chen 2022; Ghosh 2021; Rogan 2022).

As the impacts of the COVID-19 pandemic and related restrictions have contributed to one of the largest global economic downturns in generations, national governments are likely to search for additional sources of revenue to finance stimulus and recovery packages—and this may lead towards the prioritization of direct taxation on the self-employed in the informal sector. Yet, such interventions ignore the taxes and operating fees that informal workers already pay, the economic contributions that they make, and the crippling disproportional impacts of the pandemic recession on them.

There is one further inappropriate application of social contract ideas which should be highlighted here. This is the idea, promoted by multilateral institutions and often linked to the idea of a new social contract, that the presence of informality—and in particular self-employment—justifies the dismantling of employment-linked social insurance; for example, see *The Changing World of Work. World Development Report 2019* (World Bank 2019). Whilst it is true that social protection should be extended to informal workers regardless of employment status, the arguments and evidence for removing social protection from the ambit of labour regulation are not as straightforward as the World Development Report insists (Heintz 2008; ILO 2018b). Furthermore, removing the contributions of employers (or owners of capital in the case of self-employed informal workers) cuts off a potentially important source of financing for benefits above the very basic minimum provided by the state (Anyidoho et al. 2022; Staab 2020).

The testimonies of informal workers in the WIEGO-led crisis study show how all of these components of the even worse contract—predatory capital, hostile (local) states, and inappropriate regulation (and even protection)—compounded one another during the COVID-19 lockdowns of 2020 and the successive waves of the virus and restrictions during 2021 so that even where urban informal workers had been declared as essential workers, many were unable to work (Reed 2022). The danger for informal workers moving forwards is that these three elements are intensified.

4.3 A 'better new' contract

At the same time as providing a warning about what could become worse for informal workers, we have also presented, in section 3, a vision of a better new social contract: one in which informal workers are recognized as workers; laws and policies are relevant and responsive to the needs of informal workers; reciprocal relationships are established between the state, capital, formal, and informal labour at the municipal, national, and transnational levels; rights and responsibilities are redistributed between stakeholders and expanded beyond a narrow view of social protection and national taxation; and—last but not least—spaces for policy dialogue are opened up to informal worker organizations and leaders. To realize this better new social contract, two major processes of change are needed.

A change in mindsets and dominant narratives regarding the informal economy

Most policymakers and economic planners tend to see informal workers and their enterprises and activities as a problem to be dealt with, as the negative narratives suggest. Yet, most informal workers are trying to earn an honest living: often without social or legal protections; without basic infrastructure, transport, and social services; without access to public space or public procurement bids; without financial or business development services; and without tax breaks and other incentives, in the face of systemic discrimination and violence by local authorities and the police as well as stigmatization and neglect by planners and policymakers. Although there remains a long way to go, international (and, in a few cases, local) advocacy efforts have started to shift the dominant negative narratives and change the mindsets of policymakers and other stakeholders so that informal workers can be seen as part of the solution to reducing poverty and inequality and also to growing the economy. While COVID-19 has exposed and exacerbated the inequalities and disadvantages faced by informal workers, it has also shone a spotlight on the essential goods and services provided by informal workers and served, in many countries, to strengthen informal worker organizations.

Inclusion of informal worker organizations/leaders in governance and policy processes

Most fundamentally, a new social contract for the informal workers requires that policymaking and rule-setting processes are made more transparent and participatory, inviting representatives from organizations of informal workers to the policy table. Informal workers need representative voice in the processes and institutions that determine economic policies and formulate the 'rules' of the (economic) game, including both existing tripartite state–business–(formal) labour dialogues and special policy dialogues between state, business, and informal labour. Representatives of organizations of informal workers have the ground-level knowledge and experience to negotiate a new social contract that is appropriate—and better—for informal workers. The common motto of the global movement of organizations of informal workers is 'Nothing for Us, without Us'.

5. Closing reflections

The COVID-19 pandemic recession has exposed and exacerbated economic injustice and inequality around the world. But it has also shone a spotlight on frontline workers who provide essential goods and services to all of us. What is not well recognized is that many of the frontline workers who provide essential goods and services do not enjoy essential rights, including health insurance, as most of them are informally employed.

So long as informal workers, the majority of all workers globally, are stigmatized, penalized, and criminalized, both for what they do and who they are, poverty and inequality will not be adequately reduced and economic growth will not be optimal. What is required is a better new contract that redistributes wealth through appropriate tax policies; invests in strengthening local systems of production and consumption; ensures universal access to social protection and to good-quality public services, including basic infrastructure and care services, with well-remunerated workers; regulates markets to limit the power of capitalists to download costs and risks on informal workers; ends state violence against informal workers; and challenges the dominant narrative that stigmatizes informal workers as a problem rather than recognizing their contributions in providing essential goods and services as well as paying taxes and fees.

This better new social contract will require a change in mindsets and ongoing negotiations. It will require the organized strength of informal workers to demand change as well as an accountable state and responsive owners of capital who are willing to listen and respond to the demands of informal labour, that is, reflecting the principle of responsiveness Roever and Ogando 2022). Since long before COVID-19, informal workers have been organizing, negotiating, bargaining, and joining hands to make their demands known. In April 2014, in preparation for the standard-setting discussion on formalization at the 2014 and 2015 International Labour Conferences, 54 organizations of domestic workers, home-based workers, street vendors, and waste pickers from 24 countries developed a common platform of what informal workers need and want from efforts to formalize the informal economy (WIEGO 2014). The better new social contract called for in this chapter builds on this common platform of formalization demands as well as a common platform of demands for COVID-19 relief and post-COVID 19 reforms by 11 organizations of informal workers in 9 cities around the world (WIEGO 2020).

Finally, and importantly, what we and the organizations of informal workers are calling for is not a separate contract for informal workers but a new social contract for society which recognizes informal workers as central. This vision draws on a realistic view of work today, namely, that 61 per cent of all workers globally (90 per cent in most low-income and some low middle-income economics) are informally employed. It embeds informal workers within concentric and dynamic circles of relationships, rights, responsibilities, and spaces at the municipal, national, and transnational levels. This larger canvas for social contracts allows for new patterns of engagement, accountability, and reciprocity between the different faces of the state, society, capital, and labour.

References

Agarwala, R (2018). 'Incorporating Informal Workers into Twenty-First Century Social Contracts', paper prepared for the United Nations Research Institute for Social Development (UNRISD) project on New Directions in Social Policy: Alternatives from and for the Global South, Geneva: UNRISD.

Alfers, L., and Moussié, R. (2019). 'The ILO World Social Protection Report 2017–19: An Assessment', *Development and Change*, 51 (2): 683–97.

Alfers, L., and Moussié, R. (2022). 'Towards More Inclusive Social Protection: Informal Workers and the Struggle for a New Social Contract'. In L. Alfers, S. Plagerson, and M. Chen (eds), *Social Contracts and Informal Workers in the Global South*. Northampton, MA: Edward Elgar, pp.106–25.

Alfers, L., F. Lund, and R. Moussié (2018). 'Informal Workers and The Future of Work: A Defence of Work-Related Social Protection', Women in Informal Employment: Globalizing and Organizing (WIEGO) Working Paper No. 37, Manchester: WIEGO.

Alfers, L., M. Chen, and S. Plagerson (2022a). 'Conclusion'. In L. Alfers, S. Plagerson, and M. Chen (eds), *Social Contracts and Informal Workers in the Global South*. Northampton, MA: Edward Elgar, pp.216–31.

Alfers, L., S. Plagerson, and M. Chen (eds) (2022b). *Social Contracts and Informal Workers in the Global South*. Northampton, MA: Edward Elgar.

Anyidoho, N.A., M. Gallien, G. Ismail, F. Juergens- Grant, M. Rogan, and V. van den Boogaard (2022). Tight Tax Net, Loose Safety Net: Taxation and Social Protection in Accra's Informal Sector. WIEGO Working Paper No. 45, Manchester, UK: WIEGO.

Behrendt, C., I. Ortiz, E. Julien, Y. Ghellab, S. Hayter, and F. Bonnet (2019). *Social Contract and the Future of Work: Inequality, Income Security, Labour Relations and Social Dialogue*. Geneva: International Labour Office (ILO).

Berg, J., M. Furrer, E. Harman, U. Rani, and M. Siberman (2018). *Digital Labour Platforms and the Future of Work*. Geneva: ILO.

Biesecker, A., and U von Winterfeld (2018). 'Notion of Multiple Crisis and Feminist Perspectives on Social Contract', *Gender, Work and Organization*, 25(3): 279–92.

Bonner, C and F. Carré (2013). 'Global Networking: Informal Workers Build Solidarity, Power and Representation through Networks and Alliances', WIEGO Working Paper No. 31, Manchester: WIEGO.

Bonner, C, F. Carré, M. Chen, and R. Douglas (2018). 'Informal Worker Organizing and Mobilization; Linking Global with Local Advocacy'. In G. Bahn, S. Srinivas, and V. Watson (eds), *Companion to Planning in the Global South*. Abingdon: Routledge, pp. 275–86.

Bonnet, F., J. Vanek, and M. Chen (2019). 'Women and Men in the Informal Economy: A Statistical Brief', Manchester: WIEGO.

Carré, F, P. Horn, and C. Bonner (2018). 'Collective Bargaining by Informal Workers in the Global South: Where and How It Takes Place', WIEGO Working Paper No. 38, Manchester: WIEGO.

Carré, F. (2022). 'Dependent Contractor—Towards the Recognition of a New Labour Category'. In L. Alfers, S. Plagerson, and M. Chen (eds), *Social Contracts and Informal Workers in the Global South*. Northampton, MA: Edward Elgar, pp.73–84.

Cass Talbott, T. (2022). 'Extended Producer Responsibility: Opportunities and Threats for Waste Pickers'. In L. Alfers, S. Plagerson, and M. Chen (eds), *Social Contracts and Informal Workers in the Global South*. Northampton, MA: Edward Elgar.

Chen, M. (2012). 'The Informal Economy: Definitions, Theories and Policies', Cambridge, MA: WIEGO.

Chen, M, C. Bonner, and F. Carré (2015). 'Organizing Informal Workers: Benefits, Challenges and Successes', Background paper for Human Development Report 2015, New York: United Nations Development Programme (UNDP) Human Development Report Office.

Chen, M., J. Vanek, F. Lund, J. Heintz, R. Jhabvala, and C. Bonner (2005). *Progress of the World's Women: Women, Work and Poverty*. New York: United Nations Development Fund for Women (UNIFEM).

Chen, M. (2022). 'Self-Employment and Social Contracts: From the Perspective of the Informal Self-Employed'. In L. Alfers, S. Plagerson, and M. Chen (eds), *Social Contracts and Informal Workers in the Global South*. Northampton, MA: Edward Elgar, pp. 49–72.

Daguerre, A (2014). 'New Corporate Elites and the Erosion of the Keynesian Social Compact', *Work, Employment and Society*, 28(2): 323–34.

Dean, H. (2013). 'The Translation of Needs into Rights: Reconceptualising Social Citizenship as a Global Phenomenon', *International Journal of Social Welfare*, 22(S1): S32–S49.

Ghosh, J. (2021). *Informal Women Workers in the Global South: Policies and Practices for the Formalization of Women's Employment in Developing Economies*. London: Routledge.

Heintz, J. (2008). 'Revisiting Labour Markets: Implications for Macroeconomics and Social Protection', *IDS Bulletin*, 39(2): 11–17.

ILO (International Labour Organization) (2002). 'Decent Work and the Informal Economy', Report VI for International Labour Conference 2002, Geneva: ILO.

ILO (2018a). 'Informality and Non-standard Forms of Employment', prepared for the G20 Employment Working Group meeting, 20–22 February, Buenos Aires, Geneva: ILO.

ILO (2018c). 'International Labour Office Expresses Concern about World Bank Report on Future of Work', ILO Newsroom statement, Geneva: ILO.

ILO (2018c). *Women and Men in the Informal Economy: A Statistical Picture* (3rd edn). Geneva: ILO.

Maiti, D., and K. Sen (2010). 'The Informal Sector in India: A Means of Exploitation or Accumulation?', *Journal of South Asian Development*, 5(1): 1–13.

Meagher, K. (2018). 'Rewiring the Social Contract. Digital Taxis and Economic Inclusion in Nigeria', paper presented at the UNRISD Conference 'Overcoming Inequalities in a Fractured World: Between Elite Power and Social Mobilization', 8–9 November, Geneva. UNRISD.

Perry, G., W.F Maloney, O.S. Arias, P. Fajnzylber, A.D. Mason, J. Saavedra-Chanduvi (2007). *Informality: Exit and Exclusion.* Washington, DC: World Bank.

Plagerson, S., L. Alfers, and M. Chen. (2022). 'Introduction'. In L.Alfers, S. Plagerson, and M. Chen (eds), *Social Contracts and Informal Workers in the Global South.* Northampton, MA: Edward Elgar, pp. 1–30.

Rawls, John (1971). *A Theory of Justice.* Cambridge, MA: Harvard University Press.

Reed, S. (2022). 'Essential and Disposable? Or Just Disposable? Informal Workers during COVID-19'. In L. Alfers, S. Plagerson, and M. Chen (eds), *Social Contracts and Informal Workers in the Global South.* Northampton, MA: Edward Elgar, pp. 189–215.

Roever, S., and A.C. Ogando (2022). 'Recognition, Responsiveness and Reciprocity'. In L. Alfers, S. Plagerson, and M. Chen (eds), *Social Contracts and Informal Workers in the Global South.* Northampton, MA: Edward Elgar, pp. 31–48.

Rogan, M. (2022). 'Taxation and the Informal Sector in the Global South: Strengthening the Social Contract without Reciprocity?'. In L. Alfers, S. Plagerson, and M. Chen (eds), *Social Contracts and Informal Workers in the Global South.* Northampton, MA: Edward Elgar, pp. 85–105.

Rousseau, J.J. (1999 [1762]). *The Social Contract.* New York: Oxford University Press.

Sanyal, K. (2007). *Rethinking Capitalist Development: Primitive Accumulation, Governmentality and Post-Colonial Capitalism.* New Delhi: Routledge India.

Singer, H. (1970). 'Dualism Revisited: A New Approach to the Problem of the Dual Society in Developing Countries', *Journal of Development Studies,* 7(1): 60–75.

Staab, S. (2020). 'Social Protection for Women Informal Workers: Perspectives from Latin America'. In M. Chen and F. Carré (eds), *The Informal Economy Revisited: Examining the Past, Envisioning the Future.* London: Routledge, pp. 215–20.

Uzbay Pirili, M., and M. Pifpirili (2015). 'A New Social Contract: Rethinking the Role of the State towards Post-2015 Development Agenda', *Ege Academic Review,* 15(2): 253–64.

Von Broembsen, M. (2022). 'Human Rights and Transnational Social Contracts: The Recognition and Inclusion of Homeworkers?'. In L. Alfers, S. Plagerson, and M. Chen (eds), *Social Contracts and Informal Workers in the Global South.* Northampton, MA: Edward Elgar, pp. 144–68.

WIEGO (2014). WIEGO NETWORK PLATFORM: TRANSITIONING FROM THE INFORMAL TO THE FORMAL ECONOMY in the interests of workers in the informal economy. Document prepared for the International Labour Congress, June 2014, Geneva. https://www.wiego.org/sites/default/files/resources/files/WIEGO-Platform-ILO-2014.pdf.

WIEGO (Women in Informal Employment: Globalizing and Organizing) (2021). 'COVID Relief and Post-COVID Reforms: Demands of Informal Worker Organizations', Manchester: WIEGO (April), available at: www.wiego.org/resources/there-no-recovery-without-informal-workers (accessed November 2023).

World Bank (2019). *The Changing World of Work. World Development Report 2019.* Washington, DC: World Bank.

12

Reflections on Informal Employment, COVID-19, and the Future

Ravi Kanbur, Jayati Ghosh, Barbara Harriss-White, and Jan Breman

1. Introduction

As detailed in a number of the chapters in this volume, the COVID-19 pandemic has clearly had a profound impact on labour markets while, at the same time, offering an important moment to reflect on the prospects for a fairer and more prosperous organization of economies and societies. Before drawing the volume to a close, we offer the reflections and perspectives of four renowned scholars of labour markets (in general) and informal employment (in particular). We asked each author to reflect on the significance of the pandemic (based, in large part, on the findings presented in the volume) and to outline some of the key lessons from the tumultuous pandemic period and fledgling recovery.

This set of reflections is structured as follows. First, Ravi Kanbur highlights the heterogeneous impacts of the pandemic and makes two proposals for future social protection measures and financing to better insulate the workforce from future crises. Next, Jayati Ghosh directs her attention to the social contract chapter in the volume (Chen et al., Chapter 11). While questioning the use of the social contract as a lens with which to examine the interplay between labour and capital, she endorses the prerequisites for a genuinely just and inclusive post-pandemic economy detailed in the chapter. Barbara Harriss-White describes the hierarchy of actors in the waste system in India and the poor working conditions of waste pickers at the bottom of the hierarchy, both before and during the pandemic, to illustrate the type of fundamental shifts that are required to ensure decent work and environmental sustainability. And finally, Jan Breman's reflections offer a wider perspective on the unjust relationship between capital and labour, especially casual labour, and how the pandemic has further exacerbated the relationship and increased inequality.

Ravi Kanbur et al., *Reflections on Informal Employment, COVID-19, and the Future*. In: *COVID-19 and the Informal Economy*. Edited by: Martha Alter Chen, Michael Rogan, and Kunal Sen, Oxford University Press.
© Ravi Kanbur et al. (2024). DOI: 10.1093/oso/9780198887041.003.0013

2. Lessons of the COVID-19 pandemic for the next crisis, and the ones after that

Ravi Kanbur

COVID-19 has led to considerable research providing real-time empirical accounts of the impact of the pandemic on a range of sectors and household types across countries. The three chapters under consideration here are among the best examples in this vein, focusing on the informal sector and excelling in the rapidity, detail, and immediate usefulness of results. While there are a number of methodological issues that can be discussed and debated (e.g. on sampling and data collection strategies in socially distanced times), there is not enough space here to discuss these in detail, nor to offer a substantive commentary on the chapters without doing an injustice to the enormous effort and dedication that has gone into the investigations. Rather, I would like to take this opportunity to present some observations on macro-level policy response to crises, observations which are inspired by the empirical detail in these chapters.

2.1 Heterogeneity of the COVID-19 impact

For me, the biggest take-away from the detailed findings in these chapters is the sheer heterogeneity of the nature of the impact of the crisis. As Chen et al.'s 'COVID-19 and Informal Work: Degrees and Pathways of Impact in 11 Cities around the world' (Chapter 1 in this volume) says, 'The impact of the COVID-19 crisis on informal workers was not uniform: it differed across cities as well as between and within sectors.'

Box 1.1 of the chapter gives 5 types of channels across 6 subgroups, leading to 30 distinct cells of potential pathways of impact, and each of the cells is itself a rich weave of interlinked mechanisms. For Bangladesh, Rahman et al.'s 'Recovery with Distress: Unpacking COVID-19 Impact on Livelihoods and Poverty in Rural Areas and Urban Low-Income Settlements of Bangladesh' (Chapter 6 in this volume) also emphasizes heterogeneity, in particular as between urban and rural households: 'Compared to the rural HHs, urban slum HHs faced more drastic "income shock" due to second lockdown, a trend similar to that after the first lockdown. Between March and August–September 2021, income dropped by 18 per cent for urban slum HHs and by 15 per cent for rural HHs.'

Across the general reduction in standards of living, they document variations across education, skill, and occupation categories.

Through the gendered lens it brings to the impact of the pandemic, the work of Chakravarty and Nayak, 'The COVID-19 Pandemic and Intra-household Bargaining: A Case of Domestic Workers in Delhi' (Chapter 7 in this volume) also highlights heterogeneity of impact depending on very specific aspects of the balance of power within the household:

> To present a nuanced understanding, we have divided our respondents' families into three categories on the basis of the family's status before the lockdown began: Category 1: husband having a regular income, more than that of the wife; Category 2: husband having regular income but significantly less than that of the wife; and Category 3: husband with irregular earnings and irregular contributions to the household budget.

Taking a bargaining approach to intra-household resource allocation, the authors elaborate how the relatively high demand for domestic work during the pandemic (relative to the demand for male informal-sector jobs) has led to an 'emerging agency of women domestic workers in the household decision-making processes' for some households.

These micro-level findings, so fresh and timely after the pandemic struck, are absolutely fascinating and have been—and will be—important for just-in-time policymaking as the COVID-19 virus mutates and causes new waves of public health and economic crises. Indeed, Rahman and colleagues point to the challenge of '"finding out fast" in order to inform the policymakers grappling with the multiple fall-outs of the pandemic'. However, I would like to take a perspective beyond the pandemic. And I would like to think about crises in general and their impact on the poor and vulnerable.

2.2 Crises in general

By crisis, I mean an event or sequence of events with macro-level consequences for the economy. Clearly, COVID, as an infectious, disease-driven public health crisis, qualifies. But there are myriad other such possible crises lying around the corner. For a start, there are other infectious diseases, respiratory and otherwise, to which economies are vulnerable in the globalized and globalizing world. There are financial crises, of the type we had in 2008–09. A flare-up in one part for the world was transmitted very quickly elsewhere with devastating consequences for economies and the poor worldwide. There are also climate-change-driven, weather-related crises, which can have enormous impact on economies. Alongside these big factors are others such as cross-border refuge flows, spill-overs of risk assessments from one economy to neighbouring ones, global sectoral collapses (e.g. tourism), each of which can cause problems for economies that are not themselves in the initial path of the shock. And all of these will impact the poor and vulnerable, including those in the informal sector.

So, we do not know which type of crisis will hit and when it will hit, but we know it is very likely that there is a crisis of some sort around the corner. How do we prepare for it and especially prepare to avert the impact on the poor and vulnerable? To start studying the impacts and to begin designing targeted responses after the crisis hits is already too late. 'Finding out fast' may not be fast enough. Each crisis will have highly differentiated impacts on the poor and vulnerable, which I think is a major lesson to be learned from the three chapters under consideration here. We should, rather, think *ex ante* about how to address crises. In fact, this is a conclusion towards which Chen et al. push us when they ask for universal comprehensive social protection that provides both social insurance and social assistance to informal workers. With a different trajectory of argument, Rahman and colleagues argue in the same spirit:

> The four cost drivers that have contributed to the expenditure burdens of the poor and lower-income groups are all related to macroeconomic policy: health care, education, transportation, and utilities. The COVID-19 crisis has created a compelling policy window to review reform measures that can address these critical cost drivers for the poor.

In other words, addressing a range of structural issues could help us prepare for, and mitigate, the consequences for the poor of future crises.

2.3 Two proposals

With this general background, I want to rehearse two macro-level policy proposals that I have made in the realm of social protection, which I believe receive support from the findings of these studies. Start with the analytical but abstract position that universal social protection is the best *ex ante* platform with which to address crises whose nature, magnitude, and timing we cannot know in advance. The logic of this position should be clear. A general social protection system that reacts to any fall in incomes with supplementation, and is financed through general taxation, will do so whatever the source of income reduction. But logic is one thing. In practice, we have a complex web of schemes with their own histories and logics. It is this system that we have to work with, not some abstract first best world, albeit it might provide general guidance on direction of movement.

A first requirement is that we understand how the actual system of schemes on the ground will react to crises of different sorts and provide coverage to the poor and vulnerable. Such analysis will reveal gaps and, indeed, redundancies. It can be the basis of piecewise reform to protect against a range of crises. It can also provide an informational and technical platform for more remedial reform proposals which move the system towards universality. But such 'stress testing' of the existing system is the start. I have argued that such an exercise for social protection is analogous to the Financial Sector Assessment Programme (FSAP), which stress tests the existing financial system against a range of plausible shocks. If FSAP, why not SPAP (Social Protection Assessment Programme)? Every country should conduct such an exercise to identify how to enhance protection for the poor and vulnerable against crises, with help from the international community as needed. The good news is that international agencies seem to be getting on board. Once the gaps are identified, governments can move to fill them with structural changes to the system. Such changes will not be costless, and the international community has a responsibility to contribute to such investment in the protection of the poor.

However, while the reform is proceeding as an ongoing process, a second requirement is that, at the macro level, funding be available to countries to actually finance the operation of the social protection system as it reacts to the next crisis and ones after that. To scramble around looking for funding after the crisis strikes is too little, too late. Rather, what is needed is to have a system of financing which flows automatically upon key indicators being breached, without needing a prolonged round of negotiations and bureaucratic procedures of international agencies. The due diligence is all done *ex ante*, and the role of pre-crisis testing is central, along with other features, such as agreeing on the triggers. Again, the good news is that the international community has some instruments that move us in this direction. The International Bank for Reconstruction and Development's (IBRD's) Deferred Drawdown Option and the International Development Association's (IDA's) Crisis Response Window provide resources to countries to address crises. What is needed is greater focus on protecting the poor and vulnerable and greater automaticity in implementation.

2.4 Concluding remarks

These three excellent studies have enough material and insights to feed into a number of ongoing debates in development beyond the current pandemic crisis. Appropriate methodologies for investigation, gendered impacts, and rural versus urban perspectives are among the discussions that will benefit from the empirical material in these chapters. I have taken up one particular aspect of the findings (namely, the highly heterogeneous nature of the impacts and channels of impact on the poor and vulnerable) and have used this to highlight two macro-level policy proposals: to stress test social protection systems in the face of crises and to use these findings to enhance automatic funding for financing the increased needs of social protection during crises.

3. Lessons for a just and inclusive post-pandemic economy

Jayati Ghosh

This is an important book, making an often ignored and inadequately accepted point about the need to recognize the centrality of informal workers and give voice to their needs, rights, and demands. I am completely in agreement with the basic thesis of the chapters that new political economy configurations and public policies must explicitly recognize the significance (and often preponderance) of informal workers, especially self-employed workers. However, I confess to some discomfort with the idea of 'a social contract' as presented by Chen et al. in Chapter 11 as it seems to assume that there is one existing and widely accepted 'social contract', rather than a continuous interplay of different political economy forces and classes, and that the resulting social contracts or bargains can change in an absolute fashion rather than in complex, and sometimes unnoticed, ways. I am also not entirely convinced by the idea that there has been an explicit or implicit social contract between capital and wage labour; certainly, this has not been true in most of the developing world.

These nuances—and the resulting divisions within society and economy—suggest that the central idea of bringing informality of employment into the discussion must also be accompanied by greater recognition of the variety of social contracts that can operate both serially and simultaneously. As already noted in the text, there are specific social contracts operating across different levels of government, with multiple and often overlapping social contracts at local, city, national, regional, and global levels. Similarly, there are different forms of social contract operating across different economic and social actors. These are obviously affected by legal/juridical/regulatory institutions and processes. But most of all, they are determined and influenced by power relationships.

In addition, it is necessary to recognize the important distinctions between different kinds of workers within informal activities: employed workers, self-employed workers, and unpaid/unrecognized workers. They are not identical, and nor are their interests; and sometimes, and in particular contexts, their interests could even be not just dissimilar but conflicting. For example, labour regulations that attempt to protect informal paid workers could conflict with the interests of those running very small and microenterprises using such labour. Unpaid workers within households and communities (who are even more voiceless in policy discourse) are typically at the receiving end of policies that result in additional work burdens being passed on to them without these being seen as a problem, even by paid informal workers within the same households and communities.

The essential point being made here is that the very important principles described in the book, for just and viable socio-economic arrangements (universal social protection; access to public space, public services, and public procurement;

fair conditions of work; just, progressive taxation; freedom from harassment; freedom from stigmatization) should apply equally to all types of informal workers, not just self-employed workers.

This is entirely in line with the broad thrust of the argument made in this book and, indeed, would provide greater social support for the important recommendations. The very useful discussion on strategies going forwards highlights two major processes of change that are required: (a) a change in mindsets and dominant narratives regarding the informal economy and (b) the inclusion of informal worker organizations/leaders in governance and policy processes. To each of these I would add (a) a change of mindsets regarding the nature of work, and taking into account the forms of work and the workers who are essential for society and contribute to the economy, even if they are not recognized; and (b) the inclusion of unpaid workers as major stakeholders, providing them with a voice and influence in all policy decisions that affect their lives.

I believe that this is essential to ensure that a genuinely inclusive and just economy can emerge from the patterns of engagement, accountability, and reciprocity between state, capital, and labour. Given the power imbalances between them, and the crucial need for coalitions to confront these power imbalances, it is all the more important to include all workers in such a movement.

4. COVID waste and waste work in small-town India

Barbara Harriss-White

Throughout the world, the production of waste is one of the fastest growing economic sectors, though rarely labelled as such, particularly when the waste takes the form of gases. India is no exception. In India, 'peak waste'—beyond which material efficiencies will counterbalance the physical growth of waste—is thought to lie a century hence. Before then, it will do nothing but grow.

As a technical field, waste is captured by engineers and technologists, whose cost–benefit analyses, biased towards metropolitan waste, tend to be blind to workers, especially unregistered ones. As a social problem, non-governmental organizations (NGOs) and self-help groups (SHGs) dominate the literature, ignoring the potentials of frontier technology. But in India, waste is the most visible expression of caste relations, in which upper castes are still entitled to throw waste into public space and in which a workforce, still overwhelmingly made up of scheduled castes and tribes, is expected to clean it up. The informal waste labour force is also the most visible expression of local tax evasion, which diverts municipalities of the resources needed to pay a registered sanitation workforce.

Since more urban Indians live outside than inside metros, I studied the waste economy of a one-lakh town during the period 2015–19. As a local government responsibility and a major public-expenditure category, waste is not unique in being managed in several poorly coordinated territorial or networked administrative silos. With exceptions, upper-caste officials are ignorant about how the sector works, their estimates of waste generation differing by a factor of three, their contact with the urban workforce minimal.

Waste disposal is structured through a set of 'public–private partnerships' which aren't found in textbooks but which may not be special to waste. Alongside the public service workforce (which is paid directly by the municipality, is unionized, has work and social security rights, and cleans most of the town), there is a differentiated private sector. The largest companies are subcontracted to the municipality and other state organizations such as colleges, hospitals, and the railways. This public and private/corporate workforce gathers and segregates waste and transports unrecyclable waste-waste to the dump yard. Private companies can only undercut the municipality at profit by reducing wages and ignoring work-related benefits—done by casualizing contracts to their *Dalit* and tribal labour force. Next in size are urban industrial and service companies (e.g. factories making liquor, rice, and clothing accessories; private clinics; private colleges; transport companies; offices, etc.). Their specialist waste, or 'housekeeping' work force is also disproportionately *Dalit*, casual, and low paid—'permanently temporary' said one. Then comes a barely regulated hierarchy of 'scrap-capital' through which paper, card, metal, glass, and plastic is gathered, segregated, and bulked for recycling, populated by petty activity and capped by a joint family portfolio including scrap yards, a lorry fleet, urban real estate, and a labour force in four figures. Serving this hierarchy is a family monopoly in control of gunnies, cement bags, and white plastic bags essential to waste work. Operating separately are private fleets of septic tankers, owned by scheduled-caste and scheduled-tribal entrepreneurs, disposing of some of the town's completely untreated faecal waste in complicitous relations of police extortion.

For every single registered worker, there must be 10–15 unregistered, rightless workers; local or migrant, some bonded as wage labourers, others self-employed.

Bolted into this public–private sector, the informal economy of waste is essential to the urban economy. Overdetermined both by tax evasion—starving local government of revenue and forcing it to seek out the lowest-cost alternatives—and by theories of new public management, public waste workers have been laid off throughout the past decade and rehired by private companies and contractors on casual or 'semi-written' contracts. Immediately, their wages drop from, say, Rs15,000 a month (with work-related benefits) to Rs5,000–6,000 without benefits. To compensate for this catastrophic decline in income (not to mention job security), waste workers add extra shifts to their long working day. 'After hours', they sift, grade and segregate, carry, drag, and sell the recyclable elements in the detritus they collect—work previously done by self-employed informal collectors. The inexorable increase in waste means that there is still work for displaced self-employed labour—if you consider earnings of Rs3,000–4,000 per month to count as work. Workers on poverty wages and incomes are heavily dependent on the public distribution system for their staple food—even if they also criticize it. They themselves can figure out that the state underwrites the reproduction of their household and its workers while it simultaneously enables employers to deprive them of income and security at work.

The worst waste work, the disposal of human waste, is no longer the realm of female manual scavenging. After its abolition in 1993, households turned to septic tanks. Nearly 30 years later, about half the town's houses have them. Septic tanker owners regard these tanks as usually too small and not voided regularly. A municipal poster encourages waste ducts from such tanks to lead through compound walls into open drains—which is what the other half of the houses do anyway from their latrines. So consumption waste is mixed with human waste in the open drains of the town. Open-drain waste is 'wet waste': men's rather than women's work (as is dangerous sewer-work). So prior to recycling, drain waste has to be cleaned and rejects for the dump yard are greater than if consumption waste were separated from human waste. And, just like the irrigation tank and the river bed, where septic tankers dump their untreated loads, the dump yard is also a resting place for decomposing human waste.

So, much waste-work is low-status, menial work with poor control over working conditions. The highest-status workers, those directly paid by local government, have no access to lavatories or bathing facilities. Apart from the irony of public-sector workers having to relieve themselves on the very verges that they clean, the absence of 'facilities' requires a tight control over bodily metabolism. Over decades, occupation-related diseases such as kidney failure and liver disorders have been reported—over and above diseases attributable to dangerous work environments, such as skin infections, allergies, joint pain, and upper respiratory tract (URT) disease. The municipal sanitation workers (MSWs) know of the Human Rights Watch finding that 90 per cent of India's sanitation workers die before retirement age. The entire informal waste sector is stigmatized, but more oppressively so for women. Women work harder for longer hours, lower pay, and fewer social entitlements. Yet, while their waste work is low-paid, dirty, and low status, as a sector it is not a barrier to accumulation. The state has had few difficulties subcontracting this work to private and corporate capital.

Over the five years prior to COVID-19, working conditions were deteriorating. The municipal labour force was being casualized. Cheaper contracts replaced permanent ones and limited, arbitrary (and delayed) benefits replaced theoretically decent work rights. New electric trucks succeeding old tractor-trailers are inappropriately designed for the labour teams; their lower capacity requires more dump yard journeys and informally lengthened work shifts. A woman MSW explained, 'apart from the explosion in plastic waste, more and more waste is complicated and mixed in drains. Diapers, sanitary napkins, tampons and incontinence pads are muddled with recyclables and food waste. That's not to mention syringes and other infectious medical waste which is not always segregated.'

Enter COVID.

While India's biomedical waste amounts to about 600 tonnes per day, even before the tragic 2021 wave, daily COVID waste added anywhere between 101 and 230 tonnes to this total. Note that this range does not vary with the pandemic surge. It is the range of official daily estimates for a given month in 2020. A hospital patient with COVID generates between 2 and 15 times the medical waste of a general patient.

'COVID waste' has emerged as a sub-field in public health and engineering directed at themes such as the logistics of yellow bag segregation; the hazards and cleaning of infected surfaces and the management of infectious sludge, disinfection, and autoclave sterilization as alternatives to compromised incineration infrastructure; and the need for education and training in sites such as clinical institutions, quarantine centres, labs, and pollution control boards. If labour is mentioned at all, it is in media op eds deploring the lack of safety gear and social security and warning of transmission risks in housing where isolation is impossible. The discovery of roadside 'disposals' of personal protective equipment (PPE), masks, and COVID-related human tissues and body fluids is blamed on 'lack of awareness'. COVID waste is seen as a burden on the environment rather on waste labour—on the life-worlds from which the research literature is far removed.

Indeed, lockdowns made fieldwork impossible. We know that in the rush for vaccination, the waste workforce was not classified as essential, and waste workers had to weigh up the inordinate time spent waiting for free vaccines at public hospitals against the deterrent cost of private vaccines relative to their earnings. Phone interviews with MSWs revealed that they were handling ever more waste and more non-biodegradable waste. COVID-related used masks, gloves, and swabs added both to the consumption waste they collected and to their risk of exposure to the virus. Increasingly, the 'dry waste' that it falls to women to collect combined general waste with infectious 'medical' waste. Meanwhile the revenue-starved municipality diverted expenditure towards its public health response to COVID at the expense of support to the invisible waste labour force that is essential to public health. The municipality provided the subset of its 'elite' labour force still on permanent contracts with two surgical masks per day but failed to supply soap, sanitizer, or gloves, let alone hazard benefits, check-ups, or tests. For waste collectors, COVID was—and remains—not a crisis in the sense of an unexpected extreme event, nor a crisis in the sense of a turning point, but simply the marking of a serious exacerbation of the hazards of their daily work.

In 2019, with an exasperation rising months before COVID arrived, a woman union leader suggested to me that the only reform worthy of the conditions in which they work needed to be radical—waste needs a workforce organized and equipped like the Indian army. 'Waste disposal should be organised by the Government of India like the police and army and not through arbitrary schemes like Swachch Bharat, or cash-starved municipalities, let alone scattered self-help groups', she said.

But the state, embodying upper-caste, waste-throwing interests, is part of the problem. India's waste economy is a cultural artefact as well as a physical hazard. Only when the practices of waste are disengaged from patriarchy and caste, and waste management is adequately publicly funded and organized, is the waste economy likely to be technologically transformed, are work conditions likely to approach decency, and are towns likely to be cleaned with less damage to the environment and to human health. Meanwhile, waste will become one of India's most obtrusive development paradoxes, with low-caste and tribal men and women toiling everywhere at their indispensable waste work and stigmatized for their essential contributions.

5. Strangling the labouring poor in casual employment and excluding them from well-being

Jan Breman

The composite character of the workforce engaged in informalized employment impedes dealing with it under one and the same label. I shall focus, in this short note, on the bottom ranks, the people dispossessed from means of production, who, moreover, are kept adrift in footloose mobility. The relationship between capital, labour, and the state indeed needs to be urgently restructured. A drastic overhaul of their entanglement is mandatory since tinkering at the margins will not redress the ever-widening gap between accumulation and immiseration. It should be clear by now that the sort of piecemeal interventions usually proposed to repair the lacking protection and security of the working classes stuck at the bottom of the economy are not going to materialize under the reign of market-driven capitalism. This anti-labour regime treats the working poor as a reserve army and aims to push the price of their irregular employment to the lowest possible rate. The policy is backed up with modes of wage payment that are meant to keep them disposable. Although unschooled-unskilled labour power is abundantly available, it is being replaced at an accelerating pace by capital, only available at low or no cost at all to those who already own it.

Capitalism has deeply intruded into the bottom shelves of society worldwide. Its protagonists suggest that the workforce in the thoroughly informalized economy do not as much suffer from a lack of savings or property as from the opportunity to make the capital that they do have more productive. Promoted by Hernando de

Soto (1989, 2000), this brand of propaganda was highly appreciated by the World Bank and other financial stakeholders of neoconservative strictures. His advocacy that capitalism is not the cause of poverty but infallible for assuring escape from it made him the darling of politicians in favour of sizing down the scale and impact of the public economy as well as drastically cutting back on social security and protection schemes meant to raise the living standard of the working poor. Instead of harping on rising unemployment and destitution, in the new catechism, the heroic achievements of petty entrepreneurship were sung.

Praise was showered on the men and women who, through hard work and a frugal lifestyle, managed to save enough to build a house, start a small business, and succeed to become or remain self-reliant (Breman 2001; Breman and Wiradi 2002). Microfinance agencies flourished and self-help groups were set up in urban slums and rural backwaters of the Global South to pave the way to a bright future. These attempts to find a pathway to accumulation in a landscape which has routinely been subjected to disentitlement and dispossession seem slowly to have lost the glamour and spirit of perseverance against all odds attached to them. Such initiatives pushed from above to wake up and nurse the capitalist instinct among the down-and-out have definitely become unstuck during the COVID-19 pandemic, which was accompanied by massive impoverishment (Breman 2020). It is high time that the United Nations critically reviewed its cooperation with the World Bank and decommissioned this prime agency of capitalist business from authorized reporting on global poverty alleviation.

The dole sparingly, selectively, and discriminately handed out at the high tide of COVID-19 was supplied by a chain of government agencies. Pleas for proper benevolence seem to be targeted at the same address. However, as has been demonstrated wide and far, both petty and big business have gone scot-free for non-payment of the minimum wages due to the labouring poor, let alone supplying relief needed to cope with acute distress during the lockdown. As for social care benefits, my suggestion is that owners and managers of capital should be held accountable for contributing to a public fund set up to safeguard livelihood for both the labouring and the non-labouring poor. The latter contingent, much neglected and abandoned during the pandemic, comprises the chronically ill and handicapped, together with single-headed female households and most seniors beyond working age.

An equally critical comment concerns the role of the state, which is adamantly unwilling to find out what transpires in the nether echelons of economy and society. It is a system of governance which holds no brief for people who are blamed for lacking coping power to satisfy their basic needs. The government of India reluctantly collects data on employment and wages of these massive classes and desists from disseminating this unwelcome news as long as possible. Part and parcel of the same politics and policies of exclusion is the recently declared design of this state machinery to deny all relief to households which fail to exert themselves to the level of self-reliance. What is still being labelled as poverty or impoverishment should actually be reclassified as pauperism and pauperization. The use of this terminology brings us back to an era in which a doctrine of social Darwinism prevailed, castigating people in dire straits for their distress (Breman 2016). The stigmatization of the population on the downside is intensified by depriving these contingents from public visibility and voice as a degraded, abusive, and criminalized lot, sweeping them aside as the non-deserving poor.

When, around the middle of the nineteenth century, the shift from a peasant to a post-peasant economy and society came about in the North Atlantic world, it took time before the land-poor and landless workforce from the countryside settled down in urban quarters. The amended Poor Laws forced these land-poor and landless workers to bring their dependents along and set up household in the city. This Great Transformation (Polanyi 2020 [1944]), which saw the transition from an agrarian-rural to an industrial-urban type of existence, has by and large failed to materialize in the Global South. My fieldwork-based research in South and Southeast Asia between the early 1960s and 2015 coincided with the switch to a predatory form of capitalism. Casualization of employment, in combination with the rising price of real estate, means that the divide between place of living and site of off-and-on working has to be retained.

Bereft from means of production enough for viable livelihood and unable to find steady demand for their labour power where they reside, but also deprived from regular jobs and shelter where they migrate to, the classes dependent on casual employment at the bottom of the rural and urban economy are forced to remain footloose. When both males and females, adults as well as minors are put to waged work, the whole household is engaged in the search for income away from home. More often, however, their households are broken up in multi-locationality. Members considered of working age hive off for bouts of employment elsewhere and are supposed to send or bring back earnings to provide for members staying back. The erratic absence of breadwinners has had an erosive impact on the household fabric. The cohesion required for sharing and mutual caring in this basic unit of cohabitation gets lost when migrants, instead of pooling their wages with dependents, start to prioritize their own needs and wants. Rather than blaming people at the bottom of the pile for lacking in much-needed solidarity, my conclusion contends that labour is insecure and unprotected, kept adrift between or within sectors of employment as well as between rural and urban destinations. Their ongoing mobility is for the greater profit which capital derives from a cheap and pliable workforce (Breman 2019/2020).

Exposure to disentitlement is more acute in nation states, which persist to remain organized in rank social inequality. It is an official demeanour made manifest in withholding citizenship from down-and-out communities. In addition, social and human rights activists are not allowed to raise the claim of inclusion publicly. This taboo on subaltern resistance explains why most of the world's immiserated people are amassed in the South Asian subcontinent, although the rate of economic growth in this region has been quite substantial in the past few decades. The pandemic has further widened the already steep gap on both sides of the welfare fence. What used to be called the poverty line has taken shape as an unsurmountable barrier. The state of dispossession climaxes for the working poor, who have lost control over when, where, and to whom they can sell their labour power. Having received in advance sizable cash 'loans' which need to be worked off, they are often still in debt on departure resulting in ongoing precarity. Unable to make both ends meet keeps them culpable to usurious moneylenders, at home as well as at sites of their casual employment.

The politics of exclusion from well-being practiced worldwide, although in different shapes and grades, resonate in pauperized segments of the increasing workforce becoming redundant to demand. Those who sketch a future of doom and gloom are criticized for overstating the huge imbalance between capital and labour, unwilling, in their scepticism, to see that the tide is turning against the relentless exploitation of man and nature. After all, we have been told that the millennium goals were realized and that, abiding by the World Bank wisdom, within ten years from now poverty will be extinguished from our planet. This pledge has put paid to the voices of alarm. Really? Why do we still pretend that development is unfolding and that, with the announcement of some mealy-mouthed reforms, a decent and somewhat dignified life for all and sundry is round the corner, Tania Li retorts (2017). Her warning against apocalyptic thinking is well taken but so is her signal that the fault line between runaway wealth and progressive improvidence appears to be beyond repair. Exemplified, for instance, in ground-level fieldwork in Kinshasa (Trapido 2021), this is the momentum when, in a fury of rioting and looting, endangered classes transform themselves into dangerous ones.

References

Breman, J. (2001). 'Question of Poverty', valedictory address delivered at the Institute of Social Studies, The Hague.

Breman, J. (2016). *On Pauperism in Present and Past*. New Delhi: Oxford University Press.

Breman, J. (2019/2020). *Capitalism, Inequality and Labour in India*. Cambridge/New Delhi: Cambridge University Press.

Breman, J. (2020) 'The Pandemic in India and Its Impact on Footloose Labour', *Indian Journal of Labour Economics*, vol.63 (4): 901–19.

Breman, J. and G. Wiradi (2002). *Good Times and Bad Times in Rural Java: Case Study of Socioeconomic Dynamics in Two Villages Towards the End of the Twentieth Century*. Leiden: KITLV Press.

Li, T.M. (2017). 'After Development: Surplus Population and the Politics of Entitlement', *Development and Change*, 48(6): 1247–61.

Polanyi, K. (2020 [1944]). *The Great Transformation: The Political and Economic Origins of Our Times*. Boston, MA: Beacon Press.

Soto, H. de (1989). *The Other Path: The Invisible Revolution in the Third World.* New York: Harper & Row.

Soto, H. de (2000). *The Mystery of Capital; Why Capitalism Triumphs in the West and Fails Everywhere Else.* London: Bantam Press.

Trapido, J. (2021). 'Masterless Men: Riots, Patronage and the Politics of Surplus Population', *Current Anthropology,* 66(2): 198–217.

Conclusion

What the COVID-19 Crisis Tells Us about the Future of Informal Employment

Martha Alter Chen, Michael Rogan, and Kunal Sen

In this concluding chapter, we reflect on the main findings from the three sections of the volume: (a) the impact of the COVID-19 crisis on informal workers and their livelihood activities, (b) what we know about the relief, recovery, and stimulus measures that developing country governments have enacted; and (c) the future of labour markets, especially informal employment, in the wake of the COVID-19 crisis.

1. Reflecting on the impact of the pandemic on the informal economy

The chapters in the first part of this volume present some of the earliest, as well as the most recent, evidence on the impact of the pandemic and government restrictions on informal employment. Moreover, the chapters offer multiple perspectives based on 'real-time' telephonic data collection during the peak of the pandemic, small surveys which collected detailed information on the impacts on specific groups of informal workers as well as nationally representative labour force surveys, which paint a broader picture of employment impacts during the pandemic and into the 'recovery' period. Each of these perspectives offers a different understanding of the crisis while also illuminating a number of common themes.

First and foremost, the chapters illustrate the large and nearly (but not quite) universal disproportionate impact of the pandemic and related policy responses on informal employment. As outlined in a number of chapters, such a finding goes against the conventional understanding of the informal economy as absorbing formal job losses during crises and downturns. The data from South Africa's quarterly labour force surveys, for example, have shown that, over a three-year period, both relative and absolute employment losses during the pandemic were greater in the informal economy, while the rate and level of recovery have been greater for formal

Martha Alter Chen et al., *What the COVID-19 Crisis Tells Us about the Future of Informal Employment*. In: *COVID-19 and the Informal Economy*. Edited by: Martha Alter Chen, Michael Rogan, and Kunal Sen, Oxford University Press.
© Martha Alter Chen et al. (2024). DOI: 10.1093/oso/9780198887041.003.0014

employment. A multi-country comparative study, however, demonstrates that there was substantial variation in the scope and depth of the impact on informal employment. In one of the most comprehensive analyses of COVID-19 employment impacts in Latin American countries to date, Chen and Vanek, in Chapter 2, show that roughly 22 million jobs were lost across just five countries during the outset of the pandemic. However, the severity of job losses varied considerably, with a nearly 7 per cent contraction in employment in El Salvador compared with 19 per cent in Mexico at the outset of the pandemic. In four of the five countries described in the chapter, the informal workforce experienced a larger contraction than the formal workforce.

In addition, many of the chapters have raised the concern that the initial sharp downturn in informal employment may have long-lasting consequences beyond the pandemic and ongoing recovery. This observation was made perhaps most clearly by Schotte and Zizzamia in Chapter 5 on employment in urban South Africa, where the authors warn that 'the COVID-19 pandemic may not only present a temporary shock but also have lasting implications for poverty rates in South Africa' that extend beyond the lifting of lockdown measures. 'It may compromise household income-generating activities in the longer term as the labour market recovery has been incomplete and households have turned to liquidating their small savings and defaulting on insurance payments in the absence of alternative coping strategies.' Such coping mechanisms and their implications for the longer-term recovery of informal livelihoods were an additional theme across the chapters, which presented data on the large negative impact on informal jobs.

Beyond the large and disproportionate impact on informal employment, another key theme which emerges across the different chapters in the first part of the volume is what the authors of Chapter 4 refer to as 'amplified vulnerabilities'. The analyses have shown how pre-existing inequalities or 'fault lines' have been widened during the pandemic and the ensuing uneven recovery. The precise nature of these amplified vulnerabilities naturally varies by context but often features unequal outcomes by type of work, status in employment, gender, caste, and race. Again, Schotte and Zizzamia's Chapter 5, which presents national data from the South African context, shows that women in informal employment, those working in informal enterprises, and informal workers in retail and domestic work were particularly affected by the pandemic and government restrictions. In Bangladesh, informal workers and the urban poor, especially women, were disproportionately impacted. The concentration of the impact in urban areas in Bangladesh was so pronounced that unemployment went from being two percentage points lower in urban slums prior to COVID to being two percentage points higher than in rural areas in 2021.

In the Latin American context, the pandemic restrictions and recession widened inequalities between formal and informal workers but also between different sectors of the economy, by status in employment and by gender and (in Brazil) race.

With the exception of El Salvador, the differences in employment losses and gains were generally greater between women and men in the informal workforce than in the formal workforce. The data in Chapter 2 also show, however, that there were nuances to the employment dynamics among different groups of informal workers. In Mexico, for example, the initial loss of employment in 2020 was similar for women and men in formal and informal employment, but by the first quarter of 2021, women informal workers had recovered less than men informal workers. Moreover, specific subsectors of the informal economy (such as home-based manufacturing and trade) were disproportionately affected, and women are over-represented in these sectors.

Similarly, Danquah et al.'s Chapter 3, which presents survey data from Ghana, shows that earnings losses due to government lockdowns were experienced more acutely by informal workers, especially women and the self-employed (many of whom work in informal enterprises). The authors noted that these particular groups were more vulnerable prior to the pandemic such that the 'pandemic shock' led to a surge of workers who reported experiencing severe food insecurity together with a more than doubling of food poverty during the early phase of the pandemic. Indeed, a key theme across the chapters has been that informal workers who were more vulnerable prior to the crisis were more negatively affected by the pandemic and have experienced a slower recovery.

A third common theme from the first part of the volume is that of heterogeneity. The specific pathways of impact have been shown to vary substantially across different contexts and between different groups of informal workers. Chen et al.'s Chapter 1, which looked at the impact of the pandemic on different groups of informal workers in 11 cities from 9 countries, perhaps best illustrates the different ways in which the livelihoods of informal workers were impacted during the pandemic and in the immediate recovery period. Most notably, the chapter showed that the impact of the unfolding crises differed not only between but also within sectors of informal employment. Home-based workers, especially those who are subcontracted, experienced the most severe disruption to their work as the supply chains in which they operate were first disrupted by government restrictions and then by the lack of demand. Street vendors, especially those who sold non-essential items, reported a prolonged decrease in the demand for their goods and services even after returning to work. In contrast, waste pickers were the most able to work in all periods but faced a shortage of market outlets and extreme fluctuations in the prices for reclaimed waste. The one exception was those who worked in dump sites which were closed. In other words, a combination of health threats, government restrictions, and market contractions impacted differently on specific groups of informal workers.

A fourth common theme took the form of what Rahman et al., in Chapter 6 on Bangladesh, refer to as 'distress resilience'. They argue that the pandemic and policy restrictions precipitated a greater use of family labour put into vulnerable and lower-income occupations, rising expenditure burdens, and eroding financial capacity amidst 'only token social support or protection, if any' (see Chapter 6: 15). In Bangladesh, as in other parts of South Asia, lost livelihoods among the urban poor led to involuntary migration back to home villages. The analysis in the chapter found that nearly 30 per cent of urban households had involuntarily migrated during the first 18 months of the pandemic. In the absence of sufficient government support, a common theme across contexts was the variety of coping mechanisms used by workers and their households. Such responses ranged from reducing caloric intake and forgoing meals to depleting savings, selling assets, and taking on new and often unsustainable levels of household debt.

As the evidence presented in Part I of this volume illustrates, the COVID triple crisis—pandemic, restrictions, and recession—had a disproportionate impact on informal workers, while, at the same time, informal workers provided essential goods and services (food, health, transport, sanitation, recycling) during the crisis. The COVID crisis also exposed and widened pre-existing disadvantages or inequalities that informal workers face in gaining access to public services (including health, education, childcare, basic infrastructure, and transport services), to public space (to pursue their livelihoods), and to public procurement (to support their livelihoods). In policy terms, this evidence suggests that the informal economy should be a priority in economic recovery efforts.

2. Reflections on relief and recovery

The COVID-19 pandemic clearly had widespread negative impacts on informal employment in developing and emerging economies. What have governments done to provide much-needed relief to informal workers in this moment of crisis? What have been the economy recovery packages that developing country governments enacted, and what possible pathways exist to making national economic recovery plans relevant for the livelihoods of the majority of workers in developing and emerging countries? The chapters in Part II of this volume suggest that economic recovery and stimulus measures have largely ignored informal workers and their livelihood activities. Making recovery of informal livelihoods even harder, in the name of public health or economic recovery, many governments have evicted informal workers from their workplaces and/or destroyed their equipment and workplaces.[1]

---

[1] For examples, see www.wiego.org/blog/do-no-harm-why-harassment-informal-workers-hurts-public-health-and-economic-recovery (accessed November 2023).

2.1 Government relief and recovery

In Chapter 8, Danquah et al. examine the effectiveness of economic relief and stimulus packages in three countries in sub-Saharan Africa—Ghana, Kenya, and South Africa. The content of the relief packages varied quite substantially across these three countries. For example, in Ghana, the government provided tax incentives such as an extension of the tax filing date and a three-month tax holiday as well as a doubling of payments to the beneficiaries of Ghana's main social protection programme, Livelihood Empowerment against Poverty. Food relief was also provided in the most affected districts in Ghana. In Kenya, most relief measures focused on income tax and value-added tax (VAT) rebates. In addition, the government enacted a far-reaching Economic Stimulus programme in May 2020, especially targeting vulnerable citizens and business affected by the pandemic. In South Africa, the government created a COVID-19 Social Relief of Distress Grant (SRDG) as a temporary measure providing additional support to the poor and vulnerable in South Africa. In addition, the government announced an economic and social support package in April 2021, amounting to 10 per cent of gross domestic product (GDP).

However, notwithstanding these relief-cum-recovery measures, all three countries have witnessed a slow and uneven recovery. Many workers and households fell through the safety net, pointing to the inadequacy of the policies both in terms of scale and targeting. The experiences of the three countries show the difficulty in designing relief and recovery measures that ensure that the most vulnerable are not left behind in a widespread crisis such as the COVID-19 pandemic. In Chapter 10, Alfers and Juergens-Grant discuss lessons learned from the inadequate relief response in most countries.

In Chapter 9, Mhlana et al. analyse national recovery plans in two low-income countries (Bangladesh and Kenya) and two middle-income countries (South Africa and Thailand). The analysis of the plans suggest that the focus was mostly aimed at stimulating economic development: financing economic recovery; developing local value chains; facilitating international trade; boosting public investment; and supporting micro, small, and medium enterprises (MSMEs). However, there are significant differences in the recovery plans of the four countries. For example, the Kenyan Economic Recovery Strategy was mostly focused on fiscal consolidation and private-sector-led growth, while the plan for Bangladesh emphasized global value chains and export-led growth. The South African National Economic Recovery and Reconstruction Plan was concerned with the creation of jobs through public employment programmes, infrastructure investment, and delivery, in so doing achieving gender equality and economic inclusion of women and youth. In contrast, Thailand's five-year development plan foregrounded ethics and values, economic and social security, fair access to resources and quality social services, strengthening the grassroots economy, and preserving and restoring natural resources and environmental quality.

The authors argue that the plans mostly focus on the quantity of employment, not its quality, and do not centre their focus on support to informal enterprises, which comprise the broad base of the economy. The plans do not pay sufficient attention to the constraints faced by own-account workers and contributing family workers, which form a large part of the workforce in several of these countries. The authors further argue that the imbalances in the national economic recovery plans are likely to deepen inequalities and entrench the increase in poverty experienced by women and men in the informal economy.

2.2 Distress recovery from below

While there was recovery in numbers employed by mid-2021 and mid-2022 in many countries, average earnings remained lower than pre-COVID levels due, in part, to the lack of full-time work. The evidence from Chapter 1 also underscores that, by mid-2021, informal workers and their households had not been able to rebuild the savings they had depleted, redeem the assets they had pawned or sold, or repay the money they had borrowed to meet basic necessities (including buying food on credit) and faced postponed payments (often with compounding interest) for rent, utility bills, and school fees. As noted earlier, the authors of Chapter 6, on Bangladesh, characterize the efforts of informal workers and the urban poor to restart their livelihoods, against great odds, as 'distress resilience'.

In short, by mid-2021, informal workers and their households had experienced a slow recovery of earnings and an even slower recovery of assets and were receiving little (if any) relief or recovery support from government. The dramatic impact of, and slow recovery from, the COVID crisis raises concerns that, in addition to the temporary shock to employment and earnings, the crisis may result in longer-term setbacks in efforts to reduce poverty, expand employment opportunities, and grow economies.

3. The future of informal employment

The effects of the pandemic and accompanying government restrictions to contain its spread have been both dramatic and highly differentiated. In many developed countries, the pandemic and associated restrictions have given rise to even greater levels of flexible work arrangements, decreases in labour supply, and the continued expansion of the 'gig economy'. In contrast, in emerging and developing countries, informal workers have borne the brunt of employment losses and have largely been left to fend for themselves. The shifts in the structure of employment, especially in developed countries, and the catastrophic loss of employment and earnings among the informally employed, especially in developing and emerging economies, will likely have enduring implications for labour markets.

The findings presented in this volume illustrate three important points about the nature of informal employment, which constitutes over 60 per cent of all workers globally, 90 per cent in developing economies, and 67 per cent in emerging economies:[2] first, the pre-existing structural disadvantages that informal workers face in pursuing their livelihoods and securing their well-being; second, the highly heterogeneous nature of the informal workforce and, therefore, of the levels and pathways of impact of the COVID crisis on different groups of informal workers. This heterogeneity can be understood by investigating the branch of the economy, status in employment, place of work, and goods or services produced of informal workers, and, intersecting with these variables, the gender and race (as the Brazil and South Africa data show) of informal workers. The third important point raised about informal employment is the essential goods and services provided by informal workers in normal times and during crises, including food production, preparation, and distribution; health-, child, and eldercare services; sanitation and recycling services; and transport services.

The sheer size of the informal workforce, the social and economic contributions of informal workers, and the disproportionate impact of the COVID crisis on them would suggest that informal workers should be integrated into social and economic policies going forwards. However, there is a very real chance that the global community will revert to the 'bad old deal' for informal workers, namely, exclusion from public goods and exclusion from, or penalization by, public policies. Further, some governments have introduced a 'worse new deal' for informal workers, namely, eviction from and/or destruction of their workplaces in the name of public health or economic recovery. However, to reduce poverty and inequality and to generate robust and inclusive growth, what is needed is a 'better new deal' for informal workers.

Before turning to future policy responses to promote a 'better new deal' for informal workers, here are some lessons for future policy research from the studies featured in this volume.

4. Future policy research

The studies featured in this volume provide important insights about the scope, data sources, methods, and time frame of future policy research on informal labour markets.

---

[2] These estimates are from ILO (International Labour Organization) (2018). *Women and Men in Informal Employment: A Statistical Picture* (3rd edn). Geneva: ILO.

4.1 Research scope

First and foremost, more research is needed on the impact of economic trends and policies—not just economic crises—on informal workers. Second, future research on these topics needs to take into account the heterogeneous nature of the informal workforce and the different pathways of impact on different groups of informal workers. The key variables to consider are branch of economy; status in employment; place of work; products or services provided; and (intersecting with these variables) gender, class, ethnicity, caste, and race as well as place of residence (whether rural or urban, served or underserved, own or other's).

4.2 Data sources and research methods

The studies featured in this volume illustrate the value of using mixed data sources to inform and illuminate each other. A growing number of countries are using the international statistical definitions and measures recommended by the International Conference of Labour Statisticians in their collection and tabulation of national labour force data, including many of the key variables listed above. Microstudies, which illustrate the importance of these key variables in understanding the informal economy, have been used to inform these statistical definitions and measures and, thereby, the production of national labour force data. Microstudies have also been used, as in this volume, to interpret national data as they illustrate the intersection of these key individual variables with wider structural variables—economic trends and policies; practices of government, employers, and dominant economic actors; and discriminatory social norms—in driving employment outcomes, not just during crises.

4.3 Research timing and time frame

Finally, the studies featured in this volume illustrate two key temporal dimensions of research on the impact of crises. First is the need of 'finding out fast'—as dramatic impacts can happen quickly, as with the imposition of lockdowns or other restrictions at the outset of the pandemic. Second is the need to continue to monitor the impact of a crisis—as recovery is often very slow and can stall or leave informal workers behind.

5. Future policy responses

There are three major policy implications of the findings presented in this volume: first, that informal workers should be given priority in economic recovery efforts and in future economic policies; second, that policy support to the informal workforce requires a differentiated approach to address the dynamics of different groups of informal workers; and third, given the structural disadvantages faced by informal workers pre-COVID, the policy responses need to be broad-based.

5.1 Economic policies

The chapters in Part II of the volume suggest that informal workers need both ongoing relief measures to help them pay off loans, rebuild savings, and restore assets and recovery measures to restart and rebuild their livelihood activities. As outlined in Chapter 9, key elements of inclusive national recovery plans, to help informal workers recover their livelihood activities should include business support, the rebuilding of supply chains, and public investment.

The authors of Chapter 6 on Bangladesh recommend a broad-based approach to economic policies to address the cost drivers and expenditure burdens of the poor. They identify four cost drivers that have contributed to the expenditure burdens of the poor and lower-income groups—all related to macroeconomic policy: health care, education, transportation, and utilities. They make the case that the COVID crisis has created a compelling policy window to introduce policy reforms that can address these critical cost drivers for the poor, arguing that '[i]f the entrenched roadblocks to governance reforms can be confronted, leading to rationalization of such expenditure burdens, the impact on the well-being of the poor and middle-income classes alike will be as great as—if not greater than—the welfare from social protection measures alone'.

The two concluding chapters in Part III of this volume are about the future and call, respectively, for a new approach to social protection and a new social contract, both inclusive of informal workers.

5.2 Social protection

The pandemic has prompted an almost unprecedented policy focus on social protection, in part due to the lack of adequate relief and social safety nets when earnings came to a standstill in the second quarter of 2020. The pre-existing mechanisms for smoothing or protecting income largely failed, and the crisis-induced relief aid was inadequate in coverage, benefits, frequency, and duration. Although there is growing consensus around the need to develop social protection systems that can protect against future shocks and crises, there is considerable disagreement regarding the design, financing, and implementation of such systems. Key questions remain about how to include informal workers in social protection systems and where the financing for expanded social protection coverage, including to informal workers, should come from.

But in this COVID moment, as suggested by Alfers and Juergens Grant in Chapter 10, there is an opportunity to hear from informal workers and other key stakeholders regarding what works to provide universal social protection. Several suggestions emerged from chapters in this volume. Rahman et al., in Chapter 6 on the impact of the COVID crisis in Bangladesh, make the case for focusing social protection on the urban poor, who, compared to the rural poor, were relatively neglected pre-COVID and disproportionately impacted during COVID. Rogan and Skinner, in Chapter 4 on the impact of the COVID crisis in South Africa, make the case for cash transfers to the poor, citing evidence that shows that cash transfers not only reduce poverty but also increase investments in informal enterprises and boost demand. And in his reflections for this volume in Chapter 12, development economist Ravi Kanbur makes a pair of recommendations about social protection going forwards, namely, 'to stress test social protection systems in the face of crises and to use these findings to enhance automatic funding for financing the increased needs of social protection during crises'.

5.3 New social contract

Chapter 11 in this volume makes the case that informal workers need to be included as key partners in a new social contract between state, capital, and labour. It highlights the mismatch between the lived realities of informal work and mainstream approaches to social contracts and makes the case for a new social contract that includes informal workers as key stakeholders in contracts with the state as well as with capital.

What is required, Chen et al. argue, is a better new contract that redistributes wealth through appropriate tax policies; invests in strengthening local systems of production and consumption; ensures universal access to social protection and to good-quality public services, including basic infrastructure and care services with well-remunerated workers; regulates markets and supply chains to limit the power of capitalists to download costs and risks on informal workers; ends state violence against informal workers; and challenges the dominant narrative that stigmatizes informal workers as a problem rather than recognizing their contributions in providing essential goods and services as well as paying taxes and fees. As economist Jayati Ghosh writes, in her reflections on this chapter in Chapter 12, 'The essential point being made here is that the very important principles described in the book, for just and viable socio-economic arrangements (universal social protection; access to public space, public services and public procurement; fair conditions of work; just, progressive taxation; freedom from harassment; freedom from stigmatization) should apply equally to all types of informal workers, not just self-employed workers.'

The authors conclude that this new social contract will require two major processes of change: a change in mindsets and dominant narratives regarding the informal economy; and the inclusion of informal worker organizations and leaders in governance and policy processes.

6. Concluding reflections

The COVID moment is a moment to be bold—it provides an opportunity to address pre-existing structural disparities and to accelerate structural change in support of the informal workforce. The increased recognition of informal workers as essential workers should be translated into more inclusive recovery plans and an agenda for transformative change to protect and support these workers and their livelihoods. Inclusive social and economic policies in support of the informal workforce are fundamental to advancing social and economic justice.

Finally, to borrow from Martin Luther King, there is a 'fierce urgency of now' to this COVID moment. Reflecting on runaway wealth and deepening poverty before and during the COVID crisis, sociologist Jan Breman, in his reflections for this volume, underscores that 'The pandemic has further widened the already steep gap on both sides of the welfare fence. What used to be called the poverty line has taken shape as an unsurmountable barrier.'

Index